YEATS ANNUAL No. 12

Frontispiece: D. P. Moran (1869–1936), editor of *The Leader*. 'The most offensive of Irish clerical personalities, but an amiable fat man in presence' (WBY, 1913)

YEATS ANNUAL No. 12

A Special Number

THAT ACCUSING EYE
Yeats and his Irish Readers

Edited by
Warwick Gould and Edna Longley

First published 1996 by
MACMILLAN PRESS LTD
Houndmills, Basingstoke, Hampshire RG21 6XS
and London
Companies and representatives
throughout the world

ISBN 0–333–63315–6
ISSN 0278–7688

A catalogue record for this book is available
from the British Library.

10   9   8   7   6   5   4   3   2   1
05   04   03   02   01   00   99   98   97   96

Yeat Annual No. 12 was set in Garamond
and page-made using Nota Bene 4.2
by Warwick Gould. It was finished on
24 December 1995.

Printed and bound in Great Britain by
Antony Rowe Ltd
Chippenham, Wiltshire

Contents

Abbreviations

The standard works listed below are cited in *Yeats Annual* by standard abbreviations, including volume number (where appropriate), and page number. Volumes in *The Collected Edition of the Works of W. B. Yeats (CEW)*, edited by Richard J. Finneran and George Mills Harper, are cited by abbreviations of their individual titles. Manuscripts are cited using abbreviations for the main collections, listed below. Second or later citations of other works frequently referred to are usually by abbreviation or acronym as explained in the footnote accompanying the first citation in a particular essay.

Au	*Autobiographies* (London: Macmillan, 1955).
AVA	*A Vision: An Explanation of Life Founded upon the Writings of Giraldus and upon certain Doctrines attributed to Kusta Ben Luka* (London: privately printed for subscribers only by T. Werner Laurie, Ltd., 1925). See also *CVA*.
AVB	*A Vision* (London: Macmillan, 1962).
Berg	Books and Manuscripts, The Berg Collection, New York Public Library (Astor, Lenox and Tilden Foundations).
B.L. Add. MS	Additional Manuscript, The British Library, London (followed by number). Manuscripts as yet uncatalogued are cited as *B.L. Uncat.*
Bodley	Bodleian Library, Oxford.
Brotherton	Manuscript, The Brotherton Collection, Brotherton Library, University of Leeds.

CH

W. B. Yeats: The Critical Heritage ed. A. Norman Jeffares (London, Henley & Boston: Routledge & Kegan Paul, 1977).

CL1, 3

The Collected Letters of W. B. Yeats: Volume One, 1865-1895, ed. John Kelly and Eric Domville ; Volume Three, 1901-1904, ed. John Kelly and Ronald Schuchard (Oxford: Clarendon Press, 1986, 1994).

CM

W. B. Yeats: A Census of the Manuscripts by Conrad A. Balliet with the assistance of Christine Mawhinney (New York and London: Garland Publishing, Inc., 1990).

CVA

A Critical Edition of Yeats's A Vision (1925), ed. George Mills Harper and Walter Kelly Hood (London: Macmillan, 1978).

CW1-8

The Collected Works in Verse and Prose of William Butler Yeats (Stratford-on-Avon: The Shakespeare Head Press, 1908, 8 vols.).

DC

Druid Craft: The Writing of The Shadowy Waters, Manuscripts of W. B. Yeats transcribed, edited & with a commentary by Michael J. Sidnell, George P. Mayhew, David R. Clark (Amherst: The University of Massachusetts Press, 1971).

Diaries

Lady Gregory's Diaries 1892—1902, ed. James Pethica, (Gerrards Cross: Colin Smythe, 1996).

E&I

Essays and Introductions (London and New York: Macmillan, 1961).

Emory

Books and Manuscripts in the Robert W. Woodruff Library, Emory University, Atlanta.

Ex

Explorations, sel. Mrs W. B. Yeats (London: Macmillan, 1962; New York: Macmillan, 1963).

G-YL   *The Gonne-Yeats Letters 1893-1938: Always Your Friend*, ed. Anna MacBride White and A. Norman Jeffares (London: Hutchinson, 1992).

Harvard   Manuscript, Houghton Library, Harvard University

HRHRC   Books and Manuscripts, Harry Ransom Humanities Research Center, University of Texas at Austin.

I&R   *W. B. Yeats Interviews and Recollections* ed. E. H. Mikhail, (London: Macmillan, 1977), 2 vols.

J   *W. B. Yeats: A Classified Bibliography of Criticism* second edition, revised and enlarged, by K. P. S. Jochum (Urbana and Chicago: University of Illinois Press, 1990). Item nos. or page no. preceded by 'p.'.

JS&D   *John Sherman AND Dhoya (CEW XII)*, edited by Richard J. Finneran (New York: Macmillan, 1991).

Kansas   Manuscripts in the Kenneth Spencer Research Library, University of Kansas, Lawrence.

L   *The Letters of W. B. Yeats*, ed. Allan Wade (London: Rupert Hart-Davis, 1954; New York: Macmillan, 1955).

LBP   *Letters from Bedford Park: A Selection from the Correspondence (1890—1901) of John Butler Yeats* edited with introduction and notes by William M. Murphy (Dublin: The Cuala Press, 1972).

LDW   *Letters on Poetry from W. B. Yeats to Dorothy Wellesley*, intro. Kathleen Raine (London and New York: Oxford University Press, 1964).

LJQ	*The Letters of John Quinn to W. B. Yeats* ed. Alan B. Himber, with the assistance of George Mills Harper (Ann Arbor: UMI Research Press, 1983).
LMR	*"Ah, Sweet Dancer": W. B. Yeats / Margot Ruddock, A Correspondence* ed. Roger McHugh (London and New York: Macmillan, 1970).
LNI	*Letters to the New Island: A New Edition (CEW VII)* edited by George Bornstein and Hugh Witemeyer (London: Macmillan, 1989).
LRB	*The Correspondence of Robert Bridges and W. B. Yeats* ed. Richard J. Finneran (London: Macmillan, 1977; Toronto: Macmillan of Canada, 1978).
LTWBY	*Letters to W. B. Yeats* ed. Richard J. Finneran, George Mills Harper and William M. Murphy with the assistance of Alan B. Himber (London: Macmillan; New York: Columbia University Press, 1977). 2 vols.
MBY	Manuscript in the Collection of Michael Butler Yeats.
Mem	*Memoirs: Autobiography · First Draft: Journal* transcribed and edited by Denis Donoghue (London: Macmillan, 1972; New York: Macmillan, 1973).
Myth	*Mythologies* (London and New York: Macmillan, 1959).
MYV1, 2	*The Making of Yeats's "A Vision": A Study of the Automatic Script* by George Mills Harper (London: Macmillan; Carbondale and Edwardsville, Ill.: Southern Illinois University Press, 1987). 2 vols.

NC   *A New Commentary on the Poems of W. B. Yeats* by A. Norman Jeffares (London: Macmillan; Stanford: Stanford University Press, 1984).

NLI   Manuscripts in the National Library of Ireland.

NLS   Manuscripts in the National Library of Scotland.

NYPL   Manuscripts in the New York Public Library.

Norwood   Manuscripts, Norwood Historical Society, Day House, Norwood, Mass.

OBMV   *The Oxford Book of Modern Verse 1895-1935*, chosen by W. B. Yeats (Oxford: Clarendon Press, 1936).

P&I   *Prefaces and Introductions: Uncollected Prefaces and Introductions by Yeats to Works by other Authors and to Anthologies edited by Yeats (CEW VI)*, edited by William H. O'Donnell (London: Macmillan, 1988).

PR   *The Poems: Revised* edited by Richard J. Finneran (New York: Macmillan Publishing Company, 1989; London: Macmillan, 1989). (*CEW 1* replacing *The Poems: A New Edition* ed. Richard J. Finneran [New York: Macmillan Publishing Company, 1983; London: Macmillan London Ltd., 1984], *PNE*).

SB   *The Speckled Bird, With Variant Versions* ed. William H. O'Donnell (Toronto: McLelland & Stewart, 1976).

SQ   *A Servant of the Queen: Reminiscences* by Maud Gonne MacBride, edited by A. Norman Jeffares and Anna MacBride White (Gerrards Cross: Colin Smythe, 1994).

SS   *The Senate Speeches of W. B. Yeats* ed. Donald R.
            Pearce (Bloomington: Indiana University Press,
            1960; London: Faber and Faber, 1961).

TB   *Theatre Business: The Correspondence of the First
            Abbey Theatre Directors: William Butler Yeats,
            Lady Gregory and J. M. Synge* ed. Ann
            Saddlemyer (Gerrards Cross: Colin Smythe;
            University Park, Penn.: Pennsylvania State
            University Press, 1982).

TSMC   *W. B. Yeats and T. Sturge Moore: Their Cor-
            respondence, 1901-1937* ed. Ursula Bridge
            (London: Routledge and Kegan Paul; New
            York: Oxford University Press, 1953).

UP1   *Uncollected Prose by W. B. Yeats*, Vol I, ed. John
            P. Frayne (London: Macmillan; New York:
            Columbia University Press, 1970).

UP2   *Uncollected Prose by W. B. Yeats*, Vol 2, ed. John
            P. Frayne and Colton Johnson (London: Mac-
            millan, 1975; New York: Columbia University
            Press, 1976).

VP   *The Variorum Edition of the Poems of W. B. Yeats*
            ed. Peter Allt and Russell K. Alspach (New
            York: The Macmillan Company, 1957). Cited
            from the corrected third printing of 1966.

VPl   *The Variorum Edition of the Plays of W. B. Yeats*
            ed. Russell K. Alspach assisted by Catherine C.
            Alspach (London and New York: Macmillan,
            1966). Cited from the corrected second printing
            of 1966.

VSR   *The Secret Rose, Stories by W. B. Yeats: A
            Variorum Edition*, ed. Warwick Gould, Phillip
            L. Marcus and Michael J. Sidnell (London: Mac-
            millan, 1992). Second edition, rev. and enl.

Wade   Allan Wade, *A Bibliography of the Writings of W. B. Yeats*, third ed., rev. Russell K. Alspach (London: Rupert Hart-Davis, 1968). Item nos. and/or page nos. preceded by 'p.'.

WWB1, 2, 3   *The Works of William Blake Poetic, Symbolic, and Critical*, edited with lithographs of the illustrated "Prophetic Books," and a memoir and interpretation by Edwin John Ellis and William Butler Yeats, 3 vols. (London: Bernard Quaritch, 1893).

YA   *Yeats Annual* (London: Macmillan, 1982-) cited by no.

YAACTS   *Yeats: An Annual of Critical and Textual Studies* (publishers vary, 1983-) cited by no.

YL   Edward O'Shea, *A Descriptive Catalog of W. B. Yeats's Library* (New York and London: Garland Publishing, 1985).

YO   *Yeats and the Occult*, ed. George Mills Harper (Toronto: Macmillan of Canada; Niagara Falls, New York: Maclean-Hunter Press, 1975).

YP   *Yeats's Poems* ed. & ann. A. Norman Jeffares, with an appendix by Warwick Gould (London: Macmillan, 1989). Cited from the second, revised edition of 1991.

YT   *Yeats and the Theatre*, ed. Robert O'Driscoll and Lorna Reynolds (Toronto: Macmillan of Canada; Niagara Falls, New York: Maclean-Hunter Press, 1975).

YVP1, 2, 3   *Yeats's* Vision *Papers* (London: Macmillan, 1992), George Mills Harper (General Editor) assisted by Mary Jane Harper, Volume 1: *The Automatic Script: 5 November 1917—18 June 1918*, eds. Steve L. Adams, Barbara J. Frieling and Sandra L. Sprayberry; Volume 2: *The Automatic Script: 25 June 1918—29 March 1920*, eds. Steve L. Adams, Barbara J. Frieling and Sandra L. Sprayberry; Volume 3: *Sleep and Dream Notebooks*, Vision *Notebooks 1 and 2, Card File*, eds. Robert Anthony Martinich and Margaret Mills Harper.

Editorial Board

Notes on the Contributors

Richard Allen Cave is Professor of Drama and Theatre Studies in the University of London (at Royal Holloway). The author of many studies of the contemporary theatre, he has also edited George Moore's *Hail and Farewell: Ave, Salve, Vale* (Colin Smythe, 1976, 1985) .

Wayne K. Chapman is Associate Professor of English at Clemson University, South Carolina and author of *Yeats and English Renaissance Poetry* (Macmillan, 1990). He is the author of articles on Yeats's library, and its textual evidences. He is working with Michael J. Sidnell on an edition of the manuscripts of *The Countess Cathleen* for the Cornell Yeats Manuscripts Series.

John Wilson Foster is Professor of English at the University of British Columbia. His most recent books are *Fictions of the Irish Literary Revival* (1987), *Colonial Consequences: Essays in Irish Literature and Culture* (1991) and *The Idea of the Union: Statements in Support of the Union of Great Britain and Northern Ireland* (1995). He is editor of *Nature in Ireland: A Scientific and Cultural History* (1996).

R. F. Foster F.B.A. inaugurated the Carroll Chair of Irish History in the University of Oxford in 1991, where he is a Fellow of Hertford College. His books include *Charles Stewart Parnell: The Man and His Family* (1976), *Lord Randolph Churchill: A Political Life* (1981), *Modern Ireland 1600-1972* (1988), *The Oxford Illustrated History of Ireland* (1989), *The Sub-Prefect Should Have Held His Tongue: Selected Essays of Hubert Butler* (1990). *Paddy and Mr Punch* (1993) is a selection from his many essays and articles. The first volume of his life of W. B. Yeats is forthcoming from the Clarendon Press.

Warwick Gould is Professor of English Literature in the University of London, where he teaches at Royal Holloway and the School of Advanced Study. He is co-author (with Marjorie Reeves) of *Joachim* *of Fiore and the Myth of the Eternal Evangel in the Nineteenth Century* (1987), and co-editor of *The Secret Rose, Stories by W. B. Yeats: A Variorum Edition* (1992). He is co-editor of *The Collected Letters of W. B. Yeats*, Volume II, (1896-1900) (Clarendon, 1996), and is working on editions of Yeats's *Early Essays* and *Mythologies* for the new Macmillan *Collected Edition of the Works of W. B. Yeats*, and of *Yeats's Occult Diaries (1898-1901)*.

Richard Greaves is Lecturer in English at the Liverpool Hope University College. His University of London PhD thesis (1994) is on W. B. Yeats's middle period and Modernism.

Eamonn Hughes lectures in English at the Queen's University of Belfast. He has edited *Culture and Politics in Northern Ireland 1960-1990* (1991) and is working on a study of Irish autobiography.

A. Norman Jeffares has held chairs in Stirling, Leeds and Adelaide. A revised edition of *W. B. Yeats: Man and Poet* (1949), will shortly appear from Gill & Macmillan. His many studies and editions of Yeats include *A New Commentary on the Poems of W. B. Yeats* (1984, now under revision), *W. B. Yeats: A New Biography* (1989), *A Vision and Related Writings* (1990), *Yeats's Love Poems* (1990) and *Yeats's Poems* (1989, 3rd revised edition, 1996), and with Anna MacBride White he edited *Always Your Friend: Letters between Maud Gonne and W. B. Yeats 1893-1938* (London: Hutchinson, 1992). His most recent book (with Martin Gray) is the *Collins Dictionary of Quotations* (1995). He is Honorary Life President of IASAIL.

Edna Longley is Professor of English Literature at the Queen's University of Belfast. Her most recent books are *Louis MacNeice: A Study* (1988) and *The Living Stream: Literature and Revisionism in Ireland* (1994).

W. J. Mc Cormack is Senior Lecturer in English Literature at Goldsmiths' College (University of London). His most recent books are *From Burke to Beckett* (1994) and *Cease your Funning: A Bibliographical and Critical Inquiry into Discussion of a Projected Union between Ireland and Great Britain . . . 1797—1800* (1996).

Peter McDonald lectures in English at the University of Bristol. He is the author of a collection of poems, *Biting the Wax* (1989) and of *Louis MacNeice: The Poet in his Contexts* (1991). He is currently working on a book of essays about Irish poetry and culture.

Bernard O'Donoghue is Fellow of Wadham College, Oxford. His most recent volume of poems is *Gunpowder* (Chatto & Windus, 1995), which won the Whitbread Poetry Prize. He is the author of *Seamus Heaney and the Language of Poetry* (Harvester, 1994).

Alex Owen is Associate Professor of History at Northwestern University and the author of *The Darkened Room: Women, Power and Spiritualism in Late Victorian England* (1989). She is working on a study of magical sects at the turn of the century.

Eve Patten is British Council lecturer in Bucharest, Romania. She has edited *Returning to Ourselves: Second Volume of Papers from the John Hewitt International Summer School* (1995).

James Pethica is Assistant Professor of English at the University of Richmond, Richmond, Va. His edition of *Lady Gregory's Diaries 1892—1902* will be published by Colin Smythe in 1996, and his co-edition (with Jon Stallworthy) of the manuscript materials of Yeats's *Last Poems* is forthcoming from Cornell University Press.

Michael Sidnell is Professor of English at Trinity College, University of Toronto. Co-editor of *Druid Craft: the writing of "The Shadowy Waters"* and of *The Secret Rose, Stories by W. B. Yeats: A Variorum Edition*, he is author of *Dances of Death: The Group Theatre of London in the Thirties* and co-editor of *Mythologies*, forthcoming in the *Collected Edition of the Works of W. B. Yeats*, and of *The Countess Cathleen* in the Cornell Yeats Manuscripts Series.

Colin Smythe is a publisher with a unique range of interests in Irish and Anglo-Irish culture. He is currently preparing a new edition of *A Bibliography of the Writings of W. B. Yeats* for Clarendon. He is the General Editor of the Coole Edition of Lady Gregory's works, and co-editor of *Lady Gregory Fifty Years After* (1987).

Deirdre Toomey is editor of *Yeats and Women: Yeats Annual No 9* (1991), a revised and augmented edition of which is forthcoming in paperback form from Macmillan. She is co-editor of *The Collected Letters of W. B. Yeats*, Vol II, (1896-1900) (Clarendon, 1996) and is working on editions of Yeats's *Early Essays* and *Mythologies* for the *Collected Edition of the Works of W. B. Yeats*, and on an authorised edition of *Yeats's Occult Diaries (1898-1901)*.

Preface and Acknowledgements

FOR A VERY LONG TIME we have wanted to devote an issue to consideration of Yeats and his Irish readers. For an Irish writer of his time to succeed was to succeed in London, but in 1896 he threw an imperative to his translator Henry-D. Davray who was to write about him in *Le Mercure de France*: 'I want you to understand that I am an Irish poet, looking to my own people for my ultimate best audience & trying to express the things that interest them & which will make them care for the land in which they live'.

The Irish audience mattered most to him, even to the point of his refusing to send his books for inevitably hostile review in Ireland from 1902 onwards for many years. It was the audience that managed to wound him by its attention and by its indifference. It matters still, more than all others, and *Yeats Annual* is honoured to have Professor Edna Longley to co-edit a special number made up of essays by Irish critics and scholars.

Contributions for *Yeats Annual No 14* should reach me by 31 May, 1997, at our new editorial address:

The Centre for English Studies
School of Advanced Study,
University of London,
Senate House, Malet Street,
London WC1E 7HU.

E-mail w.gould@sas.ac.uk.

Professor Roy Foster, F.B.A., Carroll Professor of Irish History in Oxford (c/o Hertford College, Oxford) is working on the second volume of his authorised life of W. B. Yeats for the Clarendon Press, Oxford. Professor Ann Saddlemyer, c/o Massey College, University of Toronto, continues to work on her authorised life of George Yeats. Dr John Kelly of St. John's College, Oxford is General

Editor of *The Collected Letters of W. B. Yeats* (Clarendon Press). Colin Smythe (PO Box 6, Gerrards Cross, Bucks, SL9 8EF, UK) is completing his revision of the Wade-Alspach *Bibliography* for the Clarendon Press. An authorised edition of *Yeats's Occult Diaries, 1898-1901* is being prepared for the Macmillan Press by Deirdre Toomey and myself. All the above would be very grateful to hear of new letters, and to receive new information from readers.

Yeats Annual is now presented to the publisher in camera-ready form. Contributions should be supplied on 3.5" disks, and preferably in NotaBene 4.2, the program used in the preparation of *Yeats Annual*. We can translate from other PC programs, and from texts prepared on Macintosh machines if they have been written to PC formatted disks. It is essential to send with the disk three copies on paper, and we advise that you send submissions in two separate parcels. Further information for contributors and a style sheet are also available upon request. We are grateful to receive offprints and review copies and other bibliographical information (which is acknowledged at the end of each volume).

Our chief debt of gratitude is to Miss Anne Yeats and Mr. Michael B. Yeats for granting permission (through A. P. Watt Ltd.) to use published and unpublished materials by W. B. Yeats. Many of our contributors are further indebted to Michael Yeats and Anne Yeats for making unpublished materials available for study and for many other kindnesses, as is the Editor.

Other unpublished materials have been made available to us through the kindness of Colin Smythe, who further alerts us to an error in what we had intended as a correction on p. xx of *Yeats Annual No. 11*. AE's letter (now in the Robert W. Woodruff Library at Emory University) which contains a caricature of 'William MacYeats: | Bard of the Gael!' carrying 'a black porker' is of 29 November 1897 (cf. *YA 3* 155). The motif is repeated in 'The Banning of the Black Pig', AE's design for the contents page of the 1897 *Irish Homestead* Christmas Number, *A Celtic Christmas*, which illustrated Douglas Hyde's article of the same title.

A number of helpful librarians including John McTernan, formerly of the Sligo County Museum and Library, Catherine Fahy of the National Library of Ireland, Dr Philip Milito of the Henry W. and Albert A. Berg Collection, New York Public Library (Astor, Lenox and Tilden Foundations), Dr Cathy Henderson and Professor Thomas F. Staley at the Harry Ransom Humanities Research Center, provided us with materials and research assistance. The British

Library, The University of London Library, and Mr David Ward of the library of Royal Holloway (University of London), have also been unfailingly helpful, and Professor Robin Alston of University College, London provided invaluable assistance with on-line databases. Many other helpful scholars and librarians have been thanked within the compass of individual contributions to this volume.

Miss Riette Sturge Moore (who died in 1995) allowed us to use on the front board of *Yeats Annuals* a symbol adapted from Thomas Sturge Moore's designs for the H. P. R. Finberg translation of *Axël* (1925).

Linda Shaughnessy of A. P. Watt & Son, Professor Roy Foster, F.B.A. and Dr. John Kelly on behalf of Oxford University Press were generous with permissions. At Macmillan, Charmian Hearne, and Tim Farmiloe were particularly helpful during the preparation of this volume. Members of the Advisory Board continue to read a large number of submissions and we are grateful to them, and also to Mr R. A. Gilbert, Mr Roger Nyle Parisious, as well as to Joyce Bianconi and Valerie Murr.

Both Deirdre Toomey and Warwick Gould are immensely grateful to the Rockefeller Foundation. During a collaborative residency at the Bellagio Study Center in Italy in August-September 1995 they were able to turn to the preparation of this volume. Back in London, Deirdre Toomey as Research Editor took up the challenges which had defeated contributors and thus found innumerable ways to make this a better book. All associated with the volume (as well as its readers) will be grateful to her for her curiosity.

WARWICK GOULD

THAT ACCUSING EYE

Come, fix upon me that accusing eye.
I thirst for accusation. All that was sung,
All that was said in Ireland is a lie
Bred out of the contagion of the throng,
Saving the rhyme rats hear before they die.
Leave nothing but the nothings that belong
To this bare soul, let all men judge that can
Whether it be an animal or a man.

Introductory Reflections

I

YEATS'S ARTISTIC IMPULSE is inseparable from his sense of audience, his search for audience. From one viewpoint his poetry might be described as a running commentary on its own reception and on that of the Irish Literary Revival. The essays collected here can explore only a few aspects or instances of the reciprocity between 'Yeats and his Irish readers': a theme whose infinite permutations are exemplified by the fact that the essayists themselves come within its orbit. Among the topics not directly broached (in part, due to the studies that already exist) are readings of Yeats by such coevals as Synge and Joyce; 'theatre-business'; Yeats the politician. Yet this volume's stress on the interconnected spheres of politics, cultural politics and aesthetics may highlight some of the issues that continue to be most alive in Irish responses to Yeats: issues which his death did not resolve, and which have acquired new contexts as a result of the conflagration in Northern Ireland. Reading Yeats and his readers is bound up with contemporary history. It is equally, of course, bound up with contemporary scholarship: for instance, with the great project of editing his letters—which has often revised Yeats's editing of himself—and with Roy Foster's forthcoming biography. All in all, 'Yeats' constitutes a site of intersection and tension between many more 'interpretive communities' than most writers can muster.

To headline a phrase from 'Parnell's Funeral'—'Come, fix upon me that accusing eye. | I thirst for accusation'—is not to pre-empt the conclusion that Irish readings of Yeats are invariably hostile. Nonetheless, our choice of title characterises a poet in unusual conflict with sections of his audience. Hence the *j'accuse* of 'The Fisherman': 'Suddenly I began, | In scorn of this audience, | Imagining a man . . .' In 'Parnell's Funeral' 'that accusing eye' represents an interrogation by conscience which Yeats strategically turns upon his own persona in order to accuse the Irish who accused Parnell and now the Parnellite poet. The verb in 'accusation' points two ways. Read as a poem about the reception/rejection of culture-heroes, 'Parnell's Funeral' meshes politics, art and audience according to a long view of their interactions. It links 1891 with 'Forty Years Later' (the original title of part II), and shuttles conceptually as well as historically between O'Connellite and Parnellite Ireland. The 'crowd' that has followed O'Connell, sacrificed Parnell, and implicitly sidelined Yeats, has the usual faults of the Yeatsian mob. However, the speaker merges into its plurality during the stanza that prepares for 'Come, fix upon me that accusing eye':

An age is the reversal of an age:
When strangers murdered Emmet, Fitzgerald, Tone,
We lived like men that watch a painted stage.
What matter for the scene, the scene once gone:
It had not touched our lives. But popular rage,
Hysterica passio dragged this quarry down.
None shared our guilt; nor did we play a part
Upon a painted stage when we devoured his heart. (*VP* 541-2)

By taking on 'our guilt' Yeats asserts his status as national poet, his resultant role as national scapegoat. The theatrical metaphor thus brings together political and artistic reception by equating the (ir)responsibilities of populace and audience. The one has botched its share in national politics, the other its share in national art. 'A nation should be like an audience in some great theatre—"In the theatre," said Victor Hugo, "the mob becomes a people"—watching the sacred drama of its own history; every spectator finding self and neighbour there, finding all the world there, as we find the sun in the bright spot under the burning glass' (*VP* 836). But Irish spectators misrecognise what represents them. The recoil from Synge's plays, as if foreign to Ireland, is also on the mind of this poem.

The next stanza cites 'the nothings that belong | To this bare soul' to expose politics and art that have faked or denied 'sacred drama': 'All that was sung, | All that was said in Ireland is a lie'. Yeats's irony includes his own patriotic utterances, and the echoes of *King Lear* reinforce radical standards of 'judgement': 'let all men judge that can | Whether it [Parnell's soul] be an animal or a man'. To those incapable of judging (ethically, politically, aesthetically), the poem tosses 'the rhyme rats hear before they die'. Such people are unlikely to appreciate the art that Yeats has made in Parnell's image. Earlier, the contrasting reflexivity of 'Some master of design | Stamped boy and tree upon Sicilian coin', has evoked Yeats's senatorial as well as literary achievements. Yet the aposiopesis of part II ('Had de Valera eaten Parnell's heart . . . Had Cosgrave . . . Had even O'Duffy . . .') puts the inadequate absorption of Parnell's politics and Yeats's literary movement on the long finger of history: 'Their school a crowd, his master solitude; | Through Jonathan Swift's dark grove he passed, and there | Plucked bitter wisdom that enriched his blood'. This suggests that rejection by the crowd may enhance the artist if it dooms the politician (including the politician in the artist): Swift combines both principles. Yet Yeats's rhetoric of 'solitude' is also a crowd-pulling device, and his habitual contrast between long-term and short-term visions belies an irrevocable break with the national audience. 'Parnell's Funeral' flatters an implied, and potential, Irish reader who is not a rat.

II

The rest of this introduction will raise, in a preliminary way, the disposition of Yeats's Irish audiences by looking at his reception from three main angles: Yeats's struggle to mobilise 'Hearers and hearteners of the work'; his poetry's implied reader; the religious and political factors that still condition author-reader relations. These motifs make various appearances in the essays that follow, but to rehearse them now may suggest some general principles.

Some *a priori* principles may also be relevant. In current academic usage the verb 'read' has greatly expanded its applications—to the point of losing precision and elasticity. Nonetheless, this volume takes 'reading' to signify any form of decoding, interpretation or construction which produces a version of 'Yeats'. The version may be that of a poet, autobiographer, critic, journalist, exponent of cultural politics, literary historian—all functions fulfilled by Yeats himself and consequently challenged in Ireland. Yeats, indeed, might partly allow the latterday elision whereby, as Jane P. Tompkins says, 'Reading and writing join hands, change places, and finally become distinguishable only as two names for the same activity.'[1] 'Reading' is certainly not Yeats's only metaphor for his art, just as language is not his only metonymy, but he often presents his inspiration as the reading/writing of a sacred book, a transcription from *anima mundi*: the 'half-read wisdom of daemonic images' (*VP* 427). On the other hand, most theorists would hardly sympathise with Yeats's fixation on 'Tables of the Law', or with his efforts to make his own text authoritative by weaving in cabbalistic signs against their 'murderous moth'. Yet this does not mean that theories of reading have nothing to say to Yeats (other than to depose his textual authority) or *vice versa*.

The theories that accord somewhat with Yeats's own theory and practice are not to be found at that end of the spectrum which locates all value in the reader's activity, or all interest in the conventional signifying systems thus brought to bear. This is also the end of the spectrum where the reader (and hence writer) is generally confined to the academy, determined by 'the configuration of . . . relationships' in 'the subjective classroom'.[2] In 'The Reader in History' Tompkins argues that 'the reader-response movement', because it 'assumes that the specification of meaning is the aim of the critical act', in fact 'owes nothing to the ancient rhetorical tradition it seems at first to resemble, and almost everything to the formalist doctrines it claims to have overturned'. Tompkins herself assumes, however, that classical or Renaissance concepts of language 'as a force acting on the world' are alien to modernity: 'The first requirement of a work of art in the twentieth century is that it should *do* nothing.'[3] As it happens, this piece of modernist received wisdom pinpoints an amusing contradiction in early Yeats: his poetry telling itself to 'nowise worship dusty deeds' while its entrepreneurial super-ego has already begun the career encapsulated by John P. Frayne: 'There never seems to have been a time in Yeats's life when he was not founding a society or hatching some collective literary scheme' (*UP1* 21-2). Frank O'Connor calls him 'a blazing enthusiast'; St John Ervine, 'one of the best advertising agents in the world' (*I&R* 334, 104). In fact, Tompkins's versions of classical civilisation and Renaissance England do not seem remote from turn-of-the-century Ireland: in the one, 'literature, its producers, and consumers are all seen in relation to the needs of the polity as a whole'; in the other, it is the task of a poet like Ben Jonson 'to express an attitude toward real persons and events—praising, blaming, memorializing, petitioning, thanking . . . poems are thought of as a form of influence, a means of accomplishing specific social tasks'.[4] It is not because Yeats consciously invoked ancient Greece, or summoned Ben Jonson and the Medicis to his side during Irish culture-wars, that his writing became 'rhetorical' and 'eloquent' in the traditional sense: an 'art of persuasive communication'.[5] 'What cared Duke Ercole' is itself the rhetorical articulation of a need: 'I always rouse myself to work by imagining an Ireland as much a unity in thought and feeling as ancient Greece and Rome and Egypt' (*Mem* 251). To come into its strength his poetry required more than an audience. It had to conceive and address an entire society. Yeats, who wanted (or thought he wanted) a congregation, found himself in an *agora*. Thus 'The Fisherman' attacks 'critics' *qua* fellow-citizens. Even today, his Irish academic readers have not quite forsaken the *agora* for the subjective classroom.

Ireland's microcosmic potential was not, of course, guaranteed or stable. Yeats adduced supposedly holistic communities from the past because he could hardly count on the hegemonic identity between writer's and reader's systems which some American theorists take to be normative. Hans Robert Jauss's definition of literature as writing that extends the 'horizon of expectations', seems more apt, especially if this is not merely a literary extension but a cultural intervention bearing 'desires, demands, and aspirations . . . calling into question and altering social conventions through both content and form':[6] 'Nor may I less be counted one | With Davis, Mangan, Ferguson . . .'. Yeats was to move the horizon less politely later on. Further, his multiple time-place zones accord with Susan R. Suleiman's *caveat* about the 'different horizons of expectations coexisting among different publics in any one society'.[7] It was, indeed, this very distance between contemporaneous horizons—initially the *fin-de-siècle* and Young Ireland—that kept Yeats's poetry on the stretch. Just as his prose was challenged by the divergent expectations of the *Bookman* and *United Ireland*, so his poetry (even against its will) began to present readers with what Jacques Leenhardt terms 'the short-circuit effect . . . produced whenever a conflict of meanings cannot be resolved' and which marks 'a "hole" in the checkerwork of meaning . . . through [which] the text may perturb the preestablished reading scheme'.[8] 'The Fisherman' dramatises that 'conflict of meanings' as pain felt by the author who allays it by giving his implied reader, his ideal reception over the horizon, a tangible shape. The push-pull of different audiences generated Yeats's politically frustrating but artistically fruitful discovery that you can't please all the interpretive communities all of the time. Trying 'to explain myself' to Maud Gonne (*Mem* 142) exemplifies the ever-shifting horizon between inception and reception.

The story of Yeats's appeal to various audiences through his publications and literary journalism of the 1890s, and his theatrical activities thereafter, has often been told. But certain patterns in the appeal and the response, and in how the response changed the appeal, illuminate the agency of his Irish reception in Yeats's art. It is, of course, ironical that the founder or co-ordinator of a national literary movement should have told his publisher in 1903: 'I write to remind you of our rule to send no copies of my books to Dublin papers . . . Reviews in Dublin papers sell no copies & I don't see why I should give them the oppertunity of attacking me' (*CL3* 341-2). This decision came to symbolise Yeats's sense of the antagonism out there: 'For twenty years I never even sent my books for review in to the Irish newspapers, an ignorant form of Catholicism is my enemy' (*L* 873). It is equally ironical that the founder of 'A People's Theatre', once thrilled by 'an audience at Longford . . . shopkeepers and lads of the town, who smoked and were delighted' (*L* 476), should have inverted that term to signify 'an unpopular theatre . . . an audience like a secret society where admission is by favour and never to many' (*Ex* 254).[9] Such abdications or strategic retreats do not simply accept defeat by Irish political and religious orthodoxies. Yeats's art constantly regroups in reaction to constituencies by which it refuses to be controlled and of which its regrouping is a critique.

The showdown in 1907 over Synge's *Playboy*—Yeats on stage confronting an actual Irish audience—was not foreseen by the poet who set out in the late 1880s to maximise all his assets. Nor was the youthful Yeats who urged that 'so much in the way of writing is needed for Irish purposes' (*CL1* 191) alert to his own mixed or unconscious motives as a publicist: ambition for his own work, ambition for a collective cultural renaissance, nationalist ambitions of fluctuating tilt and intensity, not to mention the promptings of class and religion. The public for his poetry was the one he most astutely fostered, as his relations with publishers testify;[10] but it was always difficult to ensure that these ambitions would co-operate rather than collide. He had to maintain the wobbly London-Dublin literary axis, and to combat vested interests who resented his brash appropriation of cultural nationalism: 'the condition of the country [is] now too serious for madrigals', said Sir Charles Gavan Duffy (*CL1* 312n.). Frayne sees Yeats's 'propagandistic writings of the nineties' as achieving their main success in that he 'held the attention of British journals and convinced the English reading public that a "Celtic Renaissance" was actually in progress. He once more made it intellectually respectable to be Irish' (*UP1* 58). But, of course, reputations made in Britain could be suspect, and many Irish people did not consider Yeats intellectually respectable. A letter to Lady Gregory catches the tangled threads of his audiences in May 1901:

> [Bullen] told me that he was amazed to find the hostility to me of the [Dublin] booksellers . . . I am looked upon as hetredox it seems . . . Russell told me . . . that clerical influence was he beleived working against me because of my mysticism. He accuses Father Finlay & his jesuits of working behind Moran. Memory of 'The Countess Cathleen' dispute accounts for a good deal. Bullen found the protestant booksellers little better . . . Magee, the College publisher said 'What is he doing here. Why doesnt he go away & leave us in peace.' He seems to have suspected me of some deep revolutionary design . . . [Bullen's traveller] said that Carleton and myself were received with the same suspicion . . . I imagine that as I withdraw from politics my friends among the nationalists will grow less, at first at any rate, & my foes more numerous. What I hear from Bullen only confirms the idea that I had at the time of 'the Countess Cathleen' row that it would make a very serious difference in my position out side the small cultivated class (*CL3* 71).

Although Gregory's reply hardly seems reassuring ('we want all the aids to popularity we can get for the theatre, having your enemies and Moore's enemies and the Castle in general against us' [*CL3* 74n.]), Yeats's next letter both makes a characteristic compensatory switch from political to cultural mode, and reverts to the lure of a wider audience than 'the small cultivated class': 'I have always felt that my mission in Ireland is to serve taste rather than any definite propaganda . . . Bullen and his traveller may have had too great expectation of the success they would have with my books & so have exaggerated the significance of the opposition' (*CL3* 74). Also, his announcement of 'withdraw[al] from politics' proved, as so often, premature. Deirdre Toomey's essay ('Moran's Collar: Yeats and Irish Ireland' pp. 45-83) demonstrates how *Cathleen ni Houlihan*, conceived between Yeats and Lady Gregory later that year, recouped 'friends among the nationalists' from Moran. It briefly made their theatrical venture 'a kind of Holy Place of Irish nationalism'.[11] Yet the play itself can be seen as the defensive move of a Protestant republican over-stressing his fealty. And if, as Maria Tymoczko suggests, he also rose to Frank Fay's bait, the quest for a popular audience may have taken him a bridge too far. Fay had urged that, for Yeats to achieve 'greatness as a dramatic poet', he had to 'give us a play . . . that will rouse this sleeping land' (*YA10*, 38). Yeats often laboured, not only when tutored by Gregory, to keep various groups on board—or in the theatre. Yet an audience politically gained could be an audience politically lost (the 'revolutionary design' of *Cathleen ni Houlihan* definitively excludes unionists). In fact, before 'the *Countess Cathleen* row' (1899) Yeats had been conciliatory: 'the last thing I desire is to give legitimate offence to any of my countrymen' (*L* 316). He and Lady Gregory kept an anxious eye on Synge's impact, and Earnán de Blaghd thought it a virtue that Yeats 'never permitted *The Tinker's Wedding* to be played in the Abbey' (*I&R* 389). But by the time of the *Plough and the Stars* row (1926) lines were deeply drawn. Yeats seems to have deliberately used the play and his Free State senatorial clout against the audience that had vilified Synge. In Gabriel Fallon's account: '[Yeats] looked at me with the light of battle in his eyes, smiled and said: "Fallon, I am sending for the police; and *this time* it will be *their own* police!"' (*I&R* 185).

A conflict between the urges to embrace audiences and to 'scorn' them was thus written into the Yeatsian script. Roy Foster, in an essay which corrects Yeats's martyrological icon of Synge, contrasts their management skills: 'In crises like Marie Walker's alienation from the Fays, Yeats was all for vehement offensive tactics, while Synge more wisely wanted "TO LET THE HARE SIT".'[12] Before the theatre, so to speak, dramatised his relations with audience, Yeats steered more buoyantly between controversy and conciliation, though already alert to tricky shoals. For instance, he did his best to keep Catholicism on side through cultivating Father Matthew Russell, editor of the *Irish Monthly*, while having to defend his recuperation of Carleton: 'Anything that any body may be doing in the way of Irish poetry interests me greatly . . . By the way I think you are unjust to Carleton he has drawn beatifully many entirely Catholic forms of life and virtue' (*CL1* 174). In 1892 he orchestrated a lively argument as to the locus of 'Ireland's Intellectual Capital'. Debate got real and bruising, however, with the struggle for power over the New Irish Library and hence over audiences. Yeats desired to 'enlist the sympathy of the young men who will have the building up of the Ireland of tomorrow' (*CL1* 312). His reaction to the first volume issued by the victorious Gavan Duffy (Thomas Davis's *The Patriot Parliament of 1689*) was to attack the Library's political and intellectual credentials. Invoking the republicanism of Tone, Mitchel (and, implicitly, O'Leary) as a counter to Young Ireland grown old, he asserted: 'Perhaps honest criticism, with as little of the "great day for Ireland" ritual as may be, can yet save the series from ebbing out in a tide of irrelevant dulness, and keep the best opportunity there has been these many decades from being squandered by pamphleteer and amateur' (*CL1* 398).

Yet there was a potentially awkward fissure not only between Yeats's invocation of republicanism and his plea for literature as 'almost the most profound influence that ever comes into a nation' (Arthur Griffith was to be his nemesis here); but also between his crusade for 'honest criticism' and his literary 'log-rolling'. In *United Ireland* (November 1894) Yeats had classically stated his aspiration to create a 'critical' public in Ireland. Rebutting a claim that 'Americans did not mind the London critics', he insisted that 'it is often necessary for an original Irish writer, to appeal first, not to his countrymen, but to that small group of men of imagination and scholarship which is scattered through many lands and many cities, and to trust to his own influence and the influence of his fellow-workers to build up . . . a cultivated public in the land where he lives and works' (*CLI* 409). This is Yeats optimistically seeing his London reputation as a bridgehead to Dublin. However, an 'ambition . . . to make criticism as international, and literature as National, as possible' did not, it seems, preclude his 'member[ship] of a happily incestuous group of younger writers who reviewed one another' (*UP1* 32). Yeats was already sensitive to the charge of 'log-rolling' brought by his political enemies. For instance, he asked Katharine Tynan to leave unsigned one of the two journalistic pieces on him that she published in November 1893: 'the blackguards over here of the [John F.] Taylor type are ever crying out about what they call log-rolling' (*CL1* 362). Increasing fame made it less per-

sonally necessary to Yeats that 'Every new Irish writer [should]
increase the public for evry other Irish writer' (*CL1* 455), while self-
critical self-renewal made him realise that he might become a victim
of his own propaganda (an issue discussed in my own contribution
to this collection). In 1901 he explained his revisions thus: 'One
changes for the sake of new readers, not for the sake of old ones'
(*CL3* 102). Even if he always log-rolled for Lady Gregory—sometimes absurdly—Synge and Joyce introduced him to a
better class of Irish protégé. His writing conspicuously changed for
the sake of Synge, who triggered 'an explosion of all that had been
denied and refused'—by Yeats as well as Ireland (*Mem* 223). First,
the attacks on *In the Shadow of the Glen*, then the *Playboy* riots, crys-
tallised not only Synge's but Yeats's 'long, bitter misunderstanding
with the wreckage of Young Irelandism' (*Mem* 154). This sequence
of events forced an open split between his notional Irish audiences,
between 'criticism' and 'opinion', which (as John Wilson Foster's
essay suggests pp. 180-212) may not be over yet.

Yeats's therapeutic 'Journal', mostly written in 1909 and crucial
to the remaking of his aesthetic, pivots on a crisis in relations
between poet and audience. 'Wreckage' (quoted above) betrays
Yeats's own unconscious state. His sense of having been routed by
Young Irelandism led him back to the terms of his admiration for
Richard Ashe King's lecture 'The Celt: the Silenced Sister' (December 1893): '[a man of letters] should, no matter how strong be his
political interests, endeavour to become a master of his craft, and be
ever careful to keep rhetoric, or the tendency to think of his
audience rather than of the Perfect and the True, out of his writing'
(*CL1* 371). (Alice Milligan's contrary view provided the germ of
'The Grey Rock'.) Now (February 1909) Yeats writes, marvellously:
'Opinion . . . is the enemy of the artist because it arms his
uninspired moment against his inspiration' (*Mem* 170). But inspiration, too, needs an armour if Yeats is to shake off 'a kind of fright, a
sense of spiritual loss' (*Mem* 171). Central to his meditations at this
period are two words that come together in 'Parnell's Funeral':
'popular rage'. He endeavours to conceive a 'discipline': i.e. a
psychological and aesthetic strategy for coping, first, with
unpopularity; secondly, with rage. In Yeats's usage 'rage' signifies
more than anger—obsession, madness. He admires Synge's apparent
detachment (as if trying to eat his heart) and is disturbed to discover
in himself 'a kind of Jacobin rage' (*Mem* 157) which should be the
degrading mark of his populist opponents. He analyses his social

demeanour to find help: 'I fear the representatives of the collective opinion, and so rage stupidly and rudely, exaggerating what I feel and think' (*Mem* 138). With reference to other orators, authors and impresarios, he tries to see a desire for general popularity, or its attainment, as a weakness. 'Against Unworthy Praise' may take sly comfort from the current unpopularity of Maud Gonne, self-styled 'voice [and] soul of the *crowd*' (*G-YL* 166); he says of AE's coterie, 'they long for popularity that they may believe in themselves' (*Mem* 148); and his sonnet to Douglas Hyde, 'Dear Craoibhin Aoibhin, look into our case', is multiply barbed. Yeats asks Hyde for the secret of the Gaelic League's success as contrasted with the English-language wing of the Revival. He implies that the Abbey is criticised for reasons which pretend to be aesthetic but whose inconsistency proves their political motive:

> You've dandled them and fed them from the book
> And know them to the bone; impart to us—
> We'll keep the secret—a new trick to please.
> Is there a bridle for this Proteus
> That turns and changes like his draughty seas?
> Or is there none, most popular of men,
> But when they mock us, that we mock again? (*VP* 264-5)

Yeats's irony plays off Hyde's fey *nom-de-plume* ('pleasant little branch') against the officialese of 'look into our case'—a hint that an artist has been corrupted into an institution. He insinuates, too, that Hyde's popularity depends on infantilising rather than educating his followers ('dandled . . . and fed'). Following Ronsard, this poem envisages no middle way between providing the pap that public opinion wants, and returning mock for mock. 'Mock' will be another word that denotes Yeats's strained relations with Irish audiences. However, in the 'Journal' he has already elaborated the mask as a mediating 'discipline' which might regulate such relations and enable mockery without injury to the mocker: 'In pursuit of the mask I resolved to say only fanciful and personal things, and so to escape out of mere combat' (*Mem* 139); 'If we cannot imagine ourselves as different from what we are and try to assume that second self, we cannot impose a discipline upon ourselves, though we may accept one from others (*Mem* 151). The mask—persona, attitude, tone ('Dear Craoibhin Aoibhin . . .')—thus becomes cognate with 'extending the horizon of expectations'. Indeed, it recognises such

an extension not merely as an artistic and cultural good, but as
essential to artistic survival. The mask does not renounce combat,
but promises to attack from the unexpected angles which are the
prerogative of art as opposed to 'a current code'. On the one hand,
we might see that very theatricality as impelled by the power of current codes. On the other, the provocation has complicated Yeats's
aesthetic. His insistence on 'phantasmagoria' originates as a blend of
psychotherapy and politics: a means of channelling rage and out-
manouvring the crowd. The most pessimistic stanza in 'Dialogue of
Self and Soul' defines his panic lest the 'mirror of malicious eyes'
should control the artist and remake the artwork in its image:

> The finished man among his enemies?—
> How in the name of Heaven can he escape
> That defiling and disfigured shape
> The mirror of malicious eyes
> Casts upon his eyes until at last
> He thinks that shape must be his shape?
> And what's the good of an escape
> If honour find him in the wintry blast? (VP 479)

Metaphors of sea and howling winds often figure the uncontrollable
forces, external and internal, whose power Yeats fears. However,
the next stanza re-affirms and resumes the first-person mask by
proposing to 'live it all again'.

III

Responsibilities, as this text evolved, re-positioned Yeats's poetry
with reference to Irish audiences. The vocative case is prominent, in
both phillipic and panegyric. 'Ireland in the Coming Times'—that
horizon of utopian expectations—has fractured into an implied
reader at odds with an implied mis-reader or non-reader. All the
'blind' and 'ignorant' responses to the literary movement are
summed up in 'Paudeen'. The ideal alternative takes on more indi-
vidualised forms: *'silent and fierce old man'*, *'Dowson and Johnson'*,
'Cosimo', 'O'Leary', 'Three women that have wrought | What joy
is in my days', the shade of Parnell invited to decode contemporary
Ireland. At the outset *'Pardon, old fathers'* and *'Poets with whom I
learned my trade'* firmly guide reader-response. In the former, family

history provides a more culturally nuanced point of departure than national history. (Thus Yeats's enforced textual revision from the Jacobite to the Williamite side at the Boyne makes no difference.) In 'The Grey Rock' he now makes a virtue of necessity by decisively preferring the aesthetic creed of the *fin-de-siècle* to Young Ireland and opinion: '*Nor gave loud service to a cause | That you might have a troop of friends . . .*'. The uniformity of 'troop' contrasts with those imagined Italian courts where the individuality of patron matches the individuality of artist. 'To a Wealthy Man' poses a central question from the *Journal*: 'Am I not . . . un-national in any sense the common man can understand? (*Mem* 251)' Irish comment on his direction tended to agree.[13] Yeats's implied reader and mis-reader belong to a range of dialectical rather than binary structures. 'Paudeen' resembles 'A Dialogue of Self and Soul' in that the faculties of the artist-speaker are infected by unintelligent response: 'Indignant at the fumbling wits, the obscure spite | Of our old Paudeen in his shop, I stumbled blind . . .'. The audience's fumble causes the artist's stumble. Yet this debased symbiosis is redeemed by another scenario: 'a curlew cried and in the luminous wind | A curlew answered'. 'Luminous wind', which fuses clarity of sight and sound, symbolises perfect conditions for transmission and reception. The poem ultimately includes the reader's 'soul' in its 'sweet crystalline cry'. Yeats's epilogue reverses this trajectory. It moves from its author internalising the pure voice of the Muse ('*that reed-throated whisperer*') to an audience's heedless insult: '*till all my priceless things | Are but a post the passing dogs defile*'. However, convoluted syntax intertwines a mediating sentence ('*While I . . . surmise companions | Beyond the fling of the dull ass's hoof . . . I can forgive even that wrong of wrongs*') with the sonnet's other inclination towards brooding on that wrong. The companions associated with a '*sterner conscience and a friendlier home*' render Yeats's ideal reception in terms of Coole and an imagined literary community. This inner asylum, at once welcoming and critically intelligent, suggests that Lady Gregory did, in a sense, save Yeats from artistic nervous breakdown. Of course, some readings of *Responsibilities* identify with its mis-reader.

The chief masks assumed by Yeats in *Responsibilities* are those of the epideictic speaker who praises virtue and censors vice. In its hour of need his imagination has reached for the oratorical skills sharpened by journalism and by his American tour of 1903-4: 'I am beginning to understand how an actor feals' (*CL3* 534). If Yeats's poetry subsequently multiplies its masks, praise and censoriousness are always called for. Perhaps his poetic temperature varies according to what he called the 'thermometer of abuse' (*CL3* 659). Six months on from 'The Fisherman', 'The People' begins with a parodic reprise of *Responsibilities* ('What have I earned for all that work') and digests Gonne's rebuke: 'Yet never have I, now nor any time, | Complained of the people'. Gonne's letters to Yeats contain some good advice as to the difference between their publics. However, Yeats could never quite renounce the poet's claim on both; and, even if Irish audiences did not listen, the rhetorical cast of all his poetic quarrels was confirmed. These draw on the full resources of *elocutio* (Brian Vickers might have illustrated 'Rhetorical Figures and Tropes' as comprehensively from Yeats's lyrics as from Shakespeare's plays).[14] Susan R. Suleiman quotes Paul de Man on literary authority: 'the ability of the mind to set up, by means of acts of judgement, formally coherent structures is never denied, but the ontological or epistemological authority of the resulting systems, like that of texts, escapes determination'; and adds: 'For the positivists it is precisely that authority whose determination must be affirmed'.[15] Yeats's rhetoric produces texts with strong designs on positivistic readers. Yet the contextual foundations and performative force of his poetry lay it dialectically open to history: to competing reading systems beyond the subjective classroom.

Hence the argument between 'Under Ben Bulben' and 'The Man and the Echo' as last thoughts on writing and reading. The former is spoken by a positivist—'Here's the gist of what they mean'—who initially claims authority from an occultist text: 'what the sages spoke'. He also invokes western canons ('Measurement began our might'), and his imperatives insist on achieved 'forms' in life and art: 'Completeness of their passions won', 'He completes his partial mind', 'Poet and sculptor, do the work', 'By his command these words are cut'. Yeats's later poetry sometimes keeps its spirits up by casting audiences into a posture of awe: 'Why did the people stare?' Thus 'Under Ben Bulben' commands its reader to gaze at a monument. However, 'The Man and the Echo', written in a less regular version of the same couplets, subverts completion of the life, perfection of the work and command of the reader. 'Did that play of mine . . . ?', like the echo's mere repetition, admits that reception is incalculable. It also admits the destabilising shock of Irish audiences. In doubting the speaker's 'epistemological authority' and the certainty of any audience outside his own echo-chamber, the scenario anticipates Beckett's inversion of Yeatsian oratory: 'What do we know but that we face | One another in this place?' However, the poem's indeterminacy ('And its cry distracts my thought') is yet another rhetorical tactic—albeit one which breaks the closed circuit and opens a further horizon of expectations. 'Man' says: 'All that I have said and done . . . Turns into a question still'; de Man says: 'the answer metamorphoses into a question'.[16]

IV

'Under Ben Bulben' may be sectarian as well as authoritarian. Roy Foster reads the 'Journal', which contains passages relevant to 'Under Ben Bulben', in less psycho-aesthetic (or more psycho-social) terms than my own reading above: '[it] is preoccupied by aristocracy, anti-egalitarianism and occasionally anti-Catholicism . . . The baseness and and intellectual corruption of Catholic education is stressed, the adherence of Protestantism to form, and Catholicism to formlessness'. Foster also mentions the 'robust contempt of Catholic values' to be found at Coole.[17] Part of Yeats's crisis was that the *Playboy* riots made it finally impossible to surf-ride religious difference. Moran had jeered at special-category status for Protestant Home Rulers; there was a sectarian dimension to the theatre's internal divisions; the *In the Shadow of the Glen* row (1903) had led Yeats to protest publicly against 'the obscurantism of the more ignorant sort of priest' along with that of 'the more ignorant sort of Gaelic propagandist' (*CL3* 452). 'Ignorance' and Catholicism are coming together. Above all, perhaps, Maud Gonne had sealed sexual betrayal with conversion. Now, in Conor Cruise O'Brien's words, '"An insult to Ireland", cried the first set of voices, and the second set responded: "an insult to Catholic Ireland".'[18] These voices finally goaded Yeats into thinking about Protestant Ireland, even if it took the legislature of the Irish Free State to add the 'people of Burke and of Grattan' to his rhetorical repertoire.[19] Did he thereby surrender to the bigoted expectations of 'malicious eyes', or did he accept that 'cultural fusion' was always a self-deceiving ideal?

   In keeping with Yeats's conciliations, delays and repressions, scholars have only recently embraced the full awkwardness of his religious contexts. What might be termed the Anglo-Irish gentlemanly tradition of writing about Yeats (Henn, Hone, Jeffares) either

does not read him against its own grain or, conditioned by the
protocols of mid-century Ireland, keeps the lid on some explosive
matters. Moran, D. P. does not disfigure the index. It seems that
Northern Ireland has played a part in re-opening, and perhaps continuing, religiously-based perspectives. This does not apply only to
the 'Northern nationalist' critiques discussed by John Wilson
Foster—for instance, to Seamus Deane's sophistications of Moran
and perhaps of Gavan Duffy. Though also deploying other frameworks, Vivian Mercier, F. S. L. Lyons, Roy Foster and W. J. Mc
Cormack have all situated Yeats in terms of historical relations
between Protestant and Catholic Ireland. These relations are still
unfolding as the North ponders 'parity of esteem'.

For example, Yeats's affiliation to the peculiarities and insecurities
of Irish Anglicanism has been brought into the foreground. The
'pious Protestants of my childhood' (*VP* 819) had faded from
view—whether as antagonists or stimuli—along with the cultural
and political presence of southern Protestantism. Joyce, in admiring
'The Adoration of the Magi' and 'The Tables of the Law',
understood Yeats's complementary heterodoxy, although he
thought him mad to open up a second front and get embroiled with
Catholic Ireland too.[20] Mercier has persuasively charted the
influence of Anglican evangelicalism on the Revival; balancing its
bigoted and conservative (as contrasted with English evangelicals)
aspect against its 'life-enhancing' idealism and social energy, and
explaining how theosophy in Dublin could hold 'almost exactly the
status of a tiny Protestant sect'.[21] Foster, in his essay 'Protestant
Magic', translates the 'supernatural dimension of the Irish Protestant
subculture' into more political terms as 'the reclamation of an elite
authority'. Thus 'occult preoccupations . . . mirror a sense of dis-
placement, a loss of social and psychological integration, and an
escapism motivated by the threat of a takeover by the Catholic middle classes'.[22] It is interesting that Yeats never compromised on
'magic', despite the damage to his Irish reputation, and that it should
validate his literary powers. In representing Yeats as a 'marginalised'
southern Protestant subject to a Catholic Ascendancy virtually in
place by 1900, Foster interprets the power-dynamics which moulded
his mask of *aristo* facing down *sans culottes*. Mc Cormack deals with
Yeats's precarious class-position by focusing on this textual upward
mobility. He discusses Yeats's ideology of 'Protestant Ascendancy'
with reference to the aristocratic gloss that the nineteenth century
had put on 'the consolidation of bourgeois hegemony'.[23] Mc

Cormack's deconstruction of 'ancestral houses', and of their credibility for critics such as Henn, has influenced Deane's perception of Yeats as 'translating into a proud assertion an almost comically absurd historical fiction'.[24] When set the task of establishing Yeats's class-position, a group of MA students at Queen's University put it too high.

Some questions that arise from this reinsertion of Yeats into Irish Protestant history are: how does his model of Protestantism respond to the conflicts that culminated in 1907? what do subsequent historical and literary commentaries make of Yeats's model? To these I would add the questions posed earlier as to whether he had been boxed in by the sectarianism that the Revival sought to transcend.

The qualities that Yeats came to associate with Protestantism—or, rather, with a section of Irish Protestant society—were, in one sense, 'shaped' by the malicious eyes and voices that had assailed his values. He knew that 'the small cultivated class' was not wholly Protestant. Nor did he actually like most Protestant members of that class (as Eve Patten's revisiting of Dowden and Yeats reminds us; pp. 29-44). However, the hostile 'crowd' was largely Catholic and it expressed its 'hatred' in Catholic nationalist terms. Yeats began to explain the deficiencies of this audience as a set of lacks: lack of tradition, culture, form. His charges, flavoured by Anglo-Catholicism *manqué*, not only claim a deep-rooted stake in the Ireland that matters, but significantly reverse the Catholic Church's historical view of Protestantism. Indeed, Yeats distinguished between Catholicism as religion and Catholicism as education—i.e., Irish Catholicism (*Mem* 187). Frank O'Connor saw him as 'a Catholic, typically a Catholic' (*I&R* 264). Also, for Yeats, sheer weight of numbers identified the Irish Catholic 'crowd' with mass culture elsewhere. Meanwhile Protestantism, perforce, acquired the solitary, 'minority' and supposedly aristocratic virtues that Yeats was trying to internalise: the 'power of self-conquest, of elevation' (*Mem* 213). He seems to have developed an 'us and them' mentality by now; although *'their own* police' (his phrasing to Gabriel Fallon) insists that 'they' made the first exclusionary move. It cannot be over-stressed that Parnell and Synge coalesced for Yeats as instances of Catholic Ireland repudiating its 'own'. Hubert Butler writes: 'to be called an alien is far more bruising [than other forms of political attack] since you cannot change your blood'.[25] Yeats's interest in birth, breeding and race, eventually in 'stocks' and eugenics, expresses his clash with a Catholic-ethnic version of Irish cultural

identity. Hence his stylisation of O'Connell *versus* Parnell. Hugh
Kearney observes that because 'ethnic nationalists established a
monopoly over the memory of O'Connell . . . civic nationalists
found an alternative symbol in . . . Parnell'.[26]

However, Yeats has been tempted into the ethnic jungle: the
trouble with 'analog[ies] between [the] long-established life of the
well-born and the artist's life' (*Mem* 156) stems not only from snobbery but from analogy—Yeats should have remembered his objections to allegory. The analogies had run out of steam, let alone
acceptability, before he used the adjective 'base-born' in 'Under Ben
Bulben'. (The poetry is a slow release of the anguished 'Journal' as
history seems to confirm its anguish.) However, ancestral houses at
the symbolic core of such notions helped Yeats, not so much to
demonstrate that the 'sense of form' is monopolised by Protestant
Ireland, as to concentrate on the building-blocks of his art and
reconceive tradition as cultural history rather than transcendental
legend and folk-lore. One consequence, traced by Peter McDonald's
essay here, is the extraordinary durability and influence of his lyrical
structures (pp. 213-42). But Yeats also applied his sense of form to an
entire architecture—'Character isolated by a deed | To engross the
present and dominate memory'—which would impose his images of
'Ireland's history' on 'those that hated *The Playboy of the Western
World*' and other recalcitrant audiences. (Eamonn Hughes's discussion of autobiographical intertextuality shows him at work on this
agenda, pp. 84-116.) Yeats's retrospective freeze-frames are exactly
the opposite of revisionist historiography—hence the challenge to
his biographer.

McDonald quotes a poem by Seamus Heaney which asks: 'How
habitable is perfected form?' Heaney's versions of Yeats continue a
line of response which is sometimes manifested by Irish writers and
critics from Catholic backgrounds. On this reading Yeats has
implicitly succeeded in his 'masked' counter-attack, since the
insecurity and defensiveness that prompted it are not picked up.
Heaney evokes Yeats as 'an authoritative public poet . . . the finished man among his enemies' without being alert to a possible pun
in 'finished'.[27] Thus his adjective 'habitable' vestigially renews a
siege. Indeed, Heaney has recently proposed the geometry of 'an
integrated literary tradition' as a 'quincunx' constituted by male
writerly towers, although in this instance he appropriates Yeats's
strengths for the historical cause of Catholic Ireland: 'the Norman
tower [is] a deliberate symbol of [Yeats's] poetic effort, which was to

restore the spiritual values and magical world-view that Spenser's armies and language had destroyed'.[28] Here Heaney may be attempting to redress a brand of vulgar post-colonialism which bundles together Spenser, Yeats, and 'literary unionism', but he violates the soul that Yeats owed to Spenser's poetry and religion. In 1942 Sean O'Faolain, less dominated by Yeats's freeze-frames and closer to his life and times, understood that 'his political ideas . . . were incubated in self-defence'. O'Faolain knows the class-score, too: 'All his pretensions to be part of the great Anglo-Irish lineage arose from this; and they were rather pathetic seeing that he was connected rather with trade and the more easily attainable professions.' Nonetheless, this statement belongs to a somewhat confused attack which is trying not to be impressed by the edifice that it seeks to demolish or replace, and which sets 'the aloof and subjective Yeatsian self-dramatisation' against 'common life'.[29] O'Faolain, like Heaney elsewhere,[30] takes Yeats's rhetoric of solitude literally, and turns it back upon him. And he is curiously drawn to Yeats's 'lovely grey suit', as Heaney to 'the great fur coat of attitude'.[31] On both sides of this conjectural literary fence there are enormous anxieties about status, about the image presented to the Other. Similarly, the extent to which you consider Yeats a political success or failure sometimes appears to depend on your own place in the current Irish scheme of things (his presence is construed as most formidable by representatives of the upwardly mobile Catholic constituency in Northern Ireland, who are not far from the ethos which produced Yeats's original antagonists). It may also depend on the ratio between literature and history in your data base: literary readings tend to credit Yeats with greater efficacy. However, assessing his impact from the perspective of contemporary Ulster unionism, George Boyce argues that whereas Catholicism could not have sold Home Rule in an England then more consciously Protestant, Yeats provided the 'Ireland of romance, song, writing, twilight', and the melody lingers on.[32]

If Yeats misreads Catholic Ireland (sometimes on purpose), Catholic Ireland can also misread Yeats. This applies epistemologically as much as politically; for instance, when his dialectical structures are flattened by a Catholic understanding of authority: 'one is awed by the achieved and masterful tones of that deliberately pitched voice'.[33] Yeats's authority depends, rather, on a clash of tones, on the frustration of his desire to be an acknowledged legislator, and this is where he eludes some admiring as well as malicious eyes. Temperament might have made Yeats a Catholic; history made him a Protestant. To provide a different illustration: just as Yeats's early poetry will always be the most 'popular'; so, for some people (not only Romantic England), he remains an Irish republican. The flame so lovingly tended by P.S. O'Hegarty ('He was always on the National side')[34] has, in recent years, flickered through death notices in *An Phoblacht/Republican News*. According to Damian Smyth's research,[35] the most common Yeats quotation in obituaries for 'IRA volunteers' is: 'We know their dream . . . they dreamed and are dead'. If Yeats's ambiguous 'enough' drops from sight, this censorship may not be the unanimous decision of individual readers, but copied from the back-cover of *The Last Post: The Details and Stories of Republican Dead 1913-1975* (1976), the stylebook of the National Graves Association. Yeats also features occasionally elsewhere in *An Phoblacht*. 'The centre cannot hold' has been one of his most abused tags throughout the Troubles, but never so much so as when it appeared as an enormous front-page headline, involving a grim double pun, over a photograph of devastated buildings in Belfast city centre.[36]

If Yeats can figure in Irish religious and political imaginations as Protestant and Catholic, nationalist and unionist, he might also be claimed for liberal and libertarian positions. Because of his (unusually honest) reflections on violence, and the debate about his fascist leanings, the Yeats who took some impatient shortcuts in the oppressive climate of de Valera's Ireland has too often usurped the Yeats who became 'a disturber of the old life' and who defended his theatre as 'disordering the discipline of the squads' (*CL3* 447). He wrote to the *United Irishman* regarding *In the Shadow of the Glen*: 'Extreme politics in Ireland were once the politics of intellectual freedom . . . but now, under the influence of a violent contemporary paper, and under other influences more difficult to follow, even extreme politics seem about to unite themselves to hatred of ideas.' This results from trying to silence those 'who have begun that experimental digging in the deep pit of themselves, which can alone produce great literature' (*CL3* 451). In the 'Journal', after stating how 'Irish things . . . make life nearly unendurable', Yeats says: 'The feeling is always the same: a consciousness of energy, of certainty, of transforming power stopped by a wall, by something one must either submit to or rage against helplessly . . . is it the root of madness?' (*Mem* 157). It is, perhaps, the continuing Irish impasse, of which Yeats's experience with Synge was a prophetic intuition:

one that obliged him to 'beat upon the wall | Till Truth obeyed his call'. His strategies for negotiating the impasse, for fighting censorships and 'hatred of ideas', for trying to control his own rage, may speak to contemporary Irish liberalism. As for Yeats's illiberal lapses in the 1930s, Louis MacNeice notes that a 'vacillation between would-be Fascism and neutrality . . . may be characteristic of Yeats but is also characteristic of his country'.[37]

The obituaries collated by Roy Foster in 'When the newspapers have forgotten me' (pp. 163-79) had a dress-rehearsal on Yeats's seventieth birthday (13 June 1935), when Yeats told Olivia Shakespear that he was being 'generally praised and petted' (L 835). Besides the international chorus of praise, the *Irish Times* commissioned 'articles from the pens of some of Ireland's foremost men of letters'.[38] In a politic interview given to the *Irish Press* Yeats said: 'The feud now is not so bitter . . . as the old hereditary feud between Unionist and Nationalist. I can get good discussion now on anything and the people do not fly at each other's throats' (I&R 227). Nonetheless, the snapshot of his Irish reputation in the *Irish Times*, thirty-four years on from the alarmed letter to Lady Gregory, still captures considerable strains with regard to politics and cultural politics. Thus the leading article on Yeats is sharply at odds with Aodh de Blacam's contribution, perhaps included for the sake of balance. The former uses Yeats to attack contemporary attitudes to the southern minority:

> He took his inspiration from the ancient Celtic legends of the West; but he always has been proud of the fact that he comes of Anglo-Irish stock—that he belongs to that section of Irish society which some of our ultra patriots stigmatise as 'the planters' . . . . In this way W.B. Yeats has set an example to his class, far too many of whom are inclined to accept the taunt of alien aspirations . . . . There never will be any real progress in this country until the people from whom Yeats sprang have taken their rightful place in the national being—and it is not the place of aliens, or even of Irish citizens on sufferance.

De Blacam, however, shows the dutifulness of the convert in wishing that Yeats were less of a fighter. He regrets that he ever fell out with Sir Charles Gavan Duffy: 'that impatient break . . . with the inarticulate popular tradition that was on his side'. Hence the fact that the Abbey 'never became the centre of a true national revival in which the *Táin* would return'. The burden of de Blacam's complaint is that controversy, scepticism, satire and mockery damage 'the great movements of national impulse' and 'challenge sacred things': Yeats, for example, has praised 'The Midnight Court': 'a work which is a morbid freak, totally untypical of Gaelic letters, with their stern chastity'. Here Yeats's rhetoric has startlingly conjured an anti-self, but de Blacam's article, largely a disquisition on the Gaelic tradition and its unbroken 'racial memory', cannot just be seen as a morbid freak. (He was a member of the Fianna Fáil executive.) Denis Johnston, writing on 'Yeats as Dramatist', mentions 'the practice of sectarian pamphleteers [who] try to exclude or dismiss Yeats from the annals of Irish literature with the catch-cry of "West Briton"', and remarks: 'Mr Yeats, in contemplating the whirlwind advance of the Gaeltacht, must sometimes experience a few of the sensations of Frankenstein'.

In taking or reflecting the aesthetic pulse of Yeats's movement, this symposium presents a mixed picture with various political overtones. Thus de Blacam wants the Abbey to become epic; Johnston wants Yeats to abdicate and allow it to become 'vulgar'; the drama critic Andrew E. Malone states that 'the Irish National Theatre is now at the parting of the ways' and implies that 'the tradition of the peasant' may no longer be relevant to a radically changed Ireland. It is still difficult to situate Yeats in an uncontentious model of twentieth-century Irish literature, while his own propensity to epitaphs confuses the issue: Ireland has hardly seen the last of its romantics. Discussing poetic traditions (pp. 117-62), I suggest that there are few clear-cut beginnings or endings (certainly not 1921 or Yeats's death). If literary faction and reaction share in a wider history, they also depend on mechanisms of tradition, on stimulus as well as conflict within and between generations. Nor need the conflict conform to familiar party-lines. But, given the hegemonic sensitivities attached to literary history as to Irish history in general, all critics walk a tightrope between interpreting politics as aesthetics and aesthetics as politics.

For example, there are the questions of how we categorise literary period and conceive literary genre. Since the mid 1970s the word 'Revivalist' has been used to signify a past-oriented, mythic and rural mindset, despite the shifts in co-ordinates and personnel between 1900 and 1939, and despite the movement's continuing repercussions (the Irish Literary Revival may not be over yet).

Terence Brown, the leading analyst of mid-century cultural dynamics, edited a section of the *Field Day Anthology of Irish Literature* (1991) under the rubric: 'The Counter Revival: Provincialism and Censorship 1930-65'. As Brown's material shows, in fact, serious writers were more united in countering provincialism and censorship than divided between Revivalist and 'counter-Revival' tendencies. Like other critics, Brown uses an opposition between 'idealism' and 'realism' to demarcate periods: 'In such a context, realism seemed the appropriate artistic mode. Ideals had apparently diminished to a day-to-day pragmatism.'[39] But even if we could pin a date on the death of Romantic Ireland, there is a distinction between realism as social philosophy or social practice, and realism as artistic mode. Nor should poetry be seen as inherently more idealist than prose. Again, post-Treaty Ireland became not just provincially drab, but isolationist, repressive and sometimes frightening: Flann O' Brien is its Kafka. As the 'realist' prose writers O'Faolain and O'Connor also testify, religious and Gaelic idealists ran unpragmatically rampant. In 'The Future of Irish Literature' (*Horizon*, 1942) O'Connor refers to 'anguish and claustrophobia', 'emptiness and horror', 'a fanatical and corrupt middle class', 'religious secret societies'.[40] There are Yeatsian notes here, as in O'Faolain's companion-piece, 'Yeats and the Younger Generation'. For all his declaration that Yeats was a bad father who 'left no helpful guidance', O'Faolain defines the 'impasse' faced by young Catholic writers as a struggle 'between their deep-rooted love of their own people [and a] deep-rooted longing for intellectual detachment, independence of thought, converse with the world'.[41] *The Bell* was, even then, resorting to Yeatsian rhetorics and identifying his 'bitter thought' with that of its editor.[42]

In poetry the most explicit attempt to eliminate Yeats was Leslie H. Daiken's anthology *Goodbye, Twilight* (1936), an idealistic text which thinks itself realist. Full of anti-Treaty, Connollyite polemic, Daiken's introduction stigmatises the more aesthetically based rebellion of MacGreevy, Beckett, Devlin and Coffey, 'driven by the psychology of escape . . . across the wastelands of interiorisation, and technical experiment'.[43] But there may be no refuge for Yeats here either: critics who advocate the 'determined urban internationalism' of 'poets who did not take their bearings from Yeats' often repeat an extra-aesthetic nuance in the utterances of the poets themselves (Coffey, MacGreevy).[44] International modernism sometimes carries nationalist baggage.[45] Whether during his lifetime or in retrospect, an Irish stress on not-Yeats differs from an English or American stress on, say, not-Eliot. Thus Joyce has lately been brought home to deracinate Yeats. Terence Brown had to call for order in a 'critical debate' which polarised the two writers: 'Yeats, it seems, passed the Irish nation a dud local cheque—Joyce can draw on the inexhaustible credit of the European and world banks.'[46] Joyce the anti-nationalist has been reinvented to serve a theoretically street-wise, subtextually sectarian discourse which marginalises Yeats by calling his nationalism 'essentialist'. Joyce himself, of course, ignored these formal and ideological checkpoints. To quote Richard Ellmann: 'In Paris Joyce's friends . . . considered his passion for Yeats quaint, and they were startled also by his distaste for Eliot'.[47]

After the Easter Rising Yeats feared that 'all the freeing of Irish literature and criticism from politics' had been 'overturned' (L 613). This might also be unconscious fear for his own reputation and posterity, since the reader over the horizon could now be less defiantly imagined. For Susan R. Suleiman, among the advantages of Jauss's theory is that it involves following 'changes in understanding [which are] always functions of changes in the reader's horizon of expectations, changes which are themselves the result of both literary evolution and the evolution of cultural, political, and social conditions and norms in the society at large'.[48] On the one hand, Yeats's potential Irish audience has changed in a less evolutionary fashion (the virtual disappearance of his Protestant world makes it easier for him to be co-opted by American-inflected modernism). On the other, the recrudescence in Northern Ireland of 'the old hereditary feud between Unionist and Nationalist' has caused Yeats to be re-read and re-written—not only in negative terms. 'Meditations in Time of Civil War' governs the poetic landscape, renewing Yeats's themes as well as his forms. David Ward emphasises the switch from Pegasus to Proteus in the drafts of 'At the Abbey Theatre'.[49] It was by asking 'Is there a bridle for Proteus?' that Yeats arrived at his protean art. Since the 1890s Ireland has served various exclusion-orders on Yeats ('Why doesnt he go away & leave us in peace', as the Trinity College bookseller asked). It has tried heresy-hunting, Moranism, Gaelicism, Connollyism, modernism, post-colonialism, yet somehow he hangs in there—a Big Bang in whose explosion Irish literature still lives. But Yeats's audiences made his poetry, too. Perhaps his real glory was that he had such enemies.

EDNA LONGLEY

NOTES

1.　Jane P. Tompkins (ed.), *Reader-Response Criticism: From Formalism to Post-Structuralism* (Baltimore and London: John Hopkins University Press, 1980), Introduction, p. x.
2.　David Bleich, 'Epistemological Assumptions in the Study of Response', *ibid.*, p. 159.
3.　Jane P. Tompkins, 'The Reader in History', *ibid.*, pp. 201-3, 210.
4.　*Ibid.*, p. 204, p. 208.
5.　Brian Vickers, *In Defence of Rhetoric* (Oxford: Clarendon Press, 1988), p. 1.
6.　Robert C. Holub, *Reception Theory: A Critical Introduction* (London and New York: Methuen, 1984), p. 68.
7.　Susan R. Suleiman, Introduction to (eds) Susan R. Suleiman and Inge Crosman, *The Reader in the Text: Essays on Audience and Interpretation* (Princeton, New Jersey: Princeton University Press, 1980), p. 37.
8.　Jacques Leenhardt, 'Towards a Sociology of Reading', *ibid.*, p. 224.
9.　See Ian Jack, *The Poet and his Audience* (Cambridge: Cambridge University Press, 1984), pp. 150-6.
10.　Warwick Gould, '"Take Down This Book": Yeats's Early Volumes, 1895-99', lecture at the Yeats International Summer School, Sligo, August 1995.
11.　Conor Cruise O'Brien, *Passion and Cunning and other Essays* (London: Grafton Books, 1988), p. 33.
12.　R. F. Foster, 'Good Behaviour: Yeats, Synge and Anglo-Irish Etiquette', *Paddy and Mr Punch: Connections in Irish and English History* (London: Allen Lane, The Penguin Press, 1993), p. 201.
13.　E.g., George O'Neill, in the *Irish Catholic*, 23 December 1911.
14.　Vickers, *In Defence of Rhetoric*, pp. 491-8.
15.　Suleiman, Introduction to *The Reader in the Text*, pp. 43-4.
16.　Paul de Man, Introduction to Hans Robert Jauss, *Toward an Aesthetic of Reception* (Brighton: The Harvester Press, 1982), p. xiii.
17.　Foster, *Paddy and Mr Punch*, pp. 231, 224.
18.　Conor Cruise O'Brien, *Passion and Cunning*, p. 34.
19.　See Edna Longley, '"Defending Ireland's Soul": Protestant Writers and Irish Nationalism after Independence', in *The Living Stream: Literature & Revisionism in Ireland* (Newcastle upon Tyne: Bloodaxe Books, 1994), 130-49.
20.　See Richard Ellmann, 'Yeats and Joyce', in (ed.) Liam Miller, *The Dolmen Press Yeats Centenary Papers MCMLXV* (Dublin: The Dolmen Press; Oxford: Oxford University Press; Chester Springs, Pennsylvania: Dufour Editions, 1968), p. 448.
21.　Vivian Mercier, 'Evangelical Revival in the Church of Ireland, 1800-69', in (ed.) Eilis Dillon, Mercier, *Modern Irish Literature: Sources and Founders* (Oxford: Clarendon, 1994), pp. 64-85 (pp. 70, 80).
22.　Foster, *Paddy and Mr Punch*, pp. 220-2.
23.　W. J. Mc Cormack, *Ascendancy and Tradition in Anglo-Irish Literary History from 1789 to 1939* (Oxford: Clarendon Press, 1985), p. 330.
24.　Seamus Deane, *Celtic Revivals* (London: Faber and Faber, 1985), p. 30.

25. Hubert Butler, 'The Country House After the Union', *Escape from the Anthill* (Mullingar: The Lilliput Press, 1985), p. 55.

26. Hugh Kearney, 'Contested Symbols of Nationhood 1800-1995', paper given at the eighth John Hewitt International Summer School, Co. Antrim, July 1995.

27. Seamus Heaney, *The Redress of Poetry: Oxford Lectures* (London: Faber and Faber, 1995), p. 89.

28. 'Frontiers of Writing', *ibid.*, p. 199.

29. Sean O'Faolain, 'Yeats and the Younger Generation, *Horizon*, 5:25 (January 1942), 50-1.

30. See Seamus Heaney, Introduction to 'William Butler Yeats (1865-1939)', *The Field Day Anthology of Irish Writing* Vol. II (Derry: Field Day, 1991), pp. 786-7.

31. Seamus Heaney, 'Yeats as an Example?', *Preoccupations: Selected Prose 1968-1978* (London: Faber and Faber, 1980), p. 112.

32. George Boyce, '"They Have Got Yeats": Asking some more of the right questions about Literature and Politics in Ireland', *Text and Context*, 3 (Autumn 1988), 48.

33. Heaney, *Preoccupations*, p. 109.

34. P.S. O'Hegarty, 'W.B. Yeats and Revolutionary Ireland of his Time', *Dublin Magazine*, 14:3 (July-Sept. 1939), 22.

35. This material was orally communicated to me.

36. *An Phoblacht*, 9 January 1992.

37. Louis MacNeice, review of Allan Wade (ed.), *The Letters of W.B. Yeats* (*New Statesman and Nation*, 2 Oct 1954), reprinted in Alan Heuser (ed.), *Selected Literary Criticism of Louis MacNeice* (Oxford: Clarendon Press, 1987), p.190.

38. These were collected into a booklet under the auspices of Irish PEN. The other contributors, besides those I name, were Francis Hackett, Sean O'Faolain and F.R. Higgins.

39. Terence Brown, *Field Day Anthology* Vol. III, p. 90.

40. *Horizon*, 5:25 (January 1942), 59-62.

41. *Ibid.*, 50-1.

42. See 'Fifty Years of Irish Literature', *The Bell*, 3:5 (February 1942), 333. The editorial is followed by a selection from 'The Wisdom of W.B. Yeats'.

43. Leslie H. Daiken (ed.), *Goodbye, Twilight: Songs of the Struggle in Ireland* (London: Lawrence and Wishart, 1936), Introduction, p. xii.

44. Patricia Coughlan and Alex Davis (eds), *Modernism and Ireland: The Poetry of the 1930s* (Cork: Cork University Press, 1995), Introduction, p. 20. However, the perspectives of this collection of essays are usually more complex than those of Michael Smith in his preface to *Irish Poetry: The Thirties Generation*, first published as *The Lace Curtain*, no. 4 (1971).

45. See 'Poetic Forms and Social Malformations', in Longley, *The Living Stream*, 196-226.

46. Terence Brown, 'Yeats, Joyce and the Irish Critical Debate', *Ireland's Literature: Selected Essays* (Mullingar: The Lilliput Press, 1988), p. 85.

47. *Dolmen Press Yeats Centenary Papers*, p. 473.

48. Suleiman, Introduction to *The Reader in the Text*, p. 36.

49. David Ward, 'Yeats's Conflicts with his Audience, 1897-1917', *English Literary History*, 49:1 (Spring 1982), 143-63 at p. 153.

A 'general crowd of small singers':
Yeats and Dowden Reassessed

Eve Patten

IN 1888 JOHN TODHUNTER wrote to Professor Edward Dowden 'Have you subscribed for Willie Yeats's volume of poems? I believe he has now got enough subscribers to induce Kegan Paul to take it—I think it a most promising first volume. He has genuine imagination, richness of diction, and above all a power of writing easy musical verse quite remarkable in these days of Tennyson, Rossetti or their followers. . . . In fact he has poetic genius.'[1] In theory Dowden needed little convincing: as a friend of the family he had encouraged the young poet and praised his early work, but Todhunter's enthusiasm reads nonetheless as an attempt to recruit the critic who had hitherto expressed in private mixed feelings towards the emergent poet. While Yeats was still at this stage, deferential to the senior man of letters, biographer of his beloved Shelley and long-time friend and supporter of his father, Dowden had expressed quiet misgivings. 'I sometimes see Willie Yeats' he had written to Todhunter two years earlier. 'He hangs in the balance between genius and (to speak rudely) fool. I shall rejoice in the first. But it remains doubtful. Don't make public the brutalities of this letter.'[2]

The souring of the Yeats/Dowden relationship over the next ten years as recorded by Yeats in *Reveries* is shaped to a considerable extent by subsequent pressures. Dowden was readily sacrificed as the representative of a Victorian ethos which the young poet wished to reject, particularly when juxtaposed with the preferred paternalism of John O'Leary. Psychologically, too, Yeats was exercising and exorcising in his attitude to the Professor a hangover from the latent strains in the friendship between Dowden and his father. Dowden's consistent anxiety over the uncertain career of the painter whom he had long regarded as a soul-mate was met increasingly with disenchantment and criticism on the part of Yeats senior. Later, reading the letters exchanged between the two, Yeats perceived that underlying the friendship there had 'long been an antagonism'. Maintained as an occasional contact, Dowden was viewed as a disappointment to both father and son and at length abandoned to the 'barren soil' of Dublin Unionism (*Au* 85-9; 235).

In the terms of this somewhat schematic retrospect Dowden has been twice damned in the history of the Revival, his political casting in the role of dour Unionist hack providing a causal background for the literary alienation and ultimate failure of 'a man born into the world to write a life of Southey', as Yeats would describe him.[3] The public controversy which he provoked in 1895, pursued in the Saturday issues of the *Daily Express* and collected later as *Literary Ideals in Ireland* (1899), secured for him a place as chief antagonist to Yeats and his circle. The debate itself was no bad thing for the new movement, serving at least to sharpen the respective and divergent agenda of William Larminie, AE, John Eglinton and Yeats himself, while Dowden's denunciation of what he perceived as the vulgarity, lack of critical discrimination and bogus patriotism of the Revival in its early phase was a useful reminder of the need for scrupulous dealings with the ghost of Thomas Davis. But in his high-handedness, together with his use of Trinity's Historical Society as a forum from which to ridicule both the concept of a national literature and Yeats's 'Thirty Irish Books', Dowden played into the hands of his opponents.[4] The fused ideologies of Unionism and University were more than sufficient to isolate him. If Ireland's critics had failed her as Yeats claimed, Dowden, spurred on by the sour grapes of frustrated creative and political desire, was the embodiment of their collective irresponsibility.

The reduction of the controversy to a personality clash—albeit one underwritten by conflicting political drives—makes it difficult to re-evaluate Dowden's unhappy position on the margins of a Yeatsian kinesis. Certainly his negative characteristics cannot be disguised, least of all his persistent West Britonism. Thanking Todhunter for a sketch of England which he had sent, he wrote: 'Its English spirit is like that of home to one who has been a visitor, he and his kith, for three hundred years in Ireland. But I am grateful to Ireland too, for England, I fear, knows no such sea as we saw racing in the Atlantic fashion all the summer in Donegal bay.'[5] His rhetoric is equally problematic. The ironic strain which Yeats repeatedly identifies in his personality leads Dowden too often towards caricature and hyperbole. His now familiar depiction of the new movement as consisting in 'flapping a green banner in the eyes of the beholders and upthrusting a pasteboard "sunburst" high in the air' is easy pickings for the counter-attacks of Yeats and subsequent critics, and his plea for cosmopolitanism at a time of unprecedented domestic regeneration in the arts is open to interpretations of anti-nationalism.[6] Habitually overlooking his island, Dowden failed to place his trust in native creativity, leading Terence Brown to highlight in his portrait of an otherwise sympathetic and scholarly Victorian a discernible racism and a sensibility deformed by colonialism.[7]

What tends to be left out of the Dowden equation, however, are the wider social and, specifically, civic dynamics of late nineteenth-century Ireland. In the light of the coherence of Yeats's subsequent career management Dowden appears as an idiosyncratic and recalcitrant figure: a configuration which glosses over first, his importance as a link man for Dublin's *literati* and second, the existence of what was a more complex social and intellectual constituency than the essentialising denomination of Dublin Unionist Ascendancy will permit.[8] The cultural hegemony which the Revival appropriated was (and is) compelling enough to have refigured the more tentative or gradual formation of intellectual aristocracy which was its immediate predecessor. W. J. Mc Cormack is right in insisting that 'what has been less than thoroughly investigated is the historical space opening up between the apparent location of Yeats's tradition (the eighteenth century in essence) and the location of its execution (Yeats's own lifetime, Yeats's own textual being)'.[9] It is easy to miss in particular, when attempting to reconstruct the circle into which Yeats emerged as a poet, the scholarly but decidedly less charismatic fellowship of scientists, mathematicians and antiquarians affiliated to Trinity College or the Royal Irish Academy. Dowden's adverse reaction to the Revival was chiefly a defence of personal literary and political values which were to prove increasingly untenable, but it was also a last stand for the ascendancy of scholarship which he, like many of his background and generation, looked to as a basis for social stability and cultural hegemony.

Here Dowden's natural reticence to declare affiliation to any 'troop and banner-bearing' idealism served him ill, for the disinclination which he showed towards the diverse literary groupings of the period affected, simultaneously, his ability to render into prose the social dimension of his own cultural creed. Where Yeats and AE were uninhibited in their appeal to a mandate, particularly in the expansiveness of the 1895 debate, Dowden failed to project a convincing and necessary counter vision of what his community was. It was left to John Eglinton to stake a posthumous claim for Dowden which, while damning with faint praise, at least begins to endow him with some degree of national consciousness:

The Intellectuals always smiled when the 'question of religion' was dragged in. But what they advocated, and at length succeeded in setting up, was nothing more or less than a Catholic Ireland. Well, the Ireland contemplated by Dowden was a Protestant Ireland; that is to say an Ireland in which Protestant ideals were paramount. And he was perfectly entitled to conceive of a Protestant Ireland. What is more, Protestant Ireland was really the proper name for the Ireland conceived of by the Intellectuals. It was in Irish Protestantism that Ireland, dumb through the ages, had found a voice. The conception of Ireland as 'a great capacity not yet brought into action' (Grattan's words) was a Protestant conception. The ideal Ireland, as conceived of by Dowden, was the rounding forth of the English connection, a luminous filling in of a hitherto blank space, a country in a word, for which the glorious part remained of realising in these islands the perfect entelechy of an ideal for which he was ready to accept the name 'English'.[10]

If Eglinton's matrix of terms—within which both 'English' and 'Protestant' are contingent—is to be of any use, it is in exposing Dowden's relationship to a tradition of Irish Augustanism as much as West Britonism; to a Grattanite ideal of enlightened Irish Protestantism, civic virtue, scholarship, patriotism and intellectual liberty. This is a generous interpretation, perhaps, which cannot disguise the ambiguities stemming less from Eglinton's shorthand and more from Dowden's short-sightedness in attempting to translate eighteenth-century idealism into a volatile nineteenth-century reality without the benefit of Yeatsian rhetoric. Nonetheless, Eglinton provides an image of Trinity's Professor of English at least considering the need for cultural focus, and thereby the need for the cultural leadership which would provide some form of national self-definition, under the Union *and* within an international arena.[11]

Viewing Dowden from this perspective helps to reduce the apparent erraticism of his position in resisting the Revival, and relocates him within a Victorian tradition which looked to concepts of *clerisy* as central to the maintenance of strong political culture. In this respect too, Eglinton's description reinforces Dowden's proximity to Samuel Ferguson, who had consolidated by the early 1880s his own significantly more cohesive and developed version of cultural aristocracy derived from an eighteenth-century model. It is ironic that the origin of the Dowden/Yeats controversy was, in effect, Sir Roden Noel's lecture on Ferguson, which was first delivered to the Irish Literary Society in London and subsequently re-read in Dublin in February 1895. Dowden's lack of support on this occasion was construed by Yeats and others as a betrayal not only of national idealism but of friendship, an interpretation which obscured the true conditions of the long-term acquaintance which had existed between the two men.[12] Despite his disappointment in the apathy of the men of Trinity College when it came to creating a national literature, Ferguson shared with Dowden a vision of an organic scholarly community as a stabilising and enriching force within the country as a whole, and as a preface to any sustained cultural agenda.

It is worth looking briefly at those elements of Ferguson's legacy which were inevitably ignored by Yeats but which help to illuminate aspects of Dowden's reaction. For both Victorians the mainstay of any credible cultural leadership was its rootedness in interdisciplinary scholarship; in other words, in the systematic cross-fertilisation, as it were, of the scientific with the literary or historical, the antiquarian and the archaeological. Throughout his working life as a poet, critic and archivist, Ferguson was connected to a network of scholarship which extended beyond Ireland to Scotland and France, where much of the best antiquarian work on Celtic material was being done. He depended entirely on the belief that such a community was demarcated by the scientific methods and professional skills of the gentleman amateur, an ethos which he defined in his 1882 inaugural speech on taking up the Presidency of the Royal Irish Academy after the death of the scientist Robert Kane. Here he defended science, first as the basis on which the existence of societies such as the Academy could be justified, secondly as the natural companion to Philosophy, History and Poetry, central

to education and exploration in all forms. The subjects in which
Irish scholars of the nineteenth century excelled—whether
astronomy, mathematics, chemistry or philology—were combined
as the basis upon which Ireland would be established as a stable
home of patriotic endeavour and cultural pre-eminence.[13]

Ferguson's concept of an integrated intellectual aristocracy relates
to what several commentators have established as a pervasive and
distinctly Victorian discourse.[14] The constituency of such a community coincided inevitably, though not exclusively, with the membership of the Protestant Ascendancy, but it was consolidated
through practices of shared and competing scholarship, the formation and reformation of societies, institutions and clubs, and the
network of mutual interest which embraced the professional and
clerical classes in addition to the gentleman scholar. His confidence
in the effectiveness of such a body to form a dynamic and organic
civil hierarchy is expressed frequently in his writing, most convincingly in a passage which celebrates the achievements of mid Victorian Ireland as the direct result of interdisciplinary effort and
interest, generated by colleagues from a range of administrative,
engineering and scholarly disciplines:

> No stronger force of scientific and literary ability ever existed
> together in this country. Hamilton, a pure mathematician,
> metaphysician, and poet, looked out from his intellectual obser-
> vatory over all the realm of mind and matter. He stood so high that
> all who looked up at all saw and recognised his pre-eminence. James
> Pim, then junior, in introducing our first line of railway, conceived
> within prudent realisation the largest views of social advancement
> due to the locomotive and the electric telegraph. He was a man of
> ardent imagination; not a poet himself, but the associate not only of
> engineers and accountants, but of poets, and inspired with an
> enthusiasm as energetic as theirs, but an enthusiasm compounded
> with sagacity, that exerted itself in the production of works of
> mechanical and industrial organisation. He was a great diviner of
> the capacities of men. As Petrie saw and cultivated the power of
> O'Donovan and Curry, so he developed the latent workmanlike
> ability of Dargan. Larcom, then Lieutenant Larcom or Captain,
> with the statistical genius of Petty combined the higher political
> economy that we now call sociology, in its most human and
> sympathising applications. Every development of a self-respecting
> patriotism that could advance and elevate a people had a place in his

Economics. In speaking of Petrie educing the literary ability of O'Donovan, it might be questionable whether Larcom should not have been named as the nurturer of Petrie. But the truth is, that where great and congenial minds are brought together, such as Pim's, Stokes's, Larcom's, Petrie's, it is impossible to say from which intellectual centre the electric energy proceeds. The power—or rather the involuntary capacity—of imparting enthusiasm is one of the greatest gifts of great men.[15]

Ferguson's social vision was more confident than anything Dowden would have to offer; his idealism more finely tuned to the needs and promise of the national condition. Like Dowden, nevertheless, he was to be compromised by Yeats who was highly selective and conditional in the use he made of his predecessor.[16] Yeats's apotheosis of Ferguson immediately after the latter's death in 1886 appeared as a move to salvage the poet from the stifling philistinism of Irish Victorianism, but at the expense of what Ferguson had espoused in the *same* Irish Victorianism as energising and supportive. While applauding the awkward epics 'Conary' and 'Congal', Yeats significantly devalued the antiquarianism which Ferguson had considered key to his cultural programme, complaining that 'towards the last . . . when [Ferguson] had exchanged poetry for antiquarian studies, his Nationalism (in the political sense), though not his patriotism, became less ardent'.[17] The inheritance which he drew from Ferguson was in reality a process of pragmatic misrecognition which was extended to his predecessor's intellectual circle. Reviewing Mary Ferguson's posthumous biography of her husband Yeats dismissed it as a collection of the vapid opinions of dignitaries, barristers and bishops, 'a class at whose dinner-tables conversation has long perished in the stupor of anecdote and argument'.[18] The criticism reflects the ease with which Ferguson's vibrant nineteenth-century cultural aristocracy was translated retrospectively into a sterile Ascendancy hierarchy.

Dowden's response to Yeats was contextualised by the fracture of the cultural lineage which the young poet was simultaneously claiming as central to his own purpose. Yeats's elision of key discrepancies between Ferguson's inclusive cultural nationalism and the exclusive policies of the Revival served to isolate Dowden further from the literary community which the Revival had begun to circumscribe. It is interesting to see, therefore, how echoes of Ferguson's accommodating phraseology can be traced in Dowden's efforts to defend his position. In the introduction to *New Studies in Literature* (1895) he attempts to balance his strictures against the separatist tendency of the new movement with a vision of plurality, couched in the language of his former associate. We can conceive, he wrote, 'of an Irish literary movement which should command our deepest interest and sympathy; a movement in which such differences of national character as perhaps may exist should manifest themselves not of deliberate purpose, but naturally and spontaneously'.[19] If such sentiments were indeed intended as an indirect allusion, they read as a vain attempt to invoke the authority of Ferguson before that authority was conclusively usurped.

More pointedly, Dowden's anxieties concerning the shifting cultural climate frequently recall the social aspects of Ferguson's agenda. Early in 1889, the year in which *The Wanderings of Oisin* was published, Dowden wrote to Todhunter thanking him for sending good news of the Yeats household. 'JBY himself could have had a great deal of happiness without success', he wrote, 'but I am very glad that Mrs Yeats has had all these sources of hope and comfort.' He continued:

I did not mean in the *Fortnightly* article to say anything against what is genuine in any Irish intellectual movement, or against local predelictions anywhere; but I think we have always suffered from not being able to approach things in Ireland from a central standpoint—eg: the absurdities of Irish antiquaries and others who were not equipped with scientific knowledge. And I also wanted to point out that much of the best work is not adscripted to the glebe, but if rooted in any soil lives in a wider spiritual world—eg; the mathematics of McCullagh, Hamilton and Salmon. To encourage Irishmen to be masters in any and every province is the way to create a true literature in this country, and not to whip them on to a national sentiment purpose.[20]

While Dowden's personal and more emphatic grievances related to his predictions that the introversion of the new movement would eventually render it fruitless, the communal vulnerability suggested here implicates a connected group of established scholars comprised largely of his academic and, in the case of Trinity's new Provost George Salmon, political associates whose contribution was peripheral to the Revival agenda. The naming of names resembles, too, the tendency of Ferguson and later Yeats himself to list apostles and activists in an attempt to annex their respective and ideal cultural communities, a sign that Dowden was beginning to understand the nature of the contest in which he was involved.

As a representative as much as an individual, therefore, Dowden sensed the danger of being culturally short-changed. This aspect of his anxiety underlies in particular his defence of science, frequently employed as a loose term covering a range of activities integral to the collective authority of Irish scholarship. Here the nature of the clash with Yeats comes into sharper focus. For Dowden, unity of culture entailed the recognition of the scientific as integral to the creative, the scientist as compatible with the poet. His was essentially a holistic literary vision: it was in their indulgence in sentiment, passion and confessionalism rather than 'the study of outward things and of social life' that the Romantics had disappointed him; whereas Whitman, the poet of democracy and practicality, won his support. Similarly, he championed the scientific imagination of George Eliot, much to the chagrin of the young Yeats who seized upon the novelist as another stick to beat the Professor.[21]

The debate had relevance beyond the bear-pit of literary criticism, however. On several occasions Dowden defended the place of science in the university curriculum, a pressing issue in the wake of Newman and the future of Irish university reform.[22] More generally, science was germane to technical modernisation and thereby to political manoeuvering in the period. Dowden was a confirmed liberal unionist, inspired by Arthur Balfour who was appointed Chief Secretary in 1887. 'I have just read Mr Balfour's admirable speech at Manchester', he wrote to a colleague that year. 'I wonder does Mr Balfour know that no name is received with such enthusiasm as his in any loyal Irish gathering?'[23] Balfour's efforts towards stabilising the country through technological developments and economic restructuring as a prelude to the later incentives of 'constructive unionism' in the late 1890s provided Dowden—temporarily at least—with what appeared to be a viable and practical politics, a healthy alternative to the country's post-Parnellite malaise.[24]

The conflict which developed in the 1890s was clearly a battle for the terms of Irish self-perception, with science a key signifier. The emphasis on a culture which took full cognisance of scientific and technological progress inevitably featured in the *Daily Express* controversy, where it emerged as a *fin-de-siècle* squabble between Yeats and John Eglinton. Launching a full-scale attack on the 'occult triumphs' of the symbolist school, Eglinton insisted with some vehemence that 'the kinematograph, the bicycle, electric tramcars, labour saving devices etc., are not susceptible of poetic treatment, but are, in fact, themselves the poetry of a scientific age'.[25] His claims were perhaps appropriate in a decade which saw the introduction of Balfour's light railways scheme, the running of electric tramways in Dublin and the first cinematographic show, but Yeats and AE had little difficulty winning the return match. In 'The Autumn of the Flesh' Yeats would appeal for the substitution of alchemy for chemistry, and for science to be superseded by the higher arts which would 'lead us back upon our journey by filling our thoughts with the essence of things, and not with things.'[26]

This much-rehearsed dichotomy in the formative years of the Revival was inextricably bound up with what Dowden described as his fears for literature in the present day, 'especially as those hopes and fears are connected with the democratic tendencies and the scientific movement of our century'.[27] But it is in his particular urge to pre-empt the rupture which the Revival threatened to force between science and antiquarianism that he came closest to adopting Ferguson's directives towards cultural aristocracy, moving as he did so in direct opposition to Yeats. The young poet was convincing on the need to liberate Ireland's literary and antiquarian resources from the grip of fastidious scholarship: the man of science was too often, he opined, 'a person who had exchanged his soul for a formula; and when he captures a folk-tale, nothing remains with him for all his trouble but a wretched, lifeless thing with the down rubbed off and a pin thrust through its once living body'.[28] Throughout his early review articles he railed against the idea of science in relation to the treatment of Irish material to the point at which its intrusion was suggestive of an affront to nationality. The antiquarian David Fitzgerald's folklore articles for *La Revue Celtique* would not match those produced by Hyde, he claimed, for 'they are written more from the side of science than literature. Douglas Hyde's, on the other hand, will be, I feel sure, the most Irish of all folk-lore.' As far as the Revival was concerned the boat of science was, as he put it, on a different course from that of tradition and once again headed for shipwreck.[29]

Dowden's resistance to this trajectory was founded on his conviction that culture in Ireland would thrive through the integration and not the separation of disciplines; through the application of rational, democratic and enlightened scholarship. He argued, therefore, that the study of the past should draw upon a 'scientific' and forward-looking history rather than an explorative and politically orientated one. 'Let an Irish antiquary study the relics of his native land with all the resources of modern science', he wrote, 'viewing these interesting remains from the central and not merely from a provincial standpoint, and he will lead us towards the truth instead of plunging us into folly and illusion.'[30] The impetus which Yeats and his colleagues would seek to gain from the spirit of the Irish past was counterpoised, therefore, with Dowden's wish to impose the letter, the discipline of science, rather than the unrestricting liberty of national feeling and imagination.

The deflection of a new cultural nationalism may have been on Dowden's hidden agenda here—to the same end, he had encouraged both Todhunter and de Vere to indulge as much as they desired in Irish material as long as they contained it within the proper forms of English metre and verse.[31] A more sympathetic reading, however, reveals once again Dowden's collateral concerns: neither the resistance to science *per se* nor the rejection of science in anti-quarianism existed in a social vacuum. The rhetoric of the early Revival in this respect threatened to undermine the workings of a coterie of Irish scholars who formed for Dowden an important social, intellectual and civic nucleus. In loosening the hitherto close bonds between science and antiquarianism the Revival would simultaneously challenge the authority of a scholarly community or civic hierarchy which had constructed itself through such cross-reference. It was this concept which Dowden struggled to maintain in his 1895 claims for the school of craftsmen which would provide for the emergence of genius in Ireland. 'Such a body of trained scholars' he projected, 'should be the intellectual aristocracy of a democratic age, an upper ten thousand of workers. It will include in large proportion those whose studies are scientific, and who influence literature only indirectly. Their influence, although indirect, is far from unimportant.'[32]

In his mind's eye, perhaps, Dowden saw the combined strengths of the men who had dominated Dublin's intellectual life a decade or two before: Kane, Ferguson, Hamilton, Stokes, Petrie. Now, as the century drew to a close, he was attempting to maintain some confidence in the concept of a clerisy—derived as much from Burke as from Arnold—which would be grounded in modern science, culturally productive and politically effective. Cast by his critics as aloof, reticent and irresponsible, Dowden envisaged the cultural leadership of his society in quite the opposite terms, elevating the individual to a position of responsible intellectual, critical leadership which—crucially—did not seek out the popular as the easiest route. 'The chief duty of the thinker and man-of-letters at the present time and in the coming years', he wrote:

> is to save the democracy, if possible, from what is unfruitful in its own way of thinking and feeling. As topics arise which demand the attention of the people, it will be necessary to challenge the current notions, the current phrases, and the popular sentiments; it will be necessary to ply the public, willing or unwilling, with exact knowledge and well-considered thoughts. The state of half-culture which seizes upon a general principle, regardless of its limitations or relations to other principles, and which is therefore full of impetuosity and self-confidence, is a state as dangerous as we can well conceive.[33]

Despite the political underpinnings of the last line of the passage one can sympathise with Dowden's disquiet over the culture of esoteric mystification which, as he saw it, Yeats and his colleagues had begun to foster. For Dowden, the gentleman scholar of the nineteenth-century was the last line of defence, and the scholarly community the last refuge of a Grattanite civic idealism which would resist the encroachment of an insurgent nationalism. By the late 1890s his vision was already proving inadequate; no competition for Yeats who was meanwhile laying the foundations of his own cultural aristocracy, a new clerisy or fellowship of discourse 'whose basis was, in the last analysis, manorial'.[34] The civic version of intellectual ascendancy which Dowden clutched for safety was never to fulfill Ferguson's vision, nor does it now seem tenable in the impacted political and cultural context which was the fall-out of Parnellism. The architects of the Revival were already self-consciously constructing its replacement. In what is by far the best essay of the *Literary Ideals* series AE defined the tenets of the new cultural community which would render its predecessor inauthentic and obsolete. A literature, he wrote:

> loosely held together by some emotional characteristics common to the writers, however great it may be, does not fulfill the purpose of a literature or art created by a number of men who have a common aim in building up an overwhelming ideal—who create, in a sense, a soul for their country, and who have a common pride in the achievement of all.[35]

In a reply to a request that some of his own poetry be included in an Irish anthology, Dowden claimed that he would rather remain 'one of the general crowd of small singers than one of a local group'.[36] His inability to define and defend what he meant by the 'general crowd' in terms which did justice to his social vision left him vulnerable to the more persuasive rhetoric of his opponents. Only John Eglinton attempted several years later to contemplate the idea that Dowden, despite the best attempts of Ferguson, de Vere, Todhunter and John Yeats to convert him to nationalism in literature, had been right to stand his ground. The Revival had, after all, obscured many better scholars—Tyrrell, Mahaffy, Bury—than those it promoted. But in the end, Eglinton concluded, Dowden lost any authority which he might once have possessed. Having distanced himself into the relative safety of Unionist politics, he was most likely to be remembered simply as a difficult man who in later years 'denounced Rome to the delight of Protestant old ladies'.[37]

How, then, did Dowden read Yeats? The question looks for antagonism, and in retrospect it is tempting to polarise a situation which was in reality determined by more subtle shades of meaning and dissent. Divergence on several other fronts, from Duffy, Hyde and later O'Casey, was to have greater effect on the development of the young poet and the politics of the Revival. Dowden was a useful devil's advocate for a short time but never a genuine threat. In his defence it can merely be maintained that he was a better reader of early Yeats than many others: between the idiocies of Rolleston and Brooke in their introduction to *A Treasury of Irish Poetry in the English Tongue* (1900) and the misplaced adulation of Forrest Reid who by 1915 had securely defined him as the last Romantic, the poet was frequently diminished into blandness.[38] Obscured as his perspective may have been by his relationship with John Yeats and by his affiliation to Trinity College Unionism, Dowden at least took account of the potential which Yeats represented, and reacted accordingly. His struggle to articulate the terms of a late Victorian scholarly ethos, international and interdisciplinary, was in clear recognition of the fact that Yeats and his colleagues were starting to move the cultural goal-posts a decade before the end of the century.

Remembering Dowden is, finally, a means of restoring the dynamics of the late nineteenth century into which Yeats emerged. The notion of blankness on which Yeats would later capitalise as a self-enabling myth is undermined by the diversity of relationships—whether cemented through religion, scholarship or poetry—which existed in flux during the 1880s and 1890s. The

Revival must be located in the context of Irish Victorianism as
Terence Brown suggests,[39] but Irish Victorianism was a multifarious
discourse, characterised by ideals and affiliations which went far
beyond the qualifiers of 'Protestant' and 'Unionist'. Dowden's
standoff can be read, certainly, as the narrow-mindedness of a
peevish don, but it also illuminates on a wider canvas the troubled
intersection of a forceful Yeatsian incentive and a social ethos
threatened with extinction.

NOTES

1.   John Todhunter to Edward Dowden, 5th June 1888 (Dowden papers: Trinity
     College Dublin, MS 3715).
2.   ED to JT, 26 August 1886 (Trinity College, Dublin MS 3715). Hereafter TCD
     MS.
3.   John Eglinton, *Irish Literary Portraits* (London: Macmillan, 1935), p. 65.
4.   Dowden presided over the Historical Society debate on the 'Revival of Irish Lit-
     erature' in February 1895. Yeats's list of 'Thirty Irish Books' had been pub-
     lished in the *Daily Express*. For an account of the clash from Dowden's perspec-
     tive see Kathryn R. Ludwigson, *Edward Dowden* (New York: Twayne Pub-
     lishers Inc., 1973), p. 148.
5.   ED to JT, 27 December 1901, (TCD MS 3715).
6.   Edward Dowden, *New Studies in Literature* (London 1895), p. 18; hereafter *New
     Studies*.
7.   Terence Brown, 'Edward Dowden: Irish Victorian', *Ireland's Literature* (Mul-
     lingar: Lilliput Press, 1988), pp. 43, 45.
8.   George Moore, for example, mentions Dowden as a frequent host to Dublin's
     literary set, *Hail and Farewell* (Gerrards Cross: Colin Smythe, 1985), 716 n. 83.
9.   W. J. Mc Cormack, 'Yeats and Modernisation', *Linenhall Review* 5.4 (Autumn
     1988) 5.
10. *Irish Literary Portraits*, pp. 81-2.
11. Dowden was able to accept a principle of nationality co-operating within an
     overarching cosmopolitanism: see his comments on Germany, Italy and France
     in this respect, *New Studies*, p. 14.
12. See Yeats's article 'Professor Dowden and Irish Literature', *Daily Express*,
     Dublin 26 Jan. 1895 (*UP1* 346 & ff.). Earlier his criticism of Dowden featured in
     his article 'The Poetry of Sir Samuel Ferguson', *Dublin University Review*
     (November 1886), 932-41.
13. Address delivered before the Academy by Sir Samuel Ferguson, LL.D., Q.C.,
     President, 30 November 1886. *Proceedings of the Royal Irish Academy*, 16, 1879-
     1888, p. 186.

14.   See in particular Phillipa Levine's study of the phenomenon of 'hidden com-
      munities' in *The Amateur and the Professional: Antiquarians, Historians and
      Archaeologists in Victorian England, 1838-1886* (Cambridge: Cambridge
      University Press, 1986), p. 36, and Marshall Berman, 'Hegemony and the
      Amateur Tradition in British Science', *Journal of Social History* no. 8 (1975) pp.
      30-50. The phrase 'intellectual aristocracy' is developed from Noel Annan's clas-
      sic study 'The Intellectual Aristocracy', *Studies in Social History: A Tribute to
      G.M.Trevelyan*, ed. J. H. Plumb (London: Longman, 1955), pp. 241-87. For the
      tradition of 'clerisy' in general, see Ben Knights, *The Idea of the Clerisy in the
      Nineteenth Century* (Cambridge: Cambridge University Press, 1978).
15.   Cited M. C. Ferguson, *Sir Samuel Ferguson in the Ireland of his Day*, 2 vols.
      (Edinburgh, 1896), 1, p. 70.
16.   See Yeats's 'The Poetry of Sir Samuel Ferguson', (No 1) *Irish Fireside*, 9 October
      1886 (*UP1* 82-7), and Thomas Kinsella, *Davis, Mangan, Ferguson? Tradition and
      the Irish Writer*, Tower Series No 11 (Dublin, 1970).
17.   'The Poetry of Sir Samuel Ferguson' No 2, *Dublin University Review* (Nov
      1886), *UP1* 100, Kinsella, p. 43.
18.   *The Bookman* no 10 (1906), rpt *UP1* 405.
19.   *New Studies* p. 18.
20.   ED to JT, 5 February 1889 (TCD MS 3715).
21.   Dowden, 'Literary Criticism in France' (1889) *Studies in European Literature:
      Taylorian Lectures 1889-1899* (Oxford: Clarendon Press, 1900), pp. 25-6; 'The
      Scientific Movement in Literature', *Studies in Literature: 1789-1877* (London: C.
      Kegan Paul & Co., 1878). Yeats's reaction is recorded in *Au* 88. See also Brown,
      pp. 37-8.
22.   Dowden addressed the issue of science and Catholicism within university educa-
      tion on various occasions including his speech on 'Political Education', delivered
      to the Trinity College Historical Society and reported in the *Daily Express* (15
      November 1883). See his unpublished *Personalia* (TCD MS 3124 nos. 9, 38-65).
      For background to the issue see F. S. L. Lyons, *Ireland Since the Famine*
      (London: Fontana 1985), pp. 94-8. Alvin Jackson comments on Unionist
      response to the university debates of 1897 in *The Ulster Party: Irish Unionists in
      the House of Commons 1884-1911* (Oxford: Clarendon Press, 1989), pp. 181-2.
23.   Dowden to Professor Knight, 15 December 1887 (TCD MS 2259).
24.   Dowden's Unionism during the late 1880s and early 1890s consisted largely of
      power-brokering the Trinity College seat, which he secured for his candidate
      Edward Carson in 1892. For his attitude in later years, see his article 'Irish
      Unionists and the Present Administration', *National Review* xliv (October
      1904). For background on Dublin Unionism and technological development in
      this period see Jackson, pp. 184-9 and Lyons, pp. 204-6.
25.   'Mr Yeats and Popular Poetry', *Literary Ideals in Ireland* (Dublin: *Daily Express
      Office;* London: T. Fisher Unwin, 1899), p. 42.
26.   *Ibid.*, p. 74.
27.   *New Studies*, p. ix.
28.   Letter to the Editor of the *Academy* 2 October, 1890 (*CL1* 229).
29.   'Some Forthcoming Irish Books'; 'Irish Wonders' (*LNI* 14, 97). J. W. Foster
      considers Yeats's ambivalent reaction to Hyde as an over-scientific folklorist in

Fictions of the Irish Literary Revival: A Changeling Art (Syracuse: Syracuse University Press, 1987), pp. 219-30.

30. *New Studies*, pp. 11, 19.
31. See, e.g., Dowden's letter to Todhunter, 22 February 1888, on receiving a copy of Todhunter's book of verse: 'Towards the longer Irish poems I have a mingled feeling. The subject of the Children of Lir I have long known and thought full of charm, and here too it is everywhere a poet who treats the subject. But I do most firmly believe that for a poem of length there should be nothing of the nature of experiment and I look on your metre as hazardous - having its charms and its magic, but I hold, too experimental. . . . The first condition to be accepted is that it is an English poem and the form I maintain ought (at loss no doubt, but greater gain) to be an accepted English form, one of those magnificent regular metres which centuries have tried and justified. Ferguson seems to have felt this, for any metres he invents are I think in such close kinship to the regular English metres that they cannot be looked on as experiments (TCD MS 3715).
32. *New Studies*, p. 21.
33. *New Studies*, p. 10.
34. Foster, p. 31.
35. 'Nationality and Cosmopolitanism in Literature', *Literary Ideals in Ireland*, p. 81.
36. Dowden to Dixon, undated (TCD MS 2259).
37. *Irish Literary Portraits*, pp. 65, 81.
38. Stopford A. Brooke and T. W. Rolleston (eds), *A Treasury of Irish Poetry in the English Tongue* (London: Smith, Elder & Co., 1900), p. xxxii, confirm Yeats as a poet of Celtic and pseudo-Catholic mysticism; Forrest Reid's study locates early Yeats within a tradition of English Romanticism, *W. B. Yeats: A Critical Study* (London: Martin Secker, 1915).
39. See Brown's essay 'The Church of Ireland' in *Ireland's Literature*, pp. 57-9.

Moran's Collar: Yeats and Irish Ireland

Deirdre Toomey

Public opinion will compel you to learn Irish (*Au* 361)

MORAN'S COLLAR, named after an ancient Irish judge, strangled any wearer who deviated from truth or equity. David Patrick Moran, the principal architect of the influential Irish Ireland ideology was certainly (within limits) a truthful journalist, but a writer for whom tolerance and equity were empty concepts. In his weekly *The Leader*, the cause of Irish Ireland was advanced by the universal use of terms such as 'Sourfaces', 'Bigots', 'the Saved' and 'Orange lambs' for Protestants, the 'dark Brethren' for Irish manufacturers, the 'Bigots' Dust-Bin' for the *Irish Times*, the 'Great Whine' for Unionists of any religion, 'Bung' for publicans and *raimeis* [nonsense, empty talk] for all that with which Moran was in disagreement—which implicated most Irish nationalists, indeed it would seem, most Irish people (identified largely as 'Castle Catholics', 'Shoneens' and 'West Britons').

Moran, who was born in Waterford in 1869, had returned to Ireland in 1899 after a decade in England, during which time he had worked as a journalist on T. P. O'Connor's evening paper, *The Star*.[1] In London Moran had joined the Southwark Literary Society (the ur-Irish Literary Society), then the Irish Literary Society. He was strongly pro-Parnell at the split and for a time was a Branch Secretary of the National League. He was also a member of the London

45

Gaelic League and was 'an enthusiast for the dancing side of the programme. Dancing was his dissipation in those days'.² The respected *New Ireland Review*, edited by Father Tom Finlay, published between December 1898 and August 1900 six powerful articles by Moran, outlining what was to become the philosophy of Irish Ireland.³ In these articles we see Moran at his best; although they are slashing, contradictory, abusive and vituperative, they also exhibit his ability to see the weakness in all nationalist positions (save his own). They represented Moran's greatest achievement and in his following thirty-six years in journalism he could only repeat, debase and coarsen the points made in them.

Perhaps what is most remarkable about these articles is the briskness with which Moran rejected all previous Irish political movements. Moran was militantly opposed to all physical force nationalism. It was indeed a courageous man who in 1899 was prepared to say: 'The '98 processions are a grand intoxication, and no more. What, after all, was the great Wolfe Tone demonstration significant of?', to dismiss the 1798 uprising itself as merely the revolt of Englishmen who had been born in Ireland, irrelevant to the interest of the authentic 'Gaels', and to describe Wolfe Tone as a man of the Pale—'a Frenchman born in Ireland of English parents'. Moran dismissed all movements from the Dungannon Volunteers Convention onwards as being the product of the Pale rather than of the true Gaelic or Irish Ireland.

> [1782] placed the Pale at the head of Ireland for the first time in history, and ever since the Pale has retained that place. The '98 and '48 movements, the Fenians and the Parnell agitiation were Pale movements in their essence, even when they were most fiercely rebellious.

Moran was—as Yeats later put it—trying 'to convince people that a nation can drop a century & half out of its life as if Irish history ceased to be Irish history when the men who made it spoke English' (*CL3* 23). Moran's hatred and contempt for physical force movements in his own day was even more strongly expressed.

> The Irish Gael, when he does work himself up into a passion of patriotism, generates no further energy than that which enables himself to shout himself hoarse at some political meeting . . . rankest rebel claptrap . . . the little squint-eyed bit of nationality,

the squint of impotent hate and surly growl . . . some of the hillside
men will tell you that all the wild rebellious talk is nonsense, but
that it is necessary to keep up the national spirit: that if you do not
keep the prospect of bloody war with England alive in the Irish
mind Irish national sentiment will cease to be.[4]

Despite such ferocious assaults on all that Irish nationalists held
dear, within eighteen months of publishing his first Irish Ireland
article, Moran had a journal of his own devoted to this philosophy
and had recruited well-known journalists such as W. P. Ryan to the
cause. By late December 1900 Moran was able to boast to Douglas
Hyde that he had already made a great change in Ireland by *The
Leader* and had helped in 'the building up of the nation better than
anyone else had done'.[5]

This paradox is no paradox at all. Moran's initial demolition of
physical force ideology came at the end of a year of great expectations, 1898. The '98 centennial celebrations had mobilised enormous
hopes among nationalists. Indeed, as the celebrations tailed off during the autumn, expectations of political crisis rose. The popular
feeling that all the parades, meetings, and demonstrations must lead
to something—'everywhere people had looked forward, expecting,
speculating' (*Au* 418)—stimulated hopes of war, of a French invasion, a political climax. These culminated in the false hopes raised by
the Fashoda incident. In November 1898 it was possible even for
moderate nationalists such as William Redmond to assume that history would repeat itself and that 1898 would see a French invasion
of Ireland. On 29 October the *Irish Weekly Independent* published a
front-page cartoon, 'Should Auld Acquaintance be Forgot', which
depicts 'Pat' addressing 'Miss La Belle France': 'Sure, Miss, if you
have any trouble with yer neighbours you might like to step over
here for a time, bring a few traps with you'. The 'traps' at La Belle
France's feet contain guns and bayonets. The accompanying
editorial assumed an imminent invasion of Britain by France and
urged the French to come via Ireland, where they would be sure of a
welcome. T. P. Gill, editor of the *Daily Express* [Dublin] was asked,
quite seriously, '"What will you do . . . if the French land at Kil-
lala?"' Yeats's 'War' recalls this period of expectation of an
imminent French invasion via memories of Mary Battle: 'she began
to say that it would be a hard thing to see children tossed about on
bayonets, and I knew her mind was running on traditions of the
great rebellion' (*Myth* 110). However, by December 1898 it was evi-

dent that there was to be no repetition of 1798 and thus disappointed Irish nationalists were open to an ideology which rejected
physical force as futile: 'a nation in tumult must needs pass to and
fro between mechanical opposites' (*Au* 360).

Moran sought to separate nationality from politics; one could
sum up Irish Ireland as defeatism combined with nativism. He also
regularly attacked what he perceived as an endemic nationalist vice,
that of combining self-idealisation with self-pity and the passive
cultivation of victim status; '"there's some *myaw* on poor ould
Ireland"'.[6] Yet conversely he not only rejected physical force
activism, but had little respect for the Irish Parlimentary Party:

> It has been said before, and it needs to be said ten thousand times
> again, that politics is not nationality. As this view, however, is still a
> rank heresy to the multitude, it may be worth unfolding it in detail.
> An Irish political reform is got or striven for by popular organisa-
> tion, by public protest, by boycotting, by illuminating houses, by
> demonstrating, by brass and fife and drum bands, by voting, by
> going to jail, and by a vigorous party in the House of Commons.
> Out of the entire population of Ireland, however, only about
> eighty-six can hope to be sent to Parliament on the popular side;
> under Forster's *régime* the highest number called upon to go to jail
> never exceeded two thousand. Taking the nationalist population at
> 4,000,000, what is left for the remaining 3,997,914 to do?[7]

Moran urged nationalists to become Irish in 'personality', in language, in culture, in way of life, in dress and in consumption. They
were to learn Irish, to read Irish literature—i.e., literature written in
Irish— they were to live and to take their holidays in Ireland, to
wear Irish manufactured clothing, sing Irish songs, dance Irish
dances, play Irish games and buy Irish goods. Arthur Clery recalled:
'the star of Irish Ireland when it first shone forth in our sky was,
and still is, a five-pointed one: language, industries, music, dancing
and games'.[8] On the issue of language Moran was adamant; one
could not be Irish if one did not speak Irish. He looked forward to
the days when Ireland would be a bi-lingual country. Despite this
stance *The Leader* was not written in 'the kingly and melodious
Irish' but in 'so-called English'.[9] There is no evidence that Moran
himself ever became fluent enough to write an article in Irish—his
use of the language was confined to the odd Irish word, typically
raimeis.[10] By 1900 the Gaelic League had been promoting Irish for

seven years, but Moran's campaign was more dynamic, because fuelled by antagonism and scorn. It is significant that George Russell finally decided to learn Irish in August 1900: 'I am going to learn Irish. It is necessary if I am to make my boy an Irishman . . . I will I hope soon be able to sneer conscientiously at people who don't know it. It will be a great relief to my mind when I can.'[11]

On the issue of clothing, the Irish Irelander stood firm. *The Leader* urged the wearing of Irish cloth, tailored in Ireland and Yeats attempted to follow this model; 'I believed myself dressed according to public opinion, until a letter of apology from my tailor informed me that "It takes such a long time getting Connemara cloth as it has to come all the way from Scotland"'.[12] Paul Gregan, a young Theosphist, poet, agricultural organiser and follower of Russell's, wrote to the *All Ireland Review* in September 1900, lamenting the lack of Irish made cuff-links and studs to complete his All-Irish Donegal homespun suit, Belfast shirt and collar, Irish poplin tie, Castlebar boots, and long cycling stockings made by the Kilcommon Home Industries Society.[13] Subsequently ideological refinements were added to the dress issue: as Arthur Clery put it, 'there is always a tendency to suspect something wrong about a very well-dressed Irish-Irelander'.[14] Yeats's public engagement with the dress question came at the Dublin Pan-Celtic Congress of August 1901, when the issue of an Irish national costume was debated: Yeats temporised, arguing for the very gradual adoption of national dress; he pointed out that they all had to cope with the reactions of 'the small boy', who could be evaded if they 'started first in evening dress'.[15] Irish Irelanders did not advocate a national costume.

The buying of locally produced goods was a source of endless challenge to conscientious Irish-Irelanders and *The Leader* regularly reported encounters with unpatriotic shopkeepers who failed to stock, for example, Irish made paper.[16] *The Leader* advertised only Irish made goods including 'Irish-raised' tobacco and the 'Mick M'Quaid Plug', named for Colonel Lynam's serial hero.[17] Finally, foreign holidays were frowned on. In 'The Dead', a story which Joyce sets in January 1904, Miss Ivors badgers Gabriel Conroy in the stern propagandist voice of the Irish Irelander: '"O, Mr. Conroy, will you come to the Aran Islands this summer? . . . And why do you go to France and Belgium . . . instead of visiting your own land?'.[18]

Irish Ireland rejected the concept of 'Irish literature in English', which Moran blamed on 'Young Ireland': 'the '48 men put a few

more nails in the coffin of the Gael. The worst thing they did . . .
was that they brought into life a mongrel thing which they called
Irish literature in the English language'.[19] He asked rhetorically: 'Is
there any character in Anglo-Irish Literature really drawn with a
sincere desire to be true? I doubt it, with the possible exception of
Mick M'Quaid'. In 'The Battle of Two Civilizations' Moran put the
absolute case against this 'mongrel thing' and the pseudo-civilisation
which it expressed: 'In Grattan's time Irish civilization was thrown
overboard; but "Irish Nationality" was stuck up on a flag of green . .
. since Grattan's time every popular leader, O'Connell, Butt,
Parnell, Dillon, and Redmond, has perpetuated this primary contradiction'. When he moved from his general theses that an Irish
civilisation must be re-established, that on every Irish heart should
be engraved '"Thou shalt be Irish: thou shalt not be English"', he
very specifically took Yeats as his key example of 'mongrel' culture.
Further, he attacked him as a talentless attention-seeker and
obscurantist:

> A number of writers then arose, headed by Mr. W. B. Yeats, who,
> for the purposes they set themselves to accomplish, lacked any
> attribute of genius but perseverence. However by proclaiming from
> the rooftops that they were great Irish literary men, they suceeded
> in attracting that notice from the people of Ireland which the crowd
> walking up Ludgate Hill would give to five or six men who waved
> their hands and shouted on top of St. Paul's cathedral . . . . Mystics
> they were and are, for a mystic is assuredly a man who deals in
> mysteries . . . A muddled land which mistook politics for nation-
> ality, and English literature for Irish . . . was offered the services of a
> few mystics . . . However, it must be admitted that the mystics
> served a useful purpose, though it was by no means the one that
> they intended. By making a serious and earnest effort to create a dis-
> tinct Irish literature in English they pushed forward the question
> 'What is Irish literature?'. The Gaelic League took up a logical and
> uncompromising position . . . and last summer Mr. W. B. Yeats for-
> mally surrendered his sword, and Irish literature henceforth was not
> to be thought of outside the Irish language.[20]

Moran's particular loathing was for the 'Celtic note' and he had
already indirectly attacked Yeats in 'The Future of the Irish
Nation'.

A certain number of Irish literary men have 'made a market'—just as stock-jobbers do in another commodity—in a certain vague thing, which is indistinctly known as 'the Celtic note' in English literature, and they earn their fame and livelihood by supplying the demand which they have honorably and with much advertising created. We make no secret of the reason why we have dropped our language, have shut out our past, and cultivate Anglo-Saxon ways. We have done them all in the light of day, brutally, frankly—for our living. But an intelligent people are asked to believe that the manufacture of the before-mentioned 'Celtic note' is a grand symbol of an Irish national intellectual awakening. This, it appears to me, is one of the most glaring frauds that the credulous Irish people have ever swallowed. I hope no one will think I am attacking the 'Celtic note' from an English literary point of view. I am looking at it merely from the point of view of the Irish nation, of which it is put forward as a luminous manifestation. Beyond being a means of fame and living to those who can supply the demand, what good is the 'Celtic note' in English literature to the Irish nation? What good is it to any, except the owners of them, that Irish names figure largely in current English literature? I hasten to add that it secures for Ireland a little bit of English patronising praise, which is at present the breath of our Irish national nostrils. We were recently asked to swell ourselves with pride after contemplating the English debt to Irish literature. What a happy pass we have come to when we cry out with joy because of the gifts we have given our enemies. Has the Irish nation got anything for it?[21]

This is Moran's characteristically violent response to Yeats's 'The Celtic Element in Literature', first given as a talk to the Irish Literary Society in December 1897 and expanded for publication in *Cosmopolis* in June 1898. Yeats does indeed see Irish literature as the source of special qualities in English literature:

A little later the legends of Arthur and his table, and of the Holy Grail, once the cauldron of an Irish god, the Dagda, changed the literature of Europe, and it may be changed, as it were, the very roots of man's emotions by their influence on the spirit of chivalry and on the spirit of romance; and later still Shakespeare found his Puck and his Mab, and one knows not how much else of his faery kingdom, in Celtic legend . . . and now a new fountain of legends, and, as scholars have said, a more abundant fountain than any in Europe, is being opened, the great fountain of Gaelic legends; the tale of Deirdre, who alone among the women who have set men mad was at once the white flame and the red flame, wisdom and loveliness; the tale of the Sons of Turran, with its unintelligible mysteries, an old Grail Quest as I think; the tale of the four children changed into four swans, and lamenting over many waters; the tale of the love of Cuchullain for an immortal goddess, and his coming home to a mortal woman in the end; the tale of his many battles at the ford with that dear friend, he kissed before the battles, and over whose dead body he wept when he had killed him; the tale of his death and of the lamentations of Emer; the tale of the flight of Grainne with Diarmuid, strangest of all tales of the fickleness of woman, and the tale of the coming of Oisin out of faeryland, and of his memories and lamentations. 'The Celtic movement,' as I understand it, is principally the opening of this fountain, and none can measure of how great importance it may be to coming times, for every new fountain of legends is a new intoxication for the imagination of the world. It comes at a time when the imagination of the world is as ready, as it was at the coming of the tales of Arthur and of the Grail, for a new intoxication. The reaction against the rationalism of the eighteenth century has mingled with a reaction against the materialism of the nineteenth century . . . the Irish legends move among known woods and seas, and have so much of a new beauty, that they may well give the opening century its most memorable symbols.[22]

That Irish Literature could feed and transform non-Irish literatures was repugnant to Moran, for whom literatures were or should be autarkies. The 'Celtic note' remained an obsession:

Literary articles and literary discussions were studded with these words 'natural magic.' Mr. Yeats chanted them on a hundred platforms . . . then yet another Irish make-belief was born, and it was christened 'The Celtic Note,' Mr. W. B. Yeats standing sponsor for it. The 'Celtic Renaissance' was another name invented about this time.[23]

In an even more abusive attack in the Gaelic League weekly, *An Claidheamh Soluis*, Moran had described Yeats as a 'humbug' and added: 'I never knew a man who can, with such impunity, cast insults at his race and nation as Mr. W. B. Yeats'. Yeats, who had chaired a lecture by T. W. Rolleston on 'One Hundred Years of Irish Song' at that epicentre of West-Britonism, the Irish Literary Society, London, argued that in Irish peasants' passion for their own land is 'included a natural love for all the legend and story that grows like an invisible crop from stream and mountain, from the fields of old battles and the shrines of half-forgotten saints'. Yeats had insisted that 'a national literature must be based upon some strong and universal passion of the people'.[24] Yeats's prime 'insult' was to assume that there could be an Irish 'national' literature in English, but Moran also disliked Yeats's idealisation of pre-literate cultures: '[Yeats] described his countrymen . . . as he has often described them before, as a primitive people who did not read . . . who talked and talked and listened, and were very childlike and simple and far away'. Moran prophesied that the continuance of Irish Literature in English was 'unthinkable' and that 'in twenty years it will have dissolved into the great elements surrounding it, as completely as a snow-flake on the river'.[25] His position is advanced so confidently that one does not immediately notice the bizarre nature of his case. In 1900, when only Douglas Hyde was writing significant literature in Irish, Moran was advocating the rejection of most that had been written by Irish people between 1700 and 1900. Yet it was the radicalism of Moran's position which made it seductive to disappointed nationalists seeking a new departure, and Yeats was to describe this period of exclusivist nationalism as one in which 'Nationality was like religion, few could be saved, and meditation had but one theme—the perfect nation and its perfect service' (*Au* 361).

Yeats's first response to Moran's Niagara of abuse was in a long letter published in the first issue of *The Leader* (*UP2* 237-42). Moran had sent advance copies of his editorial to various prominent Irish figures. The editorial had promised 'an independent weekly review written from first to last from exclusively Irish standpoints'. It called for Ireland to become

a self-governing land, living, moving, and having its being in its own language, self-reliant, intellectually as well as politically independent, initiating its own reforms, developing its own manners and customs, creating its own literature out of its own distinctive consciousness, working to their fullest capacity the material resources of the country, inventing, criticising, attempting and doing.

Moran accepted that a politically independent Ireland must be a final goal, but advocated its achievement by cultural independence. Yeats's subtle and temperate letter replies, not merely to Moran's cautiously worded editorial, but to the more characteristic outbursts of the last two years. He conceded that it was probably necessary to turn from 'purely political nationalism' to cultural nationalism 'with the language question as its lever'. He fully endorsed the language movement, but pointed out that Irish people would still have to express 'Irish emotion and Irish thought' in the English language as it was as yet their first language. He anticipated an elite literature in Irish comparable to that of England, but envisaged the mass of Irish people responding to folk-poetry. He warned Moran that the great day of an Irish speaking Ireland would not be brought nearer by 'quarrelling about names' and by 'bringing to literary discussion . . . the exasperated and violent temper we have learned from a century of political discussion'. Yeats insisted on the reality of an Irish Literature in English, using Allingham's 'The Winding Banks of Erne' as his example, and argued that AE's poetry, despite its lack of obviously 'Irish characteristics' was 'more Irish' than those collections tediously labelled 'racy of the soil'. He wound up by responding to Moran's 'many attacks . . . upon me and upon the movement I represent', insisting that 'Celtic Renaissance' and 'Celtic note' were 'vague grandiloquent terms' which he sought to avoid and only used in quotation—from Arnold. Moran, in his temperate, even conciliatory, editorial reply, represented himself as one of the plain people of Ireland—'we are essentially mere people of common sense'. Moran conceded that he and Yeats might have some beliefs in common, even that 'the distinctly Irish genius can now and then strike a distinct note in the English language'. Moran urged Yeats to look at things from the Irish Ireland point of view:

> Our concern is with Ireland—all Ireland—as it is, not with Irish literature alone. We want to de-anglicise Ireland, and let who can produce the poetry . . . nothing can be Irish literature that is not written in the Irish language . . . Mr. Yeats's letter we regard as significant of the new spirit that has come or rather is coming into Irish controversy; that new spirit-the old, old fair and honourable spirit—was badly needed. We are—in consequence of the work we have taken in hand we are compelled to be—a fighting paper. We will put all the force and passion we can into our work; but we hope that no matter how hard we may have to hack that we will never be tempted to depart from the traditions of *Cuchullin* at the Ford.[26]

If Yeats thought that this was the end of it he was greatly mistaken. The traditions of Cuchulain and Ferdia were rapidly dropped and intemperate and personal attacks on Yeats became something of a feature of *The Leader* in its first six months, so much so that the *United Irishman* commented sarcastically: 'the great danger confronting the 20th century [is] W. B. Yeats'.[27] A former friend from the Irish Literary Society, W. P. Ryan, who wrote in *The Leader* as *Seang Siúir*,[28] established himself as an enemy of Yeats's in a jeering piece published on 3 November 1900, 'Mr. Yeats's Jug'. The article turns on an interview with Yeats in Woburn Buildings published in T. P. O'Connor's London gossip paper *M. A. P.*, in which details of Yeats's making tea for his interviewer and going out to purchase milk from a local dairy are used.[29] Ryan used this unsolicited interview to belittle Yeats's use of Irish mythology in *The Wanderings of Oisin* and *The Wind Among the Reeds*.

In what did the poet 'fetch' the milk? In a hat, a tobacco-pouch, a scooped turnip, a blue-bell, or the jug of civilization?. . . Was it, after all, a *Meigin Doilghe* in which the poet brought back not mere milk but ruthful, heart-hungering white foam from the eternal seas of Manannan? . . . Was it of earth, or after-earth, or of Orchill's under-earth, manufacture, that Jug which, 'with reverent hands,' the poet bore out into the spellful night what time the blithe nymph was tea-thirsty? And for hence, when we have fared to other stars, the two classes into which our Gaelic posterity, like all the children of men, will be divided—the realists and the idealists—will debate from *earrach* to *geimhreadh* whether it was a jug made in Germany, or one formed by adept sea-fingers from the foam on the lips of Lir.

Yeats replied with admirable restraint and brevity in the next issue, pointing out that he had not invited any interviewer from *M.A.P.* and professing not to know the author of the piece. (He realised of course that the 'interviewer' had made copy out of an unsought social encounter.) A series of attacks on the Brooke-Rolleston *Anthology of Irish Verse* also implicated Yeats in this 'Anglo-Irish' venture. In the anonymous review of 22 December, Yeats is singled out as one who 'does not understand us'—'us' being presumably the Irish—and 'has yet to write even one line that will strike a chord of the Irish heart'.[30] Despite many protests from readers, Moran refused to concede on this point. He doggedly insisted that Yeats was an 'Anglo-Irish' poet, rather than an Irish poet. This belittling term has been one of Moran's enduring gifts to Irish cultural debate.[31]

Yeats had in fact been involving himself more closely with the Gaelic League in late 1900, speaking at the Rotunda on 11 October in defence of Irish language teaching in Irish schools, and on 17 October speaking at a *Sgoruigheacht* [party] at the Central Branch of the Gaelic League, again powerfully endorsing the language movement in terms which seek to accommodate the best version of Moran's ideology and which even echo his language:

> Mr. Yeats presided during the proceedings and in the interval he addressed the audience in English . . . [and said] if they wanted a higher civilisation they should study the Irish language, and become acquainted with its literature (hear hear). It was no use disguising from themselves that they had going on now in Ireland a war of civilisation, and upon that war not only did the issue of Irish nationality hang, but the very greatest issues a man could concern himself with. The civilisation which existed in the Irish language . . . was an older and better civilisation . . . which it was their duty to preserve until the deluge had gone by (hear, hear) . . . In Ireland, where the Irish language still existed, they had a literature which was the possession of all the people . . . [they should] perform short plays in Irish . . . and build up a new drama in Ireland . . . It would be of great advantage to the movement if they gathered the songs and stories associated with each neighbourhood relating to its hills, its valleys etc (hear, hear) . . . Local songs were dear to the people, and if they only issued small books in Irish containing legends etc. of each locality it would have great effect in furthering the movement.[32]

Yet these sincere and well-intentioned moves had no effect on the new wave of Irish Irelanders who had, as Yeats later confirmed, 'the intensity and narrowness of theological sects' (*Au* 362).

By late 1900 any faint hopes that Yeats and Russell might have entertained that *The Leader* might be a positive force were gone. In the summer of 1900 Russell was 'afraid there is a warlike spirit let loose in Ireland. I suppose Moran's paper will be its organ'. He proceeded to classify the supernatural directors of the Irish press.

> To attribute the A.I.R. [*All Ireland Review*] to say Lu and the 'Leader' to Bov or some other power, and all the other papers to

their respective fountains should be one of our aims. I think the
Express is Balor's paper. It certainly has got the evil eye and turns
its readers into mummies or howling spooks.[33]

By December 1900—the Portadown Presbyterian ousting the
Theosophist—Russell dismissed Moran as a 'priest's boy' and was
prepared to set the *United Irishman* upon *The Leader*.[34] (Later, W. P.
Ryan, having jumped ship from *The Leader* and become an anti-
clerical land-reforming Theosophist, described Moran's contribution
to the journal as 'something a cautious parish priest with a rough
sense of humour might have written.)[35] Douglas Hyde tried to make
peace between Moran and Yeats. Lady Gregory recorded this
encounter in her diary:

> [Hyde] had seen Moran, who told him that he could not make head
> or tail of Yeats, or understand a word he said or wrote—however,
> he promised not to attack him (tho' he has not altogether kept that
> promise). Hyde hinted that it was unwise to attack any but enemies,
> but Moran would by no means agree to this. 'Your enemies don't
> mind what you say, but if you attack your friend, he is the boy that
> will feel it!'[36]

Yeats's analysis for Lady Gregory of the attacks in *The Leader* is
impressively objective:

> 'The Leaders' first attack on the Anthology was, like the article on
> my Jug, undoubtedly Ryan but the second attack was I feal very
> certain Moran. I would not call its passing allusion to my self
> exactly an attack—as Moran understands such things. The 'even'
> ('Even Mr Yeats has not' Etc) was meant for a form of politeness as
> Moran-understands-politeness; and from Moran's point of view, the
> point of view of a man who only cares for the mob the sentence
> was true. Had he not given Hyde his promise there would doubtless
> have been no 'even'. His reply to Rolleston was curiously week &
> irrelevant, &, I almost thought, conscious of its folly. Ryan is a man
> who wanted to send Moore a play to read a while back, & though I
> urged Moore to write to him & though Moore promised & I think
> his letter was unanswered. It was a pity for Ryan has all his life lived
> under a sense of wrongs. He had a complicated quarrel with Duffy
> & the Irish Lit Society & will I have no doubt avenge himself on all
> his enemies from behind the wall [of] the Gaelic League. He had
> some unfriendly remarks about 'The Shadowy Waters' for being in

'an alien tongue' & for attempts to carry out theories in Symons
symbolist book. It is wonderful the skill with which these people
play on subtle hints of heresey when they review A E or my self; &
after all they are right from their point of view. It is as much their
very respectable instinct for heresey, as rage against something they
cannot understand, that keeps them ever harping on symbols, only
they should be more open (*CL3* 10-11).

Ryan's attack on 'The Shadowy Waters' had dismissed it as 'a neo-
dreamer's play in a foreign speech'.[37] Yeats correctly identified symbolism as a red rag to Irish Ireland and *The Leader* continued to
berate Yeats as a symbolist long after he had changed his style: 'Mr.
Symbol was a mighty poet, philosopher, artist, litterateur and savant
. . . ghosts, fairies and annotated moonshine were the only things he
deemed worthy of notice'.[38] Yeats continued his analysis of the
phenomenon of Moran in a letter to Lady Gregory of 23 January
1901.

I think Moran is merely puzzled as so many self taught men are
puzzled at finding a mysterious heirarchy, governed by standards
they cannot understand. The first result of a man's thinking for
himself, when he has no cultivated tradition behind him, is that he
values nothing but the obviously useful, the obviously interesting,
the obviously forceful . . . The rest is to them is a trap, a mystification invented by the priviledged classes to keep the poor man out of
his rights. When the self-taught man adds to this inevitable instinct
a special doctrine of his own, whether socialism or the gaelic league,
he grows as lively as a Dancing Dervish. Moore . . . tells me he
talked to Moran like a father. He pointed out that 'The Leader'
should draw to it everybody, who beleived in intellectual nationalism & that it was no use Moran's trying to change me by abusing
me, for I wouldnt & couldnt change, but that he might keep me
from writing for him, if he went on abusing me. Moran replied why
did I not write like Burns etc etc. Moore replied 'could he change
the shape of his nose by trying' which ought to have been conclusive (*CL3* 19-20).

Moran had given a reasonably polite version of this encounter with
George Moore in *The Leader*: '[h]aving expressed the view to a well-
known literary man that the writings of another Irish literary man
were all stuff and nonsense, he demurred . . .'.[39] Yeats continued to
analyse Moran in letters to Lady Gregory:

Moran is certainly bewildering this week. His reply to Rolleston
... is a wonderful cloud of words, & his ar[g]ument in a different
article that as the Irish people are 'rude & rough & lacking in the
power of sustained thinking' or some such words, all Irish writers
should become as they are—for that is the upshot—shows an
almost pathetic ignorance of the way literature is written. Like so
many Irishmen he cannot distinguish between journalism, which is
written for a man's own day & literature which is written, however
it may fail of its purpose, for all days (*CL3* 25).

Moore—in one of his more bizarre incarnations—briefly became
an Irish Irelander in 1901. *The Leader* gave an approving account of
Moore's attempt to buy Irish goods in Dublin. He had requested
Irish-made hosiery in a shop in Grafton Street and was informed
that the 'respectable classes' did not buy Irish goods. Moore snorted,
'"Damn the respectable classes; they are the disgrace"'.[40] Moore had
already contributed an article to *The Leader*, 'The Culture Hero in
Dublin Myths', an attack on Mahaffy and Trinity culture.[41]
However, despite these overtures of friendship from Moore, the
'obnoxious' *Diarmuid and Grania* proved too much of a temptation
for *The Leader* and was predictably attacked for being 'degenerate
and unwholesome' and for being 'un-Irish'.[42] This attack was as
much on Moore as on Yeats. Moran himself praised Hyde's one-act
curtain raiser, *Casadh an tSugain*, leaving the dirty work to 'Mac
An Cuill', who tore into *Diarmuid and Grania*:

> 'Diarmuid and Grania' . . . is an Irish legend. The Irish mind made
> it, and the Irish mind preserved it, pure and fresh and wholesome
> and clean. And now the English mind takes it by force, drags it
> through the mire of the London Streets, brings it back to us
> bedraggled, besmirched, and befouled, and asks us to admire it in its
> new dress!
>   Pah!

Moore replied in the next issue at some length, but temperately and
reasonably, defending the play in terms of historical accuracy. In the
issue of 18 November, 'Mac an Cuill' fought back, concluding that
Moore, seen as the true author of the play, 'has shown us as with an
electrical searchlight the gap between the English mind and the Irish
mind'. Much later Moran gave vent to an unvarnished account of
his dealings with Moore.

We did not go after the coterie; rather the coterie, or some of it, made it its special business to come after us. The unconsciously funny old gentleman who is now 'saved' and presumably 'making his soul', sought us out and said flattering things to us; but a level-headed man with a knowledge of the world, particularly of the shallow and very human deeps of literary 'gents,' spook-seers, artists and the rest is not too easily flattered. The unconsciously comic old gentleman . . . used to come to our offices carving the air with his gesticulations. We treated him with great tact and smiled when he departed. [43]

Yeats is only intermittently attacked in the period 1901-2—once for the crime of having his birthday noted in a daily paper: 'the star of W. B. Yeats is in the ascendant'.[44] This relative lull might indicate some sense of his continuing support from the radical *United Irishman*, which, on 21 September 1901, launched a ferocious attack on *The Oracle*, a journal edited by 'D. P. Hooligan', indicating that it was thought that Frank Hugh O'Donnell, the maverick ex-MP, renegade Fenian and pamphleteer, was a director of the company which ran the journal:

DIRECTORS.

FRANK U. O'DONNELL Esq., . . . Laird of Strath Spy, and Chevalier of the Order of Ananias and Sappira. Author of 'The Real Wolfe Tone,' 'Irish Pro-Boers in Paris,' and other standard works of fiction; Pamphleteer by private appointment to the City of London Corporation and the British Empire Defence Association; President of the Kicked-out Club; High Shepherd of the Golden Fleecers and Grand Master of the Knights of the Black Mail, &c., &c.

D. P. HOOLIGAN, Esq., Concentration Camp, Rathmines, late of the *Estates Gazette* and *Star* offices, London. Author of 'James Stephens, Criminal'; President of the Conspirators' Branch of the Gaelic League, Apostle, by King's Letters Patent, to the Irish Heathen, &c.

The attack continued by describing *The Oracle* as 'founded to exploit the labours of the Irish Revivalists and divert the thoughts of the Irish people from the misgovernment of their country', and asserted that the journal was essentially a British tool and pro-

Imperial.[45] This scale of attack, in a year in which Standish O'Grady's cross-party *All Ireland Review* had also been engaged in a slanging match with *The Leader*, might have made Moran and his fellow journalists watch their backs for a while. (O'Grady had accused Moran of 'murdering thought' and of converting *The Leader* into 'a horror and abomination'.)[46] Indeed Robert Elliott's 'Criticism and the Neo-Celt', while insisting on the non-Irish character of Yeats's work, does see him as a poet of genius, if a poet whose closest affiliations are with English romanticism.[47]

Yeats was too experienced in years of cultural and political controversy to respond to Moran in *The Leader*: he did not write to the journal between November 1900 and November 1907, despite continued attacks. (He was also undoubtedly reluctant to give Moran free copy.) In 1901, when writing to William Sharp, Yeats acknowledged that the 'growing Catholic party' in Ireland was already so 'suspicious' of him that he would lose nothing were he to to come out even more strongly as a believer in practical Magic.[48] Yet Yeats does accommodate a very modified Irish Ireland position in 'Ireland and the Arts', which rejects international 'tribeless, nationless' art and argues that Irish artists should derive their subject matter from their own country and its culture if the Irish are to become 'a chosen race . . . one of the pillars that uphold the world'.[49]

Yeats's 'reply' to Moran is 'What is "Popular Poetry"?', published in the *Cornhill Magazine* in March 1902, although drafted in 1901. The essay is autobiographical, even confessional in style. Yeats looks back to his youth, to the days when, like Moran, he was opposed to 'coteries' and determined to transform Irish literature by writing '"popular poetry" like those Irish poets, for I believed that all good literatures were popular . . . and I hated what I called the coteries'.[50] In looking back, Yeats, I think, sees the Moran of 1901 as the devil's walking parody of that young iconoclast of the 1880s, whose head was filled 'with thoughts of making a whole literature'. In 1901 Yeats finds himself on the other side of the fence, identified as a member of the 'coterie' which Irish Ireland opposes. Although themes treated in this essay are familiar from 'The Literary Movement in Ireland', they have been remobilised in the service of a refutation of Moran. Yeats turns Moran's canonisation of the 'true Gael' against him by basing 'popular poetry' on the poetry of the 'unlettered', those who keep hold of 'the unwritten tradition' which binds them 'to the beginning of time and to the foundation of the world'. This truly 'popular poetry' is not opposed to the poetry of the lettered elite: '[b]oth are alike strange and obscure, and unreal to all who have not understanding'. Irish oral poetry and the poetry of the elite both presuppose a tradition—one an unwritten tradition, one a written tradition. Antagonistic to these two complementary forms of poetry is the false 'popular poetry' of the middle classes, Longfellow and Burns. With the dethroning of Burns (whom Yeats had classed as a symbolist in 'The Symbolism of Poetry') we see an open engagement with Moran, who had cited Burns as the exemplary poet able to touch 'the Scottish heart', and who had naively asked Moore why Yeats did not write like Burns.[51]

> I became certain that Burns, whose greatness has been used to jus-
> tify the littleness of others, was in part a poet of the middle class . . .
> [d]espite his expressive speech which sets him above all other popu-
> lar poets, he has the triviality of emotion, the poverty of ideas, the
> imperfect sense of beauty of a poetry whose most typical expression
> is in Longfellow (c.f. *E&I* 6).

The new middle class culture, founded on journalism rather than on literature, is condemned in terms that are very close to Yeats's estimation of Moran and his fellows on *The Leader*—'that straightforward logic, as of newspaper articles, that so tickles the ears of the shopkeepers' (c.f. *E&I* 5). Indeed the 'baker' who fails to comprehend Tennyson's '"Warming his five wits, the white owl in the belfry sits"' (*E&I* 7) is 'F.P.' who, in *The Leader*'s 'Irish Prose Composition' quoted this distych, with the query, 'will any person tell me exactly what Tennyson meant by [these lines]. What exactly are the owl's "five wits"? How are they warmed . . .?'[52] Yeats's conclusion is a rejection of Irish Ireland:

> Now I see a new generation in Ireland which discusses Irish litera-
> ture and history in 'Young Ireland Societies,' and societies with
> newer names, and there are far more than when I was a boy who
> would make verses for the people. They have the help, too, of an
> awakening press, and this press sometimes urges them to desire the
> direct logic, the clear rhetoric of 'popular poetry.' It sees that
> Ireland has no cultivated minority, and it does not see, though it
> would cast out all English things, that its literary ideal belongs more
> to England than to other countries (c.f. *E&I* 11).

What would have been the consequence of this essay's having been published in—say—the *United Irishman* rather than secreted in the conservative London *Cornhill* between serial novels and articles on social solecisms? We would now read it for what it is, a response to Moran and a defence of Yeats's position on Irish culture; but it would also have been recognised by Moran for what it was, and the reverberations would have occupied Yeats for months. Yeats was no coward in the matter of controversy in the Irish Press, having between 1897 and 1901 engaged in half a dozen lengthy and angry debates on issues of cultural and political nationalism. However, he was aware of the futility of engaging with Moran directly. Yeats later summed up the cannibalistic self-devouring character of Irish nationalism with a fable of Wilde's: 'when I have thought of the results of political subjection upon Ireland I have remembered a story told to me by Oscar Wilde . . ."If you carve a Cerberus upon an emerald . . . and put it in the oil of a lamp and carry it into a room where your enemy is, two new heads will come upon his shoulders and all three devour one another"' (*Au* 361).

In 1904, sympathising with George Russell (who had unwisely embroiled himself in a controversy with Moran) Yeats reiterated his position on *The Leader*, insisting on the journal's 'abusiveness & its hate for all ideas not part of its own very narrow programme '. He urged Russell to return to the issue of 'abusiveness' in the Irish Press, telling him that he had once had a plan for 'a thermometer of abuse—rows of adjectives & nouns . . . to be published at stated intervals—a weather chart . . . a prize to be given at the end of the year for the most copious'.[53]

The short but respectful review of *Cathleen Ni Houlihan* by 'Chanel'[Arthur Clery] might seem to show that *The Leader* was able to accommodate a "98' play, despite Moran's professed contempt for 'pikes and blunderbusses, and that sort of blood and passion'.[54] Clery, a highly committed Irish Irelander otherwise remarkable for his early advocacy of the partition of Ulster,[55] hailed a change in Yeats's writing:

Mr. Yeats . . . would appear to have begun to see the light. "Kathleen" was a true play. The action was sufficient for its small proportions. Its sudden change from the joy of the marriage eve to the sadness of war and sacrifice gave it a true tragic plot. The feelings had full play throughout. It was indeed a work of the greatest promise. As a study in the contrasts of Irish life it was particularly interesting. It brought the humdrum and the ideallic, the funny and the poetic side of Irish life together, and showed their interrelation; a topic which has hitherto been much neglected. In fine, it was a play such as the people could enjoy. Let us hope we find in it the type of the drama that is to come. If our Irish dramatists continue to seek the suffrages of the Irish *people*, whether in English or in Gaelic, they will find that, whilst literary excellence and artistic verbiage will be points in their favour with true Irish audiences, plays that are so in fact as well as in name can alone win popular sympathy and approval, and form the beginning of a really national drama.

One does get the sense that Clery—still a student at University College— wrote this inhibited praise nervously with Moran growling in the background, but a positive tone was sustained by Clery in later reviews of performances in Cork.[56]

Moran had refused on principle to attend any performances at the Abbey: 'our interest in Mr. Yeats and his following has been so languid that we never bothered to attend one of his performances till last week'. However in January 1905, Moran made his first visit to see *Cathleen ni Houlihan* and *Spreading the News*, immediately noting that the audience did not seem to be composed of true Gaels: 'we might have thought . . . that we had strayed by mistake into some prayer meeting of the foreign element in Ireland':

'Kathleen ni Houlihan' was not a play, though, with a looseness of language, it was so styled on the programme. It was the second item performed, but as Lady Gregory's farce was placed second on the programme, we, during a considerable portion of the sketch, laboured under the impression that we were witnessing Lady Gregory's farce while we were watching Mr. Yeats's tragedy. When Kathleen came on the stage we assumed that she was the old woman that was to spread the news, but her appearance and her chanting did not suggest laughter, and it dawned upon us after a while that we had mistaken one piece for another. The 'poor old woman' symbol for Ireland is too greenly sentimental for us. Vigorous Ireland has told the old weeping, wailing creature to move out of its way; but the 'poor old woman' has gained admittance to the scented drawing-rooms where they take a little green sentimentality with their coffee and gossip. 'Kathleen ni Houlihanism' makes Irish patriotism quite harmless, if not even 'respectable,' a thing about which the 'best people' might utter 'isn't it charming,' or 'how pretty;' even Tony Traill and Brother Goulding might patronise it, feeling happy that if it led the youth into green sentimentality, it would keep the hand of young Ireland off such lusty nation-killers and bigots as themselves. Let who will simper and sigh about 'the poor old woman' and her chanting; give us a modern man with a heart and a head and a strong hand, and make a play—not a Yeatsonian chant—about him . . . We fear that Mr. Yeats, shrewd man though he is, will never touch the Irish heart.[57]

'A. M. W.', who mirrored Moran's position, published a characteristically coarse parody of *Cathleen Ni Houlihan* in *The Leader* in January 1905: it attacks the usual targets—Shoneens, Freemasons, nationalists.[58] Moran's hostility to the play goes beyond a dislike of 'Anglo-Irish Literature', on which his position was by now compromised,[59] or of glorification of '98. The undercurrent is a dislike of Yeats as a man with a recent Fenian past. Yeats had been a member of the IRB from c. 1886 to c. 1894, when he and the other London-based Fenians moved to the INA. Both were revolutionary organisations dedicated to Irish Independence via physical force. The INA was more radical and was aligned with those American Fenians (the 'Triangle') who endorsed terrorism. Yeats was not a fellow traveller in these organisations, but an important activist, particularly in the period 1897-8, during which as President of the '98 Celebration Committee of Great Britain, and Chairman of the Young Ireland Society (a front for the IRB/INA) he addressed countless political meetings, including huge gatherings in Phoenix Park and Stephen's Green in March and August 1898. Yeats and Maud Gonne left the INA in late 1900 as a protest against Dr. Mark Ryan's refusal to expel Frank Hugh O'Donnell from the organisation, despite his having tried to 'felon-set' Maud Gonne on a charge of treason in June 1900. Yeats's affiliations were no secret, nor could they have been after 1898. The paradox of Yeats's position after 1900 was that, having left the INA, he was much more unprotected politically, yet continued to carry the reputation of a Fenian. This he had acknowledged in a letter to Lady Gregory of May 1901, in which he sees Moran's attacks on him as being fostered by Father Finlay, formerly a friend of Russell's: he continues, 'I imagine that as I withdraw from politics my friends among the nationalists will grow less, at first at any rate, & my foes more numerous' (*CL3* 71). Rather suprisingly, Moran seems to have had links with the older generation of Fenians, as an anecdote in 'The Future of the Irish Nation' indicates.[60] He could also have heard of Yeats's career in the IRB/INA from Frank Hugh O'Donnell, one of Yeats's most bitter enemies. In 1901, in an article occasioned by the death of James Stephens, Moran attacked Fenianism as profoundly damaging to Ireland: 'it implanted the secret society virus in the national blood, and, as secret societies are bad among any peoples, they are doubly bad amongst a people like us who are as yet half slaves'.[61] For Moran, Yeats, in *Cathleen ni Houlihan*, is engaging in what he termed 'lip Tin-pikery', that is a rhetorical presentation of a physical force position remote from any real prospect of rebellion. Fenianism was 'an airy nothing, a dream backed by such stuff as dreams are made of'.[62]

Yeats's account of the genesis of his only 'National Drama' begins with a dream:

> One night I had a dream almost as distinct as a vision, of a cottage where there was well-being and firelight and talk of a marriage, and into the midst of that cottage there came an old woman in a long cloak. She was Ireland herself, that Cathleen ni Houlihan for whom many songs have been sung and about whom so many stories have been told and for whose sake so many have gone to their death (*CL3* 321-22).

The dream was presumably of summer 1901, for he and Lady Gregory began work on the play in September 1901, when it was simply known as *The Poor Old Woman* and when Lady Gregory drafted the first section from Yeats's dream-scenario.[63] *Cathleen ni Houlihan* is perhaps the strangest physical force drama ever written. It is brief, domestic, intimate. It avoids all representation of violence and gains its force not from 'pikes and blunderbusses' but from the *unheimlich*, the uncanny: it has an almost Racinian avoidance of on-stage violence and its power comes from the combination of a peaceful setting and the presentation of the call to revolution as deriving from a supernatural figure, the country itself.[64] Previous patriotic dramas of '98 such as J. W. Whitbread's *Theobald Wolfe Tone* (staged to immense success in Dublin in December 1898) were simple crowd-pleasing melodramas, obsolete in style and idiom. *Cathleen ni Houlihan* came from a dream; but where did that dream come from? It derives not from the collective unconscious, but from the 'mongrel' Anglo-Irish literature that Irish Ireland had rejected.

When Yeats was a young man he had been obsessed with Carleton, whom he saw as the first authentic voice, in English, of the Irish peasant: '[h]e was but half articulate, half emerged from Mother Earth . . . but his wild Celtic melancholy gives to whole pages of "Fardarougha" and of "The Black Prophet" an almost spiritual grandeur. The forms of life he described . . . passed away with the great famine, but the substance which filled those forms is the substance of Irish life, and will flow into new forms which will resemble them as one wave of the sea resembles another' (*UP1* 364). The *topos* of 'The Lianhan Shee' (from *Traits and Stories of the Irish Peasantry*) is the source both of Yeats's dream and of *Cathleen ni Houlihan*. Carleton's tale, a fine study in the *unheimlich*, opens with a detailed and loving depiction of a comfortable Irish cottage interior in which Mary Sullivan, a farmer's wife sits at evening alone by her hearth; 'the shadow of a person passing the house darkened the window opposite which she sat and immediately a tall female, of wild dress and aspect, entered the kitchen'. The mysterious, semi-supernatural woman frightens Mary Sullivan with unintelligible threats and pleas centring around a thing which she carries on her back, hidden by her long cloak, which she insists is the 'Lianhan Shee' or persecuting fairy. She tries to force Mary Sullivan to accept a magical gift and in a magnificent speech describes her isolation:

> Every door is shut in my face! Does not every cheek get pale when I am seen? If I meet a fellow-creature on the road, they turn into the field to avoid me; if I ask for food it's to a deaf ear I speak; if I am thirsty they send me to the river. What house would shelter me? In cold, in hunger, in drought, in storm, and in tempest, I am alone and unfriended, hated, feared an' avoided . . .[65]

The tale's combination of the *heimlich*—the naturalistically described cottage and the simple farmer's wife—and the *unheimlich*, the strange, threatening, semi-supernatural visitor with her unintelligible speeches, is maintained brilliantly until the tale lapses into a melodramatic conclusion. When this tale resurfaces as a dream in the summer of 1901, the key elements are intact, the quiet cottage, the supernatural visitor, the simple peasants. In the play Cathleen's speeches echo Margaret's account of her wanderings and her rejections on the road, with the image of cheeks paling at the sight of her being inverted into one of deliberate sacrifice: 'Many that are red-cheeked now will be pale-cheeked . . . They that have red cheeks will have pale cheeks for my sake . . .'.[66] The uncanny element gives the play a stature above that of a typical '98 drama and this is Yeats's rather than Lady Gregory's achievement, although without her strong grasp of peasant dialogue the *heimlich* element of the play would not have been established so economically and confidently.

The play's extraordinary and immediate success has been well documented, as has its effect on Irish politics. When Yeats asked 'Did that play of mine send out | Certain men the English shot?' he knew what the answer was. What remains remarkable is that the play was written *against* the tide of Irish Ireland; that it was a physical force drama conceived in a period in which nationalist culture had moved— in part under Moran's direction— against physical force. Yet, after four years of highly effective abuse from Moran on the follies of Irish people's 'sensuous' dreams of 'the humiliation of England, a hundred thousand English corpses with Irish bullets, or pike wounds through them',[67] nationalists veered round and applauded *Cathleen Ni Houlihan*. One can well understand Moran's rage at the play's 'green sentimentality' in 1905, a year in which he quarrelled not only with Yeats, but with the Gaelic League—having in the previous year violently attacked Arthur Griffith's 'Green Hungarian Band', Horace Plunkett and George Russell.[68] In 1905 Moran was at once at his most powerful and his most isolated, *The Leader* having been boycotted by the nationalist Press and Moran himself having been forcibly ejected from the Gaelic League's 'Language Procession' in January.

The ever-expanding success and influence of *Cathleen ni Houlihan* was signalled in a manner peculiarly hurtful to Moran; it was the first work by Yeats to be translated into Irish. In 1905 the *United Irishman* serialised Father Thomas O'Kelly's translation *Caitlin ni Uallachain/Drama Naisiunta* and it was separately published later in the year.[69] O'Kelly's preface was in every sense an affront to Moran: a 'mongrel Anglo-Irish' play, which canonised '98 as the key moment in modern Irish history and which endorsed physical force nationalism, was translated into Irish because '[m]any readers of Mr. Yeats' beautiful play "Kathleen ni Houlihan" must have felt, as the writer has felt, a desire to see it clothed in the native speech of the people whom it seeks to rouse to a deeper consciousness of the duty of self-renunciation in the cause of the Motherland'.[70] O'Kelly's preface and translation, the praise of loyal Irish Irelanders such as Corkery and Clery, the regular productions of the play by little theatre societies around Ireland, all this signalled the eclipse of Moran's movement in its purist form. The play became part of nationalist consciousness, so much so that when Eamon de Valera quoted Cathleen ni Houlihan's words in 1920, in his statement on the death of Terence MacSwiney, he gave no author, as if the play were the product of Ireland itself.[71]

Moran's period of greatest influence was between 1900 and 1905, the watershed of his influence. Between 1900 and 1905, as P. S. O'Hegarty acknowledged, in a generally hostile obituary, *The Leader* was bought and read by most nationalists, alongside the very different *United Irishman*.[72] Moran's sheer abusiveness and his willingness to attack anyone and anything gave his long editorials a charge and obviously contributed to the success of the journal. (Indeed Father Peter O'Leary praised Moran's all-round ferocity by saying that 'if you have a good dog . . . he will give you an occasional bite if you're not careful'.)[73] Clery recalled 'once [Irish Ireland's] forces were mobilized, about the turn of the century, they advanced with the invincible force of a conquering army. The movement spread like wild fire through the country'.[74] Something of the continued diffusion of Moran's ideology can be seen in Frank O'Connor's autobiography *An Only Child* in which he recalls impassioned discussions in Irish on such issues as '"Is dancing national" ' or '"Is Shakespeare national"', as well as his father's determination not to accept English made matches.[75] O'Connor was very conscious of the impact of Irish Ireland on figures such as Daniel Corkery, his schoolteacher, who as 'Lee' regularly contributed to *The Leader*. Corkery's canonisation of the peasant in *A Munster Twilight*, especially in 'The Ploughing of Leaca-Na-Naomh', is a mystical-atavistic sophistication of Moran's presentation of the Irish speaking peasant as the only 'true Gael'.[76] Sean O'Faolain, a close friend of both Corkery and O'Connor, was harsher in his estimation of Corkery's ideology and aesthetic: when assessing him in 1936, O'Faolain pointed to parallels with national Socialism in Corkery's refusal to accept writers of Protestant descent as 'Irish'.[77] P. S. O'Hegarty is probably correct to see 1905 as the turning point in Moran's career, the point at which his influence peaked. Clery confirms this: '. . . after a time the onset slackened; resistance gathered from various quarters. When the first fervour had passed, say about the middle of the first decade of the century, the advance of Irish Ireland may be said to have been held up.'[78] In part Irish Ireland's success as a movement led to its becoming separated from Moran's purist conception and hybridising with other movements, including—paradoxically—physical force nationalism.

The Leader continued to attack Yeats, typically bringing in the sore issue of *Cathleen ni Houlihan*. In Moran's editorial comment on the *Playboy* Riots, he attacks Yeats as much as Synge:

> A country cannot take a criminal libel against Messrs. Synge and Yeats; and when, feeling its impotence before what it considers a painful slander, the country, or some part of it, howls, the author of 'Cathleen ni Houlihan,' with a cry of 'freedom of judgement', calls in the police.[79]

Yeats tended to ignore the *Leader*'s attacks on him—although occasionally he used other Dublin newspapers for a response. An exception is a letter to *The Leader* of 21 November 1907, responding to a piece which criticised his presence at a dinner at the Corinthian Club at which the Lord Lieutenant, Lord Aberdeen and his wife and other ascendancy figures were present. Moran had a field day:

> The author of 'Cathleen ni Houlihan,' we see, was at a 'God save the King' dinner one night last week! 'Cathleen,' we suppose, is all right in theory; but then a dinner is a dinner even to a poet . . . Sir Charles Cameron presided over the dinner, and amongst the followers of 'Cathleen ni Houlihan ' present were the Lord Chancellor, Judge Ross, the Attorney-General for Ireland, Tony Traill, Sir Christy Nixon, James Talbot Power, 'Oh, Caithleen ni Houlihan, your way's a thorny way'![80]

Yeats's letter—misdated in the heat of the moment—insisted that his presence at the dinner was a mishap: he had thought that he was being invited by Sir Charles Cameron to a private theatrical party:

> I expected to find a Bohemian gathering of perhaps twenty or thirty people. I found two or three hundred, and was already sitting in my place when I heard that Lord and Lady Aberdeen were expected . . . I have long ceased to be an active politician, but that makes me the more anxious to follow with all loyalty the general principles defined by Mr. Parnell and never renounced by any Nationalist party. He directed Ireland on the occasion of a Royal visit in 1885 or 1886 to pay no official honour to any representative of English rule until a suffecent National independence had made possible a new treaty. I could have slipped away and avoided attack, or won a little vain glory by making some protest, but I chose rather to follow those old rules of courtesy in which, as Balzac has said, we are all Conservatives.[81]

In his reference to 'the general principles defined by Mr. Parnell' Yeats directly attacks Moran's 'Collar the King' policy: from 1903 onwards Moran had argued that nationalists should not boycott state visits or reject government appointments, but rather get what they could out of the British Government and move for autonomy within the Empire.[82] Moran admitted, in editorial comment on this letter, that Yeats had cleared himself of the charge of 'knowingly and with malice intent' being present at a 'God save the King dinner'. He could not resist moralising on the folly of the exaggerated hostility of un-named 'terrorist obscurantists' to the symbols of British Rule, while ridiculing Yeats for accepting an invitation to a 'vulgar eating club' where 'beef-eaters . . . hook an actor or someone like that and hang an evening sing-song on to him'.

In his 1909 Diary—responding to Synge's terminal illness—Yeats engaged in bitter reveries on the type of the new Irish journalist:

> The root of it all is that the political class in Ireland—the lower-middle class from whom the patriotic associations have drawn their journalists and their leaders for the last ten years—have suffered through the cultivation of hatred as the one energy of their movement, a deprivation which is the intellectual equivalent to the removal of the genitals. Hence the shrillness of their voices. They contemplate all creative power as the eunuchs contemplate Don Juan as he passes through Hell on the white horse (*Mem* 176).

When writing to Lady Gregory he interpreted this note as referring to 'Griffith and his like': a subsequent entry, in which he speaks of the 'destructiveness of journalism here in Ireland' in relation to *The Leader*, indicates that Moran and his 'mechanical logic and commonplace eloquence' were as much in his mind as Griffith (*Mem* 178).

The Leader did occasionally print a positive response to Yeats; a striking example is Shane Leslie's 'The Irish National Anthem', in which Leslie urges 'Red Hanrahan's Song about Ireland'— which he describes as 'a great National poem'—as a future National Anthem, despite its not being written in Irish.[83] Leslie, an ascendancy convert to nationalism and Catholicism, was too big a catch to be subjected to censorship. However, when Yeats accepted a pension in 1911, Moran exploded:

> The Pensioner is, of course, a pure-souled patriot: in payment for his patriotism Emmet got the rope, but Pollexfen Yeats, the author of 'Cathleen ni Houlihan,' gets three pounds a week from the British Government.'[84]

In his correspondence with Lady Gregory, Yeats makes regular reference to Moran's antics and his vehement attacks on the Abbey Players, particularly during their American tour. Yeats felt obliged to respond to one editorial which recycled the attacks of an American Jesuit, Father Kenny, but he did so in the *Freeman's*

Journal.[85] This roused Moran's ire and led to a sequence of attacks on 'the Artful Dodger' 'Pensioner Yeats', the 'Green Playboy'. These culminated in a skit by 'A. M. W' which Yeats found damaging because of the religious element dragged into the issue:

> The Leader is very venomous this week & I think will from this on attack us openly on religious grounds. They put into my mouth one curious sentence (I quote from memory)—. . .' my Pollexfen relations were foolish—they said no Catholics need apply. I am wiser & say none but Catholics need apply—especially bad characters.'[86]

The skit is accompanied by a vigorous cartoon which depicts Yeats in the guise of a Dublin policeman, an allusion to his use of the police at the *Playboy* riots. The actual words of 'Constable Yeats of the Art Division, D.M.P.' are significantly misremembered by Yeats—he substitutes 'Catholic' for the offensive 'Papist':

> So the Irish Papists have stripped off the eternal mask of Art, and shown that the bird of paradise was, after all, only an ugly Carrion Crow [i.e., Protestant]. Well, let it be so. It was great art while it lasted, it was Art in the Highest sense, it was the Art that conceals Art, in the sense of using Art as a dirty weapon of offence against Irish Papists while professing to love them. Great Art is a rare thing even among its own people. Now the Pollexfens of Sligo showed a woeful want of Art in excluding Popery from their official cast, and by doing so gave the whole show away. I did the thing differently, and that is where the divine afflatus comes in. Pollexfen adopted the crude and clumsy principle of no Papists need apply, but in my establishment it was—none but Papists need apply, especially Papists of very bad characters. Now, of course, we are both found out; but, oh, what a difference was in the Art.[87]

The skit continues with Yeats trying to arrest Cathleen ni Houlihan and boasting:

> Yeats, the Artful Dodger, has played his part, but Yeats, the Dramatic Coercionist; Yeats, the Buckshot Forster and the Balfour of the pagan propaganda; Yeats, the bobby, the beadle, Yeats, the bum-bailiff and process-server of Art is on the stage still. Look out, ye low-down Irish Papists. Hands off our stage nightmares, or I'll summons ye. Who'll tread on the tail of my rhythmical twilight—huroo!

Yeats's letters to Lady Gregory demonstrate Yeats's continued sensitivity to Moran's programme and an awareness that Moran had to be circumvented. Indeed in the 1930s Yeats told Tom MacGreevy that he had sought to anticipate the *Leader*'s attacks on new plays:

> . . . if, in the old days, they had a play coming on which was likely to prove controversial he would call round to *The Leader* office, tell D. P. Moran, the editor and ostensible enemy, about it, and ask that, if the play had to be attacked it should be on some, to W. B., unimportant, ground rather than on the one that might prove damaging to the theatre effort as a whole. Always D. P. would see what he could do about it and no harm would be done (*I&R* 411).

Whatever negotiations took place between Yeats and Moran, this is a softened account, adjusted for the mild MacGreevy. Yet Yeats had asked Lady Gregory to write to Moran informing him that William Boyle's *The Eloquent Dempsey*, which was to open at the Abbey on 20 January 1906, was 'a play after his own heart "a Leader play" in fact'. (Both Yeats and Synge had thought the play 'impossibly vulgar' on a first reading.)[88]

Meanwhile *The Leader* went into a gradual decline, becoming scrappier, shorter and printed on inferior paper; to compare *The Leader* of 1905 with an issue of 1913 is to see a concrete expression of Moran's marginalisation. He was increasingly out of touch with political developments in Ireland: when invited to be on the steering committee of the Irish Volunteers in November 1913, he refused. The Easter Rising was initially unintelligible to Moran; in his brief, dazed editorial comment he admitted that 'what has happened, has happened' but insisted that he still supported 'Home Rule for Ireland within the Empire'.[89] Moran's response to 'the men who were shot' is a most pathetic example of a vigorous journalist bewildered and at a loss; he runs through the names of those executed, making brief comments on those he knew—Pearse was only half-Irish and had a rather pompous public manner, Connolly had a strong Scots accent—concluding that he only associated three of them with physical force nationalism.[90]

Yeats's endless rise paralleled Moran's decline into marginality. The Nobel prize was another blow:

> British Pensioner Yeats is an English poet, and he has won a Swedish money prize. What has that to do with the Saorstat? Nothing, of course. However Dr. Gogarty thinks the award was the most significant thing that had come to our country since the

Treaty . . . There was a time when Mr. Yeats was quite a champion
of the Irish language cause, not that we accuse him of ever having
tried to master a primer of Irish. But whatever he may be as a poet,
he was always a show publicity agent for himself, and certainly
made the most, in the material market, of his talent.[91]

Yet perhaps the most humiliating moment for Moran was when the
upward trajectory of Yeats's career led to the reprinting in *The
Leader* for 29 June 1935, in honour of Yeats's seventieth birthday,
the letter which Yeats had written to *The Leader* in September 1900,
when Moran was the coming man and Yeats the voice of 'mongrel
Anglo-Irish literature'. Yeats preserved a cutting of this remarkable
trophy.[92]

The obituary issues of *The Leader* (8, 15, 22, February 1936) reveal
the extent of Moran's decline. Each contributor speaks of a forgotten great man and they recall the Golden Age at the beginning of
the century when *The Leader* was read by 'everyone' from
University College students to the village priest and schoolmaster;
'*The Leader* was everywhere and everybody was talking about it or
quoting from it'.[93] Aodh de Blacam, a former contributor to the
journal, acknowledged that he and Moran had quarrelled over
politics and become estranged, but praised Moran as

the Gael in real life. If he had a rough side to his tongue, who got it
but the enemies of historic Ireland? That is bred in our bone and
blood and spirit. Whom did he lash but slaves, shoneens, nation-
sellers and oppressors?[94]

Other contributors preferred to emphasise Moran's extreme shyness, his dislike of public debate, his good humour, boyish spirit,
devout Catholicism and happy family life.[95]

Yet though Moran must have died a disappointed man, Irish
Ireland was not dead. It was Irish Ireland which formed Aodh de
Blacam, Irish Ireland which led Brian O'Nolan's father to insist that
only Irish be spoken in his house—with the unexpected result that
the first great work of fiction in modern Irish is *An Beal Bocht*.[96]
And an Irish Ireland ideology is behind Eamon de Valera's 1943 St
Patrick's Day speech, with its atavistic vision of a Gaelic Arcadia,
isolated from foreign influences:

Acutely conscious though we all are of the misery and desolation in
which the greater part of the world is plunged, let us turn aside for a

moment to that ideal Ireland that we would have. That Ireland
which we dreamed of would be the home of a people who valued
material wealth only as the basis of right living, of a people who
were satisfied with frugal comfort and devoted their leisure to the
things of the spirit—a land whose countryside would be bright with
cosy homesteads, whose fields and villages would be joyous with
the sounds of industry, with the romping of sturdy children, the
contests of athletic youths and the laughter of comely maidens,
whose firesides would be forums for the wisdom of serene old age.
It would, in a word, be the home of a people living the life that God
desires that man should live.

And Irish-speaking Catholics all in this ideal country. De Valera
made a plea for the Irish language as the natural speech of
Ireland—by 1943 a lost cause:

[T]he national language . . . is for us what no other language can be.
It is our very own. It is more than a symbol; it is an essential part of
our nationhood. It has been moulded by the thought of a hundred
generations of our forebears . . . As a vehicle of three thousand
years of our history, the language is for us precious beyond measure
. . . With the language gone we could never aspire again to being
more than half a nation.[97]

Moran is still largely forgotten, but as Roy Foster has noted, his
legacy survives in—for example—recent Field Day publications, in
which Seamus Deane sounds 'like an exceptionally frenzied D. P.
Moran, *circa* 1904'.[98] So perhaps Moran's collar has not yet loosened
its grip on Irish culture.

NOTES

1.   Dr. Patrick Maume's *D. P. Moran* (Dundalk: Historical Association of Ireland,
      1995) is the major study of Moran to date. I am very grateful to Dr. Maume for
      sending me proofs of his monograph and for commenting in detail on this arti-
      cle. For a briefer survey of Moran's career see Patrick Callan, 'D. P. Moran
      Founder Editor of *The Leader*', *Capuchin Annual* (1977), 274-287. For a broader
      survey of Irish Ireland see F. S. L. Lyons, *Culture and Anarchy in Ireland*
      (Oxford: Oxford University Press, 1983), pp. 57-83. See also J. Hutchinson, *The
      Dynamics of Cultural Nationalism :The Gaelic Revival and the Creation of the Irish*

Nation State (London: Allen and Unwin, 1987), pp. 173-8 for a positive account of Moran and of Irish Ireland. Conor Cruise O'Brien's *Ancestral Voices* (Dublin: Poolbeg, 1994) is idiosyncratically stimulating on Moran, *The Leader* and 'Irish Ireland'.

2. 'The Editor of the *Leader*' [W. P. Ryan], *The Irish Peasant*, 26 May 1906, [7].

3. These were collected as *The Philosophy of Irish Ireland* (Dublin: James Duffy & Co., 1905).

4. These quotations are taken from the *New Ireland Review* as follows. 'Is the Irish Nation Dying?', December 1898, 213; 'The Pale and the Gael', June 1899, 235-6, 234; 'The Future of the Irish Nation', February 1899, 354; 'Politics, Nationality and Snobs', November 1899, 140.

5. Hyde told this to Lady Gregory who noted the conversation in her diary for 29 December 1900 (Berg).

6. 'Is the Irish Nation Dying?' 210: *myaw* is a phonetic version of *mi-ádh* i.e., ill-luck or misfortune.

7. 'Politics, Nationality and Snobs', *loc. cit.*, 136.

8. See *Dublin Essays* (Dublin: Maunsel, 1919), p. 131. Clery recalls intense discussions as to whether someone who wore a kilt, spoke Irish and played hurling could still be an Irish Irelander if he occasionally attended a Rugby match (pp. 66-7).

9. For this distinction see Myles Na gCopaleen, *Cruiskeen Lawn* (Dublin: *Irish Times*, n.d. [c. 1941]), p. 1.

10. The Irish language contribution to the journal was a brief regular column, initially written by Father Peter O'Leary.

11. ALS to Lady Gregory, 13 August 1900 (Berg). Though Russell had been a friend of Hyde's for many years it took 'The Battle of Two Civilizations' to mobilise his desire to learn Irish, in the face of a professed dislike of Moran's 'sarcasm'.

12. See *Au* 361. *The Leader* carried advertisements for 'Real Irish Tweed' which could be made up by 'D. Towel (Great Irish tailor) Dublin', as well as for Irish-made boots, shoes, mackintoshes etc.. Readers of *The Leader* regularly complained of difficulties with 'Irish Tweed'.

13. *All Ireland Review*, 1 September 1900, 4. According to Frank O'Connor, this costume was the 'correct' costume of an Irish nationalist c. 1903. See *My Father's Son* (London: Macmillan, 1968), p. 87. For the passionate investment in this issue see 'Irish Hats for Irish People' (*The Leader*, 4 April 1903, 77-8.)

14. 'Chanel' [*pseud*, i.e., Clery's confirmation name], *The Idea of a Nation* (Dublin: James Duffy & Co., 1907), p. 59. This volume collects articles published by Clery in *The Leader*. Clery does not exaggerate. Moran discussed this issue in *The Leader*, pointing out—only semi-humorously—that an Irish Irelander was not the more authentic for refusing to wear a tie, for wearing baggy trousers and limiting his washing: '[i]t will not do to dub a man a *seoinin* because he washes his face at least once a week; and yet we hear that there is a tendency for the term to degenerate in that direction.' Irish Ireland women also adopted a very plain, homespun style of dress ('Concerning the Seoinin', *The Leader*, 20 June 1903, 261-2).

15. *Celtia*, 1 September 1901, 141.

16. For a characteristic piece see 'In A Kanturk Shop', *The Leader* (4 June 1901), 92. Encouragement of 'Home Industries' had been a British concern for some time,

but in translating this practice to Ireland, Moran gave it an ideological edge. Indeed some of the advertisments in *The Leader* are frankly xenophobic. John S. Kelly (furniture retailer) gave special concessions to Gaelic League members and announced that his was a 'Sinn Fein' shop which gave 'Home Manufacture the Preference' and had 'No connection with the Jews' (22 July 1904, 365).

17.   Mick M'Quaid is the hero of a long running serial in *The Shamrock* by Colonel Lynam: Mick is variously an M.P., a Removable Magistrate, an Evangelist, a Gombeen Man etc., and is always accompanied by his faithful friend Geraghty and a black bottle of whiskey.

18.   That Miss Ivors is an Irish Irelander has not been noted in most editions of *Dubliners*, although Terence Brown does indicate an Irish Ireland context; however he associates Irish Ireland with Griffith and *Sinn Fein* (London: Penguin, pp. xxvi, 309). In John Wyse Jackson and Bernard McGinley's excellent edition of *Dubliners* (London: Sinclair-Stevenson, 1993) Miss Ivors is simply seen as a Gaelic Leaguer, despite her regular and hostile use of 'West Briton', her rejection of 'Cosmopolitanism' and non-Irish culture, and her reiterated references to Gabriel's 'own language'. Irish Irelanders were members of the Gaelic League, but not all members of the Gaelic League (which in 1904 was non-sectarian, non-political and included Unionists) were Irish Irelanders. Jackson and McGinley assume that Joyce partly or wholly endorses Miss Ivors' position. Yet in this story Joyce indicates strong affection for the 'mongrel' Anglo-Irish culture which Moran condemned. Furthermore, Gretta's desire to go back to her birthplace in Galway is very distinct from Miss Ivors's ideologically driven determination to visit the West. See Jackson and McGinley, *op. cit.*, p. 170. As Conor Cruise O'Brien has recently identified his mother, a committed Irish Irelander, as a model for Miss Ivors, perhaps the case rests (*Ancestral Voices*, p. 44). For an attack on foreign holidays see *The Leader* (27 April 1901), 130 and 'Irish Irelanders and Holidays' (27 May 1905), 220-7. Andrew Gibson has made an interesting case for some accommodation of the Irish Ireland position in 'Circe': indeed given Moran's influence in 1904, one would expect to find the movement in *Ulysses*. Certainly Stephen Dedalus's 'cracked lookingglass of a servant' could be read as a humiliated absorption of Moran's contempt for 'Anglo-Irish literature'. However the creator of Leopold Bloom—'Irish Jew'—evidently rejected the central tenets of Irish Ireland. See '"Strangers in My House". . . England in "Circe"' in Andrew Gibson (ed.) *Reading Joyce's 'Circe'* (Amsterdam: Rodopi, 1994), pp. 185-6 & 205-6.

19.   'The Pale and the Gael', *loc. cit.*, 238.

20.   'The Battle of Two Civilizations', *New Ireland Review*, August 1900, 329-331. Yeats's 'surrender' was to assert, in a speech made on 16 July 1899, at the establishment of the Kiltartan branch of the Gaelic League, that 'Every nation [has] its own duty to the world, its own message to deliver, and that message [is] to a considerable extent bound up with the language. The nations make a part of one harmony just as the colours of the rainbow make a part of one harmony of beautiful colour. It is our duty to keep the message, the colour which God has committed to us, clear and pure and shining', *An Claidheamh Soluis*, 29 July 1899, 314-5.

21.   'The Future of the Irish Nation', *loc. cit.*, 352-3.

22.   *Cosmopolis*, June 1898, 684-6, c.f., *E&I* 185-7.

23. 'The Battle of Two Civilizations', *loc. cit.*, 329-330. When this essay was col-
     lected by Lady Gregory in *Ideals in Ireland* (London: Unicorn Press, 1901), she
     made him cut about 1,000 words, including this attack. Most of the cuts were
     restored when Moran collected his essays in 1905. In fact by 1898 Yeats had
     become uneasy about 'Celtic' versus 'Irish' and had changed the name of the
     projected Literary Theatre from 'Celtic', as it had been proposed in July 1897 to
     'Irish' as it was announced in January 1899. However, abuse of the 'Celtic note'
     was to remain a staple of *The Leader*. In 1904 'A. M. W.' produced a skit entitled
     'A Great Auction of Celtic Notes' in which the 'Celtic Note Limited Liability
     Company' sold off its 'opal lakes', 'Enchanted Woods' and 'Shadowy Waters'
     (*The Leader*, 27 August), 8-9. The 'Celtic note' is picked up by Joyce in
     Dubliners: in 'A Little Cloud' Chandler dreams of having his as yet unpublished
     poems praised for '"The Celtic Note"'. Oddly Arnold's name is not mentioned
     in these debates.

24. In 'Irish Nationalist Poetry' (*The Pilot*, 19 May 1900, 351), Stephen Gwynn
     partly reports Yeats's speech. In his lecture Rolleston had claimed that Yeats was
     'the most distinguished of all the spiritual children of Ferguson' and that he had
     'thoroughly absorbed the mystical dreaming spirit of Gaeldom, the spirit which
     regards all the visible "realities" of earth as manifestations of unseen and eternal
     powers' (*Irish Literary Society Gazette*, December 1900, 3-4). Moran's attitude to
     the Irish-speaking peasant was paradoxically ambivalent: he was an essentially
     urban type.

25. 'A Hundred Years of Irish Humbug', *An Claidheamh Soluis*, 19 [May] 1900, 149-
     151. *The Leader* regularly published fantasies in which in a future Ireland,
     English was to be a minority language. In one such fantasy, by W. P. Ryan, set
     in the 21st Century, French scholars were learning Irish so as to have access to
     the greatest European literature of the twentieth century.

26. *The Leader*, 8 September 1900, 28. In the *Tain* Cuchulain (the Champion of
     Ulster) fights his foster-brother Ferdia (Medb's champion) embracing him at the
     end of every battle and sending food and medicine to him across the Ford.
     Cuchulain eventually kills Ferdia and mourns him. This was taken by all nation-
     alists as the epitome of ancient Irish chivalry.

27. 26 January 1901, 2. Griffith's paper was friendly to Yeats, not least because
     Maud Gonne was its financial backer. Yeats contributed to the *United Irishman*
     regularly between 1900 and 1905.

28. i.e., 'Slender Suir', a reference to Ryan's place of birth at Templemore, near the
     river Suir.

29. The article is probably by Anna, Comtesse de Brémont, a friend of the Wilde
     family and a popular writer, whom Yeats had known for many years and who
     had propositioned him in the late '80s. She had briefly been a member of the
     Golden Dawn, as her reference to 'in the outer' indicates. Ryan, who had
     worked for T. P. O'Connor on *The Star* and who was still living in London,
     probably knew the identity of the 'interviewer'.

30. Although Moran qualified his comment with 'Even Mr. Yeats', this provoked
     protests from several readers and Rolleston himself replied vigorously, pointing
     to the absurdity of Moran's seeking to speak for Ireland: 'is it not a little
     ridiculous to see a worthy gentleman sitting at a desk in Dublin and pro-
     nouncing gravely from that watch-tower that he alone knows what reaches or

does not reach the "Irish heart"'. Rolleston went on to insist that Yeats's poetry had moved 'many Irish hearts' (*The Leader*, 5 January 1901, 296). Yeats, who had come to despise Rolleston—by now very much a Unionist—was impressed by this response: 'I thought Rolleston's reply to Moran suprizingly good. He seems to have been really angry & that kept his wits alive' (*CL3* 6). Father Jeremiah O'Donovan of Loughrea, a cultured nationalist, defended Yeats as one who had moved many 'Irish hearts' whether educated or otherwise: ' I have a dainty volume of Mr. Yeats's collected poems. One evening I missed the book from its accustomed place. I asked my housekeeper if she saw it . . . she said it was in the kitchen, where she had taken it to read one of the poems—the ballad of Peter Gilligan—to a neighbour, and, as in justification, she added, "To tell you the truth, sir, the two of us cried over it"'. O'Donovan further defended Rolleston by remarking that 'he knows his native language'(*The Leader* 12 January 1901, 315-6). Rolleston had good Irish which is more than could be said for Moran. Moran's declared position was that Rolleston was 'an educated Englishman who thinks he is an Irishman' (5 January 1901, 296).

31. In 1902-1903 a mild controversy arose in *An Claidheamh Soluis* as to whether there could be Irish literature in English and if so, what should this literature be called. The incoming editor, Patrick Pearse, responding to a letter by Seamus MacManus, rejected 'Anglo-Irish' as a descriptive term—or as a category: 'we . . . think that the manful admission of our past delinquencies is much more likely to be helped by calling literature in the English language, English and not Irish or Anglo-Irish literature' (see issues for 27 December, 1902, 709-10; 3 January 1903, 723; 10 January 1903, 740; and 17 January 1903, 761). Yeats recalled: '"It must be either English or Irish", said some patriotic editor' (*Au* 219).

32. *An Claidheamh Soluis*, 27 October 1900, 517.

33. ALS to Yeats nd. but probably late August 1900 (MBY).

34. ALS to Lady Gregory (Berg). Russell thought that Moran had a duty to keep W. P. Ryan under control.

35. See *The Pope's Green Island* (London: James Nisbet, 1912), p. 270. Ryan belittled *The Leader* as ' a moderately Irish, rather pro-clerical organ'.

36. MS Diary, 29 December 1900 (Berg). Lady Gregory with characteristic diplomacy contributed articles to *The Leader* from October 1900 to December 1902.

37. *Freeman's Journal*, 1 January, 1901, 7.

38. 'A. M. W.', [i.e., John Swift, a journalist], 'Our Puny Intellectual Tin Gods', *The Leader*, 11 February 1905, 410-12. See also 'Imaal' [J. J. O'Toole], 'A Rather Complex Personality', 26 September 1903, 71-2 and further correspondence 10 October, 100 and 17 October, 122.

39. *The Leader*, 19 January 1901, 339.

40. *The Leader*, 28 September 1901, 79-80.

41. *The Leader*, 20 July 1901, 329-331.

42. *The Leader*, 2 November 1901, 155 & 158; 16 November, 188-9.

43. 'A Sober Nationalist', *The Leader*, 10 September 1904, 38. Moore was 'saved' because he had converted to Protestantism.

44. *The Leader*, 6 December 1902, 239.

45. O'Donnell did contribute to *The Leader* under his own name in 1901. He had, in 1900, stolen funds destined for the IRB and had been forced to disgorge them.

O'Donnell had also attempted to 'felon-set' Maud Gonne by disclosing treasonable activities of hers. In addition he had published a pamphlet, 'The Harp or the Guillotine', in 1900, attacking Wolfe Tone, proving himself a man after Moran's heart.

46. *All Ireland Review*, 1 June 1910, 154.

47. *The Leader* (25 May 1901), 203-4. Elliott, an Englishman, was the journal's art critic.

48. ALS to William Sharp c. late May-early June, 1901 (MS Private).

49. Published in the *United Irishman* in August 1901. *E&I* 210.

50. The text quoted is the *Cornhill* version, p. 345 (c.f., *E&I* 4).

51. Editorial note, *The Leader*, 26 January 1901, 352.

52. *The Leader*, 8 June 1901, 233.

53.   *CL3* 658-9. After a serial attack on Horace Plunkett's *Ireland in the New Century* in *The Leader* by Michael O'Riordan, George Russell had turned on Moran for the first time in 'Physical Force in Literature'. Russell, a Buddhist, a vegetarian, and a pacifist, made a case for physical force nationalism: 'The theory of physical force has been gradually ebbing away from politics in Ireland. It required men to be brave; and for those who are willing to risk their lives we always have respect. When a man is ready to shoulder pike or rifle for an idea, he regards his ideal as more important than life, and however he may pervert these ideals in expression, I have never a doubt but that in such a case the man's heart has been made holy by some sacred fire. There are nobler ways of settling the right or wrong of a question, but the heroes of gentleness and love are few, and if a man is unable to live this life, it is better he should take some course which at least demands of him sacrifice. But while much can be said for the man who, seeing no higher way, decides to establish his right by force, there is nothing at all to be said for the physical force theory in literature which has come to be accepted by so many journalists in Ireland. To adopt it in life shows courage. To bring it into literature or argument shows the man is a coward. He runs away from the battle while seeming to take a sword . . . When a writer or speaker suggests that his opponent is a liar, or one who acts from a mean motive, when he tries to shout him down, he is not only a coward in his own cause, for he does not speak for it, but he is also a recreant of the Light, and has listed under the banner of the Dark Immortal, no matter what Holy Name he may profess to worship.' (*Dana*, September 1904, 129). Moran, enraged at being called a coward, filled *The Leader* for 10 September with three pages of abuse of Russell, Yeats, Plunkett O'Grady *et al.* ('A Sober Nationalist' 37-9). Russell replied with a long letter printed in the issue of 1 October, which provoked a repellently abusive editorial response from Moran (pp. 88-90). Russell collected the whole controversy in a pamphlet (*Controversy in Ireland: An Appeal to Irish Journalists* [Dublin: D.J.O'Donoghue, 1904]), the profits of which went to the Gaelic League.

54.   *The Leader*, 9 February 1901, 388.

55.   See Clery *The Idea of a Nation* (Dublin: J. Duffy & Co, 1907) pp. 62-74. Clery argued for 'Home Rule within Home Rule' and for an Ulster partitioned on sectarian grounds. He later became Professor of Law at the National University, Dublin, was a Republican Judge and opposed the Treaty.

56.   *The Leader*, 12 April 1902, 106. Clery was more forthright when he reviewed the Cork production: 'Each time that I have seen it my appreciation has increased

. . . A strong political interest for once brought Mr. Yeates down from the clouds and made him speak in a symbolism that is intelligible' (18 March 1905, 55-6). Corkery had also praised the play in *The Leader*, saying that he looked forward to seeing the Cork Players perform it (31 December 1904, 311).

57.   *The Leader*, 17 January 1905, 330. Tony Traill—known to *The Leader* as 'bigot Traill' is Anthony Traill, who was Provost of TCD 1904-14. 'Brother Goulding' is Sir William Goulding, a member of the family which owned the Goulding Fertilizer Company of Dublin, and, as a prominent Unionist, a frequent subject of attack in *The Leader*: 'Brother Goulding the tolerant manure manufactor . . .' (*The Leader*, 2 May 1903, 149).

58.   14 January 1905, 345-6.

59.   In 1905 Moran published an Irish novel in English, *Tom O'Kelly* (Dublin: Duffy). It is a fairly coarse satire on aspects of Irish provincial life, attacking familar targets, drink, Fenianism, snobbery and 'sunburstery'.

60.   *Loc. cit.*, 13. 'I remember visiting the Naval Exhibition some years ago with a friend of mine who had "gone out" with his rifle in the affair at Tallaght. I believe that until he had seen the stupendous engines of modern warfare there he nursed the hope that he might shoulder his rifle again in the cause of the liberty of his country'.

61.   'Fenianism', *The Leader*, 6 April 1901, 87. Conor Cruise O'Brien does not seem to have grasped Moran's hostility to Fenianism: see *Ancestral Voices* p.58.

62.   *Ibid.*

63.   James Pethica has fully established Lady Gregory's co-authorship of the play by examining drafts in the Berg Collection; see '"Our Kathleeen"' in *YA* 6, 3-31. As Yeats was the declared author of the play, I do not give both names.

64.   For the *unheimlich* see Sigmund Freud, *Collected Edition* (London: Hogarth Press, 1955) Vol. XVII, pp. 217-256.

65.   *Traits and Stories of the Irish Peasantry* (Dublin: William Curry, 1845) II, pp. 75-96. The 'Leannan Sidhe' is usually a fairy mistress who takes a human lover. Yeats describes her as 'the Gaelic muse, for she gives inspiration to those she persecutes' (*P&I* 15). However in this tale she is conceived more as a malignant parasite.

66.   *VPl* 229. Even details such as the stage direction '[An Old Woman passes the window slowly]' (*VPl* 221) derive directly from the tale, in which the passing shadow of the mysterious woman darkens the window of the cottage and heralds the shift into the uncanny.

67.   'The Battle of Two Civilizations', p. 333.

68.   Moran had attacked Griffith's *The Resurrection of Hungary* (1904) throughout 1904 and well into 1905. He also claimed ownership of the *Sinn Fein* economic policy advocated by Griffith.

69.   It was serialised from February 11 to March 11.

70.   Dublin: M. H. Gill & Son Ltd., 1905, p.[3].

71.   See Maurice Moynihan (ed.), *Speeches and Statements of Eamon de Valera 1917-1973* (Dublin: Gill and Macmillan; New York: St. Martin's Press, 1980), p.47.

72.   'D. P. Moran', *Dublin Magazine*, June 1936, 129.

73.   *The Pope's Green Island*, p. 94. Moran is not named but is clearly under discussion.

74.   *Dublin Essays*, p. 132.

75.   *An Only Child* p. 8. O'Connor's father, a drunken ex-soldier, had little political
       commitment save to William O'Brien, the member for Cork City, and was
       favourably disposed to the British Government; however he would send his son
       back to the shops if he failed to buy Irish-made matches (ie those made by Pater-
       sons of Dublin). O'Connor's father probably never read *The Leader* but was
       responding to a diffused version of its programme. O'Connor, born in 1903, is
       recalling the period up to 1916. As George Watson has recently indicated, the
       problem of what constitutes a national subject matter still bedevils Scottish writ-
       ing: Iain Crichton Smith experienced some uneasy responses after using Freud's
       name in a poem in Gaelic and was informed that a story in Gaelic about an
       American President 'was not considered to be a Gaelic theme'. See 'Celticism
       and the Annulment of History' (*Irish Studies Review*, Winter 1994-5, 6).

76.   See *A Munster Twilight* (Dublin: Talbot Press, 1917).

77.   See 'Daniel Corkery' (*Dublin Magazine*, April-June 1936, p. 54). In attacking
       Corkery's rejection of 'Anglo-Irish Literature as literature' O'Faolain referred
       directly to Nazi rejection of non-Aryan Germans. Corkery's *Synge and Anglo-
       Irish Literature* (Cork: Cork University Press, 1931) completed a process begun
       in *The Leader*, where, in 1905, Corkery gave a hostile account of *The Well of the
       Saints* as misrepresenting the Irish peasant and holding the mirror up not to
       nature but to '"nature's freaks"' ('Mr. Yeats in Cork' [30 December] 313-4). See
       Patrick Maume *'Life that is Exile': Daniel Corkery and the Search for Irish Ireland*
       (Belfast: Institute of Irish Studies, 1993) for a full assessment of Corkery's stance
       on Synge.

78.   *Dublin Essays*, 132-3.

79.   *The Leader* 9 February 1907, 401.

80.   *The Leader* 23 November 1907, 211-12. Moran's quotation is from Ethna Car-
       bery's 'The Passing of the Gael'.

81.   *The Leader*, 30 November 1907, 226. See *UP2* 356.

82.   I am grateful to Dr. Patrick Maume for his interpretation of this letter of
       Yeats's. For a clear account of the 'Collar the King' policy see *D. P. Moran*, p.
       29. P. S. O'Hegarty, in his obituary of Moran, sees the 'Collar the King' policy
       as a fatal blunder on Moran's part.

83.   24 September, 1910, 132-3. Leslie also defended Yeats as Ireland's greatest writer
       in a review of Stephen Brown's *A Reader's Guide to Irish Fiction* (29 October,
       1910, 253-4).

84.   *The Leader,* 25 November 1911, p. 348. *The Leader* had denounced the firm of
       Pollexfen for employing too many Protestants. I am grateful to Dr. Patrick
       Maume for pointing this out to me.

85.   21 November 1911.

86.   ALS to Lady Gregory after 9 December 1911 (Berg). I am grateful to John Kelly
       for providing me with a text of this letter and for permission to quote.

87.   *The Leader,* 9 December 1911, 415-6.

88.   ALS to Lady Gregory 15 January 1906 (Berg). I am grateful to John Kelly for
       providing me with a text of this letter and for permission to quote. See also Ann
       Saddlemyer (ed.) *Theatre Business* (Gerrards Cross: Colin Smythe, 1982) p. 74.

89.   *The Leader* (triple issue for 29 April, 6 and 13 May) 269-70. *The Leader*'s offices
       were burnt down in the Rising. Moran subsequently supported the Treaty.

90.   *The Leader*, 20 May 1916, 295-6.

91. Editorial, *The Leader*, 8 December 1923, 414-5. In the issue for 22 December 1923, 'Avis' [Willie Dawson] produced a parody of 'Innisfree': 'I will arise and go now, unto the Baltic Sea, | And a large cheque obtain there | For poems I have made, | Seven thousand "Beans" I'll have there . . .' (467).

92. *NLI* 31075. Yeats's reprinted letter is the largest contribution to this issue of *The Leader* and dominates the shrunken journal.

93. 22 February 1936, 89 (Louis J. Walsh).

94. 'An Appreciation: He Put Backbone Into Irish Slaves!', *The Leader*, 8 February, 36. *The Leader*'s response to Yeats's death was respectful; Seamus O'Neill's 'W. B. Yeats' praises him as a true lyric poet and a true patriot (25 February, 1939, 639). Lia Clarke's memoir (11 February, 1939, 592) is more curious. She recalls several meetings with Yeats and quotes from an interview in which he gives an utterly characteristic account of the shift in modern Irish literature: 'We had been romantic and eloquent; we became realistic and taciturn . . . we have a passion for knowing the worst of ourselves'. She then gives an account of an interview of 1936, when she was 'the official Irish correspondent of the German News Agency'. She had found it difficult to obtain a positive response to National Socialism from Irish writers, but recalled Yeats as the exception. Yeats apparently said '"I am profoundly excited by the possibilities for literature arising out of race consciousness."' He pointed to the importance of race in ancient civilisation and 'predicted a fertile union of blood and spirit in the new Germany'. Lia Clarke gives no indication of where this remarkable interview was originally printed and it certainly sits oddly with Yeats's letter to Ethel Mannin of 8 April, 1936 in which he expresses horror at 'the cruelty of governments . . . Communist, Fascist, nationalist, clerical, anti-clerical, are all responsible according to the number of their victims . . . every nerve trembles in horror at what is happening in Europe' (*L* 851).

95. Moran had married in January 1901 Teresa O'Toole, the daughter of a friend of Parnell's, Captain Thomas O'Toole, thrice mayor of Waterford in the 1890s. I presume that Moran's future father-in-law helped him to start the journal. *The Leader* was edited from 1936 to 1971 by Moran's daughter, Nuala Ni Mhorain, becoming a modest, uncontroversial Catholic journal, with good arts coverage (contributors in the 1950s included Benedict Kiely and Denis Donoghue), which supported Irish industries and an Irish way of life.

96. 'Myles na gCopaleen' (Dublin: Dolmen, 1941).

97. *Speeches and Statements*, 466-8. The speech marks the fiftieth anniversary of the founding of the Gaelic League, but it is Irish Ireland with its gospel of autarky which informs de Valera's vision of 'The Ireland That We Dreamed Of'.

98. 'Nations, Yet Again', *TLS*, 27 March 1992, 5.

'You need not fear that I am not amiable': Reading Yeats (Reading) Autobiographies

Eamonn Hughes

YEATS'S *AUTOBIOGRAPHIES* have an infamously tangled writing, re-writing and publishing history[1] which has led to debate about editions[2] and makes the task of editing them difficult.[3] However, what provokes headaches for others seems hopeful for us, in that the response to the *Autobiographies* in Ireland, as elsewhere, is spread over nearly sixty years, from the appearance of *Reveries Over Childhood and Youth* in 1916, through the various individual volumes and 'collected' editions, through to *Memoirs* in 1972. The source material for a survey of Irish responses to *Autobiographies* falls into two categories. Most obviously, there are the reviews in Irish periodicals or by Irish reviewers in other periodicals. There are also the autobiographies which come after Yeats in which we might reasonably expect to find some indication of Yeats's influence as autobiographer. In short, surveying the responses to *Autobiographies* seems to allow us to consider, both empirically and theoretically, the whole question of Yeats's audience in Ireland over half a century.

This temporal spread offsets the fact that Jochum's bibliography, which I have used as the major source for information on reviews, appears to support Yeats's own contention that 'I felt acutely my unpopularity and told my publisher not to send my books for review in Ireland, a decision kept for many years' insofar as it lists comparatively few reviews—Irish or otherwise—of the autobiographical writings (*Au* 447). Furthermore, the reviews that do exist tend to be at best naive in their response to autobiography as a genre. As Hazard Adams put it as late as 1965:

> . . . we are inclined to overlook the fact that these works [*Autobiographies* and *A Vision*] are, so to speak, books in themselves. Of course, we have read them with care, but usually as if they were mines of interpretation situated somewhere underneath the poetry.[4]

This tendency to see *Autobiographies* as an adjunct to the poetry or as a form of secondary material is common throughout the reviews (as it was for a long time in the general critical response to *Autobiographies*) and may account for the comparatively sparse response.[5] Consequently, there is often an air of thinly-disguised bafflement in the reviews about the aims and motives of the autobiographies. Perhaps the most extreme example of this comes from the reviewer who compares Yeats's autobiographies to James Joyce's *Work in Progress*.[6] I do not wish to underplay the literary sophistication of the *Autobiographies*, but this does seem to be overstating it.

There are several complicating factors which must be taken into account before embarking on a survey of responses. For a start, to leap straight into such a survey would be to take Yeats at his own valuation as the fountainhead of Irish literary autobiography, as of so much else in the literary and cultural life of Ireland in this century. Therefore, as readers of Yeats, we should be aware of him as someone who was himself a reader of autobiography. In the case of *Autobiographies* we must acknowledge that, in both the writing and the publication of its component parts, Yeats reacts not only to events but to others' representations of those events. Thinking of Yeats as reader both helps to set his own claims into context and prompts us to ask about the absences and silences in his *Autobiographies*—those events and works to which he appears not to respond. Therefore, although *Autobiographies* ends in 1923, the major political events of the period between 1908 (when he began the journal from which *Estrangement* and *The Death of Synge* are extracted) and 1923, are absent from *Autobiographies*. This can only be explained by Yeats's tact, amounting at times to evasiveness, and his consequent habit of deferring his response. While it is possible to see events from the time of writing having a determinate effect on his autobiography, it is necessary to register the insistence (in all but *The Bounty of Sweden*) on keeping his distance from the time being written about. In this manner he signals his dissimilarity from the satirical topicality of George Moore in *Hail and Farewell*, who is in turn made to look impulsive, and also from (according to this perspective) the merely documentary record of Lady Gregory's *Our Irish Theatre*. This deferred response also allows Yeats to have the last word on most subjects.

Another complicating factor is that most reactions to *Autobiographies*, from whatever textual source are by contemporaries such as AE, or younger writers such as Frank O'Connor or Sean O'Faolain, who knew Yeats, were indebted to him and, to some degree, overawed by him. Brooks Atkinson summed up the consequential difficulty as early as 1936:

> What influence he has had in Ireland no one can say; it has been prodigious; it has filtered down to many of his countrymen who are not familiar with his works yet whose lives have been changed by what he stood for.[7]

Separating out the influence of Yeats as autobiographer from his influence as poet, playwright, essayist, activist or cultural entrepreneur thus becomes a matter of some difficulty.

In addition, we are more likely to encounter discussions about Yeats's personality than about the personality as mediated through the autobiography or about the autobiography's quality and motives. This reaches an absurdist pitch in W. R. Rodgers's 'A Dublin Portrait'. Sean O'Faolain, arguing that Yeats was a poseur, instances his style of dress (the famous blue silk shirt included), to which Frank O'Connor (who consistently maintained that Yeats was a misunderstood innocent) replies:

> 'Bless my soul! . . . That a man's taste in shirts stands between him and his own natural self—Where is that getting to?'[8]

Wherever else it may lead 'a man's taste in shirts' does *not* get us to *Autobiographies*.

Further, the autobiographical response to Yeats is another complicating factor in that, while it can be proved that numerous Irish writers owned and/or had read his autobiography (whole or in part),[9] it is more difficult to elicit the literary influence that it exerted. Thus in both Séan O'Casey's and James Joyce's work the impact of Yeats's poems and plays is more obvious than that of the autobiographies.[10] Once again, we are more likely to encounter Yeats as a character in others' autobiographies than to encounter allusions to the *Autobiographies*.

Yeats as Reader of Autobiography

I turn now to Yeats as a reader of autobiography as a means of assessing his own motives and intended audience. The first point to be made is that Yeats's autobiographies emerge into a series of autobiographies. As David Wright and Gerard Moran have shown,[11] Yeats was keenly aware of autobiography as a genre from an early stage of his career and he seems quickly to have realised its socio-historical importance.

While it is possible to argue that Yeats began work on his autobiography as early as 1896 when he wrote the sketch 'Verlaine in 1894' which later appeared in *The Trembling of the Veil*, it is in 1908 that he begins to keep the journal that will later provide the basis for much of *Estrangement* and *The Death of Synge*. Thus, though it is difficult to set an exact date on the start of Yeats's autobiographical intentions, it can be said that he was writing autobiographical material up to twenty years before he finally felt the need to publish an explicitly autobiographical work. This point is reinforced by his early autobiographical fiction.[12] Why, then, was it in 1914 that he decided to put his own version of his life on record? The conventional answer is that *Reveries* was provoked by the appearance of George Moore's *Hail and Farewell*, for although Yeats had witnessed the appearance of *Ave* and *Salve* with some equanimity, the publication in *The English Review* in 1913 of passages from the forthcoming *Vale* displeased him greatly.[13] It must have seemed that in this 'disfiguring glass' Moore was not merely mocking what they had both worked for, but was also setting out a personal history of the movement which would control the perceptions of posterity (*L* 586). Since their quarrel several years earlier Moore had lived in 'spiritual exile',[14] but to the extent that he had been quiescent he had not completely escaped Yeats's control. Now, however, he was presenting his own mocking version of history and this was something that Yeats could not allow.

Others, too, were presenting their own, potentially threatening, versions of the times and Yeats's place within them. Katharine Tynan, a friend of his boyhood and youth, had published her *Twenty-Five Years: Reminiscences* in 1913 in which her portrait of Yeats, though affectionate, was ultimately condescending in its representation of him as a poetry-obsessed misfit.[15] Furthermore, Yeats was displeased by her use, without his permission, of his letters to her (*L* 586).[16] By 1914 Yeats was also aware of Synge's fragmentary and unpublished autobiography and of Lady Gregory's *Our Irish Theatre: A Chapter of Autobiography*.[17] Yeats may even have read (or heard) Lady Gregory's 'An Emigrant's Notebook', her first and still unpublished autobiographical volume, which shares many features with *Reveries*.[18] Then in 1914 Yeats read the serialisation in *The Egoist* of Joyce's *A Portrait of the Artist as a Young Man* which he regarded as 'disguised autobiography' (*L* 598-9).

Taken together (and remembering that there was much other autobiographical activity at this time; as far as I can tell some 35 Irish autobiographical texts appeared in the period 1910-1914)[19] these works represented a loss of control over that personal history which Yeats saw as being essential to the future reception of the Revival as a whole. This was all the harder to bear at a time when Yeats was also concerned that the forces of philistinism had become increasingly successful. The opposition to Synge's *The Playboy of the Western World* in 1907, Synge's death in 1909 which occasioned only 'short and for the most part grudging notices' (*Au* 510) in the Irish press, the failure of Dublin to provide a gallery for Hugh Lane's collection in the winter of 1912-13,[20] all witnessed to Ireland's continuing and apparently incorrigible philistinism as far as Yeats was concerned. The 'soft wax' that he had hoped to seal with his own image of Ireland now seemed to be hardening in the image of all that he opposed (*Au* 101).[21] There were also literary and personal circumstances which would have motivated him to autobiography. He had by this stage been written off as a writer,[22] and there was an additional anxiety about his unmarried status and the possibility that the Yeats name would die out.[23]

It was in these circumstances that Yeats began work on *Reveries Over Childhood and Youth*. His response was not, as might have been expected, an attempt at overt public apologetics, but a return to the time when the 'wax' was still 'soft' both for Ireland and for himself: a return to origins so that he might retrace his life to this point. What must be borne in mind is the inversion and consequent distancing here. The diaries begun in 1908, often provoked by public events, were first conceived as private; it was the private material—looking to his ancestry while anxious about his descendants—that he made public. Although the diaries provide a more immediate response to some of the events which also occasioned *Reveries Over Childhood and Youth*, they would not be published, even in revised form, until 1926 and 1928 as *Estrangement* and *The Death of Synge*, signalling a pragmatic use of material which marks the whole of Yeats's career. Yeats was always careful not to offend the living (or at least those whose opinion could affect his activities), not just because of tact but because he had no wish to burn his bridges as Moore had done. Moore could make such grand gestures, but for Yeats to emulate him would be an acknowledgement that he no longer saw himself as having any real part to play in Irish cultural politics. For these reasons, there is a similar gap between the time written about and the times of writing and publication in nearly all of Yeats's published autobiographical writings. But this temporal distancing should not blind us to the combative aspects of autobiography at this period; for Yeats to publish autobiography was to enter an arena already crowded with texts laying claim to be the true story of events.

'Fit Audience Found'?

What is notable about the first, initially private, responses to Yeats's autobiography is not just their hostility but Yeats's anticipation of it. Writing to his father on the day after he completed *Reveries*, he apologises for having used some of his father's conversation without permission and then, remarkably, says 'You need not fear that I am not amiable' (*L* 589). A year later he once more tries to reassure his father, who by that time had still not read the work (*L* 602-3). By June 1917 his father wrote to him: 'I congratulate you with all my heart' (*LTWBY* 334), though, according to Murphy, John Butler Yeats never liked the book.[24] Why then is Yeats so obviously apprehensive about the reception of *Reveries*? The simple answer is that he was right to be anxious. The struggle with the father which runs through *Reveries* (it had been suggested that if *Father and Son* had not been already used as a title Yeats could have used it for *Reveries* (*L* 589))[25] and which acts to unify *Autobiographies* as a whole[26] may well have made John Butler Yeats resentful on a personal level. However, as a feature of much male autobiography, it also links the apparently personal aspects of *Autobiographies* to the genre as a whole, signalling the public aspect of the work. The struggle with the father is a feature of Moore's *Confessions of a Young Man* (in which it is brutally foreshortened[27]) and of Joyce's *A Portrait*: both works in which the overthrow of the father is a necessary prelude to the development of the subject as artist. It also informs much autobiographical writing reaching back through the nineteenth century:

> A perpetual tension subsists between the desire for self-origination, to produce oneself as if without a father, and the awkward knowledge of indebtedness to what precedes and influences the subject.[28]

We must, therefore, understand Yeats's struggle with his father as more than a personal encounter. What is at stake in this story, as in *Confessions of a Young Man* and *A Portrait*, is the development of a new art, one that, in Yeats's case, has to balance respect for the past with a sense of being new-minted. In more general terms, then, we can see in the struggle with John Butler Yeats (as in the numerous other encounters with father figures throughout *Autobiographies*) an image of the Yeatsian balancing act between respecting tradition and attempting to forge something new. In time, and increasingly through the *Autobiographies*, Yeats moves to occupy the paternal role, but even at this early stage he was being challenged. Although Yeats would not have known about AE's response to *Reveries*, in a letter to George Moore in April 1916, its terms are significant here:

> His memories of his childhood are the most vacant things a man ever wrote, pure externalities, well written in a dead kind of way, but quite dull, except for the odd flashes. The boy in the book might have become a grocer as well as a poet . . . Why does he do it? We are interested in Yeats's inner mind, whatever it is, but not in anecdotes of things he saw and whose effect on his own mood is not clear. He bores me terribly now, and he was once so interesting . . . But in a way we are interested in him still because of his past. We go to hear him as we go to see the tomb of Shakespeare or the Italian garden where Keats lies. The only difference is that Yeats is his own coffin and memorial tablet. Why can't he be natural? Such a delightful creature he was when young! [29]

f Yeats belies AE's reputation for sai.
ied through the representation of hi.
.nd *Farewell*[30]), which is all the more rea
be noted, especially as it appeared in an or.
.on as a review.[31] Admittedly, the relationship
betwee.. .E was never an easy one, not least because AE
feared being swamped by Yeats's personality,[32] but these comments
date from a time when they had overcome a serious split and
effected a working reconciliation after the Dublin Lockout of
1913.[33] What is interesting from our point of view is the dichotomy
AE establishes between boyhood and death; it is as if Yeats's representation in *Reveries* of his struggle to achieve adulthood (as a
preamble to paternity) has resulted in death. AE thus turns the
account of childhood in *Reveries* into *Mémoires d'outre tombe*. Given
his long-standing relationship with Yeats, AE's comments may then
stand for the more general antagonisms and feuds that preceded and
accompanied the writing and publishing of *Reveries* during what
Yeats calls in *Responsibilities* (recognised from the start as a kind of
companion volume to *Reveries*[34]) 'these fifteen | Many-times-
troubled years' (*VP* 315). *Reveries* was, as Yeats well knew, written
and published at a culminating point of troubled times.

Perhaps Yeats's apprehension about his father's reaction lies in a
memory of his enthusiastic encouragement two years previously to
his father to write an autobiography:

> You could say anything you like about anything, for after all, you
> yourself would be the theme, there would be no need to be afraid of
> egotism, for as Oscar Wilde said, that is charming in a book because
> we can close it whenever we like, and open it again whenever the
> mood comes . . . I think you might really do a wonderful book, and
> I think a profitable one.[35]

If Yeats really thought in 1912 that autobiography meant that 'You
could say anything you like about anything', by 1914 he had reasons
for believing otherwise. Yeats knew that more was at stake than
merely telling his own story. His apprehension in regard to his
father may be said to be threefold: he represents his father in
Reveries as someone whose influence over him had necessarily to be
rejected; as part of this process he makes use of many of his father's
opinions and turns of speech; and, finally, he explains both his
father's influence and the necessity of rejecting it through a repre-

...on of his father's generation. He may ask permiss...
...ather's conversation, but does so after the event; h...
...logise for certain representations of his father's friends but
...niability is declared doubly negatively rather than positively ('You
...need not fear that I am not amiable'); and, for all his placatory comments, he still publishes *Reveries Over Childhood and Youth* as his
story. *Reveries* is therefore not only a representation of the struggle
with the father but a part of it. As Murphy has put it:

> As the time approached for the publication of *Reveries over Child-
> hood and Youth*, Papa grew more and more apprehensive, worried
> about the treatment of both himself and Edward Dowden. Willie
> tried to reassure him . . . But he knew his father's fears were really
> justified and hedged his apologies as publication day drew near.[36]

If Yeats was able to bide his time with the more public material of
the diaries, why did he run the risk of alienating his father, family
and friends through publishing in *Reveries* much that was so
apparently personal? As a reader of autobiography, Yeats follows
the model supplied by the memoirs of Young Ireland

> I have often felt that the influence of our movement on the gener-
> ation immediately following us will very largely depend on the way
> in which the personal history is written. It has always been so in
> Ireland. Our interest in the Young Irelanders was largely a personal
> interest and I doubt if we would have cared for them half as much
> but for Gavan Duffy's books. Even the Dark Rosaleen was only a
> part of a drama explained to us by Duffy (*L* 586).

In this we can see that Yeats's interest in autobiography is as a personalised history. So, despite his dislike of John O'Leary's *Recollections of Fenians and Fenianism*, fully expressed only in his own
autobiography when O'Leary was dead (*Au* 212), his review of the
work in 1897 can honestly praise *Recollections* as of value to historians (*UP2* 37). This is an instance of a remarkable consistency of
opinion throughout his life about the nature and value of
autobiography. Reviewing William Carleton's *Autobiography* early
in his career and Maurice O'Sullivan's *Twenty Years A-Growing* late
in his career (in what was to be his last-ever review) Yeats praises
both autobiographies for recording not merely an individual life but
a now lost oral world (*UP1* 394-7; *UP2* 493). He returns to this
theme in a 1922 letter to John Quinn:

Lady Gregory is writing her memoirs and has read me about half
. . . . It will be a rich book, with some chapters of historical importance, but all objective, extracts from old letters, diaries and the like
. . . . The reverse of my memoirs in every way, for I could not have
quoted a letter or diary without spoiling my effect . . . I have always
been convinced that memoirs were of great importance to our
movement here. When I was twenty years old we all read Gavan
Duffy's *Young Ireland*, and then read the Young Ireland poets it had
introduced to us. Hyde, Russell, Lady Gregory, my father, myself,
will all be vivid to young Irish students a generation hence because
of the memoirs we are writing now (*L* 684).

There is, then, a strong sense on Yeats's part that autobiography
should combine the personal with matters of more general historical
interest. That he can give credit to Gavan Duffy, Carleton, and
O'Sullivan should not blind us to the fact that they were suitably
distant in time and space and that Yeats was often signally failing to
acknowledge, except implicitly and often rebarbatively, the
autobiographies and autobiographical works that abounded when he
started to write autobiography for publication.

It would seem from the opening words of *Autobiographies* that
Yeats was modest[37] in his intentions for the work. However, a consideration of the 'Preface' to *Reveries over Childhood and Youth*
(which becomes the 'Preface' to the whole autobiography) reveals a
combative aspect to the text at odds with its surface modesty:

Sometimes when I remember a relative that I have been fond of, or
a strange incident of the past, I wander here and there till I have
somebody to talk to. Presently I notice that my listener is bored;
but now that I have written it out, I may even begin to forget it all.
In any case, because one can always close a book, my friend need
not be bored.

I have changed nothing to my knowledge; and yet it must be that I
have changed many things without my knowledge; for I am writing
after many years and have consulted neither friend, nor letter, nor
old newspaper, and describe what comes oftenest into my memory.

I say this fearing that some surviving friend of my youth may
remember something in a different shape and be offended with my
book.

Christmas Day, 1914. (*Au* 3)

On the surface this Preface invokes the reverie method proclaimed in the title; there is a claim that nothing has been consciously forgotten or manipulated. The implication is that the impulse underlying the work is merely therapeutic ('now that I have written it out I may even begin to forget it')[38] and this is supported by the tone of modesty ('one can always close a book'—which recalls his allusion to Oscar Wilde in his 1912 letter to his father) and the apparent unwillingness to offend others. Yeats has also placed himself in a context which shifts from the oral to the written (and read). In this we may be witnessing his response to Moore's compositional methods. But he is also rendering himself, like Carleton and O'Sullivan, the survivor and recorder of a lost world. Kevin Reilly's comment that Irish autobiography relies on orality, and that Yeats is part of this, is helpful.[39] Yeats is moving to writing quite deliberately and stressing the limitations of orality as talking cure. The written record that is *Autobiographies* is both an attempt to compensate for all that has been lost from the oral record, not least because of Yeats's own early indifference (*Au* 22), and to replace the now lost history stored in a silver cup (*Au* 19-20). This makes the move back to literal speech in 'The Irish Dramatic Movement' all the more poignant. If the 'Preface' shows Yeats leaving orality behind, the end of *Autobiographies*, even if contingent rather than planned, moves back to speech with the improvised and then written address[40] to the Royal Academy of Sweden. Yeats at his most public moment of triumph is formally acknowledging the possible failure of his autobiographical project. The ephemerality of speech returns and displaces the written historical record.

This is the kind of detail which makes the 'Preface', like *Reveries* and the autobiography as a whole, such a skilfully combative performance. The opening sentences represent Yeats as a kind of Ancient Mariner able to fix a listener with a 'glittering eye' and this is sustained in the phrase 'some surviving friend of my youth' in which it is reasonable to see Yeats adopting the persona of the old man that becomes increasingly common in the poetry from this point onwards. The reference to his lack of consultation with others seems designed to undercut the authority of the account. But here Yeats is being doubly skilful. His refusal to consult documentary sources is consistent with his dislike of the positivism of the nineteenth century (*Au* 82).[41] Yeats's autobiography will be memory-driven and trance-like. However, a more local reference is also implied in this passage in that Yeats may be seen to be distinguishing himself from Katharine Tynan in her use of his letters and, more surprisingly perhaps, is also distinguishing himself from the compositional methods of Lady Gregory whose *Our Irish Theatre* is largely documentary in approach.[42] If, then, Yeats is implicitly attacking those who rely on documentary methods are we to take it that he is making no claims for the authority of his account; are we to assume that Yeats faced with, on the one hand, George Moore's attempt to produce the 'sacred text' for Ireland, and, on the other, Katharine Tynan's and Lady Gregory's record, his response is one merely of personal therapy? This is of course a rhetorical question, and the key to an answer lies in the odd word 'shape' in the 'Preface'. What is odd is that Yeats is drawing attention not to the content of his memory—someone may remember some different things—but rather to the form in which those memories are presented. We are, as is often the case in autobiography, being invited to read in a certain way. As well as the strong suggestion that Yeats is, if not a lone then a rare survivor of the past he records, the shape of his memory is being drawn to our attention.

   Not only is *Reveries* divided into 33 chapters or segments and given a Christological date, it also begins with a reference to the Seven Days of Creation and ends with the death of the grandfather whom Yeats has identified with God (*Au* 8). The symbolic structural arc of the text is, then, from Genesis to Revelation (this being Yeats, the text arrives not at Revelation but at the threshold of Revelation). This shape, regardless of content, proclaims *Reveries* as a sacred text in that Yeats has adopted the narrative structure of the Bible. What is more, he has done so in a work which, unlike *Hail and Farewell* or *Our Irish Theatre*, is largely personal rather than public (thus making his childhood appear analogous to Christ's time of preparation): a work, that is, which responds to Moore in particular by stressing Yeats's family background rather than his more public achievements. While Yeats seems to be at pains to emphasise the slightness and eccentricity of his text, the 'Preface' is an apologia not for the life but for its memorial shape. That shape shows the ambition of the text to represent Yeats as Christ-like, as both unique and representative. Yeats's fear, in the closing sentence of the 'Preface', that another's memory may be different is therefore a pretence. He was only 49 at the time of this writing, and there were still many surviving friends of his youth (several of them writing other accounts), although this sentence implies that such friends are few and far between. What is at issue (as Yeats recognises in the

'Preface') is not whether Yeats has forgotten or misremembered certain things, but the shape in which he remembers. He has given his early life the ultimate pre-existing narrative shape of a Christian culture. It is, therefore, disingenuous to claim that he is afraid of giving offence; such a narrative shape declares itself to be beyond such matters.

In his use of this memorial schema Yeats may be said to be playing the Messianic game that both Moore and Joyce also play in their work, countering their declared Messianic ambitions with similar ambitions of his own. It is also possible, however, to see him working at another level, which once again shows him as a reader of autobiography, though as a reader of the genre rather than specific instances of it. Although the Messianic aspects of Irish texts have been much discussed, such discussions usually leave out of account the workings of memory, particularly its socially structured aspect, and the fact that it falls into pre-existing narrative shapes, much as Yeats's memory does here. One reason for the Messianic tradition is that a Christological structure would, in a religiously aware society, appear obvious: to remember one's life as an imitation of Christ would in such circumstances be an instance of mental economy, whether conscious or unconscious.[43] Indeed, this shape paradoxically both proclaims Yeats's singularity and his indebtedness to earlier autobiographical writings in that the imitation of Christ functions as an armature in autobiography from Augustine's *Confessions* through seventeenth and eighteenth century spiritual autobiographies into the Messianic aspects of Irish autobiographies contemporary with Yeats. This cognitive process could then be given a conative purpose: Christ's life provides the design which the 'Messianic' texts have on their readership. Significantly, Yeats avoids the conversion process central to much autobiography;[44] so although he records a similar interest in natural history (*Au* 59-60, 78-9) there is no equivalent moment of crisis to that recorded by Synge in his autobiographical fragments.[45] As against Synge's 'agony of doubt', the Yeats passages show him in an excess of belief. Memory is thus both proclaimed as individual and acknowledged as a social phenomenon.

Yeats's implication in an autobiographical tradition which stretches far beyond Ireland is further evidenced in his whole approach to audience in the *Autobiographies* which could be summed up as 'fit though few', as if he is trying to avoid the problems encountered by Moore's Messianic ambition by making his mission a more personalised one. Throughout *Autobiographies* he specifies intended audiences which generally have in common the fact that they are small but select.

Most of these audiences are specified in the dedications, and following these through we can see a move from a literally known audience: 'To those few people mostly personal friends who have read all that I have written' (*Au* Dedication to *Reveries*), to a singular audience in John Quinn who is the dedicatee of *The Trembling of the Veil* and who fulfils the condition imposed by the dedication to *Reveries* in that he had bought the manuscript of *Reveries* and read it before John Butler Yeats was allowed to.[46] The decreasing size of the audience for the first two volumes continues through the next three which have no dedicatee (*Dramatis Personae*, *Estrangement*, and *The Death of Synge*). While *The Bounty of Sweden* is similarly undedicated it does contain within its pages two implied audiences: the Royal Academy of Sweden which is addressed in 'The Irish Dramatic Movement' and the Swedish court which is invoked at the end (*Au* 571-2). As with so much else in *The Bounty of Sweden* we are witnessing a retrieval of ideals. Just as the whole work casts Sweden, the Academy and the Court as Yeats's response to Moore's Bayreuth,[47] so too it recalls his earlier, more ambitious implied audience: of Sligo people (*Au* 18). But of all the audiences implied throughout *Autobiographies* perhaps the most significant is that invoked at the end of *The Trembling of the Veil*:

> I have written these words instead of leaving all to posterity . . . that young men, to whom recent events are often more obscure than those long past, may learn what debts they owe and to what creditor (*Au* 381).

This desire to leave his version of events to posterity, alongside the gratitude for an actual audience at the end of *Autobiographies*, the multiplicity of audiences invoked throughout the text, and the efforts to control them displays Yeats's usual anxiety about audience. David Ward, writing about 'The Fisherman' sums up this anxiety:

> The poem arises out of a conflict with the men whom Yeats perceives as its real audience: it contradicts them, refuses them, negates them, but in so doing it also forces the reader to question the very

existence of the poem even as he reads it . . . It shows how Yeats'
conflict with his audiences forced him to produce poems which he
says, paradoxically, could only be produced for an audience which
does not exist in modern society. And yet the poem is here, in spite
and in scorn of the public he feared might try to destroy it.[48]

It can be said that *Autobiographies*, dedicated to actual, friendly
readers, exists to spite those whose autobiographies Yeats had read,
and to prove that he exists in his own writing as well as theirs.

The Reviewers' Response

Turning to reviews of *Autobiographies* and its constituent volumes,
we find that there is some doubt about their intended audience. In
an anonymous review of *Dramatis Personae* in 1936 Yeats is caught
in a double bind, accused of being repetitive while at the same time
the reviewer attributes his 'grand tone' to his 'new overseas public'[49]
and this despite the fact that it is a Cuala Press edition that is being
reviewed, which would lead one to assume that an Irish audience
was intended. This certainly seems to be Austin Clarke's idea in a
Times Literary Supplement review of the same year in which he
assumes that non-Irish readers may be puzzled by the move from
the 1896-1902 of *Dramatis Personae* to the diaries of 1909: '. . . to
readers unfamiliar with the intervening years of controversy and the
struggles of the Abbey Theatre their bitter topical mood will seem
curiously isolated.'[50] Clarke later changes his mind on this issue
when it better suits him to accuse Yeats of having withdrawn from
topical controversy thereby failing in his responsibilities to the Irish
cultural community:

> In "Estrangement" and "The Death of Synge," there is a suppressed
> note of bitterness, but the din of topical controversy is kept
> deliberately at a distance . . . More and more the poet retreated up
> the spiral stair to the top of his tower. . . Undoubtedly such an atti-
> tude is magnificent, but it has long since become conventional.
> Translated into practical terms, it explains why the poet failed to
> guide the Abbey rightly in its early critical phase. . .[51]

This accusation is taken up by other writers (and is surely implicit
in the phrase 'grand tone'). So already in 1916 there was a sense that

Yeats has abdicated his responsibilities and taken on a lofty and dismissive attitude to the cultural life of Ireland:

> Ferguson and O'Grady are dismissed in a couple of contemptuous sentences and it is fairly clear that the present difficulties and doubts of the literary movement here no longer interest Mr Yeats, who appears to have adopted the motto, '*après moi le déluge.*'[52]

Implicit in this is an accusation of bad faith which is most often levelled by Sean O'Faolain, whose problematic relationship with Yeats issued in accusations that Yeats 'has never dared to come too close to life. In his youth he kept it at a distance with his romance, in his old age he tries to ward it off by seeking a sort of intellectual isolation'[53] (this from the man who wrote what Terence Brown has rightly called a 'socially and culturally analytic' autobiography[54]). O'Faolain's comment that: 'We have no models to follow, we have no tradition to guide us, no criticism to help us'[55] seems to be one of Yeats's 'young men' deliberately forgetting what debts he owes and to what creditor.

If there is one area in which Yeats could not be accused of withdrawal it is in his portrayal of Moore, described in rather overheated terms by an American critic as the 'long-awaited execution of his share in the most discussed literary bout of our time . . .'.[56] Among academic critics the balance seems to have shifted from the belief that Moore's humour wins the day.[57] In response to Moore's satirical intent, there has been a determined effort to emphasise the comedy of Yeats's work starting with Vincent Buckley's not altogether convincing argument that the portrait of Moore is, though not without bitterness, wholly without cruelty, and that it is an example of Yeats' becoming 'a connoisseur of eccentricity, including his own. . .'[58] More convincing is James Olney's argument that autobiography is a comic genre because of the irony with which an autobiographer necessarily views the younger self.[59] All the characters in *Autobiographies* are therefore part of Yeats's comic drama:

> What Yeats did not want, and absolutely would not have was someone else taking over his life and his text, creating character for him when Yeats intended to be the comic playwright creating character aplenty for others: he was determined that he would control Moore and not vice versa.[60]

While there are comic aspects of *Autobiographies*, including some self-mockery,[61] Yeats's seriousness is a constant. So, while Olney sees Yeats's version of the seance described by Tynan (*Au* 103-4)[62] as an ironical and ambivalent look at his younger self,[63] he overlooks its serious purpose. Yeats is here responding to Moore's anecdote about his use of 'Of man's first disobedience. . .' as a prayer. In *Hail and Farewell*[64] Moore has AE stating that Yeats prayed thus in a ferry in a storm. Yeats's version, uniting literature and occultism, and showing him enacting his belief in poetry as true religion, wrests the incident from Moore's comedy to his own serious purpose.

The sense of Yeats as comedian does not feature in the reviews of *Autobiographies*. Although not all reviews are as extreme as the one headed 'A Portrait in Vitriol',[65] there is much comment on the bitterness with which Yeats represents Moore. Among reviewers only Walter Starkie attributes a sense of humour to Yeats on Moore: 'When we come to the second of the great personalities, that of George Moore, Mr Yeats brings a note of impish humour into his echoing prose.'[66]

Most reviewers, however, see Yeats losing what is perceived as a battle:

> Yeats's counter-attack [on Moore] in 'Dramatis Personae' does not show good generalship. He does not attempt to outflank the gigantic line of 'Hail and Farewell'—instead he attacks a little salient and the attack is not very organized.[67]

His lack of humour is implicated in this. Indeed, Louis MacNeice goes further: 'But Yeats does not appreciate frivolity, and this is perhaps (apart from the paying off of old scores) the clue to his general disapproval of Moore. Yeats, though himself in no position to deplore histrionics, likes his histrionics to be serious. Whereas Moore is a buffoon.'[68] On this reckoning, Yeats cannot be called a comedian since it is the comedic aspect of Moore that is part of the charge against him. However, MacNeice, like Austin Clarke, sees the central comment on Moore being that 'the pursuit of style . . . made barren his later years' (*Au* 437).[69] Both overlook the direct response to Moore at this point since Yeats is turning back on Moore the charge that Moore, once again via AE, had levelled against him, of pursuing style at the expense of inspiration.[70]

Not everyone is prepared to take sides, however. Horace Gregory sees *Reveries* as a symbolist response to the realist *Hail and*

Farewell[71] making them complementary rather than competitive texts. T.R. Henn takes a 'curse on both your houses' stance:

> It is certain that each was prepared, at any moment, to sacrifice any pretension to truth to the needs of a good story, a dramatic situation, a specially barbed piece of malice.[72]

And it seems to be this which causes Padraic Colum's impatience with both:

> All I want to say is that imaginative writers who want to manipulate the facts of cultural history had better leave each other alone.[73]

Donagh MacDonagh gives with one hand and takes with the other, allowing Yeats to be the more truthful but the less interesting. *Dramatis Personae* is 'the truth of Yeats rather than the fiction of Moore, and for this very reason it lacks the colour and breadth which lend such interest to the Moore world.'[74]

In the end it is Yeats's aloofness and failure to reveal himself, especially as compared to Moore, that reviewers return to:

> At the end of George Moore's *Hail and Farewell* we do know something about George Moore, of him at least as he would like to appear to us, and we do know a good deal, a malicious good deal, about his friends, but we end this book knowing nothing about Mr Yeats the man but knowing a great deal about Mr Yeats the poet. . . Let none come to this book then seeking a biography, seeking gossip, seeking the facts of a life. . . In that [the late poetry] is his autobiography, but this is merely the autobiography of his art.[75]

Padraic Colum is actually more disapproving than many about *Dramatis Personae* and its failure to give us access to Yeats:

> These memoirs, no matter what title he gives a particular volume, are a comment upon his own work, and, like most comment, they are dry. The tone of the writer's voice is essential in prose: the tone of Yeats's voice is here, but it is his lecturer's voice. In 'Dramatis Personae' he is giving an account of his work, his friendships, and his enmities, with some of his reveries, from a platform, and we feel that placed as he is there is no chance for the revelation of anything else except his public or semi-public life.[76]

However, he does realise that in the portraits of Moore and other characters we have not merely a personal opinion, but also a representation of a set of attitudes:

> Indeed, we are led to think that Lady Gregory and J. M. Synge were interesting to him because they represented attitudes that the poet wanted to make part of his life—opposite attitudes: the unconsciousness of Synge, the sense of duty that Lady Gregory had and that Yeats thinks had a feudal background.[77]

Characters in autobiography are not simply accounts of historical personages, the truth or falsehood of which we can verify from other sources, not simple instances of mimesis. They are also expressive of the autobiographer. This is why AE is wrong about the *Autobiographies* and their apparent externality and objectivity.[78] When he states that he does not recognise either Yeats or himself in their pages he fails to see that his portrait is an aspect of Yeats's self-portrait. This leads us to the whole issue of whether the *Autobiographies* are self-revelatory or not.

It is worth noting that two English critics feel the need to identify themselves as such because they think that this has a bearing on their embarrassment at Yeats's self revelation:

> A mere Englishman like myself does not know, when reading some of his pages, where to look for embarrassment.[79]

Nearly forty years later Kathleen Raine is also embarrassed when Yeats comes down from abstraction to the mundanities of life.[80]

This embarrassment is not shared by any Irish reviewer, not least because few of them seem to think that Yeats has been in any real way self-revealing. This trend starts with AE for whom the absence of the Yeats that he knew from the pages of the autobiographies is an early and consistent disappointment.[81] The rather contradictory response of an anonymous reviewer in the *Irish Book Lover* echoes in a less pointed way AE's famous comment that the boy in *Reveries* could just as easily have become a grocer rather than a poet:

> It [*Reveries*] is a remarkable self-revelation, and though dealing with early formative influences and boyish adventures, can hardly be called an autobiography—there isn't a date in it. He tells us of his

early trials at school, trials common to all shy boys as well as misunderstood geniuses. . . .[82]

AE voices his disappointment again in 1926, though acknowledging that he may be alone in it:

> What I regard as the chief defect of these autobiographies will, I think, be considered by others as their main virtue. The poet tells us but little about his internal life, but much about the people he has met, and as he has met many famous people of his time . . . his memories of these will be, for most readers, the chief interest in the memoirs. I hold that there is only one person that a man may know intimately, and that is himself. If he be a man of genius what he could tell us about his own inner life would be of much more value than anything he could tell us of the external life of others . . . I read this biography as I would look at some many-coloured shell, from which the creature inhabiting it, who might have told us about its manner of being, had slipped away leaving us only the miracle of form to wonder at.[83]

Implicit in these remarks is a set of ideas about autobiography: that it should reveal the past not the present of the autobiographer; that the past self is readily available for such revelation; and that the value of autobiography lies in personal revelation. Mary Colum, contradicting AE's judgement of what Yeats has achieved, advances another set of implicit ideas about autobiography:

> For what Yeats is concerned with is not external happenings . . . The problem with which he is constantly occupied is the problem of artistic creation and with what goes with that problem—the problem of personal realization. . . the only other book to compare it with is Goethe's *Dichtung und Warheit* . . . both autobiographies are accounts of the intellectual development and integration of poets who are also deeply concerned with abstract problems.[84]

For her it is the narrative of the development of the present self and its integration that is important in autobiography. This disagreement between reviewers is a debate about the function of autobiography, and whether it should or can be primarily self-revealing or should aim for a more general historical importance.

There is a consensus that Yeats is not only unforthcoming about himself but simultaneously in control of what we see in the *Autobiographies*, that he 'lets us see just as much of his life as he chooses'.[85] Even though Mary Colum stands aside from this consensus she, like other reviewers, sees *Autobiographies* as a willed text. Nowhere is there any sense that the text may have to be read against the grain to become revealing. However, the question as to whether what we see is integrated or not remains open:

> Glimpses of the different Yeatses can be found in this . . . volume . . . . . There is the poet as politician, the poet as mystic, the poet as social lion, the poet as theatrical manager, but the most important picture is that of the poet as poet.[86]

Louis MacNeice, like Mary Colum, would eventually write his own autobiography, and both significantly stress the emergence of the present self and the processes by which it achieves integration.

> Furious impartiality [*Au* 520]—a phrase which must sound like nonsense among all our party shirts—is an ideal implicit in some of Yeats's own writing. The idle woman, the defiant beggar are the incarnation of Yeats's desire to flout the go-getting world that is concerned with means towards ends.[87]

In spite of this distancing MacNeice agrees with Eliot that Yeats was always looking for a tradition, though not as something to conform to. His pose or mask was not, as Moore claimed, mere foppishness, but rather an internally-generated rather than an external discipline. MacNeice is excited by the passage in *Autobiographies* in which Yeats talks about this discipline and its absence in Wordsworth who answers instead to external duty (*Au* 469-70). MacNeice draws a comparison between Yeats's Wordsworth and the 'Communist poets'.[88] It is through this combination of defiance and internal discipline that Yeats achieves integrity:

> Let us pay homage to Mr Yeats and his mask. In our world almost the only coherence is that of squads which march in step; how refreshing to meet someone who is coherent with himself.[89]

Among reviewers, MacNeice may be the most explicit in his use of Yeats's *Autobiographies* for his own contemporary purposes, but he is not alone in such usage. He is, however, quite rare in being able to rise above the vacuous generalisations ('this wise and beautiful book') that characterise many of the other reviews and disguise the reviewers' bafflement, and to be genuinely excited by what Yeats does and what he has to say. What seems to attract MacNeice is Yeats's ability to retain integrity and 'furious impartiality' while also working collectively, whether in a tradition or in a group, something which others comment on:

> For he was that rare thing, a great artist who did not work in isolation; much of what he accomplished was accomplished in company, or through the achievement of others. He had no easy talent for comradeship; but he was a born leader.[90]

Even here, however, Yeats is apart, and in his 'early work' he was 'but little conscious of estrangement from national movements. He ran with the crowd, thinking their thoughts were his own, though indeed they were not'.[91]

Nevertheless, Yeats set out to write the crowd's history as well as his own. For all his other reservations about the *Autobiographies* AE sees them as an essential component of a full history—political, cultural and spiritual—of Ireland.[92] Lennox Robinson, too, recognises that *Autobiographies* is, among many other things, a history of literature and nation.[93] Even though he disapproves of it Padraic Colum also sees that the manipulation of history is important in the *Autobiographies*. Of course it is not history in a conventional sense that Yeats is writing, but legend, as Horace Gregory points out by saying that after the award of the Nobel Prize Yeats's 'need of creating a further legend of his life had vanished'.[94]

Seamus Deane has commented on Yeats's propensity for turning history into legend,[95] and, given reviewers' comments and Yeats's own view that memoirs would provide the history of the Revival, we need to consider just what sort of history Yeats was writing. Standish O'Grady's idea that archaeology was merely the preamble to history is relevant here:

> The legends represent the imagination of the country; they are that kind of history which a nation desires to possess. They betray the ambition and ideals of the people, and, in this respect, have a value far beyond the tale of actual events and duly recorded deeds, which are no more history than a skeleton is a man . . . Archæology culminates in history, history culminates in art.[96]

In these terms a documentary work, like Lady Gregory's memoirs, was merely archaeology while Yeats in writing his legend was writing true history.

The Autobiographers' Response

In their different ways writers such as Sean O'Faolain, Frank O'Connor, Austin Clarke, Patrick Kavanagh, Francis Stuart and Louis MacNeice have all had to contend with the history that Yeats left. Many, indeed, may have seen in Yeats's *Autobiographies* a prompt to autobiography in their own right. Even those writers who reject Yeatsian history have still been obliged to work within its terms.

We should not, however, assume that succeeding autobiographies owe everything to Yeats either through direct influence or as a result of a reaction against him. Similarities between his work and that of others may be a matter of influence, but are equally likely to be a response to a shared socio-cultural context, just as blatant dissimilarities may be due to changed historical circumstances rather than a conscious distancing from Yeats.

The structure and publishing history of *Autobiographies* may seem to make it a unique work. However, references to rhythm and recurrence as uniquely Yeatsian phenomena[97] run the risk of overlooking the fact that the organising principle of *Autobiographies*, by which each new addition reveals not only its own 'rhythm' but modifies that which has gone before, is shared by numerous other Irish autobiographical works. The multi-volume form of so many Irish autobiographies[98] suggests that it is shared circumstance rather than influence which is responsible for this similarity. It is as if the writers feel that the autobiographical subject cannot be contained within a single volume and that, as with Yeats, the autobiographical subject is transformed and modified continually.

If, then, Yeats's autobiography has had a formal impact it is fairer to say that it is to be found not in the imitation of his formal methods but rather in the ways that he used form to present himself as unlike his (unacknowledged) forebears in autobiography. The need, which we might say was established by Yeats, to present oneself as both of Ireland and unique, finds its reiterated expression in the dissimilarity of so many autobiographies and in the way that Yeats features in those other autobiographies, not as a model but as a figure apparently unmediated by his autobiography, as if the terms he establishes come directly from him and not from a crafted version of himself.[99] It as if Yeats's autobiographies demand that later autobiographers close his book in order to write their own.

In a similar way the struggle with the father which provides one of the unifying themes of Yeats's *Autobiographies* is a feature of numerous other autobiographies, but insofar as succeeding autobiographers represent Yeats as a father-figure whom one has to overcome to achieve artistic selfhood this cannot be said to be a matter of influence so much as an enactment of an 'unconscious master narrative'[100] in which *il faut tuer le père*.[101]

Yeats's position as literary father-figure leads to several different kinds of response in literary autobiographies. Oliver Gogarty takes a typically sideways look at the issue with his anecdote about Yeats enquiring whether Moore was impotent, as if worried that Moore may yet have literary offspring.[102] Here, Gogarty may be said to be avoiding his own autobiographical struggle with Yeats by representing Yeats as someone who has not yet overcome his own anxieties about paternity.

The case of Sean O'Faolain is much more straightforward. In his youth, he is confronted with two models:

> I think I looked like someone halfway between James Joyce and Willy Yeats when they were in their twenties.[103]

But it is Yeats who in the end is the inescapable presence, from whom one has to receive a paternal blessing which is furthermore advice to write out of, or rather into, one's own integrity:

> He intoned, or moaned, in his vatic voice, his delicate right hand slightly raised as if to give the papal *urbi et orbi* blessing: 'You must write yourself into yourself. There is no other way.'[104]

O'Faolain, like many writers of his generation, never manages to achieve such independence and integrity, and is therefore forced to the stratagem of turning Yeats into a non-presence. In the following quotation it is as if O'Faolain can only deal with Yeats, can only unarrest his pen in the presence of Yeats, by writing Yeats out of existence:

At this point I have arrested my pen as it was about to write that
few knew him as a man; it is more likely that nobody did; indeed, it
is unlikely that there was, in the common implication of the word,
a man to know.[105]

In this O'Faolain places Yeats significantly on a par with his actual
father who is associated for him with his 'locked box' and as a consequence exists for him on an impersonal level.[106]

Yeats, for O'Faolain, is a presence and a model for the cosmopolitan intellectual man of letters that O'Faolain always wished
to be, but there is never the difficulty of actual influence as there is
for Austin Clarke. Clarke's strategy in *A Penny in the Clouds* is to be
consistently deflating about Yeats; in one anecdote about dining
with Yeats, Clarke feels overwhelmed and attempts to defend his
own ideas about poetry against Yeats but the whole passage is
deflated by Yeats having to leave to catch a train.[107] This deflation-
ary procedure is more pertinently carried out, however, not on this
personal, anecdotal level but in Clarke's repeated suggestions in *A
Penny in the Clouds* that Yeats owes a debt to some lesser-known
poet. So on one occasion Yeats is linked with Mangan; on another
Gogarty's 'Leda and the Swan' 'undoubtedly influenced Yeats'; Herbert Trench is given the credit for being the first to make literary
use of the Deirdre story; Victor Plarr is said to have influenced
Yeats's 'Upon a Dying Lady', and finally Ernest Dowson 'surely
influenced' Yeats.[108] Yeats's strength as a precursor is vitiated by this
multiple acknowledgement of his precursors.

In *My Father's Son* Yeats once again figures as a father, indeed at
one point O'Connor explicitly states that Yeats is his 'real father'.[109]
However, throughout the work O'Connor makes it clear that he
quarrels with Yeats, beginning by signing a petition against him,[110]
and arguing constantly with him. O'Connor's own circumstances,
as detailed in *An Only Child*, are such that he is able to live with
Yeats as a great man and yet at the same time humanise him:

Before Death, or the Iron Curtain of legend, overtakes me, I want
to holler in everybody's ear that Yeats wasn't in the least like
that.[111]

This is very different from O'Faolain's efforts to erase Yeats by
saying that he possesses no real centre. O'Connor instead is con-

stantly attempting to present the real Yeats. There are, in
O'Connor's account of Yeats, details and qualities which few others
report; Yeats's shyness for example,[112] or—more improbably—the
idea that Yeats will accept insults to himself and his family but that
he will not allow either Lady Gregory or Synge to be insulted.[113] In
the end the version that we get of Yeats in O'Connor's work may
be no more truthful than anyone else's, including Yeats's, but it
shows that it was possible for Yeats to attract something other than
antagonism. It also, like other autobiographical responses to Yeats,
implies that Yeats never got the full measure of himself either.

I want to finish with three interlinked quotations. The
Autobiographies as we have them present a multi-faceted view of
Yeats, but the one exact aspect of the portrait is that they are
unfinished, they simply end. We can, treating them as text, look to
the significance of the ending, but we must also bear in mind that
Yeats himself, no doubt in the face of the antagonism that they
aroused, knew that finishing them was an impossibility:

> My new Autobiography—1900 to 1926—may be the final test of
> my intellect, my last great effort, and I keep putting it off (*L* 721).

It may be that he was more like his representation of his father than
he would ever have wished to admit, and that in the end the
Autobiographies have to be read in the light of the anecdote about his
father's unfinished and unfinishable painting of the pond near
Slough (*Au* 28). We should also bear in mind AE's words about the
nature not only of autobiography but of all writing about Ireland:

> Hardly anybody before entering the witness-box of literature to
> give evidence about Ireland has taken mentally the vow to tell the
> truth and nothing but the truth. The image of Ireland in literature is
> changed, either nobly or by reason of an imaginative love, or is dis-
> torted ignobly through hate.[114]

However, even taking these two points together we still have to
acknowledge the truth of Sean J. White's comment that the 'total
lesson' of *Autobiographies* is that 'the cunning subtle craftsman they
reveal is more difficult of imitation but more reliable than the
simplified effigies in use'.[115] We might, reverting to O'Grady's
terms, see those 'effigies' as the 'skeleton' and the *Autobiographies* as
providing the 'man' to read.

NOTES

1.   See Curtis Bradford, *Yeats at Work* (Carbondale & Edwardsville: Southern Illinois University Press, 1965), pp. 337-385; Joseph Ronsley, *Yeats's Autobiography: Life as Symbolic Pattern* (Cambridge, Mass: Harvard University Press, 1968), pp. 20-33; David G. Wright, *Yeats's Myth of Self: A Study of the Autobiographical Prose* (Dublin: Gill and Macmillan, 1987), pp. 115-119 which contains a useful Appendix on the 'Writing and Publication History of *Autobiographies* and Related Texts'.

2.   Joseph Ronsley prefers the 1938 New York edition (*Yeats's Autobiography* p. 33), Dillon Johnston prefers the 1926 edition ('The Perpetual Self of Yeats's *Autobiographies*', *Éire-Ireland*, 9: 4 (Winter 1974), 69-85 at pp. 69-70, and Ian Fletcher wanted an edition with the unity of the 1926 edition but which would include *Dramatis Personae*. See 'Rhythm and Pattern in Yeats's *Autobiographies*', in Denis Donoghue and J. R. Mulryne (eds.), *An Honoured Guest: New Essays on W. B. Yeats* (London: Edward Arnold, 1965), pp. 165-189.

3.   Douglas Archibald, 'On Editing Yeats's *Autobiographies*', *Gaeliana*, 8 (1986), 161-73.

4.   Hazard Adams, 'Some Yeatsian Versions of Comedy', in *In Excited Reverie: A Centenary Tribute to W.B. Yeats, 1865-1939*, edited by A.N. Jeffares, and K.G.W. Cross (London: Macmillan, 1965), p. 152.

5.   See Neville Braybrooke, 'Poetry, Magic, Mysticism', *The Catholic Herald*, 5 August 1955, 9; Donagh MacDonagh, 'Yeats Never Forgets', *Ireland To-Day*, 1:2 (July 1936), 75, 77; P. S. O'H[egarty], [Review of *The Trembling of the Veil*], *Irish Review*, 1:6 (6 Jan 1923), 7. Joseph Hone's biography can stand for more general critical works in its unproblematic use of the autobiography; so its opening words are: 'Much information concerning William Butler Yeats's family and early life can be agreeably acquired from his own telling . . . ' (*W. B. Yeats, 1865-1939* (2nd ed., Harmondsworth: Penguin, 1971), p. 1. The academic response has steadily increased over the last thirty years in line with a growing critical attention to autobiography in general.

6.   Anon, [review of *Dramatis Personae*], *Dublin Magazine*, 11: 2 (April-June 1936), 67-68.

7.   Brooks Atkinson, 'W. B. Yeats, Man of Letters', *New York Times*, 7 June 1936, Section 9, x.

8.   W. R. Rodgers, 'W. B. Yeats: A Dublin Portrait', in *In Excited Reverie*, pp. 1-13 (p. 4).

9.   Apart from the obvious evidence of reviews by various writers, there is also evidence that Séan O'Casey had read at least *Dramatis Personae*; see Séan O'Casey, *The Letters of Séan O'Casey: I 1910-1941*, edited by David Krause (London: Cassell, 1975), p. 874. Similarly we know that Joyce possessed the 1926 edition of Yeats's *Autobiographies*; see Thomas E. Connolly, *The Personal Library of James Joyce: A Descriptive Bibliography*, *The University of Buffalo Studies: Monographs in English No. 6*, 22, 1 (April 1955).

10.   For O'Casey's allusions to Yeats see Robert G. Lowery, *Séan O'Casey's Autobiographies: An Annotated Index*, (Westport, Connecticut & London: Green-

wood Press, 1983) For Joyce's allusions to Yeats see for example Adaline
Glasheen, *Third Census of Finnegans Wake: An Index of the Characters and Their
Roles* (Berkeley, Los Angeles & London: University of California Press, 1977),
p. 313.

11.   See David G. Wright, *Yeats's Myth of Self*, Ch. 8; Gerard Paul Moran, 'W. B.
       Yeats's *Autobiographies* in the Context of Other Irish Autobiographical Writ-
       ings' (Unpublished Ph. D. Thesis, University of London, 1984) *passim*, espe-
       cially Chs. 7 & 8.

12.   See Wright, *Yeats's Myth of Self*, pp. 12-34. The lecture 'Friends of my Youth'
       (1910), unpublished in Yeats's lifetime is, as Joseph Ronsley has argued, another
       intermediate stage in the move to autobiography, though it contains material
       that will be recast in *Trembling of the Veil* rather than in *Reveries*. See Robert
       O'Driscoll, 'Yeats on Personality: Three Unpublished Lectures' and Joseph
       Ronsley, 'Yeats's Lecture Notes for "Friends of my Youth"' (*YT* 4-59, 60-81).

13.   *L* 564; *Mem* 269-71. See Joseph Ronsley, *Yeats' Autobiography*, pp. 15-17; Joseph
       Hone, *W.B. Yeats*, pp. 277-279; and Richard Ellmann, *Yeats: the Man and the
       Masks*, revised edition, (Oxford: Oxford University Press, 1979), p. 209.

14.   Jack Wayne Weaver, 'An Exile Returned: Moore and Yeats in Ireland', *Eire-
       Ireland*, 3:1 (Spring 1968), 40-47 at p. 47. Weaver points out the irony of this
       situation: Moore's enforced idleness at this time gave him the opportunity to
       write *Hail and Farewell* which would have been lacking had he too been engaged
       in 'theatre business . . .'.

15.   Katharine Tynan, *Twenty-Five Years: Reminiscences* (London: Smith, Elder &
       Co., 1913), pp. 143-5.

16.   See also Pamela Hinkson, 'Letters from W. B. Yeats', *Yale Review*, 29 (1939),
       307-20, (p. 319).

17.   Richard Ellmann, *Yeats: The Man and the Masks*, p. 209.

18.   Taura Napier, 'Lady Gregory's "An Emigrant's Notebook"', Unpublished
       Paper, Queen's University of Belfast, School of English Staff-Graduate Research
       Seminar, Autumn 1994. Some circumstantial confirmation that such works were
       read aloud within the circle is given in a letter to John Quinn in 1922 in which
       Yeats states that Lady Gregory has been reading her memoirs to him (*L* 684).

19.   See AE, 'Reminiscences by Katharine Tynan', *Irish Homestead*, 25 April 1914,
       reprinted in *G. W. Russell (AE), Selections from Contributions to The Irish
       Homestead*, edited by Henry Summerfield, 2 vols (Gerrards Cross: Colin
       Smythe, 1978), 2, 884-6 for the statement that 'Ireland is more prodigal of litera-
       ture about itself in proportion to its size than any other country in the world...',
       p. 884. Some examples of other autobiographical work from this period are:
       John Denvir, *Life Story of an Old Rebel* (London: Sealy, Bryers and Walker,
       1910) an account of someone who could claim to have been politico-culturally
       active among the Irish in Britain as Yeats had been in Ireland; Sir Robert Ander-
       son, *Lighter Side of My Official Life* (London: Hodder and Stoughton, 1910), a
       high-ranking Irish police-officer who had worked for the Home Office as adviser
       on Irish matters and investigator of the Fenians; Justin MacCarthy, *Irish Recol-
       lections*, (London: Hodder and Stoughton, 1911), one of the memoirs of the
       journalist, novelist and politician who had led the anti-Parnell faction of the
       Irish Party; Patrick MacGill, *Children of the Dead End* (London: Jenkins, 1914)
       which revealed a hidden Ireland of economically-deprived peasantry that Yeats
       never registered; Sir Charles Villiers Stanford, *Pages from an Unwritten Diary*

(London: Edward Arnold, 1914), a composer who set Irish poems and whose status as practitioner of the applied arts might have attracted Yeats. One autobiographical work that we know Yeats did read was Katherine O'Shea, *Charles Stewart Parnell: his love story and political life*, 2 vols (London: Cassell & Co., 1914) from which he drew two episodes in *Autobiographies*. See Gerard Moran, 'W. B. Yeats's *Autobiographies*', p. 84.

20.   Joseph Hone, *W. B. Yeats*, pp. 269-71.

21.   Conor Cruise O'Brien, 'Passion and Cunning: An Essay on the Politics of W.B. Yeats', in *In Excited Reverie*, pp. 207-78.

22.   'The announcement of the *Collected Works* set the literary gossips of Dublin saying that Yeats would write no more, or very little.' Joseph Hone, *W. B. Yeats*, p. 227. Hone goes on to quote from Moore's *Vale* (misattributing it to *Salve*) AE's comment that Yeats 'would have written volume after volume if he had never sought a style. . .' George Moore. *Hail and Farewell*, edited by Richard Allen Cave (Gerrards Cross: Colin Smythe, 1985), p. 542.

23.   William M. Murphy, *Prodigal Father: The Life of John Butler Yeats, 1839-1922* (Ithaca & London: Cornell University Press, 1978), pp. 383-4, 422.

24.   William M. Murphy, *Prodigal Father*, p. 446.

25.   This volume was originally to be called *Memory Harbour*, after Jack B. Yeats's painting, but Grant Richards had published a book of the same name by Alexander Bell Filson Young and persuaded Yeats not to use the title. The subtitle was then promoted to the title. See Gerard Moran, 'W. B. Yeats's *Autobiographies*', pp. 33-34 and Warwick Gould, 'Singular Pluralities: Titles of Yeats's *Autobiographies*', *YA11* (1995), 205-218.

26.   Richard Ellmann, *Yeats: the Man and the Masks*, p. 21.

27.   George Moore, *Confessions of a Young Man* (1886) (London: Heinemann, 1933), p. 7. '. . . my father was dead. I loved my father; and yet my soul said, "I am glad."'

28.   David Lloyd, *Nationalism and Minor Literature: James Clarence Mangan and the Emergence of Irish Cultural Nationalism* (Berkeley, Los Angeles & London: University of California Press, 1987), p. 162.

29.   *Letters from AE*, Selected & edited by Alan Denson (London: Abelard-Schumann, 1961), p. 110.

30.   'I escaped with a halo, but halos fixed on one's brows by the wicked don't add to one's glory.' *Letters from AE*, p. 96.

31.   'The Boyhood of a Poet', *New Ireland*, 16 Dec. 1916, pp. 88-9, reprinted in *Imaginations and Reveries* (Dublin: Maunsel & Co., 2nd ed., 1921), pp. 39-42.

32.   See Peter Kuch, *Yeats and AE: 'the antagonism that unites dear friends'* (Gerrards Cross: Colin Smythe Ltd., 1986), p. 21 and *passim*.

33.   *Letters from AE*, p. 91 and Monk Gibbon's 'Foreword', p. xii.

34.   See Anon, '"Reveries" and "Responsibilities"', *Irish Book Lover*, 8: 5-6 (Dec.-Jan. 1916-17), 59-61.

35.   *L* 571-2. The last phrase indicates a motive of which we should not lose sight. Yeats certainly never did, stressing to his father the potential profitability of his memoirs, and stating that journal publication of parts of *Dramatis Personae* would supply George Yeats with housekeeping money (*L*. 820).

36.   William M. Murphy, *Prodigal Father*, p. 446.

37.   David G. Wright, *Yeats's Myth of Self*, p. 93 refers to his 'beguilingly simple prefatory remarks in *Reveries*', and L. W. Payne calls him 'exceedingly modest',

'The Inner Life of a Poet', *Southwest Review*, 13:1 (October 1927), 123-5.

38. David G. Wright, *Yeats's Myth of Self*, p. 94; and Ian Fletcher, 'Rhythm and Pattern in Yeats's *Autobiographies*', p. 166, ascribe this therapeutic motive to Yeats.

39. K. P. Reilly, 'Irish Literary Autobiography: The Goddesses That Poets Dream Of' (*Éire-Ireland*, 16:3 [Fall 1981] 57-80).

40. Gerard Moran, 'W. B. Yeats's *Autobiographies*' p. 191.

41. Herbert Spencer, a representative of the hated positivism, seems to have deliberately and explicitly abandoned memory as the primary source for his autobiography, becoming, rather, as George Landow puts it, a biographer and historian of the self; see George Landow, 'Introduction', in *Approaches to Victorian Autobiography*, edited by George Landow (Athens, Ohio: Ohio University Press, 1979), pp. xiii-xlvi at pp. xxi-xxxiii. Yeats did consult material by himself and others for later volumes of the *Autobiographies* but his revision of this material and his 'canny mode of quoting' (David G. Wright, *Yeats's Myth of Self*, pp. 66-68) mean that even when using documentary material he cannot be accused of empiricism.

42. Mary Fitzgerald, 'Perfection of the Life: Lady Gregory's Autobiographical Writings', in *Lady Gregory: Fifty Years After*, edited by Anne Saddlemyer & Colin Smythe (Gerrards Cross: Colin Smythe Ltd., 1987), p. 47.

43. See John A Robinson, 'Autobiographical Memory: A Historical Prologue', in *Autobiographical Memory*, edited by David C. Rubin (Cambridge: Cambridge University Press, 1986), pp. 19-24 (p. 23). See also Frederic Bartlett, *Remembering: A Study in Experimental Social Psychology* (Cambridge: Cambridge University Press, 1932); and Sebastiano Timpanaro, *The Freudian Slip: Psychoanalysis and Textual Criticism*, trans. Kate Soper (London: Verso, 1985).

44. See Roy Pascal, *Design and Truth in Autobiography* (London: Routledge and kegan Paul, 1960), Ch. 1; James Olney, *Metaphors of Self: The Meaning of Autobiography* (Princeton: Princeton University Press, 1972), pp. 38-42; Jerome Hamilton Buckley, *The Turning Key: Autobiography and the Subjective Impulse since 1800* (London: Harvard University Press, 1984), pp. 51-53; Jean Starobinski, 'The Style of Autobiography', in *Literary Style: A Symposium*, edited by Seymour Chatman (London: Oxford University Press, 1971), pp. 285-296 (p. 289); L. D. Lerner, 'Puritanism and the Spiritual Autobiography', *Hibbert Journal*, 55 (1957), 373-386; and Robert Bell, 'Metamorphoses of Spiritual Autobiography', *Journal of English Literary History*, 44 (1977), 108-126.

45. J. M. Synge, *Collected Works: Vol. 2 Prose*, edited by Alan Price (Gerrards Cross: Colin Smythe Ltd., 1982), p. 10.

46. William M. Murphy, *Prodigal Father*, p. 436.

47. George Moore, *Hail and Farewell*, pp. 165-76.

48. David Ward, 'Yeats's Conflict with his Audience, 1897-1917', *English Literary History*, 49:1 (Spring 1982), 143-63 at p. 148. In 'Irish Literary Autobiography: The Goddesses That Poets Dream Of' (University of Minnesota Ph.D., 1979 [Ann Arbor, Michigan: University Microfilms International, 1984]) Kevin Patrick Reilly recasts this anxiety in Oedipal terms: 'Yeats, finally, seeks the approval of his ideal Irish audience for all his writing. And he epitomizes the Irish autobiographer in seeking, by means of his autobiographical writing, an ultimate, unconditional acceptance from Mother Ireland in a recognition that his life and its meaning are integral to her own.' (p. 204).

49. Anon, [review of *Dramatis Personae*] *Dublin Magazine*, 11: 2 (Apr-June 1936) 67-

68.

50.   [Austin Clarke], 'Mr Yeats's Reminiscences: Years of Peace and the Age of Disillusionment', *Times Literary Supplement*, 23 May 1936, 434.

51.   Austin Clarke, 'Cast a Cold Eye', *The Irish Times*, 2 April 1955, 8.

52.   Anon, [Rev. of *Reveries & Responsibilities*], 59-61.

53.   Sean O'Faolain, 'Yeats on Synge', *Irish Statesman*, 11:4 (29 Sept. 1928), 71-2 at p. 71.

54.   Terence Brown, 'Literary Autobiography in Twentieth-Century Ireland' in *The Genius of Irish Prose*, edited by Augustine Martin (Dublin & Cork: Mercier Press, 1985), pp. 89-98 at p. 96.

55.   Sean O'Faolain, 'The Emancipation of Irish Writers', *Yale Review*, 23:3 (March 1934), 485-503 at p. 503.

56.   Kerker Quinn, 'Memories Differ', *Yale Review*, 26:1 (September 1936), 208-10.

57.   Meredith Cary, 'Yeats and Moore—An Autobiographical Conflict', *Eire-Ireland*, 4:3 (Autumn 1969), 94-109.

58.   Vincent Buckley, 'Yeats: The Great Comedian', *Malahat Review*, Pt 5 (Jan 1968), 77-89; see also Hazard Adams, 'Some Yeatsian Versions of Comedy'.

59.   James Olney, 'The Uses of Comedy and Irony in *Autobiographies* and Autobiography', *YAACTS* 2 (1984), 195-208.

60.   James Olney, 'The Uses of Comedy and Irony', p. 201. Others, such as Wilde, Shaw and Tynan, though also treated as comic or minor characters, had not tried to take control of Yeats's life to the same extent as Moore and so are treated more gently (pp. 203-5).

61.   For example, Yeats's plan for a mystical Order that will buy Castle Rock is gently mocked by his acknowledgement that the locals use 'The Castle on the Rock' as a synonym for 'white elephant' (*Au* 253).

62.   Katharine Tynan, *Twenty-Five Years*, pp. 208-9.

63.   James Olney, 'The Uses of Comedy and Irony', pp. 206-8.

64.   George Moore, *Hail and Farewell*, p. 277.

65.   Richard Church, 'A Portrait in Vitriol', *New Statesman*, 14 March 1936, 398.

66.   Walter Starkie, 'A Great Irish Poet Looks Back. Mr Yeats Gives Us a Book of Memories', *Irish Independent*, 14 July 1936, 6. Frank O'Connor gives an account (*My Father's Son* [London: Pan Books, 1971], pp. 88-89.) of Yeats reducing Osborn Bergin to hysterical laughter with a 'wonderful series of malicious anecdotes [about Moore] that later appeared in *Dramatis Personae* along with a number of scabrous ones that haven't appeared anywhere yet.' However, O'Connor stresses the specific motive behind this—that Yeats was attempting to win over Bergin who hated Yeats but hated Moore more—and acknowledges it as a unique 'performance' on Yeats's part. We should therefore still be wary of assuming a straighforwardly comic motive in *Dramatis Personae*.

67.   Padraic Colum, 'Yeats Looks Back', *Saturday Review*, 16 May 1936, 7. Most reviewers, in their obsession with the Moore-Yeats bout, fail to comment on the even more damning portrait of Edward Martyn—the peasant saint rather than the peasant sinner—who seems to be the real villain of *Autobiographies*; after all as a sinner Moore is possibly redeemable as an artist: 'A good writer should be so simple that he has no faults, only sins' (*Au* 527).

68.   Louis MacNeice, [review of *Dramatic Personae*] *Criterion*, 16:62 (October 1936), 120-22 at p. 121.

69.   Austin Clarke, 'Mr Yeats's Reminiscences', p. 434 .

70. George Moore, *Hail and Farewell*, p. 542.
71. Horace Gregory, 'Yeats Revisited', *Poetry*, 84:3 (June 1954), 153-57 at p. 153.
72. T. R. Henn, 'Moore and Yeats', *Dublin Magazine*, 4:2 (Summer 1965), 63-77.
73. Padraic Colum, 'Yeats Looks Back', p. 7.
74. Donagh MacDonagh, 'Yeats Never Forgets', p. 77.
75. P. S. O'H[egarty], [Rev of *The Trembling of the Veil*.] p. 7. The idea that Yeats's 'true' autobiography lies somewhere else in his writing is also quite common: 'In the Cuchulain plays he continued to write autobiography till at last, on his deathbed in France, he wrote "The Death of Cuchulain" for his monument.' Frank O'Connor, 'A Lyric Voice in the Irish Theatre', *New York Times Book Review*, 31 May 1953, 1, 16 at p. 16.
76. Padraic Colum, 'Yeats Looks Back', p. 7.
77. Padraic Colum, 'Yeats Looks Back', p. 7.
78. AE, 'The Memories of a Poet', *Irish Statesman*, 4 December 1926, 302-3.
79. R. H. C., 'Readers and Writers', *The New Age*, 2 November 1916, 15-16.
80. Kathleen Raine, 'The Discipline of the Symbol', *Listener*, 24 March 1955, 540.
81. AE, 'The Boyhood of a Poet' pp. 39-42.
82. Anon, [Rev of *Reveries & Responsibilities*] pp. 59-61.
83. AE, 'The Memories of a Poet', p. 302.
84. Mary Colum, 'The Conqueror Artist', *Forum and Century*, 10:5 (November 1938), 226-7.
85. Donagh MacDonagh, 'Yeats never forgets', p. 77. Paradoxically MacDonagh sees *Estrangement* and *The Death of Synge* as the most interesting parts of *Autobiographies* because they somehow escape Yeats's control and let us see where the poems come from. See also: Monk Gibbon, [review of *If I Was Four and Twenty*] *Bell*, 1:2 (November 1940), 91, 93 at p. 91; L. A. G. Strong, *London Magazine*, 2:6 (June 1955), 83-86 at p. 83; and John O'Riordan, 'The Mask of Yeats', *Library Review*, 24:1 (Spring 1973), 34-36 at p. 34.
86. Gerard Fay, 'The Poet', *The Manchester Guardian*, 25 March 1955, 10.
87. Louis MacNeice, [review of *Dramatis Personae*.] p. 121.
88. Louis MacNeice, [review of *Dramatis Personae*.] pp. 121-2. Yeats would have agreed (*L* 836-7).
89. Louis MacNeice, [review of *Dramatis Personae*.] p. 122.
90. Stephen Gwynn, 'W. B. Yeats: A Great Personality, The man and his measure', *The Observer*, 5 Feb. 1939, p. 8.
91. AE, 'Estrangement', *Irish Statesman*, 4 Sept. 1926, 713-4 at p. 713.
92. AE, 'The Memories of a Poet', p. 303.
93. Lennox Robinson, 'On "Autobiographies" by W. B. Yeats', *Library Review*, 115 (Autumn 1955), 162-4. Robinson also makes the point that Yeats's memory was very accurate, and says that this is corroborated by his sisters; therefore he thinks that all facts should be taken as true. See also Lennox Robinson, 'W. B. Yeats: Personality', in *In Excited Reverie*, pp. 14-23.
94. Horace Gregory, 'Yeats Revisited', p. 157.
95. Seamus Deane, *Celtic Revivals* (London: Faber and Faber, 1985), p. 29; *A Short History of Irish Literature* (London: Hutchinson, 1986), p. 143.
96. Standish James O'Grady, *Early Bardic Literature, Ireland* (London & Dublin: Sampson Low, Searle, Marston & Rivington, 1879), pp. 27, 42.
97. Ian Fletcher, 'Rhythm and Pattern in Yeats's Autobiographies', p. 165; see also Dillon Johnston, 'The Perpetual Self of Yeats's *Autobiographies*', p. 70.

98.   Among literary autobiographers only Sean O'Faolain and Mary Colum have written single volume autobiographies. Even writers such as Elizabeth Bowen or Louis MacNeice who appear to have only one volume (*Seven Winters, The Strings Are False*) have written other volumes which can be defined as autobiography (*Bowen's Court, Collected Impressions, Autumn Journal*, 'Landscapes of Childhood and Youth'—a significantly Yeatsian title).

99.   See Mary Colum, *Life and the Dream*, revised edition with additional material (Dublin: Dolmen Press, 1966), pp. 112-113 for an account of Yeats talking to students about the tragic generation in just the way that he will write or has written about them.

100.   See Fredric Jameson, *The Political Unconscious: Narrative as a Socially Symbolic Act* (London: Methuen, 1981), pp. 179-80. This is not to be confused with Harold Bloom's idea of 'the persuasive misinterpretation of the precursor'. (*Yeats* [London: Oxford University Press, 1970], p. 11). Jameson's remarks instead usefully suggest the ways in which shared social circumstances lead to biographical and other data being readable as re-enactments of underlying patterns.

101.   Sean O'Faolain, 'The Literary Scene in Ireland', *New York Times Book Review*, 5 January 1936, 8, 19. See also Sean O'Faolain, 'Four Irish Generations', *Commonweal*, 1 May 1929, 751.

102.   Oliver St John Gogarty, *As I Was Going Down Sackville Street* (London: Sphere Books, 1968), pp. 116-19.

103.   Sean O'Faolain, *Vive Moi!: An Autobiography*, edited by Julia O'Faolain (London: Sinclair-Stevenson, 1993), p. 137.

104.   Sean O'Faolain, *Vive Moi!*, p. 260.

105.   Sean O'Faolain, *Vive Moi!*, p. 279.

106.   Sean O'Faolain, *Vive Moi!*, pp. 31-2.

107.   Austin Clarke, *A Penny in the Clouds: More Memories of Ireland and England* (Dublin: Moytura Press, 1990), pp. 82-3.

108.   Austin Clarke, *A Penny in the Clouds*, pp. 96, 97, 166-8, 172-3, 202.

109.   Frank O'Connor, *My Father's Son*, p. 92.

110.   Frank O'Connor, *My Father's Son*, p. 26.

111.   Frank O'Connor, 'A Lyric Voice in the Irish Theatre', p. 1.

112.   Frank O'Connor, *My Father's Son*, p. 31.

113.   Frank O'Connor, *My Father's Son*, p. 94. This is supposedly the root cause of his malice towards Moore.

114.   AE, 'Reminiscences by Katharine Tynan', p. 884.

115.   [Sean J. White] 'Foreword', *Irish Writing*, 31 (Summer 1955), 7-8 (p. 8).

'It is time that I wrote my will':
Anxieties of Influence and Succession

Edna Longley

I

DID YEATS'S CREATIVE STAMINA exhaust or inspire the several 'younger generations' of Irish poets who appeared during his lifetime? 'Anxiety of influence' is often invoked, rarely elaborated, in this connection. Although Harold Bloom's theory grew out of his Yeatsian studies, its relevance to Yeats's posterity in Ireland has yet to be teased out and tested. Bloom identifies William Blake's 'Covering Cherub' with the 'negative or stifling aspect of poetic influence', and sees Yeats's 'revisionary readings of his precursors as . . . a series of swerves away from [them], swerves intended to uncover the Cherub, to free Yeats from creative anxieties'.[1] However, obsessed with the Anglo-American afterlife of certain Renaissance and Romantic themes, Bloom neglects the Irish contexts that make Yeats an even richer test-case for his own emergent theory: a veritable spaghetti-junction where precursors and successors jostle for position.

For example, he criticises Louis MacNeice's remarks about the 'autumnal, almost . . . morbid, languor'[2] that Yeats absorbed from Keats and Tennyson *via* Rossetti, without recognising MacNeice's need to swerve away from possibly seductive paths blocked by his 'strong precursor'. Further, Bloom's impatience with MacNeice's 'fail[ure] to describe . . . a central aspect of Romantic tradition' typically sees poetic tradition in the retrospective light of scholarly canon, rather than as an unpredictable play of energies between aesthetic reinvention, the critical spirit, and the historical moment.[3] As MacNeice notes: 'The critic tries to fit a particular artist into a niche in history as if history were a long corridor with all its niches there already . . . History for the artist is something which is evolving and he himself is aiding and abetting it' (PY 26). Nor was Yeats disposed to be languid in the 1930s. Bloom briefly notices Yeats's initial context in Ireland, and is interesting on his 'uneasy' relation to Mangan. Nevertheless, other elements in the Irish literary hinterland and political foreground make it inadequate to say: 'Yeats's problem as an Anglo-Irish poet was . . . in part, having to commence *ab ovo*, but as though an actual achievement lay behind him'.[4] Yeats made significant choices among the available Irish models, and exaggerating the magnetism of a weak precursor—whether Irish or English—may have helped his swerves from the strong.

From another angle, Yeats's belief in an Irish beginning circumvented the worry about 'belatedness', *vis à vis* English and European literature, which Bloom's thesis inherits from American modernism. The special position Yeats created for himself in literary history dramatised poetry as simultaneously ancient and newborn. He insisted that the woods of Arcady are never quite dead: it was still possible to be Oisin or Homer. More practically, as founder of a movement whose indigenous credentials were soon questioned, he remained anxious in a double sense about precursors, contemporaries and successors. He could not afford to be jealous and all-engrossing, a 'great Inhibitor',[5] a Saturn who devours his progeny, since his own work might perish if it did not procreate. Robert Farren calls Yeats 'the broad-awake kind of artist . . . the one who is interiorly compelled not only to innovate but beyond innovation to say what it is he innovates . . . This sort of artist needs others; his work must be buttressed, spread and prolonged'.[6] Bloom's contrast between a prelapsarian epoch when 'influence was generous' and an aggressive post-Renaissance drive towards strength in 'solipsism' may, in any case, interpret artistic dynamics according to highly specific cultural assumptions.[7] But if we re-align his terms, generosity and solipsism are integral to the Yeatsian dialectic and to the extroverted psycho-drama of Yeatsian poetics—'The people of Burke and of Grattan | That gave, though free to refuse' (VP 414). I will suggest that the anxiety of influence felt by younger Irish poets had its counterpart in Yeats's anxiety of succession, and that the tension between them came to a head during the 1930s.

In 1921 Padraic Colum declared in the *Dial*:

> Mr. Yeats . . . is not only a first-rate poet, but he is an abundant
> poet. And no poet writing in English in our time has given out so
> many fruitful influences. Thomas Hardy is a first-rate poet also. But
> Thomas Hardy has few sons in Apollo. Mr Yeats has fathered most
> of the Irish poets of today. And by his insistence upon the impor-
> tance of local life, local speech, and local traditions, he created in
> English-speaking countries the movement to which is due John
> Masefield in England, and Edgar Lee Masters and Vachel Lindsay in
> America. (*CH* 246)

This was before the impact of *The Waste Land* and of the war poets:
both destined, indeed, to get short shrift in Yeats's *Oxford Book of
Modern Verse*. Nonetheless, Colum's genealogy (which might be
expanded) underlines Yeats's pervasive presence in English-language
poetry at that period, while seeing it as bound up with his Irish
objectives. The poets who will be my main concern in this essay
(Austin Clarke, F[rederick R[obert] Higgins, Patrick Kavanagh and
Louis MacNeice) did not always respond to Yeats as one 'native' to
another. But it was to Irish poets that this exceptionally strong
precursor posed—and poses—the most comprehensive challenge,
whether deliberately ('learn your trade') or unconsciously. Stan
Smith has discussed W. H. Auden's 'Oedipal' relation to Yeats,[8] but
here literary anxiety was not compounded by cultural or political
anxiety. When Yeats dares his successors in 'Under Ben Bulben',
'ancient Ireland' (i.e., contemporary Ireland) conditions Bloom's
Freudian scenario whereby 'Weaker talents idealise; figures of
capable imagination appropriate for themselves'.[9] Yeats's Irish
'ephebes', to use Bloom's terminology, play out strong and weak
reactions: a mixture of aesthetic, cultural and political readings, in
which the psychology of creativity is entangled with historical
forces.

II

For Yeats, the problem of succession is bound up with the problem
of audience. Thus in 'The Tower' his 'Fisherman' becomes more
purposive ('*until* | The fountain leap'), less passively 'wise and
simple'. He now personifies, not the ideal muse-reader of Yeats's
poetry, but the bearer of its ambition and tradition:

> I choose upstanding men
> That climb the streams until
> The fountain leap, and at dawn
> Drop their cast at the side
> Of dripping stone . . . (*VP* 414)

This testamentary passage, fusing creation with procreation, itself spawns further images of virility and fertility: 'the headlong light', 'the fabulous horn', 'the sudden shower | When all streams are dry'. Yeats's willed vision eases the proleptic death of the author, subsumed into his 'last song' and 'the deepening shades' (perhaps the underworld of the precursors). But if 'The Tower' overcomes the artist's ambivalence about will-making, anxiety of succession shows itself elsewhere in doubts as to whether 'upstanding men', a potent literary elect, will be forthcoming. Samuel Beckett caustically agrees when he notes that Yeats's bequest of 'pride and faith . . . has something almost second-best bed, as though he knew that [the available candidates] would be embarrassed to find an application for those dispositions'.[10] Earlier, 'In Memory of Major Robert Gregory' (*VP* 323) had recast the genre of self-interested elegy for another poet or artist, turning it into a drama of the lost heir. The aborted finale, the rhetoric of the poem's uncompleted design ('but a thought | Of that late death took all my heart for speech'), marks the absence of a son-figure—one who might 'have published all to be a world's delight'—from the lineage of 'All those that manhood tried, or childhood loved | Or boyish intellect approved'. 'Late' does not only mean 'recent' but 'late in the day'; and Synge, Yeats's junior, is also dead. Read as a poem about anxiety of succession (implicating Protestant deaths in the Great War), the elegy signals Yeats's need to beget himself: not only in Bloom's sense of wrestling with the genes of strong precursors, but 'Myself must I remake' in default of heirs. Here Bloom's 'aboriginal poetic self', the aesthetic selfish gene, may be blind to its own overweening motives. Nonetheless, Yeats's phoenix-like rebirths were fired both by the presence (Synge, Pound) and the absence (Synge) of filial pretenders. Hence his persistence in seeking out 'forgotten . . . by youth, some bitter crust' (*Myth* 342).

More precisely, the poetry raises the issue of literary succession in three principal ways. Firstly, there are Yeats's much-resented dismissals of imitators and inferiors: 'was there ever dog that praised his fleas?', 'But the fools caught it . . .', 'Dear fellow-artist, why so free . . .?' Secondly, there is his interest in the survival of traditional forms and of form itself. At one level 'A Prayer for My Daughter' prays for a father-approved formalist suitor to a daughter-Muse: 'And may her bridegroom bring her to a house | Where all's accustomed, ceremonious' (*VP* 405). 'Meditations in Time of Civil War' elaborates dynastic metaphors for the transmission of aesthetic values. This sequence dramatises the antinomies of Yeatsian anxiety by playing on the gap between 'lonely mind' and 'bodily heirs' (*VP* 420). Sato's 'changeless sword', lying by 'pen and paper', symbolises the ideal working of tradition, the desired dynamic for all that Yeats has originated:

> Our learned men have urged
> That where and when 'twas forged
> A marvellous accomplishment,
> In painting or in pottery, went
> From father unto son
> And through the centuries ran . . . (*VP* 421)

The darker possibility projected by 'My Descendants' (*VP* 422) is that art is indexed to unpredictable life. Not metallic but organic, not a sword but a 'flower', it might succumb to environmental hazards which suggest the degeneration of artistic tradition rather than of family virtue: 'natural declension of the soul . . . too much business with the passing hour . . . too much play'. Here what has been accomplished by the speaker's 'vigorous mind' must provisionally stand as self-sufficient 'monument'. Finally, there is a heightened type or phase of anxiety: fear that history is irrevocably altering the conditions necessary for both the transmission and reception of Yeatsian art. Any poet must eventually 'become his admirers' (or detractors). But Yeats's elegies for 'Coole', like his myth of recurrence to 'that unfashionable gyre' (*VP* 565), mark his sense of an ending, his prophetic worst scenario in which modernity and post-Independence Ireland will conspire to prevent certain kinds of literary continuity: 'And I am in despair that time may bring | Approved patterns of women or of men | But not that selfsame excellence again' (*VP* 602).

III

In deference to Lady Gregory, Yeats places women first. However, like Bloom and most of the writers quoted in this essay, he represents influence and succession in mainly patrilinear terms. Patrick Kavanagh's androgynous or Marian twist—'Yeats was the god, the authority, the Mother Mind'[11]—stands out amid a prevailing obsession with 'father unto son' and with (sometimes patriotic) notions of artistic virility. F. R. Higgins boasts: 'English poets were losing not only their ears but their mouths. They lolled their tongues in unmanly verse . . . .'[12] This macho strain amusingly perpetuates Yeats's own tensions with regard to poetry and gender as disclosed in 'Coole Park, 1929': 'one that ruffled in a manly pose | For all his timid heart' (*VP* 489). While Elizabeth Butler Cullingford rightly stresses that 'Yeats was unable to identify with the norms of masculinity dominant in the late nineteenth century', his patriarchal self-assertions were not 'always an *ironic* mask' (emphasis added).[13] In Irish contexts, as the subliminal allusion to duelling implies, he associated his 'manly pose', his mature rhetorical stiffening, with necessities of defence and attack—not 'a man running' (*E&I* 161) but a man fighting to protect something vulnerable. Even in 1978 Seamus Heaney could not see beyond an armature which he characterised as 'bullet-proof glass', 'priapic', 'bare-fisted', 'domineering', and ultimately equated with Ben Bulben: 'that dominant promontory . . . the father projected into the landscape'.[14]

Among southern Protestant aspirant poets in the 1920s, the case of Monk Gibbon exemplifies hyper-anxiety of influence. His significantly named memoir, *The Masterpiece and the Man* (1959), obsessively rehearses Gibbon's failure to impress the father-poet (really a distant cousin): 'I was never at my best in his company. In fact I was always at my worst.' This masochistic retrospect persists in demanding god-like qualities of the father: that he should be self-consistent, supernaturally authoritative, benign: 'I was continually weighing him in the scales against AE, and against his own earlier self as expressed in his poems. If I challenged him on something, it was generally the challenge of the over-zealous disciple who thinks certain opinions unfitting to the master . . . I expected him to be prophet and teacher as well as poet . . .'.[15] Gibbon (b. 1896) was not alone in perceiving Yeats as the hard father, AE (George Russell) as the soft. AE also figures as nurse or supportive mother or unthreatening eunuch. Robert Farren says: 'If we think of Yeats as, in some way, the fertile but careless father of some of these writers, then AE may be called the careful midwife who delivered them alive, and the wet-nurse who suckled them to strength. He even had by him the sheets on which to lay them: the sheets of [the] *Irish*

Statesman.[16] Austin Clarke remembers AE's Sunday evenings: 'AE would praise our poems to [visitors] and quote entire passages . . . "I am only an extinct volcano", he would explain . . . The young poets—F. R. Higgins, Monk Gibbon, Lyle Donaghy or myself—each would sit there in happy embarrassment, feeling that he was rumble and fire within, sparks and smoke without.'[17] Sean O'Faolain speaks of AE's 'sweet toleration' : 'He was mild and kind . . . The main difference between him and [Yeats] was that he looked at life with the eyes of innocence, and the other looked at life with the eyes of desire.'[18] But there was, surely, more intricate collusion and competition at work. Gibbon senses, indeed, that the poets acted out rival concepts of mentorship, which derived from their antagonistic aesthetics:

> It was only when it came to his dealings with the younger gener-
> ation [as opposed to contemporaries] that Yeats seemed to sow
> dragon's teeth; whereas AE was a unifying force, absolutely
> determined to ignore all vendettas and to dissolve all animosities
> under the rays of his benevolent gaze at Rathgar Avenue. Indeed,
> part of the explanation of Yeats's propensity for throwing the apple
> of discord . . . was probably that AE was this centre of calm, this
> point round which opposites could circle and even presently
> coalesce.[19]

Yeats had long been suspicious of 'AE's canaries'.[20] He wrote to AE about his anthology *New Songs* (1904) in a letter (*L* 433-5) which justifies his own tendency to 'give unbridled expression to my dis-likes, moved perhaps by my knowledge of the strength of my likings and my loyalty to them'. (*New Songs* is singled out for satire in the 'Scylla and Charybdis' chapter of *Ulysses*.) He calls AE 'the other side of the penny, for you are admirably careful in speech, having set life before art, too much before it as I think . . .' and continues: 'Some of the poems I will probably underrate (though I am certain I would recognise a masterpiece come out of any tempera-ment) because the dominant mood in many of them is one I have fought in myself and put down.' Yeats defines this mood as 'unmanly . . . a womanish introspection'. So his struggle for a dif-ferent aesthetic, influenced by Synge's 'masculinity' and by Nietzsche, induced critical toughness and a sterner paternal attitude towards the feminised offspring of his early manner (such as, in *New Songs*, Seumas O'Sullivan, Alice Milligan and George Roberts): 'We possess nothing but the will and we must never let the children of vague desires breathe upon it nor the waters of sentiment rust the terrible mirror of its blade.' (Sato's sword waits in the wings.) In 1906 he wrote to Katharine Tynan about 'our young writers':

> They are vague, self-conscious, literary . . . They have not however yet learnt how to work at a poem. They play with words and have no organic structure . . . I once hoped a great deal from George Russell's influence . . . [but he] cannot bear anything that sets one man above another. He encourages everyone to write poetry because he thinks it good for their souls, and he doesn't care a rush whether it is good or bad (*L* 477).

Douglas Hyde's *Love Songs of Connaught* sabotaged as much as complemented Yeats's influence. Also, in succession to the pan-Celticism of the *fin-de-siècle*, there was interchange (not always approved by Yeats) between Ireland and the English poets who would later be called 'Georgian'. Reviewing David Morton's *The Renaissance of Irish Poetry 1880-1930*, Austin Clarke points out to its author (an American): 'Mr W. H. Davies, Mr Ralph Hodgson, and other English poets, have also contributed to our Gaelic mode'.[21] In 1932 James Joyce told Colum: 'too much fuss has been made about the work of recent Irish writers. "If we lift up the back-skirts of English literature we will find there everything that we have been trying to do".'[22] Underlying doubts bred over-insistence: the rift between Seumas O'Sullivan and Yeats resulted from O'Sullivan's perception that Yeats had betrayed his own revolution: the combined literary and national cause. In 'To A Poet' (1908) he accuses: 'You could have made of any other air | The little, careful, mouthfuls of your songs'.[23] So, from the early 1900s Yeats's self-renewal conflicted with his idealisation by ephebes and connected with unease about Irish literary autonomy.

Colum, although he admired Yeats's own 'capacity for renewing his poetic life' (*CH* 246) is a revealing case of semi-arrested development, and perhaps a hidden referent in the recent tendency to patronise the Revival for its supposed 'rural idiocy'.[24] This Catholic poet's imagined Ireland may also have been arrested by domicile in the United States (from 1914). Colum chose to organise his 'Collected Poems of Ireland' (1960) as *The Poet's Circuits*: as utterances set in an archetypal countryside defined by 'Field and Road', 'Things More Ancient', 'The Glens', 'The Town', 'Women in the

House', 'People on the Road'. Even the town is peopled by nostalgically evoked honey-sellers, basket-makers and whistle-players. Colum's poems have value as a preservation of *mores* threatened in 1900, and are closer to the soil than Antoinette Quinn allows when she says: '[he] adhered servilely to Revivalist [here identified with Protestant] conventions in his representations of Irish countrymen'.[25] Colum knew his local ground, he went directly to Gaelic sources, and he hardly means what Yeats means by 'traditional' when he claims that his *oeuvre* 'come[s] under traditional influences: many of the personae are engaged in traditional occupations; some of the poems are reconstructions of traditional songs and are fitted to traditional music; others are translations of pieces that have traditional existence in Gaelic'.[26] What limits this poetry is not representation, but scope and structure: the cosy absence of dialectic, the premium on celebration: 'I made poems out of glimpses I was given | Of days and nights of women and of men' ('Fore-piece'). Yeats advanced Colum's career and was 'overjoyed' by the success of his verse-play *Broken Soil* at the Abbey in 1903, since 'my position would have been impossible if I had had to snuff out the work of young men belonging to the company. It would have always seemed that I did so from jealousy or some motive of that sort. Now, however, one can push on Colum and keep one's snuffers for the next.' (*L* 417) But in 1909, as Colum's circuits became more clearly impervious to criticism and change, if in a different sense from AE's mystically timeless verse, Yeats recorded darkly: 'Colum . . . is the one victim of George Russell's misunderstanding of life that I rage over'. He calls AE's salon 'a world where no technique is respected, no merely laborious attainment applauded, but where all the bad passions of the disappointed sit like crows' (*Mem* 147-8).

Poets born between 1895 and 1910—among them Clarke (b. 1896), Higgins (b. 1896), Kavanagh (b. 1904), Padraic Fallon (b. 1905), MacNeice (b. 1907)—found themselves in a more obviously problematic literary environment. Yeats's presence loomed larger, as did his disconcerting shifts of style. Clarke, the poet most often associated (by himself and others) with Yeats-inflicted trauma, said in W. R. Rodgers's radio-portrait (1949): 'So far as the younger generation of poets are concerned . . . Yeats was rather like an enormous oak-tree which, of course, kept us in the shade and did exclude a great number of rays of, say, the friendly sun; and of course we always hoped that in the end we would reach the sun, but the shadow of that great oak-tree is still there.'[27] This Covering Oak-tree undoubtedly suggests 'the negative or stifling aspects of poetic influence'; but we might note that Clarke's much-cited simile actually resents its shade as inhibiting *reputation* rather than creativity. It was the Yeatsian mask or pose, not the Yeatsian canopy, that truly traumatised Clarke. Constructed for other reasons, the pose became a test (or externalised the test) for ephebes. L. A. G. Strong comments:

> The technique of seeming . . . the manner that, when several people came into the room, changed from intimacy to a performance: all were expression of that dominant myth, which preserved from attrition the greatest poetic personality of our time. Yeats's public manner was in no way insincere. It was a performance in which could be expressed every relevant belief and power, but it was projected.[28]

But, in the radio-portrait, opinion remains divided. Sean O'Faolain, as in most of his retrospects on Yeats, stresses distance, barriers: the 'way he had of not recognising people' [he forgets Yeats's eyesight], 'fake Brahminism', 'the lovely grey suit, the carefully chosen colours, the long hair, the flowing tie'. He contends: 'All that theatrical pose must have come between him and his own natural self.'[29] Frank O'Connor (echoing Strong) disputes O'Faolain's premiss, and Clarke actually defends the flowing tie: 'Yeats . . . had a magnificent black tie, which we could copy in other colours'. He adds that if the Georgian poets had worn such ties it might have 'saved [their art]' from 'the terrible rush and pressure of the modern world'.[30]

The difference between Clarke's and O'Faolain's obsessions with Yeats is that Clarke copies his Apollonian tie, O'Faolain covets the whole suit. Clarke is mesmerised by Yeats's Muse, whereas O'Faolain's 'eyes of desire' are turned towards his broader intellectual authority. However, there was also inter-genre competition between fiction and poetry: in 1938, discussing AE's legacy, Clarke refers to 'the meanness of our new so-called literary realism'.[31] At the same time, by (mainly) adhering to Yeats's genre, he had embraced the difficult paradox of copying the tie in other colours. His struggle to split from the paternal poetic body and negotiate the mirror-phase is now overt, now subtextual, in his autobiographical poetry and prose. Yeats bulks literally large in Clarke's recurrent images, and also tends to be seen from a concealed, voyeur's position: as a figure on the Abbey stage; rising 'to his full height' to chant 'The Lament for Owen Roe' at the Thomas Davis centenary; glimpsed through the trees at Coole as 'a tall sportsman, wearing an unusual raincoat of sky-blue watered silk, and carrying the rods and fierce tackle of his craft . . . Bewildered by that unexpected encounter, I hurried through the underwoods and, in a few minutes, had lost my way.'[32] In this chapter from *A Penny in the Clouds* (1968) Clarke partly sends up his youthful desire to 'trespass in the solitude where the poet had found so much of his inspiration'; but the text, if less conspicuously than Gibbon's *The Masterpiece and the Man*, is not fully in control of its Oedipal (and resentful) resonances. In the actual encounter that follows Clarke portrays himself as hypnotised by 'the gleam of the great signet ring, upon his waving hand' (dress fetishism again) while 'trying to defend myself from the religious novelty which he was evolving'.[33] Later, he describes how Yeats reacted to a question about Maud Gonne (Clarke in the mid-1930s hoped to write a biographical study of Yeats): 'His manner changed, and looking down at me like an eminent Victorian, he exclaimed: "Sir, are you trying to pry into my private life?"' The answer might be that Clarke, a *voyeur* uncertain of his own creative masculinity and suddenly disconcerted by a returned gaze, by 'a brown eye straining at its tiny muscles as if trying to peep into my very thoughts', was vicariously shadowing Yeats's life and art.[34] Yeats retaliated by blocking a successor who tried to come too close.

W. J. Mc Cormack argues that 'accomplished artistry' and the skills of 'an adult stylist' mediate the recurrent episodes of terror, timidity and anxiety in Clarke's autobiographies, and that the 'significance of a frequently noted gap between [the collections of poetry] *Night and Morning* (1938) and *Ancient Lights* (1955) should not be exaggerated'.[35] That is, the omission of Clarke from Yeats's *Oxford Book of Modern Verse* (1936) should not be seen as rejection by the literary father felt so deeply as to induce blockage. However, Yeats and other shades haunt Clarke's later poetry as well as his memoirs. 'In the Saville Club' also rehearses the trauma of asking the private question about Maud Gonne. 'Abbey Theatre Fire' takes Yeats's side and tone against the unnecessary razing of the partially damaged building: 'He would have called them knave or clown, | The playwright, poet, politician, | Who pull his Abbey Theatre down.' Another version, 'The Abbey Theatre Fire', appears more ambivalent about guards carrying out 'portraits in their gilded frames, | Yeats, Lady Gregory, Synge, Màire | O'Neill, Fay, F. R. Higgins, blindly | Staring in disapproval', and about the evacuation of stage properties, 'All the dear mummocks out of Tara | That turned my head at seventeen'. On the surface these impotent images enable release and exorcism: 'So, I forgot | His enmity'. However, empathetic irony ('an unstubbed butt' has precipitated the fall of Yeats's theatre) shades into *Schadenfreude*. Other poems about the Revival and Clarke's literary youth—'The Echo at Coole', 'AE', 'James Stephens'—mingle loyalty, nostalgia and anger; the father(s) neither wholly buried nor wholly praised. 'A Centenary Tribute' to Yeats has Clarke back on Yeatsian territory (not only the poet's changed house at Rathfarnham) still seeking for a sign: 'Bewildered, I tried to find the hall door.'

Clarke's difficulties about gaining access to Yeats, or to himself, may not originate in *literary* psychology alone. His autobiographies implicate other problematic father-figures, such as Thomas Mac-Donagh and Stephen MacKenna, 'a difficult parent', who praised his first book but 'couldn't get through' his third.[36] The long poem *Mnemosyne Lay in Dust* (1966), Clarke's rendering of his nervous breakdown in 1919, contains a stanza-break which turns on the duality of the father: 'Love | fathered him with their happiness. | Always in terror of Olympian doom, | He climbed, despite his will, the spiral steps . . .'. Mc Cormack suggests that *Mnemosyne* involves guilt for, unlike MacDonagh, missing the Rising (a parallel with generational guilt about the Great War). Irish writers may displace on to Yeats, feared as Olympian and Parnassian father, hidden problems with authority—familial, religious, political. Susan Halpern[37] and others have highlighted resemblances to Joyce in Clarke's Catholic background. But his conflicts were principally cast into verse, and the pattern of Clarke's career broadly and deliberately imitates Yeats's: mythic scenarios in lyric, narrative and dramatic verse; a satirical rebound in the 1950s; 'wild, wicked old man' sexuality in later poems like *Tiresias*. For years, Clarke valiantly tried to keep verse-speaking theatre alive. The trouble about this pattern is that it is not only imitative but belated, if less arrested than the loop-tape of twilight tunes.

Gregory A. Schirmer tries to make a case for Clarke's subversiveness: 'No previous teller of the tale [*The Vengeance of Fionn*, 1917] causes Grainne to wake "in sweating heat"'.[38] But Yeats had changed his own tune by that date. Similarly, the heroic period for satirical realism was in the 1930s and 1940s. There is consensus that Clarke cleared a space for himself in the early lyrics charged by his interest in Gaelic assonance and the Celtic-Romanesque period, but their melodic potential may be limited by nostalgia: 'the watery hazes of the hazel | Brought her into my mind' ('The Lost Heifer'). The 'religious novelty', proposed by Yeats, had been 'a neo-Catholic school of young poets in this country'.[39] Clarke's 'defence' against the idea that he should copy the right-wing Péguy and Claudel may have helped him to more congenial mythic ground—Yeats's push producing a healthy swerve. In *Night and Morning* Clarke's historical narratives develop into more autobiographically nuanced meditations on religion and sexuality. Yet even in a praised poem like 'The Straying Student' (1937) awkward rhythms and an uneasy compromise between everyday and archaic diction reflect a failure to mesh psycho-drama with persona:

> Awake or in my sleep, I have no peace now,
> Before the ball is struck, my breath has gone,
> And yet I tremble lest she may deceive me
> And leave me in this land, where every woman's son
> Must carry his own coffin and believe,
> In dread, all that the clergy teach the young.

The opening phrase merely fills space, as does the cliché 'every woman's son', while 'tremble' and 'In dread' are description, not manifestation. The presumed conflict is displaced into semi-mythic limbo. Terence Brown makes a doubly academic distinction between 'Yeats's vision of the Irish past . . . mediated through a profound nostalgia' and Clarke's myth 'authenticated by scholarship' and 'involved significantly with history'.[40] (Medievalising, also encouraged by Gaelic League denial of the 'English' centuries, may actually have been more regressive than Yeats's myth: myths based on history tend to run out of time.) Mc Cormack, too, avoids critical evaluation when he classifies Clarke as 'anomalous'; or, given Yeats's enthusiasm for Joyce, when he says: 'A young middle-class and Catholic urbanite did not easily conform to the Yeatsian design.'[41] It was *Clarke* who yearned to conform: so much so that his swerve in the 1920s, to material and metrics uncolonised by Yeats, may not have taken him quite far enough.

IV

Louis MacNeice begins his essay 'Subject in Modern Poetry' (1936) with the admission: 'The literary critic includes the literary historian, but it is notoriously difficult to write a history of one's own times.'[42] This is so, even where the critic does not consciously give history a nudge. I will outline some 1930s literary contexts as a prelude to suggesting how Clarke, MacNeice and Beckett approach the intertwined questions of Yeats and 'Irish poetry' in their critical writings of this period. Meanwhile Yeats himself went on writing literary history, and making it: most notoriously, that kamikaze dive into the war-zone of influence and succession—*The Oxford Book of Modern Verse*. Monk Gibbon piteously evokes the legacy-hunting that surrounded the anthology in Ireland: 'Those of us who were not between its covers could dwell on the melancholy reflection that we had lost not sixty thousand but three or four or five or six times that number of readers by our exclusion.'[43]

The *Dublin Magazine*, edited by Seumas O'Sullivan, may not have received its due as a channel between literary generations. Terence Brown's judgement seems too severe: '*The Dublin Magazine* in the 1930s was more notable for its sense of an insecure, self-regarding coterie remembering past glories and for its academic tone than for literary energy and commitment to a coherent, vital, editorial policy . . . Once more Dublin was a place to leave.'[44] While AE, alive and dead, is an unduly hallowed presence, and the featured poets—Clarke, Higgins, Fallon—often recycle old motifs, Kavanagh's contribution livens things up. Peter Sirr comments that O'Sullivan, 'a keen Francophile', kept the journal 'well stocked with critical material on Eliot and Pound and also on French and German poets'.[45] (In 1933 Blanaid Salkeld published an essay on Anna Akhmatova, together with translations.) These different perceptions may be explained by the fact that Brown looks back to the self-confident literary Dublin of earlier decades, whereas Sirr notices flashes of cosmopolitanism in a literary era that has been designated provincial. In 1934 O'Sullivan published Beckett's iconoclastic poem 'Gnome', and Beckett's mentor at Trinity College, T. B. Rudmose-Brown, was a contributor. So was Beckett's friend A. J. Leventhal, who succeeded him as Rudmose-Brown's assistant. Leventhal wrote about Dada[46] and about the modernist journal *transition*, to which

Joyce and Beckett contributed. If, in 1933, the *Dublin Magazine* could still print a clumsily conservative attack on Eliot ('no more than the waggling grinning skeleton of a great poem'[47]), by the end of the 1930s it was including material on Surrealism, the Spanish Civil War, and relations between the Communist Party and artists such as Gide and Breton. It published Alun Lewis's long poem 'Anschluss'. There is, indeed, something sporadic and lagging about this profile. Nevertheless, the magazine in other ways lived up to its subtitle: A Quarterly Review of Literature, Science and Art. It included sharp comment on the theatre,[48] articles on the visual arts, welcome for Robert Lloyd Praeger's naturalist odysseys, well-informed reviews of fiction, poetry and criticism in Britain, P.S. O'Hegarty's bibliographies of Irish authors, and—predating the foundation of *Irish Historical Studies* in 1938—spirited debate about new and old tendencies in the writing of Irish history.

Nor did the *Dublin Magazine* avoid literary and cultural controversy. In 1936 it published Sean O'Faolain's angriest attack on his former mentor, Daniel Corkery. O'Faolain contrasts Corkery's undue influence on 'our political evangels' with his failure, since he cannot speak 'the language of literature and literary values', to make any impact on creative people. He also underscores the wider resonances of Corkery's 'nationalisation of culture' in *Synge and Anglo-Irish Literature* (1931): 'With a little alteration it would equally well trumpet encouragement to all Nazis, Fascists, Communists, and every other type of exclusivist for whom the essential test of literature is a political, racial, or religious test.'[49] Earlier, *Synge and Anglo-Irish Literature* had been savaged by O'Hegarty (unusual in combining republicanism with devotion to Yeats) as 'carrying bigotry and intolerance into literature . . . a denial of the Irish Nation . . . a bad book and a mischievous book'.[50] Austin Clarke took a similar line in the *Times Literary Supplement*, with a special eye on Corkery's extension of anathema and expatriation to 'those modern Irish writers who by birth and upbringing are "initiates" of . . . Roman Catholicism'. He concludes: 'His book will enable English readers to realise the difficulties against which modern Irish writers who demand mental freedom and the right to criticise the prevalent ideas of their country must contend.'[51] Thus *Dublin Magazine* writers intervened in cultural politics, and Corkery's polemic renewed their solidarity with Yeats.

The journal's main poet-critics were O'Sullivan himself, Clarke and Padraic Fallon. Fallon's poetry at that time, as Peter Sirr's analysis confirms, helplessly idealised features of Yeats's and AE's style. His poems are jumbles of Revival tropes since the 1890s: 'Who, having come to sense, | Tenting with her but comes to know | As mere illusions | These dark eyes heavy with dream | Of lost kingdoms . . . ?' ('Wisdom') Nevertheless, Fallon's long rave-review of *The Winding Stair* praises Yeats's ability to cast 'skin after skin of opinion till now, at the age of sixty-eight, he emerges as nearly naked as a poet may, as bewilderingly fresh as the Old Woman of Beare might, youth in her veins again, an old skin already yellowing in the dew beside her'.[52] Presumably this reacts to Yeats's newly androgynous self-image as Crazy Jane. Yet the degree to which Fallon's critical, as well as poetic, idiom depends upon Yeats's own imaginative world leads to a muddled sense of his cultural whereabouts and artistic direction:

> Whatever regret we may have for the Gaelic epics that died that the strange angry, laughing lyrics in this book should come to life, we cannot fail to admire the integrity of one who finding the vision of evil as integral a part of his humanity as the mystic self whose kin is among the gods seeks to express equally the whole personality. What the Gaelic tradition loses, the Anglo-Irish tradition gains; for if he is in any line at all, it is that of Swift and Berkeley. Certainly, he is not among those negative stoics, the internationalist poets who are flocked in Ezra's little Pound.[53]

Clarke often wrote about Yeats during the 1920s and the 1930s, for the most part perceptively and positively. His years in London as a literary journalist (1922-1937) also meant that he helped to interpret Yeats for English audiences: A. N. Jeffares includes three examples in the *Critical Heritage* volume. His *TLS* review (1928) of *The Tower* deals more subtly than does Fallon with 'the dismissed reader', i.e. the lover of Yeats's earlier style: 'Although there is no philosophic peace in this new book . . . one becomes aware of a deeper sorrow at the roots of being . . . a freedom of the poetic elements, an imaginative and prosodic beauty' (*CH* 282-3). During the 1930s, especially after the *Oxford Book*, Clarke introduced more reservations into his criticism. For instance, an allusion to 'Mr Yeats's adolescent admirers in Oxford'[54] signals doubt, aggravated by the anthology, as to where Yeats's allegiance—and audience—now lies. His *Dublin Magazine* obituary for Yeats concludes with a felt tribute: 'the loss of Yeats and all that boundless activity, in a country where the mind is feared and avoided, leaves a silence which it is painful to contemplate'; but the dismissed reader still 'cannot escape [his] own surprise' at Yeats's metamorphosis—or defection:

> he returned to the major currents of English poetry and found free-dom in traditional metre . . . there is very little indication even in his critical essays that Yeats before the age of fifty was interested in historic English literature . . . In this new composite style the organ notes of English poetry are heard . . . But this new eloquence is not, I think, completely English. It has that individual Anglo-Irish note that one finds in Burke and Grattan and through all this later work there runs the earlier *tremulo*, starting here and there to surprise us in a sudden snatch.[55]

Clarke finally articulates his anxiety as to what this 'composite style' might mean for literary tradition: 'Yeats's attitude to home rule in Irish letters in his later years is somewhat of a mystery.'[56]

It is instructive to compare essays on poetry written by Clarke, MacNeice and Beckett in the mid 1930s. Clarke's 'Irish Poetry Today' (1935) also applies the terminology of political nationalism to the Revival's course: 'The *fin de siècle* movement was almost simultaneous with the rise of the national and language movement . . . With the next generation of poets the movement had gravitated towards its true centre, and happy days had come for we had home rule in our literature.' As in his Yeats obituary, he politicises poetic structure: 'It was pleasant to escape from the mighty law and order of English poetry into [the Celtic Twilight] that shadowy, irresponsible world of delicate rhythm and nuance.' Yeats's popu-larity in England already worries Clarke: 'These young English poets find expressed in his later work their own spiritual problems, and with typical insularity ignore the Irish quality in it as something foreign to their mentality.' While not yet blaming Yeats for this, he sees his 'later work [as] steeped in the rich imaginative associations of English literature' and thus 'we may well feel that the very ground on which we once stood so firmly has been undermined'. The anxieties that he and Fallon share about ascribing a clear-cut national identity to the later poetry are temporarily resolved by the back-handed ethnic compliment that Yeats's 'flightiness belongs to the adventurous, restless Anglo-Irish type of the past, those writers who, lacking lares of their own, were extraordinarily responsive and adaptable to any environment . . .'.[57]

Yet an essay that begins by lamenting Irish poetry's 'state of destitution' must accuse its absentee landlord. Clarke complains that the poetry has lost its English audience—although the 'critical tariff against Irish verse' might seem a logical riposte to de Valera's economic war (the demise of Irish publishing was also a factor in this period).[58] Less inconsistently, he regrets that 'our youngsters, with a few exceptions, are attracted to the predominant school of English contemporary verse'.[59] The latter cap might fit MacNeice, as might Anglo-Irish flightiness. MacNeice's essay 'Poetry Today.' (1935) takes in America and the English nineteenth century, and positions itself to champion—though far from uncritically—Auden, Spender and Day Lewis. His longest passage on Yeats begins: 'Mr Yeats is the best example of how a poet ought to develop if he goes on writing till he is old.' More patronisingly than in *The Poetry of W. B. Yeats* (1941), MacNeice admits that 'he has, in his own way, kept up with the times', and notes his technical affinities with the 'youngest English poets'. However, he represents Yeats as 'esoteric' and as 'further away from the ordinary English reader or writer than Eliot is . . . because of the dominance in him of the local factor. His rhythms and the texture of his lines are inextricably implicated with his peculiar past and even with the Irish landscape.'[60] So Yeats's current aesthetic appears more 'Irish' to MacNeice than to Clarke or Fallon.

Nevertheless, there is common ground between the two essays. MacNeice says: 'We now laugh at the Celtic Twilight and at the self-importance of these dilettante nationalists, but their *naïveté* and affectation had manured the ground for poetry. Where it is possible to be a hypocrite, it is also possible to be a hero, a saint, or an artist.' He also states: 'I am not one of those who have nothing to say for [Yeats's] earlier poems and everything to say for his later poems.'[61] Clarke praises Yeats's 'integrity', MacNeice his 'identity in difference', although the former has his truth to Anglo-Irish 'type' in mind (as a model for those with other *lares*), the latter his unmistakeable artistic signature. Finally, both criticise some of the excesses of modernism. 'Poetry Today' stresses Eliot's significance, which includes the reaction against him in the early 1930s, but attacks Pound: 'Mr Pound lacks grip; professing to offer us poetry he is always falling back on easier substitutes'.[62] Clarke is less hostile to modernism than are Fallon and Higgins; in fact, he rebukes English literary conservatism. But he opts, perhaps fatally, for protectionism and isolationism: 'I think that our attitude towards the present pandemonium in English poetic life should be that of neutral interest.'[63]

Such temporising tepidity would have enraged Beckett. Vivian Mercier calls Clarke Beckett's '*bête noire*': he is satirised in *Murphy* with the calling-card: 'Austin Ticklepenny | Pot Poet | From the County of Dublin'.[64] (Mc Cormack's analysis of 'this atrocious mal-representation' may overlook a straightforward literary-critical answer to the 'question: why Clarke as the butt of Beckett's ill-humour?'.)[65] Clarke and Higgins are more than personal targets of Beckett's review-article 'Recent Irish Poetry' (1934), which famously dismisses 'the antiquarians, delivering with the altitudinous complacency of the Victorian Gael the Ossianic goods'. Beckett's critique of 'poets of the Revival and after' finds Yeats more 'alive' than the aspirants to his second-best bed, but still privy to a 'flight from self-awareness'. He says: 'At the centre there is no theme . . . But the circumference is an iridescence of themes—Oisin, Cuchulain, Maeve . . . segment after segment of cut and dried sanctity and loveliness.' His charge is, of course, that the modernist 'breakdown of the object' has yet to dawn on 'twilighters' still 'adoring the stuff of song as incorruptible, uninjurable and unchangeable, never at a loss to know they are in the Presence'.[66] However, Beckett falls down in picking his own team. Despite continued special pleading,[67] Denis Devlin's and Brian Coffey's imitations of American modernist poetry, as well as Beckett's own 'Whoroscope', have generally borne cut and dried tubers. Yet Mercier may partly err in claiming: 'On the whole, W. B. Yeats was right and Beckett was wrong: by cutting themselves off from a native tradition, these Irish poets of the 1930s condemned themselves to pastiche. Austin Clarke . . . by persisting in his Irishness eventually became, like Yeats before him, a model for poets fifty years his juniors.'[68]

It is the perspectives of MacNeice's essay, rather than Mc Cormack's suggested formula 'modernists of conflicting generations',[69] that deconstruct the aesthetic opposition of Clarke and Beckett, and undermine such typically binary generalisations as Peter Sirr's remark: 'The relative backwardness in international terms of so much Irish poetry in this period must be understood in the light of the Irish Revival' (from which Sirr detaches Yeats).[70] 'MacNeice is ironical at the expense of 'aphasic' 'Americans in Paris'—evidently the *transition* writers—who want to 'scrap tradition from A to Z'.[71] Geoffrey Grigson's *New Verse* meant that the

Dublin Magazine and the 'Verticalist' manifesto of *Transition* were not inescapable alternatives. I have argued elsewhere that MacNeice mediated between traditional forms and 'modernism' in English contexts where the stuff of song could hardly be seen as unchangeable.[72]

'Irish Poetry Today' is more concerned with Irishness than with poetry (its agenda for Gaelic metres tackles only one element of form). 'Recent Irish Poetry' is brilliantly destructive polemic. But 'Poetry Today', alert to the elusive negotiations between 'impulse', 'pattern' and history, involves a dialectic about poetic structures. Unlike Clarke, MacNeice does not prescribe particular history or particular patterns, although he outlines a spectrum of technical possibilities. Thus his 'Today' has a wider and deeper resonance than Clarke's. Of poetic tradition he says: 'If we do our duty by the present moment, posterity can look after itself. To try to anticipate the future is to make the present past; whereas it should already be on our conscience that we have made the past past.'[73]

V

The *Oxford Book of Modern Verse* is Yeats's most controversial will and testament—often contested on grounds of eccentricity, if not insanity. It ends with Cecil Day Lewis, Margot Ruddock, Louis MacNeice, W. H. Auden, Julian Bell, Stephen Spender, Charles Madge, George Barker. Clarke lamented that Yeats had thrown 'his powerful influence and interest' behind 'the modern English school'.[74] MacNeice agreed, but approved, here aligning himself with the 'Anglo' camp and claiming that, while Yeats had promoted 'a steady and remarkable output of poetry by Irishmen',

A 'school' . . . implies more than this. Most of his Irish successors followed him in eschewing the industrial world and in writing their verses carefully, but they followed him in little else. There is rarely much meat on their poems. Yeats himself seems at times to have felt impatient with them, to have turned away towards English poets who were breaking his own rules (PY 179-80).

Joseph Hone, like most of the (relatively few) Irish reviewers, notes the 'strange omissions [of] Seumas O'Sullivan . . . and Austin Clarke . . . both members of the Irish Academy of Literature' founded by

Yeats; whereas, 'Mr Yeats has apparently preferred to theirs the work of two other Irishmen, MacNeice and [Cecil] Day Lewis'.[75] No review appeared in the *Dublin Magazine*. However, the contrastingly vocal reaction in England and the US complained that the Irish had done best out of the *Oxford Book*. For example, Stephen Spender, who twice attacked the (in)famous absence of Wilfred Owen and other 'war poets', refers to 'that Irish fen dominated by twin giants, Lady Dorothy Wellesley and Mr W. J. Turner', and states: 'All Mr Yeats's geese have to be swans, especially if they happen to have been born in Ireland.'[76] Day Lewis equally bit the hand that picked more of his work than of Auden, Spender and Mac-Neice. His review praises Owen as 'more than anyone else the real ancestor of our new revolutionary verse' and deplores the relegation of 'social function' in an anthology 'capricious to the verge of eccentricity, scandalously unrepresentative, as arrogant in its vulnerability as any aristocrat riding in a tumbril'.[77] Yeats's Irish swan-geese include Wilde, AE, Colum, Synge, James Stephens, Joyce, Joseph Campbell, Thomas MacGreevy and F. R. Higgins. Oliver St John Gogarty (b. 1878) is given more pages than any 'younger' Irish poet—twelve, the same number as T. S. Eliot and Yeats himself. This provocative back-formation evades a bet on 'my descendants'. However, the six poems by Higgins are significant, as is Yeats's regard for Day Lewis's thumping rhythms. MacNeice is the youngest Irish poet to be represented.

In sum, Yeats more radically provoked the English, and not just by omitting Wilfred Owen. For most reviewers, Wellesley, Turner, *et al.* constituted neither the state of the art nor of their tradition. G. W. Stonier exclaimed:

> Three pages of Hardy to twenty-eight of Edith Sitwell, fourteen lines of Rupert Brooke to 450 of Herbert Read, thirteen lines of Edward Thomas to 430 of Lady Gerald Wellesley—and so on, and so on . . . Mr Yeats's choices from Auden and Spender, from D. H. Lawrence, are as wretchedly bad as his choices from Hardy and Housman. It might still represent a strong idiosyncrasy. It does not.
>
> What the book suffers from most is not so much bad taste as an incoherent tastelessness.[78]

A. Desmond Hawkins cannot have assuaged Yeats's anxieties of succession: 'An anthologist should be a great eater of other men's work, and this is precisely what Mr Yeats is not . . . He is one who culminates in himself, a final and retrospective man, concluding a tradition and penetrating through it . . .'.[79] Although Yeats certainly ignored too much work (especially from America), his consciousness of poetic generations, of 'schools' and school-masters, indicates that he has no notion of being 'a final and retrospective man'. He seeks to perpetuate his lyrical genes by misreading or repressing English lineages; by asserting the 1890s origins of 'modern' poetry; by finding his own image in certain poets; by challenging American modernism; and by engaging with the 1930s poets 'who were breaking his own rules'—the point where he gets serious.

In promoting Turner, Wellesley, Gogarty and Higgins, Yeats looks into the mirror and reads influence or simulacra as succession. In Turner he sees both a congenial metaphysician 'rid[ing] in an observation balloon, blue heaven above, earth beneath an abstract pattern' (*OBMV* xxix) and an anti-modernist ally who is 'fighting all our battles' (*L* 846). The aristocratic cachet and archetypal pretensions of Wellesley's verse, together with her peculiar charm when 'magnificent in her masculine rhythm' (*OBMV* xxxii), have been much canvassed.[80] ('Fire', one of Yeats's selections from Wellesley, includes the lines: 'Set the tapers spick-and-spanly, | Candles burn erect and manly'.) It is equally obvious that personal rather than literary style earns Gogarty the accolade of 'heroic song'. Gogarty's insouciance 'under a shower of revolver bullets', a product of Irish poets' 'simple and exciting' public life, is also designed to put trench-poetry in its place (*OBMV* xv-xvi). Further, Gogarty's Catholicism allows his poetry to represent the kind of dynastic transfer blocked, for Yeats, by the assassination of Kevin O'Higgins. Between them, Gogarty and Higgins (a Protestant who quarrelled with his unionist father and refused to enlist in 1914-18) symbolise the desired afterlife of Yeats's Irish cultural politics, the heroic and folkloric aspects of his aesthetic. With Wellesley, they form a triptych that mimics the 'approved pattern' laid down by Lady Gregory, Yeats and Synge.

Higgins, author of *The Dark Breed* (1927) and *Arable Holdings* (1933), contributed most directly to Yeats's reflexive unity of poetic being. He was centrally involved in the Irish literary milieu of the1930s where he acted out, at least in Yeats's mind's eye, some of Yeats's obsessions. In 1935 Yeats made him manager of the Abbey Theatre. The most credible witnesses in W.R. Rodgers's radio-portrait of Higgins confirm Patrick Kavanagh's devastating judgment: '[Yeats] invented Synge and Lady Gregory and he was largely responsible for F. R. Higgins.'[81] Frank O'Connor describes Higgins as 'always so anxious to be Irish when [he was] writing . . . the County Meath Protestant had to dress himself up as a wild Irish Celt before he could begin to write at all, and he had to write things about the bards of whom he knew nothing and about Irish prosody'.[82] (Kavanagh's essay 'The Gallivanting Poet'[83] accuses Higgins of dressing himself up not only as a Celt, but as a Catholic.) In symbiosis with Yeats's creative needs—for a sexually spiced-up Synge—Higgins figured as a 'warty lad', his contact with the soil supposedly ratified by bawdy talk, folk-song and fornication. In fact, Yeats's short-sighted notion that (the very fat) Higgins sometimes came to him 'sweating from his whore' was wide of the mark. Higgins's manly verse, itself a reversion from an earlier twilit style, is innocent if sexist in its pursuit of 'bracing virgin females' ('The Ballad of O' Bruadir'). As Elizabeth Cullingford shows, Yeats's 'erotics of the ballad' included the idea that folk-song is inherently virile.[84] But Higgins has more in common with the beery wing of Georgianism. He wrote a naively phallic ode to his blackthorn stick: 'Bare skinned and straight . . . flaunting out the fierceness | That bristled through your hide'. One tramping poem is called 'The Gallivanter to his Boots'. In another celebration of male-bonding out of doors ('The Boyne Walk'), 'Adam's red apple hops dry in my throttle'. This at least rings truer than some uncomfortable couplings under blackthorns and 'creaky whin' ('The Victim'). O'Connor further conveys the mutual unreality between Yeats and Higgins—one mask begetting another—when he says of their bonding in balladry: 'There was something extraordinarily funny about . . . this man who was tone-deaf writing songs, and another man who was a public-house singer setting them to Irish airs of a sort, and then a third man writing them down in staff notations.'[85] Donagh MacDonagh contends that Yeats got the better of the bargain (as if both giving and taking a legacy): 'at the end of the period Yeats had acquired this racy ballad quality and Higgins had nothing left.'[86] 'Porter-drinkers' randy laughter' may be Higgins's epitaph.

A lateral comparison with MacNeice suggests the extent to which Yeats hypnotised Higgins, and to which the poetic environment in Ireland was still controlled by rules that Yeats himself had bent or broken. The contrast between Yeats's selections from the two poets is stark enough.[87] The Rev. Neil Kevin cautiously welcomed 'these *moderns*', but saw MacNeice's vocabulary in 'Eclogue for Christmas' as a demarcation-line: '[He] manages to introduce into a poem (as passionately conceived as scepticism will allow) the following odd assortment of words: *taxis, gramophone, carbon, diabetic, ordnance maps, stylised profile, pekingese, private property, machine-guns, traffic-islands, saxophones, technical excellence, grilled steak.*[88] Here is a corresponding list from Higgins's poems in the anthology: horse-drays, 'secret joinery of song', lightenings, wizen, 'glens of brightness', 'bardic mind', herds, 'an old weir | Of my people's', cutlass, 'grassy streets', clatter bones, 'the knife-grinder plying his treadle', 'grey juice of the barley'. The comparison is neither unfair, nor just a matter of city and country. As MacNeice says: 'The diction of a poet is very intimately connected with his subject-matter. When the diction has outlived the subject-matter it becomes a burden.'[89] Higgins generally observed a linguistic quarantine that excluded much of his inner and outer life, as well as modernity and a conceptual vocabulary. MacNeice may mean Higgins when he mentions 'an Irish poet' who asked: '"Do poets of your school never *sing?*" His assumption was that a poet should sing rather than think.' MacNeice then stresses how Yeats's 'period of hard, if perverse, thinking' tightened his lyric (PY 141). Higgins's Yeats-inflected 'Song for the Clatter Bones' has not only proved politically incorrect ('God rest that Jewy woman, | Queen Jezebel, the bitch | Who peeled the clothes from her shoulder-bones . . .'); it wholly lacks the psychological and symbolic reach of MacNeice's 'Circe': 'Something of glass about her, of dead water, | Chills and holds us . . .' Higgins's often-anthologised 'Father and Son' is a partial exception. As he approaches his actual father, the literary paternal surrogate and the manly mask—a sublimation of infantilism—fade:

> And walking longside an old weir
> Of my people's, where nothing stirs—only the shadowed
> Leaden flight of a heron up the lean air—
> I went unmanly with grief, knowing how my father,
> Happy though captive in years, walked last with me there.

Yet Higgins also eludes Yeats, and *vice versa*, where his language and mythic ground are influenced by Hyde and the second-generation Revival poets. MacNeice states that O'Sullivan, Colum and others 'did not copy the broad sweep of Yeats and their poetry lacks brainwork but they succeeded better than Yeats [in expressing] the folk elements of Ireland' (PY 181). Be that as it may, Higgins was inspired by Colum's 'Drover': 'And the crowds at the fair, | The herds loosened and blind, | Loud words and dark faces, | And the wild blood behind!' When he identifies with this notional 'dark breed', Higgins goes beyond Yeats in claiming kin with 'peasant', Gaelic, and hence national life—there was now less mileage in dreams 'of the noble[man]'. Yeats's 'wild Jack' represents sexuality; the 'manly pose' of his later poetry challenges his fellow-countrymen; the nuance of 'race' becomes oppositional rather than inclusive. But Higgins affiliates his own poetry to a totalising, macho race-consciousness in a way that, *inter alia*, tries to deny Protestant insecurity after 1921 (a denial cruelly exposed by Kavanagh). In trumpeting Yeats as 'always arrogantly the Irish poet', he joins what Yeats's subtexts put asunder: 'O'Leary's people—the Gaelic people, who lived dangerously to die jestful-ly—were his first and lasting influence.' He also remakes Yeats in the image that Yeats had made of him: 'most frank, full of zest and humour'.[90] In 1929 Higgins reviewed *Gaelic Literature Surveyed* by Aodh de Blacam, who paints the Gaels of the Red Branch cycle as 'large, splendid men, living recklessly for honour's sake', 'a virile race', of 'exuberant force' and 'wild, grotesque humour'. This image, too, may have helped to make Higgins. He likes the idea of 'Galls turned Gaels . . . fully assimilated by a more robust culture', de Blacam's 'virile turns of phrase', and his Freudian picture of 'Palesmen living inside their walled towns unconscious of the vast and virile life and literature that surged outside their battlements'.[91] Higgins's elegy for Padraic O'Conaire attaches the speaker as well as his subject to the male 'mind' of a primordial, transcendental Ireland which unites the Gaelic and Celtic modes of the Revival (in a pub):

> An ale-house overflowing with wise Gaelic
> That's braced in vigour by the bardic mind,
> And there his thoughts shall find their own forefathers—
> In minds to whom our heights of race belong . . .

On poetic maps these patriarchal 'heights of race' are often located in the west of Ireland. Higgins salutes O'Conaire as 'Dear Padraic of the wide and sea-cold eyes' and says: 'The very West was in his soft replies'.[92] MacNeice's 'Turf-stacks', also in the *Oxford Book*, attaches no racial or national significance to the west, but rewrites 'The Lake Isle of Innisfree' for the politically insistent 1930s:

Among these turf-stacks graze no iron horses
Such as stalk, such as champ in towns and the soul of crowds,
Here is no mass-production of neat thoughts
No canvas shrouds for the mind nor any black hearses:
The peasant shambles on his boots like hooves
Without thinking at all or wanting to run in grooves.

MacNeice salutes the western 'peasant' neither as mindless, nor as a repository for 'the bardic mind', but as un-ideological: as having access to resources, symbolised by the 'tawny mountain, the unregarded buttress', which resist 'the | Shuddering insidious shock of the theory-vendors'. 'The Individualist Speaks' must also have appealed to Yeats's hatred of Marxism. His Introduction states: 'MacNeice, the anti-communist, expecting some descent of barbarism next turn of the wheel, contemplates the modern world with even greater horror than the communist Day Lewis, although with less lyrical beauty' (*OBMV* xxxviii). Here Yeats over-identifies with a left-wing successor-poet who, in these lyrics and in 'Eclogue for Christmas', was starting to ask new questions about 'responsibilities' in the context of forces which reduce the poet to a marginal figure, 'playing with paint and filth' or with 'looking-glasses and beads'. Nonetheless, Yeats recognises that MacNeice shares some of his attitudes, and that the 'waiting for the end' of 'Eclogue for Christmas' invokes the gyres as well as *The Waste Land*: 'We shall go down like paleolithic man | Before some new Ice Age or Genghiz Khan'.

As with Marxism, so with modernism. Yeats's reasons for favouring MacNeice, Day Lewis and Auden (English reviewers noted his playing-down of Auden's 'leadership') involve special pleading, self-interest and self-contradiction:

Ten years after the war certain poets combined the modern vocabulary, the accurate record of the relevant facts learnt from Eliot, with the sense of suffering of the war poets, that sense of suffering no longer passive, no longer an obsession of the nerves . . . Day Lewis, Madge, MacNeice, are modern through the character of their intellectual passion . . . I can seldom find more than half a dozen lyrics that I like, yet in this moment of sympathy I prefer them to Eliot, to myself—I too have tried to be modern. They have pulled off the mask . . . Here stands not this or that man but man's naked mind . . . I have read with some excitement poets I had approached with distaste, delighted in their pure spiritual objectivity as in something long foretold . . . it is perhaps a belief shared that has created their intensity, their resemblance; but this belief is not political. If I understand aright this difficult art the contemplation of suffering has compelled them to seek beyond the flux something unchanging, inviolate . . . I would, if I could, have dealt at some length with George Barker, who like MacNeice, Auden, Day Lewis, handled the traditional metres with a new freedom—*vers libre* lost much of its vogue some five years ago—but has not their social passion, their sense of suffering (*OBMV* xxxv-xli).

The manoeuvre is to admit that the thirties poets have been influenced by Owen and Eliot (the latter being typically misrepresented), but to claim that they have transformed these influences in a Yeatsian direction. Thus, suffering is no longer passive; beliefs are no longer political; flux yearns for transcendence; intellectual and social 'passion' virtually attains the condition of personality; the new poetry has been 'foretold' (by Yeats's system?). In fact, Yeats may have understood these poets better than they understood themselves; just as he was right, in a casual but deadly aside, to stress their reaction against free verse. He does not discuss Higgins, or any other Irish poet, in terms so crucial to his aesthetic posterity. MacNeice returns a compliment whose implications he has absorbed: 'We had found music in *The Waste Land*, but we found music more to our purpose, on the whole, in the later Yeats'; '[the thirties poets] can be grouped with Yeats rather than with Eliot . . . Whatever their system was, they stood with Yeats for system against chaos, for a positive art against a passive impressionism' (PY 157, 191). When, in July 1939, MacNeice and Higgins disagreed about poetry in a radio-discussion later made emblematic by Paul Muldoon, the wars of Yeatsian succession during the 1930s lay behind their argument.[93]

VI

Relations between Yeats and his Irish 'ephebes' confirm that Bloom too hastily dismisses tradition and context from his Oedipal scenario. He writes: 'By "poetic influence" I do not mean the transmission of ideas and images from earlier to later poets. This is indeed just "something that happens", and whether such transmission causes anxiety . . . is merely a matter of temperament and circumstances.' But if 'Ideas and images belong to discursiveness and to history, and are scarcely unique to poetry', poetry uniquely makes them functions of that 'formalising activity' (MacNeice) whereby a poet's 'Word, his imaginative identity' (Bloom) is realised in words.[94] In the Irish case, sectarian and political factors interfere with the transmission of forms. Premature idealisation or premature swerves may pre-empt psychic encounter. And there are, of course, problems about acknowledging Yeats as a precursor at all. Earlier sections of this essay have indicated the uncreative misreadings that arise when poets are less aware than MacNeice that 'One has to be careful not to accept literally what Yeats says about himself' (PY 31). Poets read Yeats (and poetry) literally when they think he has abandoned the 'Gaelic' tradition for the 'Anglo-Irish' (Fallon, Clarke) or that he has synthesised them (Higgins) or when they are petrified by his mask. Such readings in terms of cultural nationalism produce a broader muddle: between ideas of literary and political Home Rule. The most salient equivalence between these ideas may be the sense that a leader has abdicated and his successors are unprepared for authority. In 1951 Patrick Kavanagh was still mourning the division and diaspora of the 'republic of Irish letters which under Yeats had achieved some kind of unity—a clearly defined polarity of bad and good'.[95] Bloom makes a rare acknowledgement of cultural context when he says: 'British poets swerve from their precursors, while American poets labour rather to "complete" their fathers. The British [i.e., English] are more genuinely revisionists of one another.'[96] Perhaps the religious contour of Irish patriarchy conditions the structure as well as the content of anxiety, bringing completion and revisionism into conflict: obedience to Yeatsian authority (Higgins); apostasy or the Joycean heresy (Beckett); deadlock beween obedience and apostasy (Clarke); apostasy mourning the death of authority (Kavanagh).

Even if the precursor's inner sanctum necessarily remains veiled, a strong poet will surely comprehend as well as swerve, interpret as well as misinterpret. Access to Yeats means peeling away the 'techniques of seeming' which shape his literary masks and public pose. Yeats may be unmasked either explicitly in criticism or implicitly in the successor's forms. I want to argue, finally, that MacNeice and Kavanagh brought special resources to this unmasking.

In *The Poetry of W. B. Yeats* and elsewhere MacNeice speaks as an intermediary between Yeats and English or American audiences—an intermediary whose own status is on the line. He is highly conscious of the need for mediation: 'Since Yeats's death Irish intellectuals have gushed about him in print and continued to mock him in private.'[97] His own approach publicly blends admiration with irony—a readiness to say 'come off it, Yeats', which Clarke and Higgins lack: 'If you believe a man was a genius, it is an insult to him to ignore his deficiencies and peculiarities . . . in judging his services to Ireland and Art, we shall be very shortsighted if we reapply his own heavily blinkered concepts of either.'[98] In *I Crossed the Minch* (1938) MacNeice parodies Yeats and satirises his reverence for Dorothy Wellesley: '[Lady Flora Barsac] showed me a poem which she had written with a wild goose quill and it seemed to me to be more profound, more exquisite, than the other poems of our century'.[99] MacNeice's tone of amusement, at once intimate and detached, epitomises a relation to Yeats that avoids extremes of accusation and awe. From the outset *The Poetry of W. B. Yeats* asserts a strategic distance from its subject: 'familiarity breeds a certain obtuseness, whereas a certain amount of strangeness is stimulating to criticism. I feel that in Yeats I have met a poet who is strange enough to excite my interest but is near enough to me myself to preclude my misrepresenting him too grossly.' MacNeice thus reassures those 'who know my own expressed views on poetry [and] might consider me unqualified for writing on Yeats, whose expressed views are so often the opposite of mine' (PY 27). The Preface and Introductory chapter vigorously express views on poetry. This establishes poetry—rather than Yeats or Ireland—as the book's primary focus, together with MacNeice's credentials to assess Yeats's practice and theory. The critic also, of course, speaks as a poet, and as a poet of 'my generation . . . a generation that had rediscovered the importance of subject matter'; although he proceeds to correct 'over-simplification' of literary 'realism' (PY 18).

MacNeice's 'my generation' answers Yeats's 'my generation' in the *Oxford Book*. It responds to Yeats more as a modern than as an Irish poet. MacNeice derives some of his critical-creative authority, to assail the father, from a peer-group of poets with shared principles. However, he also disagrees with the group, or with grouping ('Poets are commonly grouped together, or opposed to each other, according to rules of thumb'(PY 27)), and stresses that the pace of history makes relations between Yeats and the thirties generation an open and evolving question:

> I had only written a little of this book when Germany invaded
> Poland. On that day I was in Galway. As soon as I heard on the
> wireless of the outbreak of war, Galway became unreal. And Yeats
> and his poetry became unreal also.
>   This was not merely because Galway and Yeats belong in a s e n s e
> to a past order of things. The unreality which now overtook them
> was also overtaking in my mind modern London, modernist art,
> and Left Wing politics (PY 17).

MacNeice's maturation as a poet between 1930 and 1939 is corre-
lated with deeper understanding of Yeats, with the shift from con-
gratulating him on 'keeping up with the times' to recognising that
neither historical reality nor literary realism are stable concepts. It
was not only in Ireland that Yeats had naive readers: witness the
responses of Spender, Day Lewis and 'Left Wing politics' during the
1930s. Spender's confused essay 'Yeats as a Realist' (1934) praises
Yeats's poetry for 'its passion, its humanity, its occasional marvellous lucidity, its technical mastery, its integrity, its strength, its
reality and its opportunism'. But Spender only demolishes 'the
romantic facade' to discover a vacuum 'devoid of any unifying
moral subject . . . no philosophy of life, but . . . a magical system
[which is] not socially constructive'. His subsequent claim that the
Owen of 'Strange Meeting' was 'already a poet of far deeper human
understanding' may have been noted by the editor of the *Oxford
Book*.[100] Day Lewis's memorial essay, 'Yeats and the Aristocratic
Tradition', retains thirties reservations about 'the aristocratic poet
who feels a passionate love for the Cause but also a certain
impatience and contempt for the human instruments with which he
has to work'.[101] Auden, like MacNeice, was only minimally dis-
tracted from the aesthetic force of Yeats's poetry, and famously saw
its contemporary relevance in a new light on the cusp of the decade.
In 1948 he praised Yeats for tackling 'problems . . . central to the
tradition' and 'produc[ing] results which are available to his successors'; but he confines those results to Yeats's transformation of 'the
occasional poem . . . into a serious reflective poem of at once personal and public interest' and his release of stanzaic poetry from
'iambic monotony'.[102]
  The wartime context of *The Poetry of W.B. Yeats* informs Mac-
Neice's deeper identification with Yeats's 'positive art': 'Yeats's formalising activity began when he *thought* about the world; as he

thought it into a regular pattern, he naturally cast his verse in regular patterns also' (PY 157). At the same time, he preserves generational distance by keeping in view both the new aesthetic and Yeats's 'oddity' and 'limitations'. This is partly tactical, since he is offering a revisionist account of Yeats to an English audience conditioned to think of his poetry as irrelevant, reactionary, quasi-fascist, preaching a gospel 'not only obsolete but vicious' (PY 192). Mac-Neice himself does not excuse the 'elegant brand of fascism' (PY 48), but he also insists that most poets thrive on 'theoretical half-truths' and 'we should be mistaken if we inferred that *Yeats* could have written better poetry if he had had the "right" ingredients: he probably could not have assimilated them' (PY 194-7). Yet the thirties poetic norms which measure Yeatsian oddity enable MacNeice both to see Yeats whole and to move away from him, when he finally returns to 'identity in difference': 'I would say . . . that Yeats, as a poet, is characterised by integrity. He talks a lot of nonsense, he poses, he suppresses, exaggerates, misrepresents' (PY 196). Ten years later, MacNeice's review of Yeats's *Collected Poems* celebrated 'this most paradoxical poet chopping and changing through half a century . . . fey in his youth, rumbustious and hardheaded in his old age, symbolist and rhetorician, mystagogue and gossip, near-fascist and anarchist, lutanist and trumpeter by turns, yet always remaining himself'.[103]

MacNeice was well aware that any poet has difficulty in gaining access to another poet's imaginative 'self': 'I must, if I am an artist, be especially careful not to read my own questions into another artist's complex of question-and-answer' (PY 27). This, of course, does not eliminate unconscious motives or creative misrepresentation: MacNeice's critical readings push Yeats towards a congenial drunkenness of being poetically various. Similarly, he stresses Yeats the 'sceptic' (PY 79) and Yeats the covert internationalist: 'When he borrowed something (say) from India, he would excuse himself by the supposition that India is essentially Irish' (PY 49-52). Unlike Clarke, MacNeice relishes Yeats's sly breaching of Home Rule literary horizons. But the English 1930s may have raised more apt and searching questions about Yeats than the Irish 1930s: questions which ultimately allow the son to put a liberating commandment—a license to swerve—into the father's mouth: 'The spiritual lesson that my generation (a generation with a vastly different outlook) can learn from Yeats is to write according to our lights. His lights are not ours. *Go thou and do otherwise*' (PY 197).

As for Yeats and Ireland, here MacNeice emphasises closeness rather than distance; and he uses Yeatsian language to define Irish nationality as another dialectical complex of question-and-answer: 'best . . . expressed in a set of antinomies' (PY 51). MacNeice's qualifications to interpret Yeats's 'Irish Background' are set out in strongly autobiographical terms: 'It is notoriously dangerous to generalise about Ireland, but there are certain things which I can point out, either because they are patent facts or because I myself have experienced them. Like Yeats, I was brought up in an Irish middle-class Protestant family' (PY 50); 'When I read Yeats's account of his childhood I find many things which are echoed in my own or in that of other Irish people I know' (PY 52). That MacNeice can assert personal and cultural proximity, while measuring ephebic distance, guards against literalness and shows his grasp of the Yeatsian mask as well as of Yeatsian dialectic.

Patrick Kavanagh, ever-willing to generalise about Ireland, finds few echoes and no antinomies. Antoinette Quinn illustrates his Corkeryite leanings by quoting from 'The Anglo-Irish Mind', written for the Catholic *Standard* in 1943:

> From Swift to Yeats the mouthpieces of this limbo-stranded class have had to search diligently wherever they might for the spiritual food of their creative need. Yeats was the fruit of many generations resident in Ireland, yet he was forced to adopt Ireland as his country. . . . Yeats was not pushed up by the under-drive of a nation; he saw the force and he allowed it to drive *him*. It was the same with Synge.[104]

Kavanagh makes religion the badge of ethnic exclusion, as he does later in 'The Gallivanting Poet': 'They were trying to by-pass Rome on their way to the heart of Ireland.'[105] In 'William Butler Yeats' (1962) Kavanagh calls Yeats 'Irish of a certain kind' but says: 'he never was at ease'.[106] Quinn is right to read Kavanagh's expatriation of Yeats and other Protestant writers in Bloomian terms: 'In challenging Yeats's credentials as Ireland's national poet, the writer of *The Great Hunger* is implicitly asserting his own claim to that office. He is the poet raised up by his countrymen's "silent necessity", "pushed up by the underdrive of a nation" . . . the voice of oppressed Catholic Ireland.'[107] Evidently, this contrasts with 'my generation' as a back-up 'force' which powers a swerve from the precursor.

Yet Quinn may overdo the metaphors, and the reality, of anti-colonial alienation when she compares Kavanagh's demeanour towards Yeats to the advent of 'the rough beast subverting custom and ceremony' or writes: 'Kavanagh's polemic against the Revival was an act of dispossession which was the literary equivalent of the burning of the Big House.'[108] The terms of the polemic, influenced by Monaghan sectarianism as well as by Corkery, are primarily religious and rural. Kavanagh's appeal to the nation was short-lived—in part, because the nation paid scant attention. Subsequently, his anti-nationalism precluded anti-colonialism. Secondly, Kavanagh's critical writings on Yeats are riven by contradiction and recantation. Unlike MacNeice, he has no objective or dialectical means of holding Yeats in a steady shimmer. Thus 'The Poetry of W. B. Yeats', after criticising the 'bawdy of the *Last Poems*', continues: 'Having written this, something smote my conscience and I looked up the *Last Poems* and some of them are really splendid'. Kavanagh then shrewdly remarks that it is not 'those poems . . . which are bawdy and noisy about wild women [that] show Yeats's youngness but rather those in which he is his own serene authoritative self'.[109] In 'Poetry in Ireland Today' Kavanagh had yearned for a Yeatsian second coming to set authoritative standards: 'During the lifetime of Yeats that living poem appeared again and again; and as it flashed the dead bodies stirred with desire . . . nearly all the literary activity which gave the country a name was due in some measure to Yeats. What is weak now is faith in the validity of literature.' This essay shows an unusual comradely compassion for 'all who walk the barren fields where the master reaped'.[110] Yet Kavanagh not only sought space for his own work but, however incoherently, an intelligent critical reception (of the kind more accessible to Mac-Neice in England). *Kavanagh's Weekly*, the journal that he co-edited with his brother in 1952, naively tried to revive Yeatsian authority, to place poetry at the centre of Irish life, and to legislate for cultural and aesthetic value (the metaphor of death and resurrection recurs):

We have no wish to compare our position to that of Yeats and his followers in the graveyards of 1900, for that would give a number of people the opportunity of saying: you are not Yeats. Neither for that matter was Yeats when he was crusading for Life. There was practically no name that he wasn't called by the corpses of his time.[111]

Kavanagh identifies with Yeats against Yeats's imitators or unworthy ephebes, particularly Higgins and Clarke. In 1954, pressed in court about his rejection of 'the pigmy literature that was produced by the so-called Irish literary renaissance', he denied that he meant Yeats: 'No, Yeats is Yeats. In the last analysis I would not include him.'[112] In 1936 MacNeice cherished 'Yeats and his mask' amidst political and literary 'squads which walk in step'.[113] Perhaps his Irish successors invoke Yeats the father when they feel that poetry itself is on trial.

Kavanagh's literary relation to the *Dublin Magazine* complicates the term 'counter-revival' as a synonym for 'anti-colonial'. AE introduced him to the Irish literary world, and his work appeared amidst poetry and prose by Protestant and Catholic writers. Nor do poems such as 'Beech Tree', 'Morning', 'Dark Ireland' and 'Shancoduff' look incongruous there, although they might be livelier than most of their surroundings. Quinn separates tendencies which were, in fact, jumbled together (not only for Kavanagh) when she says: 'Literary Revival ideology began to compete with Georgian neo-Romanticism as an influence on his country verses . . . Irish rural poetry in the wake of the Literary Revival was inhospitable to Roman Catholic transcendentalism and, especially, to agricultural realism.'[114] *Dublin Magazine* poetry combined the rural, the Romantic and the transcendental in various structural and theological mixes: it remained for Kavanagh to create a concrete blend. In 'Shancoduff' 'sleety winds', 'rushy beards' and 'poor' poet deflate a variety of father-poets' idioms, including *The Wind among the Reeds* and Colum's 'Drover' (already satirised in *Ulysses*). But the visionary pursuit is reanimated as well as 'shaken' by extra-literary voices:

> The sleety winds fondle the rushy beards of Shancoduff
> While the cattle-drovers sheltering in the Featherna Bush
> Look up and say: 'Who owns them hungry hills
> That the water-hen and snipe must have forsaken?
> A poet? Then by heavens he must be poor'
> I hear and is my heart not badly shaken?

The images of Kavanagh's earlier poetry—including 'hungry hills', 'Clay-faced sucklers of spade-handles', 'a dark people' despoiling Eden—are, of course, transmuted in the synthesis of *The Great Hunger* (1942). This powerful swerve was less immediately from Yeats—although Yeats's Sligo localism counted so much that

Kavanagh had to misread it as alien—than from AE, James Stephens and Colum. It had been fostered by the prose realists, O'Faolain and O'Connor, as well as by more direct experience of Dublin's 'peasant-poets'. In section XIII the poem ironically claims its anti-pastoral authenticity and authority, turning 'little lyrical fields' into claustrophobic 'little acres'. Kavanagh's satire encompasses Yeatsian cultural theory ('Without the peasant base civilisation must die'), the small farmer extolled in state-iconography, and the 'star-lovely art' of his own *juvenilia*. But the contemporary poetry blasted out of the water is that of the rival ephebes, Higgins and Fallon: 'He loves fresh women . . . Unless the clay is in the mouth the singer's singing is useless'. The Cuala Press (thanks to O'Connor) published the poem.

The Great Hunger and MacNeice's *Autumn Journal* (1939) are very different works. But, in the context of Yeats and of Irish literary shifts between 1930 and 1942, they constitute long swerves by strong poets in complementary directions. Both poems are aware of T.S. Eliot as a foil to Yeats: Kavanagh devises his own free-verse rhythms and defining symbol ('clay'); *Autumn Journal* picks up the *Waste Land*'s London fragments and resolves MacNeice's inner dialectic between Yeats and Eliot with reference to the intensifying need for 'a positive art'. Both poems mention the unmentionable. Masturbation and 'boil[ing] the calves their gruel' affront the virile, wild Irish folk-landscape. *Autumn Journal* is the apotheosis of Mac-Neice's desire to go further than Yeats to meet the man in the street by 'breaking the barrier' not just between 'poetic and common syntax' but between 'poetic and common *material*' (PY 78). He notes that in 'Beautiful Lofty Things' Yeats 'is now able to take trains and banal dinner-parties and exalt them into mythology' (PY 152). Austin Clarke's review of *Autumn Journal* (along with Spender's *The Still Centre*, in which he finds technical sloppiness and 'passive suffering') is interestingly cool. He finds the poem 'very readable' but minimises its aesthetic interest: 'Most of it is keyed down to conversational level and held together by rhymes . . . The poem belongs to what has been called the new poetic school of reporting . . . a bright breezy vernacular surface'. Then Clarke takes political issue with MacNeice:

His work, like that of Mr Spender, expresses the mental predica-ment of the English intellectual, that ineffectual Fabianism, which usually leads merely to intellectual dilettantism or a romantic inter-

est in other people's revolutions. Ireland still continues to worry
Mr MacNeice and he devotes a section to this benighted country.
Mr MacNeice is prepared, apparently, to plunge Europe into a
catastrophic war to save the Czechs and other small nations, but
becomes the complete moralist when it comes to his own country
and adopts a manner which we usually associate with the typical
West Briton.[115]

With regard to reportage or journalism: just as Kavanagh draws on
contemporary prose-narrative when he floods the lyric poem with
untidy life; so MacNeice similarly reaches for modes of 1930s
realism when he re-orders the work of a decade. Clarke's defensive
perception of MacNeice's politics may also be relevant to how
Autumn Journal turns the lyric inside out. Yeats haunts section XVI
in which 'Meditations in Time of Civil War', 'Easter 1916' and the
arguments between Yeats and Maud Gonne inform the dilemmas of
1938-9:

> Nightmare leaves fatigue:
>   We envy men of action
> Who sleep and wake, murder and intrigue
>   Without being doubtful, without being haunted.
> And I envy the intransigence of my own
>   Countrymen who shoot to kill and never
> See the victim's face become their own
>   Or find his motives sabotage their motives.
> So reading the memoirs of Maud Gonne,
>   Daughter of an English mother and a soldier father,
> I notice how a single purpose can be founded on
>   A jumble of opposites . . .

It is a tricky question as to whether isolationism/ neutrality
affected Irish poetry as it did Irish society. Perhaps here again Yeats
had usefully broken a rule and provided a model, while pretending
not do do so. (In omitting Owen *et al.* from the *Oxford Book*, he
was, in part, protecting his residual credentials as Irish 'national'
poet.) It is because the sequences of the 1920s implicitly meditate on
European as well as Irish war that their dramatic and dialectical
precedent energises *Autumn Journal*. Presumably Clarke's Irish
Ireland jeer ('West Briton') reacts to MacNeice's critique of the Free
State (alongside the North): 'Let the round tower stand aloof | In a

world of bursting mortar! | Let the school-children fumble their
sums | In a half-dead language; | Let the censor be busy on the
books . . .' The echo of Yeatsian denunciation links a ubiquitous
adjective for Yeats—'aloof'—with an icon of Irish antiquarianism to
accuse contemporary cultural and literary nationalism of evading
history. F. R. Higgins had difficulty in striking a similar note when
he wrote poems about censorship and neutrality. 'Exhortation'
(1933) tries the strategy of fulsomely celebrating the ancient Irish
saints and scribes who 'caught . . . God's sweetness', as a preliminary
to requesting 'Books without censors; so shall our island be | A
shrine of living mightiness'; but the *plamás* draws the sting. 'O,
Hawks Claw-Clinched', published in the *Dublin Magazine* (July-
September 1939) is a veiled attack on neutrality's 'pastured slopes'. It
conjures Yeats ('our last bard') from his French grave, while being
poetically and politically weakened by the idiom it takes to be
Yeats's legacy:

> O, hawks, claw-clinched and bronze-plated
> On your sun-splintered forts,
> Brave winds be your perch to blaze on
> The crows in our pastured slopes.
>
> War-footed and braced by blood-music—
> Your poise is on perilous steps,
> Remote from the grass-quiet humours
> Of magpies in evening dress . . .
>
> Here willows with timbers for harpers
> Are lively; and yet our last bard
> Lies under the grin of a gargoyle,
> With potions once brewed by the dark . . .

'Blood-music' which, like the symbolic hawks, seems a quasi-fascist
retort to fascism, is a term also used by Higgins in his radio-dispute
with MacNeice earlier that year (July). After repudiating 'English
verse-speech' as 'chaotic', and celebrating Ireland's unbroken 'racial
rhythm' and 'ancient, yet everlasting, soil', Higgins continues: 'I am
afraid, Mr MacNeice, you, as an Irishman, cannot escape from your
blood, nor from our blood-music that brings the racial character to
mind. Irish poetry remains a creation happily, fundamentally rooted
in rural civilisation, yet aware and in touch with the elementals of

the future.' MacNeice, perhaps vindicated by the future and by the deconstruction of Irish 'rural civilisation' in *The Great Hunger*, replies: 'I have the feeling that you have side-tracked me into an Ireland *versus* England match. I am so little used to thinking of poetry in terms of race-consciousness that no doubt this was very good for me.' Earlier he has remarked that, on Higgins's criteria, 'there is more likelihood of good poetry appearing among the Storm Troopers of Germany than in the cosmopolitan communities of Paris or New York'.[116]

One product of MacNeice's trip to Ireland—thinking about Yeats, meeting the Dublin intelligentsia, visiting the west and the Glens of Antrim—was 'The Closing Album'. In this sequence Yeats's principal locales, Dublin and the west, once again become landscapes of European war. Thus in 'Sligo and Mayo' a series of apparently casual impressions—'turkeys | Gobbling', 'falling earrings | Of fuchsias red as blood', 'stumps of hoary bog-oak'—undermine security until touristic décor is transformed into a symbolism that points beyond Ireland: 'The coal-black turf-stacks rose against the darkness | Like the tombs of nameless kings'. More bluntly in 'Galway' 'a hundred swans | Dreaming on the harbour' encounter the refrain 'The war came down on us here'. The sequence ends with a 'nameless', and hence displaced, poem about poetry and (western) pastoral made 'unreal' by history. 'Muslin' picks up on a milkmaid image of fields 'sprigged with haycocks' in the earlier 'Sligo and Mayo':

> And why should the sea maintain its turbulence, its elegance,
> And draw a film of muslin down the sand
> With each receding wave?
>
> And why, now it has happened,
> Should the atlas still be full of the maps of countries
> We never shall see again?

Published (as 'The Coming of War') in MacNeice's Cuala Press collection, *The Last Ditch* (1940), 'The Closing Album' might even be read as his elegy for Yeats. Peter McDonald notes that the first poem, 'Dublin'

> is cast in one of the characteristically Yeatsian metres, identified by MacNeice as 'the short-line poem with three or four stresses to a

line', in which the technical difficulty is 'so to control the rhythms that the poem does not get into a skid'. 'Dublin' recalls . . . 'Easter 1916' with its imagery of stone and water, and its equivocal attitude . . . to the historical characters who harden into figures of national myth ('O'Connell, Grattan, Moore').[117]

The opening lines, 'Grey brick upon brick, | Declamatory bronze | On sombre pedestals', also characterise the architecture of Yeatsian style; and the equivocally viewed statues seem carefully divided between a poet, Catholic and Ascendancy political leaders and 'Nelson on his pillar | Watching his world collapse'. The various worlds collapsing include the early twentieth-century interaction between literature and history, beauty and terror, evoked by 'The bullet on the wet | Streets, the crooked deal, | The steel behind the laugh, | The Four Courts burnt'. Stone and water are fundamental to Mac-Neice's own dialectic and to his conflicts regarding Ireland. When he appropriates the river of 'Easter 1916', the 'living stream' that questions revolutionary necessity, he insinuates how an architectural aesthetic might indeed give way to the more fluid model that Yeats's ballad secretes under historical pressure. Thus 'the brewery tugs and the swans | On the balustraded stream' also poise the two aesthetics that part company in 'Galway'—'balustraded stream' balances architecture and water. 'Dublin' revises Yeats, not only where it introduces tugs and porter, but in its approach to history:

> And the mist on the Wicklow hills
> Is close, as close
> As the peasantry were to the landlord,
> As the Irish to the Anglo-Irish,
> As the killer is close one moment
> To the man he kills,
> Or as the moment itself
> Is close to the next moment.

'Close' mutates from atmospheric oppressiveness to socio-cultural proximity and symbiosis, to the ironic intimacy of murder, to the anti-climax of mere temporal succession. The chiasmic rhyme 'moment' reinforces the critique of Irish claustrophobia, while the last two lines endorse 'Changes minute by minute' in 'Easter 1916' and diminish the preceding images to 'a past order of things'. This, indeed, forbids a hardening into myth and implies openness to the future. Yet MacNeice's elegiac salute, 'Augustan capital | Of a

Gaelic nation . . . You give me time for thought . . . O greyness run to flower', underlines what the poem has taken from Yeats | Dublin as 'the toppling hour' changes literary bearings.

Change is also the theme of Auden's pre-war 'In Memory of W.B. Yeats': 'In the nightmare of the dark | All the dogs of Europe bark'. Stan Smith suggests convincingly that this elegy 'takes up and extends Yeats's debate with death and historical responsibility in "The Man and the Echo"'.[118] But if Auden, too, places Yeats's legacy in an ominous European context, 'the Irish vessel' and 'mad Ireland' are fairly abstract counters (the former imbued with too little agency, the latter with too much) in his opposition between 'dark cold day' and poetry's 'healing fountain'. MacNeice points out the Yeatsian character of Auden's 'stylisation' (PY 157), but this is precisely the element of Yeats's technique that the strategic impressionism of 'The Closing Album' suspects. He cut five poems from the sequence, as first published, which are less oblique about public and personal crisis. A range of ways in which Yeats's poetry negotiates the 'curse' of history are 'modified in the guts' of Mac-Neice's multiple valediction.

The Poetry of W.B. Yeats engages with Yeats on more levels than do comparable critiques by MacNeice's Irish and English con-temporaries. It replies to misunderstandings of the mask: '"So I am to speak only as myself," the poet might say, "my whole self, and nothing but myself?" If you know what my whole self and my only self is, you know a lot more than I do'" (PY 146). (Earlier, Mac-Neice argued: 'the fact that [Yeats] sees the world through a series of eccentric home-made frames . . . does not mean that he sees it false; if there is a glass in those frames to save him from the winds which afflicted D.H. Lawrence, it is only plain glass, not stained or frosted'.[119]) And it reaches beyond culture and politics to the crucial zone where form and metaphysics intersect: 'Yeats's formalising activity began when he *thought* about the world . . .' Equally, as in his poetry of the 1930s, MacNeice registers the philosophical and historical pressures that have made it so hard for 'my generation' to conceive the relation between thought and form in such terms. ('Dublin' refers to itself as 'a juggler's trick'.) He is the only ephebe both to receive Yeats dialectically and to develop the Yeatsian dialectic.

MacNeice's remark that Yeats's Irish successors wrote 'their verses carefully' but there 'is rarely much meat on their poems' implies the need to rend what Yeats had made 'sole or whole'.

Similarly, Kavanagh put meat—images, cadence and speech-rhythms—on a type of quasi-mystical rural lyric which had not kept pace with Yeats's own development. Thus both poets found literary and cultural resources which fortified them against 'idealisation'. I have suggested that, during the 1930s, Clarke (the rejected *voyeur*) and Higgins (the favourite son) were inhibited from 'capable imagination' by over-literal readings of Yeats: Higgins was incorporated into his later aesthetic; Clarke could not make Celtic-Romanesque and Gaelic metre more than variants within an existing field. Further, such 'idealisation' is tied in with ideological horizons fixed by Irish nationalism in general, rather than by the half-fragmented, half-evolutionary 'Revival' in particular. Of course, this elder pair of Protestant and Catholic poets grew up in the period of literary-political optimism. For Kavanagh, as irrationally and rationally hostile to Clarke as to Higgins, this was 'an Ireland which had only recently been invented . . . a general bedlam going on which gave everyone the notion that great spiritual activity was in the air'.[120] It may be relevant to painful disjunctions between poetry and nationalism that Bloom calls the Covering Cherub 'a demon of continuity; his baleful charm imprisons the present in the past'.[121] The Second World War proves unexpectedly significant in underlining protectionist attitudes to language, subject-matter and 'English' or European poetry. These attitudes suggest how deeply isolationism could be internalised. Kavanagh's swerve was, in part, a journey to the interior of 'All Ireland that froze for want of Europe' (*Lough Derg*). So while some poets—including Yeats himself at times—followed the Yeatsian letter, the spirit decamped elsewhere.

NOTES

1.   Harold Bloom, *Yeats* (New York: Oxford University Press, 1970), pp. 6-7.
2.   Louis MacNeice, *The Poetry of W.B. Yeats*—henceforth PY—(Oxford: Oxford University Press, 1941; rpt. London: Faber and Faber, 1967), p. 61.
3.   Bloom, *Yeats*, pp. 108-9.
4.   Bloom, *Yeats*, p. 86.
5.   Harold Bloom, *The Anxiety of Influence* (New York: Oxford University Press, 1973), p. 32.
6.   Robert Farren, *The Course of Irish Verse* (London: Sheed and Ward, 1948), p.78.

7. Bloom, *Anxiety of Influence*, p. 122.
8. Stan Smith, 'Persuasions to Rejoice: Auden's Oedipal Dialogues with W.B. Yeats', in *'The Language of Learning and the Language of Love' : Auden Studies 2* (Oxford: Clarendon Press, 1994), 155-63.
9. Bloom, *Anxiety of Influence*, p. 5.
10. Samuel Beckett, 'Recent Irish Poetry', *The Bookman* (August 1934), rpt. in (ed.), Seamus Deane, *The Field Day Anthology of Irish Literature*, III (Derry: Field Day, 1991), 244-8 (p. 245).
11. Patrick Kavanagh, 'William Butler Yeats', in *Collected Pruse* (London: Macgibbon and Kee, 1967), 254-6 (p. 256).
12. F.R. Higgins, 'Yeats as Irish Poet', in (ed.) Stephen Gwynn, *Scattering Branches* (London: Macmillan, 1940), 145-55 (p. 149).
13. Elizabeth Butler Cullingford, *Gender and History in Yeats's Love Poetry* (Cambridge: Cambridge University Press, 1993), p. 13.
14. Seamus Heaney, 'Yeats as an Example?', in *Preoccupations: Selected Prose 1968-1978* (London: Faber and Faber, 1980), 98-114 (pp. 99-113).
15. Monk Gibbon, *The Masterpiece and the Man* (London: Rupert Hart-Davis, 1959), p. 106; p. 207.
16. Farren, *Course of Irish Verse*, p. 79.
17. Austin Clarke, *A Penny in the Clouds: More Memories of Ireland and England* (London: Routledge and Kegan Paul; rpt. Dublin: Moytura Press, 1990), p. 53. This memoir repeats material on Yeats from *First Visit to England and Other Memories* (Dublin: The Bridge Press, 1945). Clarke's similar contribution to *Irish Literary Portraits* (see below) suggests that certain impressions had set, unexamined, in concrete.
18. Sean O'Faolain, 'Yeats and the Younger Generation', *Horizon*, 5:25 (January 1942), 43-54 at p. 48.
19. Gibbon, *The Masterpiece and the Man*, p. 168.
20. 'Yeats came along with a sneer, and said: I hear, Lord Dunsany, that you are going to supply groundsel for AE's canaries. The sneer brought the project [to found a literary review] to naught . . .' (George Moore, *Hail and Farewell*, edited by Richard Cave [Gerrards Cross, Bucks: Colin Smythe, 1976]), p. 580.
21. *Dublin Magazine* [henceforward *DM*], 5:1 (January-March 1930), 56. In another review 'Y. O.' (AE) protests, with a different emphasis, 'against a tendency . . . to reject as un-Irish, as not of the main stream of Irish culture, those writers who are more inspired by the old or new thought of the world outside Ireland . . .'. He also says: 'We have had too much of this poetry decorated with recognisably Irish symbols . . .'. *Irish Statesman*, 28 December 1929, 337-8.
22. 'Portrait of James Joyce', *DM*, 7:2 (April-June, 1932), 48.
23. See Jane Russell, *James Starkey/ Seumas O'Sullivan: A Critical Biography* (Mississauga, Ontario: Associated University Presses, 1987), p. 50, pp. 79-87.
24. See Patrick Sheeran, 'The Idiocy of Irish Rural Life Reviewed', *Irish Review*, 5 (Autumn 1988), 27-33, for a critique of this tendency.
25. Antoinette Quinn, *Patrick Kavanagh: Born-Again Romantic* (Dublin: Gill and Macmillan, 1991), p. 160.
26. Padraic Colum, *The Poet's Circuits: Collected Poems of Ireland* (Oxford: Oxford University Press, 1960; rpt. Mountrath, Portlaoise: Dolmen Press, 1981), Foreword, p. xii.

27.   *Irish Literary Portraits: W. R. Rodgers's Broadcast Conversations* (London: BBC, 1972), p.19.

28.   'William Butler Yeats', in Gwynn, *Scattering Branches*, 183-229 (p. 196). Strong's seems the most subtle analysis in this memorial tribute. He emphasises how Wilde taught Yeats the uses of the mask, and says: 'Reverence chilled and irritated him . . . Like many a shy man who hides behind a formal manner, he relied on the discernment of his companion' (pp. 225-6).

29.   *Irish Literary Portraits*, pp. 2-5.

30.   *Ibid.*, pp. 5-6.

31.   *DM* 13:1 (January-March 1938), 63.

32.   Clarke, *Penny in the Clouds*, pp. 11, 81.

33.   *Ibid.*, p. 83.

34.   *Ibid.*, p. 206. Prior to their meeting, Yeats refers to Clarke, in ominous inverted commas, as '"my biographer"' (ALS to Ethel Mannin, June 1936, Sligo County Library).

35.   Austin Clarke, *Selected Poems*, edited by W.J. Mc Cormack (Harmondsworth, Middlesex: Penguin Books, 1992), pp. 1-3; 14.

36.   Clarke, *Penny in the Clouds*, p. 21.

37.   Susan Halpern, *Austin Clarke: His Life and Works* (Dublin: Dolmen Press, 1974), pp. 23-7.

38.   Gregory A. Schirmer, *The Poetry of Austin Clarke* (Notre Dame, Indiana: University of Notre Dame Press, 1983), p. 14.

39.   Clarke, *Penny in the Clouds*, p. 82.

40.   Terence Brown, 'The Counter-Revival 1930-1965: Poetry', *Field Day Anthology of Irish Writing*, III, pp. 129-34 at p. 130.

41.   W. J. Mc Cormack, 'Austin Clarke: The Poet as Scapegoat of Modernism', in (eds) Patricia Coughlan and Alex Davis, *Modernism and Ireland: The Poetry of the 1930s* (Cork: Cork University Press, 1995), pp. 75-102 at p. 77, see n. 69 below; Austin Clarke, *Selected Poems*, p. 2.

42.   See Alan Heuser (ed.), *Selected Literary Criticism of Louis MacNeice* (Oxford: Clarendon Press, 1987), pp. 57-74 at p. 57.

43.   Gibbon, *The Masterpiece and the Man*, p. 183.

44.   Terence Brown, *Ireland: A Social and Cultural History 1922-79* (London: Fontana Paperbacks, 1981), p. 167.

45.   Peter Sirr, 'Myth and Reality in the Poetry of Padraic Fallon', unpublished thesis, Trinity College, Dublin (1985), p. 7.

46.   *DM* 10:4 (October-December 1935), 24-9.

47.   Herbert E. Palmer, DM 8:2 (April-June 1933), 19.

48.   For example, Andrew E. Malone's round-up of 'The Irish Theatre in 1935': The year 1935 revealed in a most remarkable manner the poverty of the Irish theatre.' And on the *Standard*'s view of *The Silver Tassie* as 'propaganda against the Christian faith': 'Thus was the return of Sean O'Casey to the Abbey Theatre celebrated in his native city.' *DM* 11:1 (January-March 1936), 48.

49.   Sean O'Faolain, 'Daniel Corkery', *DM* 11:2 (April-June 1936), 49-61 at pp. 61, 54.

50.   *DM* 7:1 (January-March 1932), pp. 53-6. For O'Hegarty and his 'exciting double life', see Wayne K. Chapman and James Helyar, 'P.S. O'Hegarty and the Yeats Collection at the University of Kansas' (*YA 10*, 221-38). O'Hegarty was equally tough on Aodh de Blacam's Corkeryite *A First Book of Irish Literature*: 'This

business of trying to cramp literature within arbitrary limits, at first getting a theory and then cutting up facts to fit it, is merely a part of the fanatical narrowness which is poisoning social and international relations all the world over' (*DM* 10:1 [January-March 1935], 65).

51. *Times Literary Supplement*, 23 July 1931, 578.
52. *DM* 9:2 (April-June 1934), 58.
53. *Ibid.*, 65.
54. DM 13:1 (January-March 1938), 63.
55. 'W.B. Yeats', *DM* 14:2 (April-June 1939), 6-10 at pp. 8-10.
56. *Ibid.*, 10.
57. 'Irish Poetry Today', *DM* 10:1 (January-March 1935), 26-32.
58. See Brown, *Ireland: A Social and Cultural History*, p. 124.
59. 'Irish Poetry Today', p. 26.
60. *Selected Literary Criticism of Louis MacNeice*, pp. 10-44 at pp. 40-1.
61. *Ibid.*, p. 15; p. 40.
62. *Ibid.*, pp. 18-19.
63. 'Irish Poetry Today', p.29.
64. See Vivian Mercier, *Beckett/Beckett* (New York: Oxford University Press, 1977), p. 39.
65. Mc Cormack, 'The Poet as Scapegoat of Modernism', *Modernism and Ireland*, pp. 89, 96-7.
66. Beckett, 'Recent Irish Poetry', *Field Day Anthology of Irish Literature*, III, pp. 244-5.
67. For example, Michael Smith (ed.), *Irish Poetry: The Thirties Generation* (Dublin: New Writers Press, 1971); J. C. C. Mays, 'Flourishing and Foul: Ideology, Six Poets and the Irish Building Industry', *Irish Review*, 8 (Spring 1990), 6-11; *Modernism and Ireland*. On political aspects, see above pp. 25-6.
68. Mercier, *Beckett/Beckett*, p. 39.
69. 'The Poet as Scapegoat of Modernism', p. 81. Mc Cormack's proposal that Clarke might represent 'the anti-modern prejudices of modernism [such as] its cults of mediævalism and primitivism', while Beckett 'is cosmopolitan, disaffiliated and prosaic', begs the question of whether, and how, the problematic category 'modernism' applies to Yeats as well as to his various Irish poet-successors.
70. Sirr, 'Myth and Reality in the Poetry of Padraic Fallon', p. 8.
71. *Selected Criticism of Louis MacNeice*, p. 14.
72. See Edna Longley, 'The Room Where MacNeice Wrote "Snow"', *The Living Stream: Literature and Revisionism in Ireland* (Newcastle on Tyne: Bloodaxe books, 1994), 252-70.
73. *Selected Literary Criticism of Louis MacNeice*, p. 13.
74. Clarke, 'W. B. Yeats', p. 10.
75. 'A Letter from Ireland', *Poetry*, 49:6 (March 1937), 336. J. J. Hogan also mentions 'strange omissions', *Ireland Today*, 2:1 (January 1937), 83.
76. 'Notes on the Way', *Time and Tide*, 19 December 1936, 1804; *Daily Worker*, 16 December 1936, 7.
77. 'Poetry Today', *Left Review*, 5: 16 (January 1937), 899-900.
78. 'Mr Yeats Fumbles', *New Statesman and Nation*, 5 December 1936, 942.
79. *New English Weekly*, 11 March 1937, 431.
80. See Cullingford, *Gender and History*, ch. 14.

ANNUAL 12 161

YEATS ANNUAL 12 161

81. Kavanagh, *Collected Pruse*, p. 225.
82. *Irish Literary Portraits*, pp. 173-4.
83. 'The Gallivanting Poet', *Irish Writing*, 3 (November 1947), 62-70. 'The trouble is that Higgins was self-deceived by his fake world' (p. 65).
84. Cullingford, *Gender and History*, p. 169.
85. *Irish Literary Portraits*, p. 178.
86. *Ibid.*, p. 180. On the other hand, O'Connor portrays Higgins as a shrewd operator who deceived him and Yeats in Abbey Theatre affairs (*I&R* 345).
87. From Higgins: 'The Little Clan', 'Father and Son', 'The Old Jockey', 'Padraic O'Conaire—Gaelic Storyteller','Song for the Clatter Bones', 'The Ballad of O'Bruadir'; from MacNeice: 'The Individualist Speaks', 'Circe', 'Turf-stacks', 'An Eclogue for Christmas'.
88. 'Modern and "Modern" Poets (1892-1935)', *Irish Ecclesiastical Record*, 49: 3 (March 1937), 249.
89. In *Modern Poetry: A Personal Essay* (rpt. Oxford: Clarendon Press, 1968), p. 139. Yeats, in a conversation of 1914, had articulated his belief in a traditional vocabulary: '"Ireland has an imaginative peasantry . . . and there is a predominant tendency on our part to lay stress on association. Poetry comes, I believe, from associative values. Among a peasantry, life changes so little from generation to generation that every article one possesses takes on a heavy charge of personal meaning. Note, for instance, what a host of human experiences is called forth by the mere mention of a wooden spade. The very word 'spade' has a value strictly spiritual which the word 'sewing-machine' has not. To your own self repeat the words 'spinning-wheel' and 'thread factory.' Which one has its associative value? The one is saturated with poetic meaning; the other conjures up industrial slavery."' (*I&R* 128).
90. Gwynn, *Scattering Branches*, pp. 147-54.
91. Aodh de Blacam, *Gaelic Literature Surveyed* (Dublin and Cork: Talbot Press, 1929), p. 37; Higgins, *DM* 4:3 (July-September 1929), 62.
92. Compare Kavanagh on O'Conaire: 'that celebrated synthetic tramp . . . with his goat tethered outside the Bailey Restaurant', *Collected Pruse*, p. 232.
93. Muldoon uses an excerpt from 'Tendencies in Modern Poetry', printed in the *Listener* (27 July 1939), 185-6, as epigraph for the *Faber Book of Contemporary Irish Poetry* (1986) to imply differences between an atavistic and a pluralistic aesthetic. In fact, MacNeice became friendly with Higgins after the broadcast, and he refers to him as an 'excellent craftsman' (*PY* 183). See quotations from the broadcast, pp. 151.
94. *Anxiety of Influence*, p. 71.
95. 'Poetry in Ireland Today', *The Bell*, 16:1 (April 1948), 36-43 at p. 39.
96. *Anxiety of Influence*, p. 68.
97. Review of Yeats's *Collected Plays*, *Selected Literary Criticism*, p. 182.
98. Review of *Last Poems and Plays*, ibid., pp. 116-17.
99. Rpt. in (ed.) Alan Heuser, *Selected Prose of Louis MacNeice* (Oxford: Clarendon Press, 1990), p. 33.
100. Rpt. in *The Destructive Element* (London: Jonathan Cape, 1935), 115-131 (pp. 128-30). Samuel Hynes's article, 'Yeats and the Poets of the Thirties', in (eds) Raymond J. Porter and James D. Brophy, *Modern Irish Literature* (New York: Twayne, 1972), is misleading in that it quotes Spender's retrospective view in *World Within World* (1951).

101. Gwynn, *Scattering Branches*, p. 178.
102. 'Yeats as an Example', rpt. in James Hall and Martin Steinmann (eds.), *The Permanence of Yeats* (New York: Macmillan, 1950), 344-51 at p. 350.
103. *Selected Literary Criticism*, p. 171.
104. See Quinn, *Patrick Kavanagh*, pp. 166-9.
105. 'The Gallivanting Poet', p. 63. See Hubert Butler's riposte in '*Envoy* and Mr Kavanagh', *Escape from the Anthill* (Mullingar: Lilliput Press, 1985), 153-62.
106. *Collected Pruse*, p. 254.
107. Quinn, *Patrick Kavanagh*, p. 167.
108. *Ibid.*, p. 170.
109. *Collected Pruse*, p. 255. MacNeice also thought 'the septuagenarian virility . . . sometimes too exhibitionistic' (unworthy of father?), *Selected Literary Criticism*, p. 117.
110. 'Poetry in Ireland Today', pp. 37-8.
111. *Kavanagh's Weekly*, 1: 5 (10 May 1952), 2.
112. *Collected Pruse*, p. 187.
113. Review of *Dramatis Personae*, *Criterion*, 16:62 (October 1936), 120-2 at p. 122.
114. Quinn, *Patrick Kavanagh*, p. 41.
115. *DM* 14:3 (July-September 1939), 82-4. Clarke's patronising review of *The Poetry of W. B. Yeats* continues in the same nationalistic vein, and clearly resents Mac-Neice's remarks about his own Irish generation: 'Apart from Yeats, he dismisses most of contemporary Irish poets in a few lines of ill-disguised contempt and, though it is obvious . . . that he is little acquainted with Irish letters as a whole, this does not prevent him from indulging in disparagement. He regards the Irish literary movement as merely a side issue . . . . Mr. MacNeice's real object is to classify Yeats among the modernists . . . . The modern problem of English poetry in recent years is an interesting study in itself, but it has been responsible for a great deal of topical criticism which is too often frivolous when it is not doctrinaire.' (*DM* 16:2 [April-June 1941], 75-7.
116. See note 93 above.
117. Peter McDonald, *Louis MacNeice: The Poet in his Contexts* (Oxford: Clarendon Press, 1991), p. 100.
118. Smith, 'Persuasions to Rejoice', p. 162.
119. *Selected Literary Criticism*, p. 66.
120. 'The Gallivanting Poet', p. 67.
121. *Anxiety of Influence*, p. 39.

'When the newspapers have forgotten me': Yeats, Obituarists, and Irishness

R. F. Foster

ON 28 JANUARY 1939, W. B. Yeats died at his long-established home on Cap Martin. He had previously lived 'several years' in New York, where 'socialists flocked to him as an intellectual leader and standard bearer'; then, 'with his greatest work *The Wind Among the Reeds* behind him he retired to the seclusion of the South of France'. Previously he pursued 'a brilliant academic career' at Cambridge where his students included John Masefield. 'He had one son, who died'.

This splendidly counterfactual version of Yeats's life retailed by the *Cleveland Press*[1] comes as something of a diversion after the blanket coverage dispensed by the Press Association to the world's newspapers in early February 1939. Literary evaluations and special numbers of journals piled up; reminiscences accumulated; one is left with the impression of a continuous memorial service, in default of a public burial in Ireland. Certainly, the absence of such an occasion was sharply felt. Even the Taoiseach's telegram of sympathy had ended pointedly: 'We hope that his body will be laid to rest in his native soil',[2] while the Abbey Theatre directorate had been even more peremptory : 'Ireland insists that Yeats be buried here Dean of St Patrick's offers grave in Cathedral'.[3] But there had never been any question of that, as George Yeats made clear to close friends. 'He returns, by sea, to Sligo in September', she told Thomas Mac-

Greevy. 'That is earlier than he had asked. His actual words were "If I die here bury me up there and then in a year's time when the newspapers have forgotten me, dig me up and plant me in Sligo." He did not want the sort of funeral AE had.'[4] A family conference amplified this, as his sister Lollie confirmed. 'We all agreed there must be no public funeral. Also he said "I want to be buried as a poet, not as a public man".'[5] There was, in fact, a service in St Patrick's Dublin on 7 February, where Lollie sharply noted that her brother's Catholic friends were constrained not to enter the church ('they should work now to get that obsolete law of the Church done away with. Now that they are "on top" & also in the majority it seems to me so foolish'[6]); and later on, a London memorial service at St Martin's in the Fields on 16 March, arranged by John Masefield.[7] But in one respect at least, the dying poet's expectations were not fulfilled; for the newspapers showed little sign of forgetting him.

For their different audiences, journalists produced different versions. American papers were heavily swayed by Macmillan's recent publication of the one-volume *Autobiographies*, entitled *Autobiography of William Butler Yeats*, which had come out in September 1938; some articles combined the function of review and obituary, and most stressed the early life and family background as presented in those disingenuous masterpieces. (This, as will be seen below, exercised a decided influence on discussion of Yeats's family tradition and influences in Ireland.) The *New York Times* honoured him with a first leader, as 'the first Irish and perhaps the first English man of letters of his time'[8]—followed by a lengthy appreciation from Padraic Colum in the *Book Review* a fortnight later.[9] This dealt knowledgeably with Yeats's career in its many phases, making several points which would not be missed by *cognoscenti*: the Fays and others who had been squeezed out of the theatre movement after quarrels with Yeats were given their full due, though Colum admitted that the establishment of the Abbey remained 'an event in the history of the Irish mind'. In the end, he judged, Yeats was himself 'a Byzantine, one, like El Greco, strayed into the western world, and expressing in our time that unaccountable affinity that the Ireland of the ninth and tenth centuries had for Byzantine civilisation'. As a subtle evasion of the thorny question which would dominate many of the post-mortem evaluations—how Irish was Yeats?—this was worthy of the magus himself.

Others had similarly special interests to advance. The *New York Evening Post* was lapidary:

He ranked at his death as the First Poet of English. He was known more widely than any living Irishman except George Bernard Shaw. He was a writer of shining prose, poetic Irish plays, elegant essays, and constructive criticism of Irish art and letters. He was a Nationalist patriot when that took courage; he was a Senator of the Free State from 1922 to 1928; in 1923 he won the Nobel Prize.

Beyond that, he was a little daft.[10]

The *Providence Journal and Rhode Island Bulletin* recalled the poet's early contributions to the *Providence Sunday Journal*, and inferred from these that 'he held a warm spot in his affections for Providence and its people';[11] its obituarist owed much to Horace Reynolds, and ignored all Yeats's work since the 1890s except *Purgatory*, apparently included only because one of the paper's journalists had attended the Abbey first night. John Devoy's *Gaelic American* similarly followed its own agenda: the 'Irish renaissance of the 1920s' was emphasised, and Yeats's greatness was located in his influence on others (with a particular and rather surprising emphasis on Eugene O'Neill). His 'inability to be natural even when in the company of friends and associates brought him much sorrow and discomfort, in the later years of his life . . . his visible eccentricity of conduct and manner of dress seemed to annoy political and literary associates'.[12] Otherwise, most of the *Gaelic American*'s space was devoted to a reprint of Yeats's speech on the centenary of Robert Emmet, delivered at the New York Academy of Music on 28 February 1904—from the paper's viewpoint, the high point of Yeats's creative career (rather reminiscent of recent biographies of Maria Callas which imply that her chief achievement was to lose a lot of weight). Above all, however, he was a patriot—English contacts notwithstanding. 'He was ever active in the cause of freedom.'

On the other side of the Atlantic, the emphasis tended to be on his towering personality. There was some demurral about his arbitrary symbolism and wilful commitment to strange gods; *Cathleen ni Houlihan* was judged his greatest play, and the early work generally preferred (or at least emphasised) above the bewildering profusion of his last poems. (A rare exception was David Garnett in the *New Statesman*, who hailed the poems recently published in the *London Mercury* as his best work.[13]) *The Times* produced a lengthy, straightforward and comprehensive piece, choosing to stress Yeats's quarrels with conventional Irish nationalism from the time of *Responsibilities*; finally, though, 'Yeats's differences with his own countrymen seem insignificant when we take into view not merely what he gave Ireland but what Ireland, through him, has given to the world'.[14] A magisterial evaluation came, predictably, from Desmond MacCarthy in the *Sunday Times*, who still managed to strike the personal note. 'He was the only poet I ever talked with whose talk and attitude (pose if you like to call it) never allowed you to forget that he was a poet';[15] characteristic phrases were recalled or adapted ('I ought to spend ten years in a library and Lionel Johnson—ten years in a wilderness without a book') and the 'enigmatic impressiveness of his romantic appearance'.

Thomas Bodkin in the *Birmingham Post* again stressed the appearance, the personality, and the deliberate elaboration which 'sometimes irritated those who might have wished to be familiar with him'; there may be an autobiographical resonance here, which would explain the otherwise incomprehensible statement that Yeats was 'not a man who enjoyed friendships'.[16] Gogarty, writing in the *Evening Standard*, offered a fulsome contradiction.[17] But, generally, those who knew him took the opportunity to make clear why they had not been allowed to know him better.

The Irish note was different, and allowed the expression of some intimate enmities. In the *Observer* Stephen Gwynn concentrated on Yeats as 'a great personality', and recalled his impact from early meetings at Dowden's house. Beneath the artistic pose he was capable of shrewdness 'even to cynicism'; but his artistic sincerity was uncompromising.

> First and last he was smashing idols in the market-place; at first, the cheap rhetoric of drum-beating ballads, false models in poetry; later, justifying work which his artistic sense approved as vital, while the crowd denounced it as 'an insult to Ireland'. First and last, he was a champion of freedom—but, above all, against the tyrannies of democracy. And in the end, the democracy which he never spared to resist and rebuke, marches, to its credit, behind his coffin.[18]

St John Ervine also wrote from a personal angle, emphasising Yeats's affectation and lofty approach to life: 'He had no common qualities, no small talk, no familiarities'; in conversation he preferred monologue, either holding the floor or leaving it; he was completely unable 'to be familiar with his friends'.[19] This provoked Smyllie of the *Irish Times*, writing as 'Nichevo', not only to deny that Yeats's Christian name was out of bounds (AE always called

him 'Willie') but also to give a memorable description of attempts to
teach Yeats golf at Carrickmines in the mid-1920s. ('Occasionally,
having played a shot, he would allow his club to fall to the ground
and stalk away after the ball, leaving me or [Alan] Duncan to
retrieve it. He would roar with laughter when Cruise [O'Brien]
foozled a shot; and in the clubhouse afterwards, when he insisted on
buying drinks for the three of us, although he took none himself, he
would regale us with vastly entertaining stories of his younger
days'.[20]) P. S. O'Hegarty wrote for the *Dublin Magazine* a piece that
appropriated Yeats in a different way, relating him to 'Revolutionary Ireland of his Time', stressing his commitment to the 1798
Centenary commemorations (where O'Hegarty had first
encountered him), and discussing *Cathleen ni Houlihan* as 'a play of
the captivity', whose impact was impossible to recapture in the independent Ireland of 1939.[21] And the *Irish Press* (currently serialising
Maud Gonne's *A Servant of the Queen*) produced a leader which
traced the canonical connection between Yeats, the literary revival
and Easter 1916.[22]

Overall, except for MacCarthy and a few other professional
critics, obituarists showed a distinct reluctance to evaluate the work,
except in a way that fitted the general interpretation of a man of
masks (Bodkin remarked that 'his prose writings are often tainted
by a slight affectation of a learning he did not really possess'). This
task was left to special issues like the commemoration number of
The Arrow, and a series of articles in *The Bell* the following year.
Here, a judicious review of the work and its development was
counterpointed with memories of the extraordinary personality
behind it, who would—it was generally accepted—dominate Irish
literature for the foreseeable future. Strikingly, a deliberate effort
was made to reclaim Yeats from the 'English' identification stressed
by MacCarthy, Garnett and others (even the *Irish Times* mischievously remarked that 'when, in 1930, the English Poet
Laureateship became vacant, he was made a candidate by leading
literary authorities in England'; and Lord Dunsany, asked for a reaction to the poet's death, likened his loss to that of Kipling, Barrie,
and Housman).[23] This approach was deliberately countered by P. S.
O'Hegarty, speaking for his generation, when he remarked: 'we felt
that Yeats and Russell were Ireland's in an intimate sense in which
Shaw and Moore were not'. Lennox Robinson also stressed that
'beside his gifts as poet, thinker and philosopher, he was pas-
sionately Irish—Irish, from his first meeting with John O'Leary

thirty-five years ago; Irish in his work as Senator of the Irish Free State; Irish to the last day of his life'.[24] (The implication that Yeats achieved Irishness only by political commitment was probably unintentional.) F. R. Higgins asserted that Yeats's artistic inspiration was authentically native-born, drawing as heavily and uncritically on the *Autobiographies* as nearly everybody else. The late poetry 'became more Gaelic in feeling', influenced by translations of Irish verse and songs (mediated, naturally, by Higgins himself). 'When we were together he sang in his own uncertain, shy, way some of these poems . . . In writing his own songs we worked together welding his occasionally meandering words to Gaelic tunes. That exercise was latterly his constant delight'.[25] Austin Clarke, in his very different way, also chose to stress Yeats's Irishness: 'no poet could be less representative of English genius than this Anglo-Irish poet'. Clarke went on to emphasize Yeats's openness to influence, a 'susceptibility to eddies and currents . . . increased by an astute awareness of literary fashions', but related his English dimension to Irish influence.

> In England the sheer art of [his] poetry has proved a useful influence and has schooled even the best known of the younger modernists. In Ireland, where the artistic tradition of the literary revival has not been broken, it is an imaginative incitement and great example rather than an influence. . . . English critics have tried to claim him for their tradition but, heard closely, his later music has that tremulous lyrical undertone which can be found in the Anglo-Irish eloquence of the eighteenth century.[26]

Thus the Irish critics of the next generation contested the claims of English obituarists to appropriate Yeats's death as a loss to 'English literature'.

There was, however, an exception. Thirty-five years before Yeats's death a profile had mischievously remarked: 'Mr Yeats has probably too little coarseness in his composition ever to become a national poet—even of Ireland—in the accepted meaning of the term'.[27] The validity of Yeats's credentials as the voice of his fellow-countrymen had for long been a matter of debate. In a leader celebrating his seventieth birthday nearly four years before, the *Irish Times* had confronted the question openly and rather defensively.[28] The same preoccupation was shared—for very different reasons—by old enemies who wrote for the Catholic press. For fifteen years before his death, Yeats's claims to Irishness had been vituperatively disputed; 'Pollexfen Yeats', the 'Pensioner' of the British government, and unabashed celebrant of the Freemason ritual at George Pollexfen's funeral, had by these very tokens disqualified himself from claims to nationality, even without the evidence of 'the foul Swan song' and the campaign on behalf of divorce. Daniel Corkery, apportioning literary citizenship in *Synge and Anglo-Irish Literature*, made much of the fact that Yeats spent a good deal of the year outside Ireland: even his residential qualifications were suspect. By 1939 the campaign against 'Anglo-Irish literature' was in full flood in the *Catholic Bulletin* (dominated by its editor, Father Timothy Corcoran, Professor of Eucation at University College) and the *Irish Monthly*; the death of Yeats declared open season on the enemy culture. In February 1939, discussing 'How to oust English literary influence', the *Bulletin* had cause to denounce 'the Outlanders' Academy of Literary Litter, who assembled at the call of Yeats and Shaw, and who have in more than one of their alluring statements taken pains to present themselves as dabblers in dirt, scholars in the sordid succession to the Sewage School of fifteen years ago';[29] and though no obituary of the late poet appeared, his name was pulled into articles such as 'The Freedom of the Press—Should Newspapers Be Controlled?'

> Let us take an example of the wrong proportion which many news-papers impose upon the news of our time. During the last month the Anglo-Irish poet, William Butler Yeats, died. Immediately every newspaper on which we could lay hands, Irish and foreign, pub-lished enthusiastic accounts of this writer's work as a poet, playwright and critic. He was represented as the supreme man of letters writing in English in our time.
>
> Now, we have no wish, when the man is newly dead, to deny him any credit to which he was entitled as an artist or a public man. We do not propose to recall in detail the many occasions on which con-scientious Catholic writers were obliged to condemn his works and to warn young Ireland against his influence. It is neither our wish nor our intention to usurp the place of Yeats's judge and to strike the balance of his account. Posterity will judge him in this world and he is already judged in the next. What we do insist upon is that a completely false idea of the man and of his achievements was given by those newspapers which published enthusiastic praises of his work and said nothing at all about his quarrel with the nation

and his quarrel with Christianity. . . . An account of him which said nothing whatsoever about his long war upon sacred things is not a truthful portrait of the man at all.[30]

The *Bulletin* decided to redress the balance: not through a general evaluation, but by recapitulating on a long-running campaign. Since the foundation of the *Irish Statesman* in 1922 the journal had denounced AE's and Yeats's 'essay to control Irish interests', which is how it interpreted Yeats's remark that 'Ireland has been put into our hands that we may shape it'.[31] In the *Bulletin*'s view that 'we' represented a Protestant claim on behalf of a 'New Ascendancy'. The scandal over *To-morrow* in 1924 fixed the battle lines.[32] The *Bulletin*'s strategy had been to claim that a Northern Protestant and the scion of Sligo Unionism had no right to speak for Ireland; much was made of the un-Irish sound of 'Pollexfen', as well as the non-Catholic nature of Yeats's and Russell's mystical beliefs. 'Some readers may have at that period felt that our emphasis on the un-Irish and utterly exotic character of these motives and aims was over-stressed', admitted the *Bulletin*; but since the demise of the *Statesman*, they felt that publication of correspondence[33] and the nature of Yeats's later writing fully vindicated them. And the poet's death enabled them to concentrate on what had long been an obsession: the fact that the greatest Irish poet was not, in point of fact, Irish at all.

The pieces by Higgins and Clarke in the *Arrow* indicate that Irish opinion in other quarters had already been slightly irritated by the way that English obituarists annexed Yeats for their own; even David Garnett's perceptive tribute had ended: 'his death is the greatest loss English literature could suffer'. Sean O'Faolain took a characteristically larger line in the *Spectator*: 'though he is by minor definition an Irish poet, he is by major definition a world poet'.[34] Even the *Irish Press*, while admitting Yeats's frequent absences from Ireland, made clear that 'not all the flattery of the outside world, not even the conferring of a Nobel prize, could tempt this poet away from his preoccupation with the life of his own country. . . . As a mystic he may have followed doubtful gleams and hovered on the verge of dim frontiers, but sooner or later he returned to Irish soil, there to find new material and fresh inspiration'.[35]

But the *Bulletin* took the opposite view, being all too ready to cede ownership on Ireland's behalf. In the first instalment of an article ominously entitled 'The Position of W. B. Yeats', Stephen

Quinn trawled through the obituaries to find the many 'special notices of his character as an English writer, and of the formative influences which went to give him his position in England'.[36] *The Times*'s notice provided valuable corroboration, being 'prominent and pointed in its affirmation of the dominant note: that note was less Yeats than Pollexfen'. The statement that 'Yeats belonged by birth to the Protestant Anglo-Irish' was triumphantly quoted; moreover, the *Daily Telegraph* was 'very definite as to the proper placing of this essentially English writer'. The *Telegraph* was particularly apposite for the *Bulletin's* purposes: its notice had begun 'English literature suffers a heavy loss in the death . . . of William Butler Yeats, the famous Irishman, who was the greatest living English poet . . . English because while he was Irish by birth and a passionate patriot, his language was English and as poet and artist he was the heir of a great English tradition'.[37] The *Autobiographies*, with their emphasis on the Pollexfen strain, and the celebration of Anglo-Irishry in the later poetry, provided further grist to the mill. Instancing the early influences of pre-Raphaelitism, Coleridge, Keats, Blake and Morris added up to only one thing: 'in no vital way was Mr Yeats entitled to be designated an Irish writer'. Better still, from the *Bulletin's* point of view, was an ill-judged tribute by Lennox Robinson (whose own satanic record as the author of 'The Madonna of Slieve Dun' in *To-morrow* was well known). In an interview Robinson remarked obscurely that Yeats 'was certainly among our Irish poets the equal of Moore, Mangan and Ferguson'.[38] Stephen Quinn took this to be an unintentional but cruelly accurate cutting down to size.

> [Robinson] ranked the poetry of W. B. Yeats with the poetry of—Thomas Moore, Esquire! No such note of discord, assuredly, would have been struck in the English literary world. That world knew its Yeats better than to mete out to him such cruel candour of appraisal.
> But as far as Catholic Ireland went, the evaluation was just about right.[39]

All this was too good to leave alone, and a month later Quinn returned with 'Further Placings for W. B. Yeats'.[40] The same issue contained an enraged article on 'The Sham Literature of the Anglo-Irish', sparked off by Father Stephen Brown who at the University College Literature Society had dared to take the affirmative side in debating 'Do We Owe Something To Anglo-Irish Literature'.[41] Perhaps incensed by this, Quinn threw all caution to the winds, denouncing the late poet for 'aping an aristocratic attitude, combining as its basis the Cromwellian foxhunter and other weird specimens such as the intrusive picture-jobber'. By now, moreover, a similar tone was heard elsewhere. Probably spurred on by the publication of Yeats's letters to AE,[42] Aodh de Blacam published a long denunciation of Yeats's un-national credentials in the *Irish Monthly* of March 1939. At the outset of Yeats's career 'we did account him one with our masters'; he had apparently devoted himself to Ireland; his great personality cast a magnetic spell; he was 'the most consummate of advertising agents' (notably over 'the grotesque Synge'); but in the end, his actual achievement was no more than that of a minor poet. In fact, he was corrupted by morbidity and supernaturalism. 'He was delicate in youth, he was not "a man's man", and his over-introspective nature made him aloof from the wholesome world'. Finally he emerged as 'the repudiator of the Gael'. De Blacam instanced damning evidence such as his arrogant letters issued from the Ascendancy fastness of Coole, and his 'mock-mysticism' ('he liked symbols as a child likes coloured stones: not for meaning but for sensuous effects'). His philosophical work was 'worthless'.

For one golden moment in the early 1920s he had seemed influenced by the new French Catholic writers. 'It almost seemed that Yeats, the man we had loved long since, was turning towards the Catholic Faith.' But it was not to be, and de Blacam's record of the poet's latter years presented him in a light more lurid than Aleister Crowley:

> Yeats became more bitter than ever before, against what we hold
> most sacred. The indecency which marred so many of his past
> books now grew more horrid, and the latest book which he pub-
> lished, less than a year ago, was a repulsive play that we can excuse
> only by assuming that the mind which conceived it was unstrung.
> His poems, in the last dozen years, were morbid. He wrote of the
> blood of Calvary some lines so horrible that I could not quote
> them: one wonders how a publisher printed them. He described
> Bethlehem as the birthplace of a monster, and lamented the coming
> of Christianity. How ill this became the poet who had once
> charmed us with lines about the child that the Little People stole,
> the mice bobbing round the oatmeal chest in a country house, and
> the merry playing of the Fiddler of Dooney!

In such exposures, the *Bulletin* felt, 'good service has already been done'. But it was less satisfied with the record of the liberal Jesuit journal, *Studies*. In previous battles, the Jesuits had weighed in on what Professor Corcoran conceived to be the side of the angels; though the magazine had published a eulogy of AE in September 1935, this had been neutralised by a debunking article by Michael Tierney, and one of the weightiest contributions to the long-running debate about the un-Irishness of Yeats was Father Francis Shaw's two-part article on 'The Celtic Twilight'. Shaw asserted that Yeats's supposedly Irish inspiration found its basis in a pseudo-Oriental dream-world, far removed from anything properly called Celtic, and based on 'much mutual borrowing and uninspired imitation'.[43] Shaw had taken particular issue with F. R. Leavis's assertion that Yeats's Irishness made 'his dream-world something more than private, personal and literary', and conferred on it 'an external validation'.[44] In contrast, Shaw denounced Yeats for turning upstanding Irish heroes into effeminate dreamers and Anglicised lotos-eaters. He further demonstrated Yeats's inability to appreciate not only the reality of the Celtic experience, but the achievements of mediæval Christianity in Ireland. His vision of a dim and narcoleptic other-world owed much to Renan and Arnold, but had nothing to do with

> expressing national character and feeling. . . . The fact of the matter is that while Mr Yeats went to O'Grady and Lady Gregory for his heroes, he went to the 'Brahmin philosopher' and Madame Blavatsky for his inspiration. Is it not a little surprising to find 'the great fountain of Gaelic Ireland' pouring forth, by some strange perversion, a pure stream of Oriental theosophy?

However, at the time of Yeats's death *Studies* chose not to denounce the poet for 'perversion', but to celebrate him as an Irishman. The issue for March 1939 carried two long and sympathetic articles about the poet and his work. Mary Macken's affectionate recollections of Yeats, O'Leary and the Contemporary Club,[45] which summoned up the world of Protestant Home Rulers like C. H. Oldham and John Butler Yeats, were roundly anathematised by the *Bulletin*; even worse, to Corcoran's suspicious eye, was J. J. Hogan's evaluation of the poet and his times.[46] Hogan took a judicious and fairly critical line about some of the work, making an interesting comparison to D'Annunzio, 'the great poet of insolence, cruelty and lust—the prophet, incidentally, of certain current philosophies of life'. (Those who ran, might read.[47]) At his best, however, Hogan judged that Yeats's true European peer was Goethe. His kind of Irishness was carefully defined: 'Yeats is specially the poet of the Anglo-Irish. But he has lived in Ireland and taken part in every Irish cause and quarrel for nearly forty years. He has fallen in with Nationalist movements, and has fallen out with them and lashed them from the Anglo-Irish, the planter's side.' But this did not go nearly far enough for the *Bulletin*, which could not forbear to quote Hogan's summing-up with apposite italicisation:

> The first great poet of modern Ireland; the poet who will command our literature as long as we use the English tongue. He was great, too, in other literary fields; a fine prose-writer and critic, a dramatist, and the chief creator of *our* theatre. He was perhaps also, though this cannot be said with certainty yet, a great public man, and a principal shaper of *our* recent history.

That 'our' rankled badly enough; but even worse was Hogan's innocent remark that in some of his early work Yeats 'catches the very mind of the simple Catholic people'. At this assertion, the *Bulletin* could not restrain itself.

> Yes; he was always an adept at that. Why, not little short of a score of years ago, that man was enabled to place himself before a public audience, in a Catholic hall, for an expressly Catholic cultural cause, to discourse on that most characteristic theme, his own style, himself. He there held forth before an audience mainly fetched from their strict suburban seclusion, convoyed by a stream of taxicabs.[48]

Readers will find themselves in full agreement with Professor J. J. Hogan's engaging ingenuousness of descriptive phrase. The Professor's second statement, some four pages later, is still more apposite, were that possible. It is a couplet, 'W. B. Yeats' his very own, a couplet printed in italics for Professor Hogan,

> We the great gazebo built;
> They convicted us of guilt.

What gazebo? None other than that gross imposture, that the mouthings of the two Mahatmas, Russell and Yeats, were in any way compatible with the mind of this Catholic and Irish people of

Ireland, and a fit theme to be fostered by the young adorers at the Merrion Square shrine, the holders-forth of the Plunkett House eleemosynary hat, the promoters of the Plunkett policy of self-help from the public pocket, of cash from the seekers of social titles of honour, diverted into the Organisation coffers by the crafty crew of calculating cadgers. The story has been told in full, has been treated with complacent pen as well as on the air, by a well-satisfied performer on the Plunkett platforms. It will soon be time for *Studies* to secure once more the services of Professor Tierney, MA, with another set of four selected slingstones. The gazebo of Yeats should be saluted with a salvo in these sedate pages of *Studies*, as fully effective as those launched, after undue delay, against the gazebo of Russellism and of Plunkettism.

Studies did not rise to this challenge.[49] Discussion of the dead giant shifted to his inheritance. Sean O'Faolain published a coruscating essay in the 1942 Irish number of *Horizon*[50] on 'Yeats and the Younger Generation'; to read his analysis of Yeats's intellectual origins is to realise how much Joseph Hone missed, and to regret the biography of Yeats which O'Faolain began but abandoned unwritten. Within the same covers Frank O'Connor wrote on the significance of Yeats's death.[51] A year before, in *The Bell*, O'Connor had drawn an unforgettable portrait of the Yeats he knew.[52] The images are those of a high priest—his rooms characterised by 'the long orderly table, the silver candlesticks, the dim light', 'the touch of dandyism in the lofty ecclesiastical stare, the vital motion of the hands, the unction of the voice'. At the same time O'Connor affirmed the poet's blazing enthusiasm and incandescent excitement, contradicting 'the pomposity and arrogance Dublin people never tired of talking of'. O'Connor went on to identify Yeats (in contrast to AE) as

a rabid Tory; he professed himself a member of the Church of Ireland, though he had much more of the Catholic in him; he was a fascist and authoritarian, seeing in world crises only the break-up of the 'damned liberalism' he hated; an old I.R.B. man, passionate nationalist, lover of tradition, hater of reason, popular education, and 'mechanical logic'.

This is a partial view, based on public performances of the late 1930s and reflecting the perspective of 1941; but it deliberately identified

Yeats's artistic personality as not only Irish, but objectively Catholic. Moreover, Hogan's assertion that Yeats could catch the mind of native Irish Catholics was reaffirmed: O'Connor finally stated that, faced with the uniquely Irish note present in Yeats's poetic voice, 'generations of country blood in me responds and I am ashamed of writing as I seem to do in a foreign language'. Thus for all the poet's hieratic, snobbish, exotic affectations, not to mention his Protestant background and Unionist family, he emerged as more Irish than the Irish themselves.

By then, in any case, the *Catholic Bulletin* was no more. Through 1939 it had continued its campaign against such 'sinister moves' as 'the curious effort to impose the "study' of the pointless outpourings of William B. Yeats on all schools',[53] but on 4 December 1939 the sudden death was announced of its editor and proprietor, Senator Patrick T. Keohane (motto: 'We stand by our friends—living or dead'). In a special appendix the journal extolled his staunchness: 'Senator Keohane's mind stood where the mind of the Gael always stood. For him the schismatic island which lies between our island and the Continent might be said not to exist.'[54] However, that was the last number of the *Bulletin*. By then, in any case, it was schismatic England which was embroiled in the mainstream of European history, while Ireland lay passively moored offshore. Discussion of the late poet's reputation in the journals had been displaced by analysis of a continental war which would—among other effects—ensure that he lay buried in Roquebrune eight years longer than intended.

Meanwhile discussion of his reputation had been reclaimed from the realm of squabbling obituarists by the disciplines of biography and literary criticism—though another effect of the war was to put most of his books out of print.[55] In looking at the reactions immediately after his death, what remains most striking is the concentration on the issue of who owned his literary body, the fierceness with which the claim was contested, and the prominence of religious criteria in the argument. 'Outside of Ireland his place is safe on Parnassus', wrote Robert Speaight; 'but inside of it he would perhaps prefer a place in the memory of his people's soul'.[56] That place would not yet be unanimously awarded, though it was ceded in full measure when the occasion of his re-interment at Drumcliffe in 1948 was made a great national celebration. He had been conveyed from France by the Irish navy, and honoured by leading politicians and the head of state. The ceremony was emphatically constructed to praise a pre-eminent national figure; the fact that it took place under the auspices of a Coalition government (including Maud Gonne's son) which had just declared its intention to sever the constitutional link with Britain, may not be irrelevant. Those who claimed Yeats for Ireland had won the day. The battle over his literary remains, however, would not have surprised the poet's shade; he had already had the last word, in 'A General Introduction for my Work' left behind him for posthumous publication.

> . . . no people hate as we do in whom [the] past is always alive. There are moments when hatred poisons my life and I accuse myself of effeminacy because I have not given it adequate expression. . . . Then I remind myself that though mine is the first English marriage I know of in the direct line, all my family names are English; that I owe my soul to Shakespeare, to Spenser, to Blake, perhaps to William Morris, and to the English language in which I think, speak and write; that everything I love has come to me through English. My hatred tortures me with love, my love with hate.[5/]

NOTES

1. 30 January 1939.
2. Typed copy, *NLI MS* 30, 772.
3. *NLI MS* 30,801.
4. *TCD MS* 8104/77, 6 Mar. 1939. She had already made detailed enquiries from shipping companies about transporting the remains from Marseilles to Sligo, and arrangements about the plot at Drumcliffe were in train by June.
5. In a letter to P. S. O'Hegarty, 11 Feb. 1939 (*Kansas MS* Ea 52). 'He said to her [George Yeats] "If I die out here bury me up in Roquebrune & then in a year or so when I am forgotten by the newspapers take me (rather his words were 'dig me up') to Drumcliffe. . ."' Also see George Yeats to W. Force Stead, 14 May 1939 (*Yale*): 'WBY will be "planted" in Drumcliffe, Sligo, about the first week of October.'
6. E. C. Yeats to P. S. O'Hegarty, as above.
7. Masefield's initiative in the matter is recorded in a draft letter to George Yeats (*HRHRC*, Austin). 16 March 1939 was the hundredth anniversary of the birth of John Butler Yeats. The music was the slow movement from Beethoven's Ninth; prayers and psalm 23 were follwed by V. C. Clinton Baddeley reading 'The Withering of the Boughs' and 'A Dialogue of Self and Soul'. The Lesson came from *Isaiah* ch. 55. In between two hymns ('Praise to the Holiest in the Height' and 'The Day Thou Gavest, Lord, Is Ended') Baddeley read 'Under Ben Bulben'. The service closed with the Benediction, and the Dead March from Saul.

The family did not feel it was, overall, a success.

8.   31 Jan. 1939.
9.   12 Feb. 1939.
10.   30 Jan. 1939. This may have been a last shaft from his old schoolmate Charles Johnston.
11.   30 Jan. 1939.
12.   4 Feb. 1939.
13.   4 Feb. 1939.
14.   30 Jan. 1939.
15.   5 Feb. 1939.
16.   30 Jan. 1939.
17.   30 Jan. 1939.
18.   5 Feb. 1939.
19.   *Ibid.*
20.   7 Feb. 1939.
21.   14:3, July-Sept. 1939.
22.   30 Jan. 1939.
23.   *Irish Times*, 30 Jan. 1939.
24.   *Irish Press*, 30 Jan. 1939.
25.   'An Irish Poet', *The Arrow* (Summer 1939).
26.   'Poet and Artist', *ibid.* Similar opinions were expressed in Clarke's parallel piece in the *Dublin Magazine* 14:2 (Apr.-June 1939).
27.   A. S. Forrest in *Today*, 27 Apr. 1904.
28.   13 June 1935.
29.   *Catholic Bulletin*, 29:2 (February 1939).
30.   *Ibid.*, 29:3 (Mar. 1939), p. 151.
31.   In his Senate speech on 'The Child and the State' (*SS* 168).
32.   Perceptively discussed in Elizabeth Butler Cullingford, *Gender and History in Yeats's Love Poetry* (Cambridge: Cambridge University Press, 1993), pp. 140-51.
33.   Particularly 'Some passages from the letters of W. B. Yeats to AE' in the *Dublin Magazine*, 14:3 (July-Sept. 1939).
34.   3 Feb. 1939.
35.   *Loc. cit.*
36.   *Ibid.*, pp. 183 & ff.
37.   30 Jan. 1939.
38.   *Irish Times* and *Irish Press*, 30 Jan. 1939.
39.   There was, in fact, a certain contemporary effort to rehabilitate Moore's Irish credentials: see W. Stockley, 'Moore's claim as Anglo-Irish poet', *Dublin Magazine* 14:4 (Oct.-Dec. 1939).
40.   *Catholic Bulletin*, 29:4 (Apr. 1939), pp. 241-4.
41.   *Ibid.*, 213 ff. As the compiler of a valuable guide to Irish fiction in the English language, Brown had a position to defend.
42.   See n. 33, above.
43.   *Studies*, 23:89 (Mar. 1934), pp. 25-41, and 90 (June 1934), pp. 260-278.
44.   *New Bearings in English Poetry* (London: Chatto and Windus, 1932), p. 34.
45.   *Studies*, xxviii:109 (Mar. 1939).
46.   *Ibid.* Hogan later reviewed *Last Poems* and *Scattering Branches* (*Studies*, 29 [1940], pp. 650-3), defining Yeats as 'this greatest of our poets', but the *Bulletin* was no longer around to be offended.

47. The D'Annunzio parallel was also made by David Garnett in the *New Statesman* (4 Feb. 1939): 'but Yeats's spirit was the opposite of the filibustering Italian'.

48. The encounter is described by Yeats in a letter to Ezra Pound, 3 Feb. 1919 (see my *Paddy and Mr Punch* [London: Allen Lane, 1993], p. 232). He had made 'a sensation' by publicly debating spiritism with a Catholic priest, and 'finished him off'.

49. Though Michael Tierney wrote on 'Nationalism and revolution' in the June number (pp. 362-374), and covered general European politics from a mildly pro-Axis viewpoint from 1940.

50. 'Yeats and the Younger Generation', 5:25 (Jan. 1942).

51. 'The Future of Irish Literature', *ibid*.

52. *The Bell*, 1:5 (Feb. 1941).

53. *Catholic Bulletin*, 29:7 (July 1939). This issue had been raised early on by M. J. MacManus (*Irish Press*, 1 Feb. 1939): 'Today the poet's voice is more needed than ever, for of all writers and teachers he is the most individualistic. The world has seen the approaching menace of a new barbarism, in which that soulless thing, the State, is deified and in which the individual counts for nothing. The generous impulses of youth are being quenched and the slavery of mass thinking is being imposed. Germany has expunged the lyrics of her sweetest singer, Heine, from her school-books because a racial heresy is in the ascendant. That, to us, may seem abhorrent. But let us not take a smug pride in our own rectitude. Has Yeats ever reached the Irish school-books?'

54. 29:12 (Dec. 1939).

55. 'All Willy's books are out of print', wrote Lily Yeats on 15 Jan. 1945. 'The scarcity of paper prevents them being printed until after the war. George tells me that she only got £10 on the English editions. She doesn't know what the American is yet.' (To Ruth Lane-Poole; my thanks to W. M. Murphy for his transcription.) Also see Marion Witt to A. P. Watt, 15 June 1949 (Scribner Archive, Princeton), making clear that Macmillan had only *Collected Poems* (1933) available. 'All other volumes are out of print; most have been so for years.'

56. *Commonweal*, 31 Mar. 1939.

57. Edward Callan, *Yeats on Yeats: The Last Introductions and the Dublin Edition*, *New Yeats Papers XX* (Dublin: Dolmen Press, 1981), p. 63.

Getting the North:
Yeats and Northern Nationalism

John Wilson Foster

I

STRANDS IN YEATS'S BACKGROUND might lead a beginning student to suppose his broad sympathy with the people and culture of the North of Ireland. After all, until two generations before the poet's birth, his English forebears had included merchants, and the North had always been busily mercantile. After 1800, those forebears had also been demonstratively Protestant, with several ancestors Church of Ireland clergymen, one a rector in County Down, where his father, John Butler Yeats, was born. The North had always been predominantly Protestant in numbers and ruling ethos. The poet's mother was a Pollexfen, member of a mercantile family in the north-west county of Sligo who were loyal Protestants, active Freemasons, suspicious of Roman Catholics and Irish nationalists. In short, here is a family history that in its cultural components many Irish unionists shared and many Northern unionists still share.[1]

In his boyhood and early youth, Yeats was obedient to the blueprint. He later remembered wanting as a boy to die fighting for the Orangemen against the Fenians. Yeats's later recurrent imagining of Cuchulain's death while fighting for the Men of Ulster against the Men of Ireland was an odd transposition of the boyhood fantasy, both a version of it and an inversion of it. (Cuchulain as an Ulster champion has recently appealed to hardline loyalists in Northern Ireland, to which a gable mural in east Belfast testifies; but of course Yeats was to identify the mythic figure with Patrick Pearse and Irish republicanism.) And as a youth, the poet displayed a passion in Sligo for the collection and study of lepidoptera (*WBY* 28, 32-33, 35). He might, it would have seemed, have gone on to emulate one of those nineteenth century Protestant clergyman-naturalists, or even become a Robert Lloyd Praeger, that younger contemporary who became the island's leading naturalist though only one among a veritable swarm of Northern scientific students of Nature.

However, not only did the maturing Yeats discard the blueprint (though not as decisively as is sometimes thought, a point upon which contemporary Northern nationalists and I agree), but the blueprint was in fact partitionist in its tendency. The latter is a claim that Northern nationalists have not as far as I know advanced, since for them unionism is unionism and can be partitionist only from the direction of the North, not from the direction of the South, from which direction Yeats felt and spoke. Nor are they likely to admit that Yeats's nationalism grew out of his Southern unionist background, like Standish James O'Grady's, Lady Gregory's and Douglas Hyde's; normally it would have been against the grain of that background, but under the conditions of the time cultural nationalism was the natural, if illicit, progeny of unionism. Nor are they likely to agree that his was an identifiable species of Irish nationalism—of an articulate, forceful, executive kind—one that Pearse at first repudiated and then shrewdly made common cause with. Or that there is a partitionist strain in the Southern Irish nationalism that triumphed against Britain in 1920, be it Yeats's or Eamon de Valera's, Pearse's or Hyde's.

Yeats's grandfather William Butler Yeats, the rector in Co. Down, disliked Presbyterians, Hone tells us, 'and could never come to an understanding with the aggressive North, because his Evangelicalism belonged to the cultivated classes . . .' (*WBY* 5-6). Social class and religious denomination would have early instilled in Yeats a distaste for the bulk of his co-religionists in what in his lifetime became Northern Ireland. When young George Russell (AE) visited the Yeats household in Dublin, John Butler 'was a little critical of this friendship, for he detected in Russell, already spoken of as the religious leader of the future, the ethical complacency of the Ulster Protestant. "A saint but raised in Portadown", he would say' (*WBY* 46).

So Yeats inherited his distaste for religious Dissent (especially Presbyterianism), and would have likewise inherited a distaste for industry, the factory city, the labouring class and the clerical workforce, all of which contributed to the regional distinctiveness of the North of Ireland. To explain Yeats's finding Northern Protestants 'alien' in terms of a 'mutual incomprehension between northern and southern Protestants'—as Edna Longley has recently done—is perhaps to posit an equality of respect between these two Protestantisms which Southern Protestants would have rejected, and still do reject.[2]

Quite early, of course, Yeats's inherited prejudices and inclinations played their parts in the poet's developing and ever more complex philosophy and poetic. Some of them were overturned; thus science, especially the scientific study of Nature, was banished, Protestantism disavowed. However, if the repudiated science found its counterpart in the mystical pseudo-science of *A Vision*, Hone (and Maud Gonne) was surely right in seeing Yeats's enthusiasm for secret societies—from hermetic orders to republican brotherhoods—as a transposition of the Pollexfenian Freemasonry (*WBY* 29, 47, 85-86). In like manner, Ulster for Yeats was chiefly the embodied opportunity for both rebellion against the ancestors and a disguised expression of ancestral attitude.

Before the Yeatsian system generated its own momentum, there would have been an element of pleasurable shock-value in the youthful inversions. An even more graphic example than Yeats's is the career of Charlie Johnston who was the son of the 'staunch' (as they say) Unionist Westminster M. P. for South Belfast—celebrated throughout the pro-Union North as 'Johnston of Ballykilbeg' (his memory was green for my grandmother and her true-blue Unionist cohorts in Belfast even as late as the 1950s). Johnston *fils* was a fellow pupil with Yeats at the High School (Dublin), who was converted to Buddhism, interested Yeats in the subject and started—with the poet—a hermetic society. He travelled to London to interview Madame Blavatsky in 1886. (This was the year of the first Home Rule Bill and of the potent symbolic expression of future Ulster resistance, when Lord Randolph Churchill rhymed, 'Ulster will fight, and Ulster will be right'—which political situation young Johnston was clearly fleeing.) He married the great woman's niece (Yeats remarked, 'If you only heard Madame Blavatsky trying to pronounce Ballykilbeg' [*CL1* 101]), later gave Yeats introductions to the London theosophists, and later still wrote tirelessly for American magazines in the furtherance of mystical Irish nationalism (*WBY* 47, 49, 69; *LTWBY* 26). Here was Orange Ulster (as Yeats called it) upended indeed, and by a son of one of its most illustrious embodiments. Whether this was, as I suspect, a case of a son's rebellion against a respected father might only be determined by a biography of this remarkable but little-known figure, a biography that would necessarily engage with many of the chief components of the Irish scene at a crucial time in the island's history.

Yeats spent a week in July 1891 at Ballykilbeg, Co. Down, visiting the Johnstons. He relished the notion of being in alien country, not just because it was Orange Order territory but also because it was Ulster-Scots territory. He recalled later: 'I left Dublin next day to stay somewhere in Orange Ulster with the brilliant student of my old Dublin school, Charles Johnston . . .'. ('Somewhere' is characteristic: the grand general threat of the place occluding its particular location.) After the visit, he reported: 'I have been away in County Down, looking almost in vain among its half-Scotch people for the legends I find so plentiful in the West'. He was to recall another visit to the North as 'an expedition into Ulster', as though Ulster were like the wilds of Connemara or Kerry (*Mem* 45; *LNI* 53).

At this time Yeats clearly thought that through Ulster—the birthplace not just of Cuchulain in antiquity but of Sir Samuel Ferguson and William Carleton in modern times—coursed 'that wild Celtic blood' which, the poet claimed in 1892 (in a letter to *United Ireland*), coursed through his own veins (*UP1* 256). Ferguson's work was praised by Yeats in 1886 for its 'barbarous truth' and the poet described as 'the greatest poet Ireland has produced, because the most central and most Celtic', his Protestantism and unionism swept aside as irrelevant (*UP1* 87, 103). Yeats wished Ulster to mean an inspired peasant Carleton and an aristocratic Ferguson in the real world, and Cuchulain in the unreal world, a place that had produced the figures that mattered most to Yeats: peasant, artist, aristocrat and hero.

But such a view of modern Ulster could not be sustained and Yeats gave up on the North as a bad job. Scots Ulster, Presbyterian Ulster, became indeed a kind of antithetical cultural self. In 1895 he thanked Sarah Purser for an embroidered 'book cover [which] is at this moment helping to civilize a novel all about North of Ireland presbeterians & succeeding as well as could be expected under the

circumstances' (*CL1* 474). Yeats did not invent his abstract portrait
of Protestant Ulster: Daniel O'Connell before him, and many a
celebrated Southerner after him, found the place galling, refractory.
Those beliefs, values, modes of thought, bodies of expression to
which Yeats became converted—Irish nationalism, Celticism,
mysticism, folklore, nationality of literature—largely and perforce
excluded Ulster. Of course, even for Yeats these were beset (Yeats
might have said enriched) by ambiguities and contradictions, but in
the midst of all 'the North' remained a simple and uncongenial
place. There were attempts to make contact, going there to help
start a branch of the Irish Literary Society, or joining Maud Gonne
on one of her errands of political mischief (*Mem* 58, 59, 131), but
they were half-hearted or inappropriate: lecturing to the Belfast Nat-
uralists' Field Club on 21 November, 1893 on fairies, for example.[3]
(It's an entertaining talk, almost a parody of biological systematics,
but what must the amateur scientists have thought?) It became clear
that as far as Yeats was concerned, any involvement of the Northern
Irish in his Revival meant their self-transformation in order to
satisfy the requirements of the Revival, and it is a measure of the
magnetism of Yeats and the Revival that certain Ulster writers
changed their names and went, figuratively but usually literally too,
to Dublin: Samuel Waddell remade himself as Rutherford Mayne,
Alice Milligan (on occasion) as Iris Olkryn, Anna Johnston as Ethna
Carbery, George Russell as AE, Harry Morrow as Gerald Mac-
Namara, Joseph Campbell as Seosamh Mac Cathmhaoil.

There was in Belfast a radical tradition that might have been congenial to Yeats. Charles Gavan Duffy had edited the *Belfast
Vindicator*, an O'Connellite organ, and he had also co-founded with
John Dillon and Thomas Davis the *Nation*, the management of
which he handed over to John Mitchel, an Ulster Presbyterian
nationalist (*CL1* 483). But this tradition did not much engage Yeats.
Nor was he much exercised by the partition of Ireland as far as I can
tell, having been engrossed by the War of Independence (as it came
to be called) and about to be engrossed by the imminent Irish Civil
War. On October 17th, 1924 after the dust settled on the island, he
did speak wisely in the Irish Senate on the subject of Northern
Ireland when he said: 'I have no hope of seeing Ireland united in my
time, or of seeing Ulster won in my time; but I believe it will be
won in the end, and not because we fight it, but because we govern
this country well. We can do that, if I may be permitted as an artist
and writer to say so, by creating a system of culture which will

represent the whole of this country . . .' (*SS* 87). This was perhaps too much to expect from an overwhelmingly Catholic country celebrating its cultural as well as political independence by enshrining in law its differences from Britain (and therefore Northern Ireland), but Yeats knew that if it was too much, then the claim to Ulster should be dropped.

However, I cannot think Yeats was entirely ingenuous in the matter of Northern Ireland, which may have provided a pretext by which he could doubly defend Protestants in the Free State. In 1925 he made his celebrated Senate speech accusing the new state of infringing upon Protestant freedoms in preparing to pass anti-divorce legislation. But his noble and often quoted defence of Irish Protestants as a racial stock with a great cultural tradition was not intended to include Ulster's Protestants who in his eyes were decidedly *not* the people of Burke, Grattan, Swift and Parnell. In fact, they were beneath his notice. His warning that by passing Catholic legislation the Free State would never 'get the North' (a phrase he repeats) seems not to challenge but to express an irredentism that culminated in the 1937 Constitution of the Irish Republic (*SS* 92). It may be that Yeats was tactically affecting the language of irredentism, hoping to appeal to that sentiment in order to sabotage legislation bearing directly upon Southern Protestants.

Either way, the North in Yeats never materialises. In his brief retrospect, 'Ireland, 1921-1931', published in the *Spectator* on 30 January, 1932, Northern Ireland is never mentioned. The article contains some expression of regret that he had once seen nothing in Protestant Ireland but its faults, but the Protestant Ireland that he rehabilitates is strictly Ascendancy Ireland, and he declines to turn his gaze north (*UP2* 486-90). In the late 1930s, when the IRA staged an anti-partition campaign, Maud Gonne sought his support for it. Yeats told her that, in the words of Hone, 'he found the inhabitants of the lost province of Ulster so disagreeable that he hoped they would never reunite with the rest of Ireland' (*WBY* 469). After all, he felt (as Hyde did), that the Protestant north-east ruptured the continuity of Irishism and made impossible that 'unity of culture' he hopefully refers to in his *Vision* papers:

> When people have unity of culture the transference of thought & image goes through the whole people. In the past pure races have been made by blood, but bloods are now so mixed that in the future they will have to be made by culture (*YVP3* 63).

The political unity of an Ireland sundered from Britain would have been an ideal expression of that unity of culture and might have permitted or facilitated that 'unity of self' and 'Unity of Being' he also extolled during his preparation for *A Vision* (*YVP3* 27). The disobliging reality of Ulster has pained and irritated more Irish figures than Hyde and Yeats, often leading them to eclipse it from their minds.

II

Until recently, there were no identifiable Northern attitudes to Yeats, his life, art and thought, with the exception of Patrick Kavanagh's. AE, Forrest Reid and St John Ervine were all Ulstermen but because Yeats's national politics were not admitted as an issue, they wrote from no regional or sectional point of view. Like Louis MacNeice in the following generation, they assumed an all-Ireland perspective which freed them to respond in appreciative or explicatory modes, the poetry and plays in the forefront of their attention.

A new note was added to the critical reception of Yeats in Ireland by the coming to maturity of the first generation of Catholics in Northern Ireland to receive higher education courtesy of the Butler Education Act (1944, extended to Northern Ireland in 1947). It may have been their distrust of Protestants, because of their early experience in Ulster and their later experience of the Troubles from 1969 onwards, that caused them to look askance at the nationalist credentials of a Protestant from the South. While those who see in Northern unionists the chief obstacle to a desired island unity ought to be gratified by Yeats's disregard for Northern unionists, I do not recall ever hearing such gratification expressed. Rather, the chief issue has been how far Yeats was a real nationalist and how far he truly escaped his Protestant, unionist background. Given Yeats's received stature as a culture-giver to the new Ireland, this is ironic. There is also irony in the fact that whereas Yeats rather ignored the North because of his dislike of Protestant unionists, a cold (that is, scrutinising) eye has been cast on him by the other Northerners whom he abandoned as readily as did the new Free State—those from the community of what we might loosely call Catholic nationalists. Now he is 'getting the North' in a way that must astonish his shade.

The local pressures operating on readers in Northern Ireland in the past quarter century have been augmented by the general pressures operating on literary critics, especially those in British and American universities. Such pressures, issuing from fashionable feminist and postcolonialist readings, have resulted in the 'interrogation' of major figures, especially from ideological perspectives unlikely to be congenial to a male writer who wrote what can be construed as Romantic work, who has been seen as fascist, and whose nationality was not of an unalloyed minority kind. Only Yeats's claim to Irishness and a presumed continuity between his Irish nationalism and the contemporary IRA may have prevented him, in the current chilly Anglo-American critical climate, from being ideologically arraigned more than he has been. (Anglo-American humanities students are sentimentally attracted to the glamour of Irish 'revolutionaries'.)

An Irish university teacher such as Seamus Deane inhabits that climate, though he knows when it is not applicable to Ireland: knows the difference, for example, between Yeats and the IRA. Given the chance by Northern nationalism (in the shape of the Field Day Theatre Company, of which Deane is the guiding light) to gauge the political direction of Yeats's work, Edward Said (whose knowledge of Ireland is admittedly modest) must have surprised the editors by analysing Yeats as 'a poet of decolonization' (i.e., a poet who furthered the cause of decolonization), when he might have been expected to follow its own lead and seen through the poet's nationalism; the consolation must have been that Said trounced imperialism and colonialism and therefore by indirection (it could be imagined) British policy in Northern Ireland.[4] More congenial to Field Day would have been recent remarks on Yeats by Terry Eagleton, another Field Day guest pamphleteer: 'In seeking to replace the detestable abstractions of politics . . . with the concretions of myth and image, he seems unaware that this is just another form of politics—that a conservative politics is usually one which denies the very category of the political itself'.[5]

There has been fallout from Northern Ireland in the rest of the island too. Perhaps a truer sense of where the Irish think Yeats stands on the 'National Question' can be achieved through a kind of critical 'triangulation', to borrow a concept from surveying. I am aware that the three perspectives I am about to list might remind Irish readers of the three Irelands that F.S.L. Lyons identifies in his controversial book, *Culture and Anarchy in Ireland* (1979), but it is

no surprise either that Lyons's three Irelands should have generated
their own critical perspectives or that those perspectives should be
apparent in studies of Yeats in Ireland. Yeats's career coincided with
(indeed, on occasions helped, however marginally or indirectly, to
create) great and terrible events in the life of Ireland—rebellion,
secession, division of the island in two, civil war, enduring suspicion
between the two reconstituted Irelands—and his voice sent its
echoes into the future to trouble the ears of those struggling to
understand and help solve the problem of Northern Ireland. More
than any other Irish writer in history, Yeats, his art and thought,
has become a *locus* as well as a focus, an *arena* as well as a field of
study.

From our first of three 'stations', one might see in the responses
to Yeats of Edna Longley, Roy Foster and Terence Brown a family
resemblance, though these three critics are individualistic, subtle and
of varied backgrounds. In their reading, Yeats is unambiguously
Irish and benignly nationalist, and their painstaking historical
revisionism would defend him against a sectarian and excluding
nationalism. From our second 'station', one might term the second
perspective unionist and it would be my own; in this perspective
Yeats is both a cultural nationalist and a literary unionist, at first
promoting extra-constitutional nationalism in the mistaken belief
that it could be contained by the literati, then retreating from hard
nationalism when it proved its sectarian and recalcitrant insularity
and philistinism; all the while he partitioned off Ulster yet helped to
create the climate of attitudes and feelings in which hard nationalists
have waged unrelenting war against it. Conor Cruise O'Brien
represents a less exonerative anti-nationalism (which does not
become explicit unionism, and leaves breathing-space for moderate
nationalism), whereby Yeats's mystical nationalism is seen to have
led him into a deplorable fascist enthusiasm.[6] The third perspective
is that of a more importunate but often disguised nationalism and it
is this perspective to which I devote the rest of this essay. We find it
graphically but not exclusively articulated by literary critics of
Northern Catholic background. In this perspective Yeats—the
merit of his poetry bracketed off—is a literary unionist but not an
authentic cultural nationalist, nor even a literary unionist who
unwittingly promoted the cause of authentic nationalism.

Patrick Kavanagh (1904-67), the poet from Monaghan, held such a
view, though he might have derived it in part from Daniel Corkery.
There have been extenuating historical and biographical circum-

stances for this view, and it must be clear by now that recent Irish criticism of Yeats has a demonstrable autobiographical dimension. Kavanagh's smacks at Yeats were unco-ordinated, personal and eccentric. Kavanagh brought a sense of grievance and envy from his backwater North and resented Dublin and metropolitan reputations such as Yeats's (which is perhaps why he famously extolled the virtue of parochialism); it was as if his northernness was too remote from Dublin for him to accept the narrative of Irish nationalism that had installed Yeats as hero. Kavanagh's views of Yeats and the Irish Literary Revival were bound up in complicated ways with his own poetry, a poetry that had a liberating effect on the youthful Seamus Heaney.[7] And they do represent a critical point of view that can be, and has been, expressed in a sophisticated manner by Seamus Deane, who was also keenly aware of Kavanagh.

It may be, then, that Kavanagh, Deane and Heaney inhabit a similar problematic northernness even though all three removed to Dublin as their natural capital. Deane and Heaney, after all, grew up in Northern Ireland, which had been separated from the rest of Ireland for nearly forty years by the time they entered university; Belfast not Dublin was their administrative capital, and the Northern city of Derry was in some ways their cultural headquarters (the founding of Field Day in Derry rather than Dublin being recognition of that fact).

The career since 1920 of Catholic-Gaelic Ireland (one of Lyons's three Irelands alongside Anglo-Ireland and Protestant Ulster) explains the quandary of Northernness, and it created the circumstances out of which the sophisticated elaboration of Kavanagh's attitude emerged. A major faultline in this Ireland was created by partition in 1920, after which Northern and Southern Ireland grew apart, the North becoming more officially Protestant and marooning Northern Catholics who more or less abstained from participation, the South more officially Catholic—against Yeats's initially loud protests and the diminishing protests of the Anglo-Irish, themselves diminishing in power and population.[8] Sadly, the cut-off Catholic population of the North came culturally and in other ways to resemble an ox-bow lake, history like new water failing to course through it.

Ironically, it was the British education system that stirred and fertilised the waters, though Protestants also benefited from the Butler Act. But when the grievances, talents and ambitions of the Northern Catholics were given voice in the 1960s (when the first

beneficiaries of higher education reached their twenties), the emerg-
ing voices were out of harmony with Catholic voices elsewhere in
Ireland. They sounded in the beginning fresh, indeed alarmingly
fresh to Ulster unionists, but as time went on, they began to sound
on certain issues curiously old-fashioned, baying startlingly after
quarry everyone assumed had been long since captured, despatched,
or liberated. When the Field Day Theatre Company began its
pamphlet series, there must have been many who were surprised to
find William Butler Yeats (reborn as gentleman, unionist,
Protestant, enemy of Catholic Ireland and, even if nationalist in
some peculiar way, nevertheless at heart West Briton) listed among
the legitimate targets.

   Yet these were not simply unkennelled hounds from the past,
outmoded nationalists giving tongue after half a century of enforced
silence in an Orange state. They were sophisticated readers and
gifted writers, indeed poets themselves some of them, and they
helped to create a literary scene in Ulster that was sometimes
referred to as the Northern Renaissance. And the Field Day
pamphlets, as well as the critical books of those I have in mind, were
welcome stimulants to thought in Ireland. But on the 'National
Question', the effect of these new figures in the landscape nonetheless was to suggest, almost subliminally (they made no explicit constitutional claims or demands), the illegitimacy of Northern Ireland
and the legitimacy of the reunification of Ireland. The Irish Republic, having apparently moved on from partition, satisfied with its
twenty-six counties (more than enough of a handful), was suddenly
brought with a shock back to 1920 or something passingly like it.

   Never mind the Irish body politic, it was all an injection of
adrenalin in the Irish body poetic, and Seamus Heaney's achievement, for example, has been acknowledged far beyond the borders
of Ulster, far beyond Ireland. But the authentic tension of Ulster, an
intense localism of engagement, has remained nevertheless in the
work of Heaney and Seamus Deane. Even Heaney's poetry achieved
a paradoxical newness in the beginning by 'resuming the dark' like
Kelly's unlicensed bull in Heaney's poem 'The Outlaw', setting in
verse notions of Ireland—female, mythic, undefeatable, boggy,
resurgent—that the Republic of Ireland had all but abandoned, and
that more resembled those of early Yeats than, say, of MacNeice,
Kavanagh, Austin Clarke or Thomas Kinsella, and that might be
partly explained by the time-warp of Catholic Northern Ireland and
the way in which Northern Catholics had become 'unlicensed'

nationalists, as far as many Southerners were concerned. To demonstrate this it is only necessary to compare the criticism of Heaney and Deane (and of Longley) on the subject of Yeats with the criticism of Declan Kiberd, a Field Day pamphleteer and an athletic intelligence. Because there is less politically and personally at stake (and because, I am compelled to say, he is largely ignorant of Northern Ireland—a wonderfully liberating condition if one is writing on the subject), Kiberd's criticism can afford more *jouissance*, and it is not surprising that he is more creatively exercised by Oscar Wilde than by Yeats. His criticism has a spring in its step that the criticism of Deane, Heaney and Longley does not, freighted as theirs is with the problems of articulating the North.[9]

The tensions and intensities of engagement were buried in the work of another critic and were exhumed less by the urgencies of the Troubles than by the challenge posed by the Northern Catholic writers and readers of Yeats. Denis Donoghue, born in the South of Ireland and eventually Henry James Professor of English and American Literature in New York University, might have been content to ply his reputable international wares, had not the Field Day pamphleteers reminded him by example that he, too, had been reared a Northern Catholic (in Warrenpoint, Co. Down) and had suffered disabilities now to be freshly voiced if not freshly remembered. However, he had been a sympathetic critic and admirer of Yeats, and so his aroused fellow feeling for other Northern Catholics was complicated by the matter of where he stood on Yeats. To take issue with Field Day, as he did, was to take issue with them on the subject of Yeats. For at times in Ireland, the 'Yeats Question' can seem very like the 'National Question', a measure of the crucial importance of that poet in Irish cultural and even political dispute.

III

Seamus Deane's unruffled account of Yeats's art in *A Short History of Irish Literature* (1986), with its nimble transitions and summary eloquence, can only appear approving. Having quoted the famous last stanza of 'The Statues', with its fellowship of Pearse and Cuchulain, the critic is content to explain:

> Momentarily the hero and the race are in accord with one another. In the poems on his own life and his great friends, Yeats had rewrit-

ten his account of modern Ireland as a place haunted by heroes. At the end of his life, he called for that heroism again, both from Irish writers and from the Irish people at large. Although he also saw that heroism was at a discount, that was merely in the oppositional nature of things. The murderers of Cuchulain, the convicted cowards, the representatives of the common mob, find their opposites too: 'They had changed their throats and had the throats of birds'.[10]

This evenness of tone is a far cry from the heated scrutiny to which Deane had subjected Yeats's idea of heroism in his celebrated Field Day pamphlet, *Heroic Styles: The Tradition of an Idea* (1984).[11] The difference may not be just one of occasion and genre (a short history versus a polemical pamphlet, professional explication versus engaged critical reading) but of deep-seated ambivalence about Yeats at the heart of Deane's ongoing response to the writer.

Yeats's 'heroism' in *A Short History* was in *Heroic Styles* 'spiritual heroics' and Deane's neutral explication was then harsh judgement. Deane claims in *Heroic Styles* that there are two dominant ways of reading Irish literature and history: the Romantic way and the Pluralistic way; these are also two modes of Irish writing, the first represented by Yeats, the second by Joyce.

The romantic mode when it is engaged in 'restoring dignity and power to what had been humiliated and suppressed', can work in the service of nationalism. One hears in the phrase 'humiliated and suppressed' an autobiographical note sounding from Derry City (where Deane was born and reared), but Yeats is not the figure who can redress the wrongs. For in the Ascendancy Revival, 'the restoration of native energy to the English language is seen as a specifically Irish contribution to a shared heritage'. 'Cultural nationalism', writes Deane, 'is thus transformed into a species of literary unionism'. In this regard, Deane allows no difference between Yeats and Ferguson, since both beat the strategic retreat of the Ascendancy from political to cultural supremacy. Whereas Catholic Ireland could provide Yeats with a language of renovation ('regeneration', Deane calls it elsewhere[12]), the art and civilization of Yeats's new Ireland came from the political connection between England and Ireland. Whatever its connection with Irish nationalism, Yeats's programme 'was not, finally, a programme of separation from the English tradition'. Deane then quotes (from 'A General Introduction for My Work' 1937) 'I owe my soul to Shakespeare . . .' to exemplify 'the pathology of literary unionism'.

The inference is clear: unionism is a disease. Also: nationalism is the cure, but only a nationalism that is literary as well as political, that is full-blooded and liberationist and admits of no reservations or complications. Aside from the milkier satisfaction of pointing out certain incongruities in Yeats's philosophy—and for what ideological gain?—why else would Deane assail Yeats on the grounds that he was not a real nationalist unless he, Deane, felt *himself* to be a real nationalist?

Clearly some of Deane's premises are unexceptionable. I have seconded Deane's proposition, first advanced by Conor Cruise O'Brien in 1966, that the Anglo-Irish nationalism of the Cultural Revival was the attempted transformation of Anglo-Irish power, not its surrender. (It failed, and became a surrender.) Moreover, Yeats's nationalism was in many ways problematic. He 'became definitely a nationalist' in the 1880s (Hone), but claimed in 1937, the year when de Valera's anti-Protestant constitution for the Irish Free State was adopted, that 'I am no Nationalist, except in Ireland for passing reasons'—an astounding retreat from responsibility (*WBY* 54; *E&I* 526). He promoted Gaelic but said English was his mother tongue (*E&I* 520). One moment he would speak for 'we Irish', the next claim merely that he was '*joined* to the "Irishry"' (my italics, his inverted commas), a rather different notion of alliance instead of self-identification (*E&I* 526). He thought, or affected to think, of the English as foreigners but was much among them and claimed that 'everything I love has come to me through English'—and he meant the literature written by the English not literature in the English language (*E&I* 519). He sought to encourage the formation of a national literature in Ireland yet complained to Lady Gregory that the Easter rebellion overturned 'the freeing of Irish literature and criticism from politics' (*L* 613)—he who was even then contemplating the poem that became 'Easter 1916', though it is arguable that the impulse of that poem is precisely the transformation of political action into myth, courtesy of the dynamic removals of the poetic imagination.

These cross-currents are evidence of Yeats's fierce energy and involvement in Ireland, though some of them are psychologically and socially explicable in ways that may not always endear the poet to an Irish reader, especially perhaps a Northern Irish reader. No one was more aware of the anomalies than Yeats himself who attempted to absorb them into a system that rested on the very notion of contradiction, opposition, antithesis. The poet often wrote in the rag-and-bone shop of the system, where mere doubts

had not become things as grand as antitheses: 'we sing', Yeats wrote
of poets, 'amid our uncertainty' (*Myth* 331). Yet Deane is correct in
seeing a fundamental unsatisfactoriness in Yeats's understanding of
and role in the 'Irish Question'. The condition of the Anglo-Irish
after Catholic nationalism got into full swing from the 1880s
onwards *was* a kind of pathology. My own view is that Romantic
nationalism, not unionism, was the source of the disease and that the
incoherence Deane attributes to Yeats in 'Yeats and the Idea of
Revolution' would have been lessened had Yeats been more unionist
and less nationalist, been truer to a cultural reality that Romantic
and mystical nationalism helped to disguise.

The blank that the North constitutes on Yeats's inner and outer
map of Ireland guarantees the unsatisfactoriness. Deane is right
when he complains, as he did recently, that 'the island Yeats knew
excluded the Northern Ireland I knew. I had to find out how he
managed to invent the place so that I might possess it for myself in
terms that seemed to me more responsive to its realities'.[13] His conclusion ought to have been that the map of Southern nationalism,
not just of Yeatsian nationalism, is blank where Northern Ireland is.
Despite the reference to reality, I detect in Deane the chronic and
romantic disappointment of Northern nationalism in Southern
nationalism, a disappointment which possibly underpins Deane's
rejection of Yeats's 'hot rhetoric' of Irish nationalism. It may also
underpin his rejection in *Heroic Styles* of what he calls Joyce's alternative 'cold rhetoric', which he finds to be a 'harmony of
indifference'. Underneath the dissatisfaction with pluralism, does
one detect here the note of abandonment sounding from Derry City
or (an allusion that will become clear later) from Warrenpoint
revisited and, by extension, from Catholic Northern Ireland?

If Yeatsian nationalism is really unionism and a pathology, might
it not explain the 'disease' of Ulster unionism? Yes, says Deane, and
proceeds to claim that 'the cultural machinery of Romantic Ireland
has . . . wholly taken over in the North', that unionism is Paisleyism
and that Paisleyism is romanticism and therefore comparable to
Yeatsianism, indeed somehow the spawn of Yeatsianism, but a Yeatsianism partitioned off and grown stagnant. Elsewhere I have
pointed out the trouble with these equations.[14] But I would draw
attention here to a certain inequality of example. Deane calls in
salutary fashion for the rejection of the romantic mystique of
Ireland; to accept this mystique 'is to be involved in the spiritual
heroics of a Yeats or a Pearse'. But whereas Deane is detailed in his

assault on Ulster unionism as romantic mystique (a largely unsustainable thesis), he is next to silent on the obviously more applicable case-study, that of Sinn Féin/IRA, a movement that produced the cult of Bobby Sands. Instead, the equivalent of Paisley is held to be John Hume, 'the minority's agent of rational demystification'. The IRA is explained away by one terse phrase: the IRA as the minority's 'agency of millenial revenge', a phrase that manages to excuse while apparently indicting. Deane claims that Pearse was 'our' (*sic*) 'last romantic' in politics as Yeats was our last romantic in poetry, which makes odd his subsequent claim that Ulster politics is rife with romanticism, unless 'our' means 'Catholic Ireland's' and the implication is that Catholic nationalism is now rational, leaving only the unionists as romantic anachronisms. Indeed, one suspects that Deane's real target is unionism, whether Yeatsian unionism (as Deane sees it) or Ulster unionism, and *not* romanticism or nationalism.[15]

To put it another way, it is Yeats's particular *kind* of nationalism to which Deane takes great exception. He calls Yeats 'dangerous' because 'his work had found an originating impulse in a theory of racial essences and identity' and promoted '*a brand of nationalism* [my italics] which was the product of a colonialism of which it thought itself the opposite'.[16] This interpretation is given an extended outing in 'Yeats and the Idea of Revolution', during which the adjectives 'hysterical', 'effete', 'authoritarian', 'strident' and 'incoherent' are attached to Yeats's project and later poetry. Yeats's spiritual heroics are explained as deriving from his colonialist mentality. Deane would agree with O'Brien on Yeats's 'savage politics', but whereas O'Brien traced them to Yeats's fascism, Deane traces them to his colonialism (i.e., his unionism) which his fascism was in reality. But on the issue of whether Yeats's colonialist nationalism actually furthered the cause of Irish liberationist nationalism (helping to bring into existence the Irish Free State), as Said believes it did, Deane turns peculiar. 'To describe Yeats's politics, and to a large extent his achievement, as colonial is not at all to diminish it.' (How does Deane expect his Yeats to survive the barrage of those epithets?)

[H]is demand was always that Ireland should retain its culture by keeping awake its consciousness of metaphysical questions. By doing so it kept its own identity and its link with ancient European culture alive. As always with Yeats, to be traditionalist in the

modern world was to be revolutionary. . . . It is a conviction which
has a true revolutionary impact when we look at the history of the
disappearance from the Western mind of the sense of eternity and
of the consciousness of death. . . . In its consciousness of death, the
culture would become truly alive . . . [Yeats] was a revolutionary
whose wars took place primarily within himself . . . .[17]

It is bewildering to find Deane re-admitting the very metaphysics
and solipsism he elsewhere labours to repudiate. And what the
revolutionary nature of death-consciousness is, much less its application to Irish politics, I hardly dare to contemplate.

Because Yeats's nationalism was colonialist, not native or
Catholic, it was not the genuine article: that is Deane's implication;
it was forged from above, not from below through humiliation or
suppression. Deane is opposed to nationalism *only when it is Yeatsian*: that is the conclusion I have come to after reading his work
over the years. Deane's reading of Yeats is a case not of Marxist anti-
colonialism colliding with romantic colonialist nationalism but of
one nationalism colliding with another, one being Anglo-Irish
(colonialist, in Deane's phrase), the other being Northern Catholic.
The collision causes Deane's often brilliant readings to buckle and
deform. Given Deane's great intelligence, we can explain his
inconsistency on the subject of Yeats only by reference to—dare I
say it?—the pathology of Northern nationalism. It is an ideology
which feels itself pre-empted by Southern, indeed Anglo-Irish,
nationalism, but which nevertheless must be advanced, though (in
the light of nationalist excesses by Sinn Féin/IRA) by oblique means
and in the terms of academic discourse.

The troubling irony of Deane's response to Yeats is that when he
leaves Yeats in order to contemplate other Irish writers (including
Joyce) or other aspects of Irish culture, he sounds to this ear like a
nationalist, and a nationalist moreover who mystifies by omission—as he has accused Yeats of being and doing, particularly in the
matter of the North. Deane closed *Heroic Styles* by calling for an
anthology of Irish literature from the beginning that would in total
effect de-mystify Yeatsian Irishness (deriving in part from Ferguson
and Arnold), revealing a literature 'unblemished by Irishness', but
also secure a sense of Irishness so as to avoid Joycean pluralism and
disinterestedness. The anthology would supersede Yeats's 'literary

unionism' and install a literary nationalism. The distinction between a blemished and a secure Irishness is too nice for me. In any case, in its conception and execution, the project actually bore much resemblance to Yeats's own early attempt to rescue from the past (and from the West British professors), and to encourage in the future, an Irish national literature, whose writers would 'include only those who have written under Irish influence and of Irish subjects', but, of necessity, in the English language (*UP1* 360). Yeats's project, though fitful compared to Field Day's, was so successful that in planning his anthology, Deane used the same criterion, merely extending it in order to re-read as Irish, writers whose work Yeats initially ignored as failing the nationality test (Swift, Berkeley, Sterne), writers normally subsumed under English literature (Wilde, for example), even British writers who merely wrote about Ireland (Giraldus Cambrensis, for example, and Spenser) and whose claim to Irishness, made on their behalf, resembles that of certain Republic of Ireland soccer players.

The anthology came to pass as the huge, three-volume *Field Day Anthology of Irish Writing* (1991), with Seamus Deane as General Editor.[18] But there was a limit to the extensions Deane was prepared to entertain. Most of the omissions are traceable, I suspect, back to the Northern nationalism that pervades the anthology.[19] It is an immensely useful assemblage and Deane laboured on it with great fortitude of love and duty, but among its many omissions, one must register in the present discussion an 'unblemished' Ulsterness. Ulster and unionism are offered to the reader only as a pathology. (In Ireland we seem to have developed germ warfare as a supplement to guerrilla and electoral warfare.) Deane does to unionist Ulster (i.e., the bulk of the North) what he accused Yeats of doing to Northern Ireland. Like Yeats, Deane inscribes on the thither (north east) edge of his known Ireland 'Here be strange beasts'. Whereas Deane's repudiation of essentialism in *Heroic Styles* was a potentially liberating and reconciliatory intervention in the Irish cultural debate, he chose in that pamphlet and in the organisation of his anthology to invest the Northern unionists and Protestants with a negative mystique and to erase them categorically. Unfortunately neither the Southern Protestant nationalist nor the Northern Catholic nationalist can bear very much reality where the Ulster Protestant is concerned, an ironically convergent antipathy for Yeats and his critic Deane to meet in.

IV

The internal difficulties of Northern nationalism have lately been revealed in another and surprising location: the Irish criticism of the worldly Denis Donoghue. In that criticism, no less than in Deane's criticism, those difficulties find their curious counterpart in the internal difficulties and contradictions of Yeats's attitude to Ireland and Irishness. Donoghue's long-standing loyalty to the poet has been challenged by affairs in Northern Ireland, including the advent of Field Day, and caused him both to revise earlier readings of Yeats and to resist having to make such revisions.

To give title to his 1986 collection of Irish criticism, Donoghue wrote an essay called 'We Irish'.[20] The phrase is from the last stanza of 'The Statues' ('We Irish, born into that ancient sect' [*VP* 611]), inspired by Berkeley's repudiation in his journal of English abstractionism *and* English materialism ('We Irishmen cannot attain to these truths'). Donoghue appropriates the phrase too, in order to reclaim his own Irishness, prompted in part, surely, by the long years in semi-exile. But in the reclamation is preserved an expatriate ironic distance: Donoghue, unlike Deane, does not wish to get mauled by the Irish situation, an experience Cruise O'Brien offered as a virtual definition of Irishness.

Yeats, Donoghue tells us, believed there is a special Irish mentality, deriving the idea partly from Berkeley, for whom 'the Irish', Donoghue concludes, meant powerless but prestigious upper-class Protestants. Donoghue calls the notion 'bizarre' and reduces it to Berkeley's wish to counter English philosophy. Yet Donoghue defends Yeats's preoccupation with a distinctive Irishness against Deane's attack in his Field Day pamphlets on the romantic mystique of nationhood, defending even the essentialism from which it issued. Indeed, Seamus Heaney, also a Field Day man, is shown to have the same preoccupation as recently as *Station Island* (1984). In 'We Irish', Donoghue is reluctant to concede the incoherence of Yeatsian Irishness to Deane, whom he construes as an anti-nationalist revisionist instead of a different kind of nationalist, which further inquiry would have revealed.

Like Deane, Donoghue regards Joyce's view of Irishness as an alternative to Yeats's. He takes issue with Joyce's ghost in *Station Island* (i.e., with Heaney) for telling Heaney that the issue of Irishness doesn't matter, yet praises Stephen Dedalus in *A Portrait* (i.e.,

Joyce) for riskily attempting to escape his Irishness. Donoghue concludes that there *is* a distinctive Irish experience but that it is an experience of proliferating 'division'.

'We Irish' ends with a reminder that Berkeley lost interest in defining an Irish mentality and increasingly regarded himself as English. Donoghue quotes the philosopher wondering aloud if it isn't the duty of the Irish after all to cultivate their love for England, and the critic adds: 'The only way he had in view was that of being unfailingly biddable'. The reader might wonder aloud if this is meant to be a nationalist sneer at a West Briton. In any case, in this one essay as elsewhere, nationalism and romanticism in one corner and pluralism and revisionism (a reactive, more culturally versatile liberal humanism) in the other can be seen contesting the field of Donoghue's Irish criticism and in a way that might baffle the reader.

Yeats's ambiguities (as Donoghue sees them) are analogues, as it were, of Donoghue's own ambivalences on the matter of Yeats and Ireland. In 'Romantic Ireland' (1980), Donoghue sets Yeats's career-long Romanticism against the poet's recognition that Romantic values had failed. In 'Yeats: the Question of Symbolism' (1977), Yeats's symbolism, with its attraction to essence and vision, is countered by 'the scruple which prevented him from making his entire art with Symons and the Symbolists', that scruple arising from 'the roughage of daily experience, chance, choice, and history' (*WI* 39, 44). In 'On *The Winding Stair*' (1965), Yeats is seen as running his course between extremities, of which his dialogue between self and soul, and all they imply, is the case in point.

Donoghue attempts on Yeats's behalf to resolve these ambiguities. He sees Yeats as a legendiser, legend being a middle term between symbolism and history, essence and existence: Yeats absorbs history into his *own* history, situating himself between contraries. Deane had said something similar in 'The Literary Myths of the Revival' in *Celtic Revivals*, but went farther when he identified as one of Yeats's appropriations of history his 'seductive historical fiction' of the dignity and coherence of the Ascendancy, which amounted to a myth *of* history, and which distorted history in the service of continued Ascendancy power. (Unlike Donoghue, product of a more dominantly liberal humanist era in criticism, Deane does not concede the sovereignty of the subject.) More problematic is Donoghue's defence gambit in 'Romantic Ireland' that the idea in the essay's title is one that has been endlessly celebrated or satirised in Irish literature, and has now (1980) been temporarily 'sequestered', removed from dispute until a calmer, more hospitable future. Four years later, Deane's *Heroic Styles* and the Field Day project showed him in error. Deane assailed Romantic Ireland—though in no unproblematic fashion, as I have tried to demonstrate.

Having loyally defended Yeats, Donoghue proceeds a few years later in 'Yeats, Ancestral Houses, and Anglo-Ireland' (first printed in *We Irish*) to undermine the poet's romantic concept of the Big House with a few well-chosen observations on the ground from Arthur Young, Carlyle and Froude. Perhaps sensing some contradiction, Donoghue attaches a personal postscript. We are told that Yeats's politics and occultism caused the critic difficulty from the start, though he was reading the poet under the aegis of New Criticism, an American methodology that required the reader to extend latitude to the work of art as artifact. It seems that young Donoghue accepted Blackmur's notion of doctrine-as-emotion. Nowadays, Donoghue admits uneasily, latitude is denied by Marxist and Irish anti-colonialist critics alike. 'My own stance is that of a latitudinarian, and I would hold to its concessiveness until a particularly extreme outrage makes me ashamed of it' (*WI* 66).

Yeats is a test case for latitudinarianism. At the outset of both 'We Irish' and 'Yeats, Ancestral Houses, and Anglo-Ireland', the most outrageous, violence-mongering, anti-democratic Yeats Donoghue can recruit (the Yeats arraigned on these nominal charges by Deane) establishes the threshold of Donoghue's tolerance for Yeats. He manages to find Yeats's occasional late hysteria 'touching in its appalling way'; Yeats was at the end of his tether, allows Donoghue, and therefore exonerable; it was society's fault for provoking Yeats's violent anti-democracy; it was not the subject's vice.

Latitudinarianism and sequestration are defensive concepts Donoghue has been forced to deploy to defend Yeats against his hostile readers, among whom he has counted the Field Day folk (wrongly) as pluralists and revisionists, left-leaning anti-authoritarians. More than Yeats is at stake, as he knows, for the poet is simply one example of 'the subject' which is under a barrage of attack in the American university literature classroom under the banners of Women's Studies, Feminism, Gender Studies, Gay and Lesbian Studies, African-American Studies, Marxist Criticism, Psychoanalytic Criticism, Deconstruction, New Historicism, Cultural Studies, Post-Colonial Studies. All of these he has recently taken on gamely if briefly in 'Doing Things with Words: Criticism and the Attack on the Subject', in which the countering concepts of latitudinarianism and sequestration become an object of study for literary critics: i.e., Bakhtinian dialogism.[21]

Under pressure of contemporary criticism, Donoghue's response to Yeats has become marked by increasing ambivalence. On the one hand he has become a revisionist in an Irish sense; that is, he is now inclined to a pluralist notion of Irish culture and chary of Yeats's mystical nationalism. He is, after all, a man of international perspective, living and teaching in a cosmopolis. This has caused him to re-think his attitude to Deane and Field Day whom he had at first repudiated *because* he thought they were pluralists and revisionists. (And yet in any case, Yeats for Donoghue is a privileged, different-order figure who escapes the strictures of revisionism.) On the other hand, his original review of Field Day (which he was honest enough to re-print above his second thoughts, in Hutchinson's hardback version of the pamphlets) shows him to be a nationalist yet, not ready to leave the field to 'revisionist pedagogy' (as he calls it in 'At Swim', a 1983 essay in *We Irish*) or loosen his grip on Romantic Ireland and the 'legend of sorrowful Ireland', as Stephen Dedalus cynically called it.

His quarrel with Field Day is more of an illusion than Donoghue believes. He fails to see that these Marxist and anti-colonialist critics are, in Ireland, neo-nationalists, and so he believes he is defending Yeats from attacks from the fashionable left rather than from new Irish nationalism that assails Yeats, nominally for being ultra-conservative but really for being a Protestant, an Anglo-Irishman—a colonialist—and an *inauthentic* nationalist. Latitude and sequestration would normally be evidence of a liberal humanism in its New Criticism (serious) or quasi-Bakhtinian (playful) guises, and closer kin to pluralism and revisionism than the nominal pluralism and revisionism of Field Day. But instead, I believe Donoghue's loyalty to Yeats is a loyalty to Irish cultural nationalism of the Anglo-Irish kind that before academic new Marxism, postcolonialism and Field Day came into existence, used to be the only respectable variety for a critic or professor. In other words, it is not simply loyalty to that notion of the aesthetic which underpinned Anglo-American critical practice when Donoghue came to maturity, and which then was the alternative to the pluralism and revisionism of today. Under protection of the notions of the aesthetic and of the inspired individual, Yeats was then a great and complex world writer to be explicated and appreciated and, when necessary, excused. (Actually, at that time the aesthetic response, which ought to have stood over against it, cohabited with a polite routine Irish nationalism, for appreciators and explicators of Yeats simply accepted the poet's ideas on Ireland.) Whereas Donoghue wishes to extend latitude to Yeats the mystical, romantic nationalist, he disapproves of latitude when he spots it in Irish revisionist historians such as T. W. Moody, F. S. L. Lyons and Roy Foster who have wrongly 'played down the story of revolution and drawn more attention to the latitude of personal, social, and political experience which the history of Ireland entails'.[22]

What we overhear in the quarrel of Donoghue and Field Day over Yeats is an unadmitted quarrel between two kinds (and two generations) of Irish nationalism, both forged in Northern Ireland, but Field Day's forged under pressure of the Troubles, Donoghue's forged in quieter days. There is, then, a generational difference and perhaps a rivalry. 'I left Northern Ireland before it became necessary for me to deal with its wretched system,' Donoghue tells us in 'Castle Catholic', a revealing book review in *We Irish*, and so he is forced to watch from the sidelines while the younger generation tries to see something through. It is an irony that it was an enterprise Donoghue mistook for an anti-nationalist enterprise—Field Day (as he thought, cleverness at the expense of the suffering fore-bears)—that stung Donoghue into re-examining sympathetically his Irishness, at first primarily through the medium of Yeats and most recently through the medium of autobiography, in which Yeats nevertheless looms large.

When I reviewed his collected Irish criticism in 1988, I wrote:

We Irish has a psychological subtext: a belated and faltering redress. Quite what is being redressed is never spelled out. The subtext's provenance, however, is probably autobiographical and it breaks the surface of the text at those points where politics and ideology, even the critic's own life, demand expression, a thrashing-out.[23]

Two years later, the autobiography of his childhood and young manhood appeared, as if on cue.

Whereas *Warrenpoint* (1990) exploits 'the latitude of personal, social, and political experience', it does so in order to set straight from an autobiographical point of view the record that the revisionists (among whom he still numbers Deane) have distorted. And part of the record distorted is the work of Yeats. He allows that 'it is a difficult issue', but believes that Yeats, even though 'poetic images harbour a corresponding disposition to carry their energy into action', was not responsible for violence in Northern Ireland, that poetic language 'holds the reader's mind for as long as possible in a fictive or otherwise gratuitous space' (sequesters the political issues, one might say) (*W* 167-8). Here we see adherence to the aesthetic (he recruits Langer's concept of 'virtuality') consorting with unreconstructed nationalism, as of old; for 'what the revisionist spirit in the reading of Yeats mainly shows [especially in Deane] is the reader's resentment' (*W* 168).

This is odd, for *Warrenpoint* is full of barely repressed resentment. Not only does Donoghue defend the Catholic ethos instilled in him by the Christian Brothers, with its Anglophobic nationalism and rejection of Northern Ireland ('the sorrowful legend of Ireland' with its unquenchable 'flame of freedom' and 'heroic men')—this ethos that is derided in the fashionable quarters that Donoghue resentfully derides in turn—but he relives and promenades anti-Protestant sectarianism which the intervening years have not softened through examination or reservation. (Donoghue cares to know as little about Ulster unionists as Deane—or Yeats.) A childhood once fled has now been re-accepted in its entirety, along with the story of his country told to him in childhood. It is a story of the indomitable Irishry acted out grimly by Bobby Sands and imaginatively propelled by Yeats. Indeed, Donoghue believes the entire country (i.e., the Republic of Ireland) needs the story: without it, he says with a Yeatsian flourish, Ireland 'is merely a member of the EC, the begging bowl our symbol' (*W* 172).

This childhood is re-anchored in the father, and the book's central act is homage to him. And the father, we are told, embodied 'purpose' and 'truth' and, it transpires, political conservatism. Although at times similarly moving, *Warrenpoint* is the mirror image of Gosse's *Father and Son* (1907) in which the son wins liberation from the father: here, Donoghue surrenders his freedom to the father. There is, though, a resemblance: against the odds, the father is in the end immensely sympathetic, as was Philip Henry Gosse. Because the father, a Catholic, born in Kerry, member of the disbanded Royal Irish Constabulary, went north after partition and joined the Royal Ulster Constabulary, Donoghue cannot find it in himself to denounce the RUC in which his father served, which his neo-nationalism requires, though he maintains that his father's religion prevented his promotion. The father's situation necessarily modifies the son's from what it might have been, an unlicensed republicanism, into a constitutional, quietist nationalism, which inside the text seems to sublimate its frustration through the virtual revolutionism of Yeats's poetry and plays.

What also complicates Donoghue's nationalism is his resentment at the Irish Free State and Irish Republic for abandoning Northern nationalists: 'the rhetoric of Irish politics since 1932 has been a cynical exercise in bad faith. It is dishonourable for Irish governments to persist in a claim upon the unity of Ireland and to make that claim . . . with studied silence' (*W* 161-2). His resentment is so great he finds himself defending Yeats's *Cathleen Ni Houlihan* against Cruise O'Brien and comes close to defending the Provisional IRA.

Somehow Yeats the nationalist Southern Irishman is the depository of the deep ambivalence felt, or suffered, by the Northern nationalist who refuses the invitation of the physical-force tradition. Even in *Warrenpoint*, a remarkable document of reversion and reaction, there are hesitations about Yeats beyond the ones I've mentioned. Donoghue was born, he tells us, in a small Southern town, and adds, seemingly gratuitously on the first page of his story: 'it is the kind of town that Yeats hated'. Why drag in Yeats? Well, Yeats would have hated it, we are told, as he passed through it with distaste 'on his way to Coole Park, Lady Gregory's estate in Gort, County Galway'. In his quarrel with Deane, Donoghue tells us that Yeats was not interested in understanding Irish history in terms of class or social formations, and we are meant to assume that Donoghue believes Yeats to have been right: Yeats's is the world of transcending mythology, of intensified narrative, the anti-bourgeois story of Ireland that allies virtual peasant with virtual nobleman. Yet earlier in *Warrenpoint*, Donoghue remembers with resentment the subtle way in which the Yeats scholar T. R. Henn slighted him and did so from the vantage point of Protestant cultural superiority, the vantage point, in fact, of Yeats's adopted Anglo-Irish Big House culture (*W* 49-50). We know that Yeats would have slighted him in a similar manner had the occasion arisen; Donoghue's resentment at (Yeatsian) Protestant superiority smoulders throughout *Warrenpoint*.

V

When I reviewed *We Irish*, I somewhat whimsically likened the Yeats of the Northern Catholics to Freud's primal father, a figure invested with an undesirable but irresistible authority. Their battle with him is beginning to resemble that Irish tale type, The Everlasting Fight. He is the nationalist they want and the higher-class Protestant nationalist they don't want, the pre-eminent purveyor of a myth of Irishness that they know has enthralled them and that has nevertheless insulated them in their Northern Ireland existence and given their life there—since they refused participation in the society of the province—meaning. He is the Ireland they have 'betrayed', either by leaving—like Donoghue—or by staying and outgrowing the old simple nationalism—like Deane, but the Ireland they still wish to propitiate; but he is also an impostor, being a Protestant.

Donoghue has, after some anguish, explicitly accepted Yeats's authority as he has accepted the authority of Irish nationalism and of his own re-imagined father. At the end of his memoir he admits that his father's characterisation is not well-rounded but reduced (in my opinion, by the diet of his son's reactivated nationalism—though he is still a moving figure) to the dimensions of authority, purpose, conservatism, single-mindedness, duty, 'truth'. In my review I said that, like Jacob, these critics are grappling with Yeats the father to discover their real names (the name of their country). But in *Warrenpoint*, Donoghue expressly rejects the Freudian theory that the son's struggle with the father is necessary to avoid neurosis. And so Donoghue writes his book in order to affirm the father without struggle. And for 'father' read also Yeats and Ireland, 'a nation once again'.

I suggested in my review that there are three ways in which Irish critics from a Catholic/Nationalist background can come to grips with Yeats and solve the 'Yeats Question'. They can 'kill' him symbolically after an authentic struggle and walk way into freedom and maturity. O'Brien has tried this and succeeded; Deane has tried it and failed. Or they can engage him in the deferential, essentially exegetical way in which North American academics used to engage him. Or they can go on grappling painfully and inconclusively with him (which Deane is doing), which is brave and honest as long as it is clear that there is not some other struggle going on, which in the case of Deane I believe there is, and it has to do with Northern Ireland. Donoghue would seem to offer a fourth course: acceptance of Yeats after self-interrogation; but I believe that the painful, inconclusive struggle is yet going on with him and it has to do likewise with Northern Ireland. I see no end in sight.

Which is what makes the prospect of Seamus Heaney's intervention in Irish Yeats Studies so appealing. Heaney as a poet will surely recuperate the aesthetic response (the poem as artifact; poetry as a sovereign space and discourse) and re-confirm the necessity of the realised self, detaching both from ideology, be it the old ideologies of romanticism (the transcending self) and nationalism or the new ideologies of pluralism and revisionism. His, one expects, will be the successful fourth way of engaging with Yeats that Donoghue was not able to achieve and that Heaney can, because he is a poet.

Heaney's interest, like Donoghue's and Deane's, is of course that of a reader, of a professional teacher and critic, and of an Irishman. But it is also that of a fellow poet, teaching himself all that can be learned from a master; he has, as he remarks of his interest in Hopkins, 'the slightly predatory curiosity of a poet interested in the creative processes of another poet'.[24] This being the case, and Yeats's poetry being self-evidently exemplary as creative achievement, Heaney will have no truck with any ideological or political belittlement of Yeats. 'Fifty years after the death of Yeats . . . it would be both stupid and insensitive to think of him or his art or the figure he cuts as being anything less than dignified, heroic and epoch-making'.[25]

Above all, Yeats was a poet and his interests and his statements—many of them troubling in their propaganda quotient—'refer to the ambitions of a poet, not to the operations of a promoter' (FD2 785). The latitude Heaney extends to Yeats here is in the first instance an unfashionable sequestering of the poetry, not just by a reader like Donoghue (Warrenpoint has some poignant and honest pages on Donoghue's lack of creativity), but also by a fellow poet. Heaney's exemplar was no ideologue, nor did his imagination 'function like an obedient seismograph', even if 'the historical shocks that ran through the world did affect Yeats' (FD2 787). Apart from anything else, Yeats 'possessed a robust, sceptical intelligence and his grasp of what was happening in his own times was at least equal to that of the most secular and topically focussed minds of his generation' (FD2 787). Yeats as a masterful voice is in active, even aggressive transaction with society and history; he is no mere amanuensis through which society and history dictate themselves. Therefore we can't simply read back from the poetry to history and society without distorting the uniqueness of the poetry, i.e., both of the poem (poem as artifact, as embodiment of the aesthetic) and of the poet and the ultimate privacy of his agenda (poet as autonomous self). One senses here Heaney's memory of critics who in the 1970s wished Heaney and others to write directly and reactively about the Troubles in Northern Ireland and how he sought to deflect their desire.

This is an essential but insufficient part of the story for Heaney, however. In fact, Yeats was in search of a third space, which both denied and utilised the importunities of the self and of society (which through time is history). And 'space' implies both breathing-space and clearance for action and flight, at once empowerment and closure. Yeats 'merged history and his biographical self into the representative figure of the poet/seer, and he spoke as one both empowered and responsible beyond the limits of a private self' (*FD2* 788). This too sets up echoes for readers of Heaney's poetry, with its claim to the vatic in the poetic speech and act, and with its declaration of poetic independence from the taxations and unwanted citizenships of society and nation. Poetry is poetry, a country unto itself.

Heaney's latitude would seem to resemble Donoghue's and to be opposed to the interrogationist, de-mystifying approach to Yeats practised by Deane. Besides, Heaney is a poet whose own effects have been often those of a powerful mystique, and whose poems reconstituted an Ireland mythic in its power and, in some ways, a Northern Catholic updating of Yeats's poetic mythology of Ireland. Not just as a poet, but as a poet of a certain tendency and temperament, Heaney has a vested interest in defending the accomplishment of his great predecessor. Whatever Yeats's social standing or pretensions might be, whatever his politics might be and whatever his religious background might be, Yeats was first and foremost a poet, membership in which masonry or guild must command Heaney's first loyalty. There is something noble about a Northern Irish poet's conviction that poetry transcends the otherwise fierce and deep differences of sect, politics, class.

Yet very early into his Introduction to Yeats for his selection of the poet in the *Field Day Anthology*, Heaney shows eagerness to bring Deane on-side. 'Quite recently', Heaney writes,

> Seamus Deane (in his *Celtic Revivals*, 1985) has insisted that there is a disparity between the social, political and intellectual realities of the eighteenth-century Anglo-Irish world and the mythic version of them that Yeats's poems both derive from and project.

And yet, he asserts, 'Deane would be the first to acknowledge the unique necessity of Yeats's work in the evolution of the consciousness that would criticize it' (*FD2* 784). But if this is true, it is a claim that imputes no real attraction by Deane to Yeats: it is akin to saying that the bourgeoisie were necessary to the triumph of the proletariat or that the vole is necessary to the marsh-harrier. And Heaney continues in this unwise vein: Deane, he allows, does indeed expose 'the recalcitrance of Yeats's mind. Yet, equally, he displays a relish and a gratitude for the integrity of the recalcitrance itself'. I have ransacked Deane's criticism in vain for evidence of that relish and gratitude.

Is this a contributing editor's loyalty to the General Editor? A wish to present an unbroken anthological front? The informal obligations of an old camaraderie? A well-learned reluctance to show division to the enemy (whoever they might be)? A gentle desire to influence an old friend? Or is it a wish to put in words what he believes Deane really feels about Yeats but cannot for ideological reasons state? For it may be that Deane and Heaney converge more than is apparent in their response to Yeats. According to Heaney, national regeneration (of Ireland) was of vital and original importance to Yeats, and it survived failures to give it political form. 'Yeats's radical devotion to the potential and otherness of a specifically Irish reality should never be underestimated', Heaney tells us in his Introduction (*FD2* 785). This surely echoes Deane's sentiments in 'Yeats and the Idea of Revolution' (it is also the ontological statement of the Field Day project), both critics managing to rarefy Irish nationalism beyond offence while attempting a usable metaphysics of republicanism.

I have discussed at length elsewhere the implication of Heaney's own poetry in the social and political realities of Ireland, despite his notion of the sovereignty of poetry.[26] Moreover, even though Heaney has utilised to eloquent, even visionary poetic effect the admission of such implication, and has poetically marked the progress of the implication *en route* (i.e., within the preoccupations—stylistic and thematic—of the poems) to an attempted third space, the truest poetry, even the space he has achieved is not without its political implications. Fascinatingly, the process so far has accompanied Heaney's almost continuous readings of Yeats.

Heaney has identified Yeats with the actions and ambitions of 'control', 'alerting strain', 'equestrian authority', 'urge to mastery', 'bony structure' and 'masculine elements', and elsewhere in his scheme of things has interpreted the Vikings, the Anglo-Saxon language, North, the English, the Anglo-Irish and the Ulster

Protestants—in short, invasions, overmasterings, colonisations, imperialisms—as exemplifying maleness. The earth (Nature), Ireland, Irish Catholicism, poetry in its most natural express-ion—these are exemplars of the feminine. Heaney has identified himself with the feminine set of imbrications but has expressed admiration for the 'masculine' (including decisive political interven-tion, for instance in Northern Ireland) and has lamented—with paradoxical eloquence—its rarity in his work.[27] (It seems fair to assume that his directorship in Field Day must have satisfied the expressed desire in him for Yeatsian political partisanship.) His sug-gestion in one early essay that Yeats entertained at last 'a motherly kindness towards life' is hardly convincing.[28] Yeats remains in Heaney's criticism the proud Protestant and his work remains politically (because culturally) infused, and therefore applicable, like it or not, to Northern Ireland.

Manifesting an almost Yeatsian engagement with antithesis though perhaps at a more unconscious level, Heaney has struggled against the tide of evaluation of Yeats that Heaney's own scheme of things helped to create, whereby Yeats is implicated in the Protestant *misrepresentation* of Ireland (in several meanings of that word), and in the Protestant subjugation of Catholic Ireland, as a man arrogates to himself the lawful right to subjugate a woman. He has struggled against the tide of nationalist desire by which as an Ulster Catholic he is naturally carried. He has shouldered, though without spelling them out, the difficulties of being a Northern Catholic. But the outcome is still in doubt.

A recent solution essayed by Heaney coincides with the express aspiration of his recent poetry to a new spirituality, a 'neuter allegiance', truancy, freedom, 'ungovernment'. In his inaugural lec-ture as Professor of Poetry at Oxford, he identified 'transcendent equilibrium' as the preferred destination of poetry, and offered examples.[29] Lately, Heaney has begun to re-read Yeats in the grip of this new preoccupation. *Through* history and *through* nationalism (and *through* maleness and femaleness, one might add), Yeats's poetry reached and created 'the place of meditation, the place of writing, the place where the second, imagined life is possible'.[30]

I have suggested in 'Heaney's Redress' that the place of trans-cendence unavoidably has political dimensions. The ideal republic of poetry is indistinguishable under the evolving circumstances from the ideal republic of Ireland; its political philosophical version can be found in the work of another Field Day pamphleteer, Richard

Kearney, as Ireland's 'fifth province', the republic in Platonic guise.
I believe my suggestion is vindicated by Heaney's own recent claim
for the utility and applicability of Yeats's 'nobility' (as Heaney
names the state of Yeatsian poetry): 'There is surely political meaning, *at once realistic and visionary*, in his sense of life as an abounding
conflict of energies; in his recognition of the necessity as well as the
impossibility of the attempt "to hold in a single thought reality and
justice"; and in his conviction—overriding his sense of hierarchy
and election—that even among the Paudeens of this earth, "There
cannot be . . . A single soul that lacks a sweet crystalline cry"' (*FD2*
790, emphasis added). What reality must the place of transcendence
assume? Heaney offers only one political reality. He paraphrases
what Yeats admitted ('I am no Nationalist, except in Ireland for
passing reasons')—'His nationalism,' Heaney tells us, 'was essentially another avenue towards an ideal if unattainable "Unity of
Being"'(*FD2* 790).

But from the perspective of a Northern unionist (routinely erased
by all of the writers and critics I have discussed), these would-be
unities of being, culture, and island are not quite the good they seem
to Yeats and Heaney. The story I have tried to tell in this essay has
been the progress of, and reasons for, the engagement of Northern
Catholic critics with the work of W.B. Yeats. It has been a dialogue
of peculiar intensity, but it has also been an *intimacy* of peculiar
intensity. It has been a rivalry rather than a radical opposition. The
point at which Yeats's unities would converge is the point at which
these Northern readers of Yeats would converge. It is also the point
at which they in turn would converge with Yeats, however genuine
the differences before that point is reached.

NOTES

1.   I borrow the details of Yeats's ancestry from Joseph Hone, *W. B. Yeats 1865-
      1939* (London: Macmillan, 1943, 1965). Hereafter *WBY*.

2.   Edna Longley, 'W. B. and Cultural Politics Today', *Yeats: A Fortnight Anniver-
      sary Supplement* (*Fortnight Magazine* [March 1989], 4.

3.   *Irish News and Belfast Morning News*, 22 November 1893, 8.

4.   Edward W. Said, *Nationalism, Colonialism and Literature: Yeats and Decoloniza-
      tion.* Field Day Pamphlet No. 15 (Derry City: Field Day Theatre Company,
      1988).

5.   Terry Eagleton, *Heathcliff and the Great Hunger: Studies in Irish Culture*
      (London: Verso, 1995), p. 308. Eagleton wrote a Field Day pamphlet in the

same series as Said (*Nationalism: Irony and Commitment*, pamphlet no. 13) but did not discuss Yeats.

6.   The work of Longley, Brown and Roy Foster is widely available; Foster is writing the authorised biography of Yeats, and Brown an unauthorised critical biography. My own views are set out in *Fictions of the Irish Literary Revival: A Changeling Art* (Syracuse: Syracuse University Press, 1987). I find a view of Yeats not dissimilar to my own in Norman Vance, *Irish Literature: A Social History* (Oxford: Basil Blackwell, 1990). See also Conor Cruise O'Brien, 'Passion and Cunning: An Essay on the Politics of W.B. Yeats', in *In Excited Reverie: A Centenary Tribute to William Butler Yeats*, ed. A. Norman Jeffares and K.G.W. Cross (London: Macmillan, 1965), pp. 207-78.

7.   John Wilson Foster, 'The Poetry of Patrick Kavanagh', *Colonial Consequences: Essays in Irish Literature and Culture* (Dublin: Lilliput, 1991), pp. 97-113.

8.   See Clare O'Halloran, *Partition and the Limits of Irish Nationalism* (Dublin: Gill and Macmillan, 1987) and Dennis Kennedy, *The Widening Gulf: Northern Attitudes to the Independent Irish State 1919-49* (Belfast: Blackstaff, 1988).

9.   See, for example, Kiberd's *Anglo-Irish Attitudes*. Field Day Pamphlet No. 6 (Derry City: Field Day Theatre Company, 1984).

10.   Seamus Deane, *A Short History of Irish Literature* (London: Hutchinson, 1986), pp. 159-60.

11.   Seamus Deane, *Heroic Styles: The Tradition of an Idea*. Field Day Pamphlet No. 4 (Derry City: Field Day Theatre Company, 1984).

12.   Seamus Deane, 'Yeats and the Idea of Revolution', *Celtic Revivals: Essays in Modern Irish Literature 1880-1980* (London: Faber and Faber, 1985), p. 38.

13.   *Guardian* Symposium on W. B. Yeats (27 January 1989), quoted by Longley, 'W. B. and Cultural Politics Today', see above n. 2.

14.   John Wilson Foster, 'The Critical Condition of Ulster', *Colonial Consequences*, pp. 215-33.

15.   A demystified unionism is advanced throughout John Wilson Foster (ed.), *The Idea of the Union: Statements and Critiques in Support of the Union of Great Britain and Northern Ireland* (Vancouver: Belcouver Press, 1995).

16.   Quoted by Longley from the *Guardian* symposium on Yeats in 'W. B. and Cultural Politics Today', see above n. 2.

17.   Deane, *Celtic Revivals*, pp. 49-50.

18.   Seamus Deane (gen. ed.), *The Field Day Anthology of Irish Writing* (Derry City: Field Day Publications, 1991). Hereafter abbreviated as *FD1,2,3*.

19.   Glaring omissions or inadequacies include nature writing, women's writing, feminist writing, and serious unionist apologetics. See Edna Longley, *The Living Stream* (Newcastle upon Tyne: Bloodaxe Books, 1994), pp. 22-44.

20.   *We Irish: The Selected Essays of Denis Donoghue. Volume 1.* (Brighton: Harvester, 1986). Hereafter abbreviated as *WI*.

21.   'Doing Things with Words', *TLS*, 15 July 1994, 4-6. Bakhtinian dialogism is tested out in an essay written especially for *We Irish*, 'Bakhtin and *Finnegans Wake*'.

22.   Denis Donoghue, *Warrenpoint* (New York: Knopf, 1990), p. 167. Abbreviated hereafter as *W*.

23.   The review is reprinted in *Colonial Consequences* as 'A Complex Fate: The Irishness of Denis Donoghue'.

24.   'The Fire i' the Flint: Reflections on the Poetry of Gerard Manley Hopkins',
      Preoccupations: Selected Prose 1968-1978 (London: Faber and Faber, 1980), p. 79.
25.   Seamus Heaney, 'William Butler Yeats', *Field Day Anthology of Irish Writing*, II,
      p. 783.
26.   'Heaney's Redress', *Colonial Consequences*, 168-205.
27.   These equations are discussed at length in 'Heaney's Redress'.
28.   'Yeats as an Example?' *Preoccupations*, p. 113.
29.   Quoted in my essay, 'Heaney's Redress', in *Colonial Consequences*.
30.   'Yeats's Nobility', *Yeats: A Fortnight Anniversary Supplement*, 3.

Yeats, Form and Northern Irish Poetry

Peter McDonald

I

'HE BECAME HIS ADMIRERS': W. H. Auden's reflection was perhaps unduly sanguine.[1] Poets do indeed become their admirers in their posthumous careers, but they also become their critics, a rule which Yeats's artistic afterlife illustrates particularly well, not least in the context of the 'mad Ireland' which Auden's poem tries to account for and transcend. The name of Yeats means a number of different things in the discourses of contemporary Irish literary criticism, some of them a very long way from what might be understood by admiration. A sense of this may be gained quickly from the following selective (but not unrepresentative) gathering of remarks:

> An idea of art opposed to the idea of utility, an idea of an audience opposed to the idea of popularity, an idea of the peripheral becoming the central culture—in these three ideas Yeats provided Irish writing with a programme for action. But whatever its connection with Irish nationalism, it was not, finally, a programme of separation from the English tradition. His continued adherence to it led him to define the central Irish attitude as one of self-hatred . . . The pathology of literary unionism has never been better defined.[2]

213

In Ireland, it is fair to say, Yeats is resented . . . because he claimed
to speak in the name of 'the indomitable Irishry.' . . . In the present
confusions, readers of Yeats resent his appeal to Irishness, and his
assertion that he knows the quality of Irishness when he meets it.
That resentment is so inclusive that little or nothing survives in its
presence.[3]

The battle with Yeats is beginning to resemble The Everlasting
Fight. He is the nationalist the Irish critics want and the higher class
Protestant they don't want.[4]

Nowhere is this more obvious than in Yeats's hopeless rehabilitation of the modes of Irish deference . . . The deepest insults could
now be happily internalized in the postcolonial mind . . . Despite
repeated resolutions to 'walk naked' he [Yeats] found it impossible
to commit the ultimate revolutionary deed of speaking with his
own face instead of performing through a rhetorical mask.[5]

'Now Ireland has her madness and her weather still': again, Auden's
ironic observation, however light in its urbanity, might still be said
to hold good after more than half a century. 'The battle with Yeats',
which the remarks above both witness and embody, continues in
literary criticism within and outside Ireland; it is a serious debate,
sometimes a learned and stimulating one, which the present essay
can address only as background. However, the fact of the debate, its
intensification in recent years, and the inevitable transformation of
Yeats from a *corpus* of finished poems into a complex system of historical and critical meanings, which the debate effects and thrives
upon, are important elements bearing upon any discussion of a Yeatsian influence on Northern Irish poetry, especially if that influence
is considered to be, at least in part, a 'formal' one.

The recognition that the forms of poetry can have something to
do with other aspects of its literary significance needs to be made by
any intelligent critical writing; but a crude version of such an awareness, in which poetic form becomes simply a cypher for ideological
content or historical placing, is a danger attendant on some of the
more spirited and committed contributions to Irish critical debate
on Yeats. In this respect, it is possible to notice a measure of the pervasive suspicion being directed, not just at Yeats's forms themselves,
but at the very idea of poetic form as something unamenable to the
more urgent kinds of ideological demand. A concern with poetic

form may thus be refracted to become 'formalism', and this theoretical position, rather than the precise and particular concerns which gave rise to its labelling, can now be the thing addressed by the post-structuralist, historicist, or post-colonial critic. Against the background of this kind of argument, it is necessary to insist that poetic form remains distinct from 'formalism', and that Yeats's forms, as they are transmitted to subsequent Irish poetry, are more significant and fertile than the other meanings—critical, historical, or ideological—which the name Yeats, like the notion of 'formalism', has accrued. Just as 'Yeats' can mean, under certain circumstances, 'The pathology of literary unionism' or a 'hopeless rehabilitation of the modes of Irish deference', so 'form' can be represented as a set of theoretical assumptions and impositions rather than the lines, timings, rhymes and stanzas which, unlike pathologies or deferential modes, can be heard and seen openly in the poetry.

The question of form in contemporary theory has a special relevance for Northern Irish poetry since the early 1960s, and the various curiosities and anomalies in the theoretical ways of addressing form might well be said to have their bearing upon the wider reception of poets like Derek Mahon, Michael Longley, and Seamus Heaney. In a recent study of poets from Northern Ireland, Clair Wills begins with a chapter on 'The Politics of Poetic Form', and sets out certain problems with a useful clarity:

Poetically, the difficulty with both the postmodernist and 'Irish identity' readings of the significance of poetic form is that the poetry is thereby reduced either to symptomatic or reactive status. The form of the work is deemed to arise out of a particular set of social co-ordinates, but its function is considered to be a reflection in the realm of the aesthetic of an image of future possibilities in the social arena.[6]

The unease evident here is justified and, even if Wills's concern with form does not lead her to discuss or examine any actual poetic forms in the chapter, she does begin here to show how poetry and its critical function can be at odds, especially at the level of formal attention and understanding. The mismatch between critical intelligence and poetic formal resource is often evident in criticism of Yeats, as when David Lloyd, a theorist of the post-colonial school, addresses 'A Dialogue of Self and Soul' and its use of 'remorse':

We need, I believe, to understand remorse as that emotion which, beyond the predetermined gyres of Yeatsian time, chooses to assert that things might have been otherwise. It is an appeal to the history of the possible, of what might have been . . . . The loose ends produced by such a history are incompatible with the formal drive of Yeats's poetic, as indeed they are equally with any representative aesthetic, asserting the irruption of a content that is in excess of any form and unassimilable to narrative time.[7]

Like the 'image of future possibilities' which Wills detects in the insistence upon form as function, Lloyd's 'history of the possible' in Yeats must be 'in excess of any form', the inevitable 'irruption of a content'. But the 'formal drive' can bear closer scrutiny than Lloyd provides, for the shapes of Yeats's stanzas, their accommodations of rhyme and syntactic structure, allow for an irruption of something inherent in, rather than in excess of form. To take the last stanza of the 'Dialogue', upon which Lloyd concentrates:

> I am content to follow to its source
> Every event in action or in thought;
> Measure the lot; forgive myself the lot!
> When such as I cast out remorse
> So great a sweetness flows into the breast
> We must laugh and we must sing,
> We are blest by everything,
> Everything we look upon is blest. (*VP* 479)

Yeats's eight-line stanza unit sub-divides in terms of its rhyme pattern, holding two four-line shapes within its *abbacddc* scheme. Yeats completes his first sentence within three lines, with the result that the rhyme for 'source' will, in terms of syntax, figure in a new sentence, and lead into a second sequence of rhymes (*cddc*). 'When such as I cast out remorse', the new syntactic start which carries along the rhyme of the sentence it succeeds, prepares for the irruption of new rhymes to conclude the stanza; Yeats accommodates the 'excess' that is his theme here in the stanza's formal renewal towards completion: the stanza is, after all, a pattern of rhyming which, in repeating its shape, changes its rhymes (*abba* repeats as *cddc*). It is part of Yeats's rhetorical achievement here to involve the syntax in this plotting of renewal, changing in the process the personal pronouns, from 'When such as I . . .' to 'We must laugh . . . '. Lloyd's 'loose ends' are only incompatible with Yeats's 'formal drive' here in that they are nowhere to be found; the stanza's completeness, its reconciliation of argument, syntax, and rhyme-scheme, ensures that 'remorse' is inseparable from 'sweetness'.

A full engagement with Yeats's poem, and with Lloyd's reading of its 'formal drive', would of course require much more detailed analysis of the patterns of formal arrangement and complication in evidence there. For the present purposes, the point to be noted is that 'form' is a perilous critical category when employed in its more abstract or theoretical senses; to invoke 'a content that is in excess of any form' is to risk very serious underestimation of how much form can do in poetry: it is also, of course, to invest in notions of 'content' which are dangerously disembodied. Yet such approaches to Yeats's poetic forms are not at all uncommon, and it is noteworthy that many combative engagements with what Yeats represents tend to allow the poems themselves to fade off the page and become aspects of a 'discourse' in which the boundaries between poetic texts and their surrounding elements of history, reception, and ideology simply dissolve away.

A critique of this principled neglect of actual poetic form, with the consequent substitution of the bogey of formalism in its place, is certainly necessary in Yeats studies and will result, it is safe to suppose, in a more complex sense of the poet's various kinds of achievement. However, the inadequacy of the de-formed version of Yeats may be made manifest by more than just literary-critical discussion, and it is within Irish poetry itself that some of the most significant understandings of Yeats, and engagements with him, are to be found. In poetry from Northern Ireland, in particular, such kinds of reception are often to do with form, and can be traced through study of the kinds of formal resource exploited by poets in the course of the 'influence' Yeats has provided. In this essay, it will be sufficient to raise one formal concern in particular, that of the stanza, and to trace Yeats's importance in this respect through some work by Seamus Heaney, Derek Mahon, Michael Longley, and Paul Muldoon. First, however, it is necessary to sketch some preliminary propositions regarding Yeats and stanzaic form.

II

Yeats's most influential stanzaic poems come, broadly speaking, from later in his career; they begin with the volume *The Wild Swans at Coole* (1919) which, besides its title-poem, includes the formal stanzaic elegy 'In Memory of Major Robert Gregory'. Of course, Yeats had been writing in stanzas before this, but with the Gregory elegy a new sense of formal resource is drawn upon, one which comes to dominate the last two decades of the poet's career. Stanzas in the earlier Yeats had often featured refrains, and were made up of shorter lines than the five-footed measure of the poet's more rhetorically-elevated voices: many such stanzaic poems gestured back, in one way or another, towards ballad form. Where the early Yeats does use larger stanzas, it is as a means of narrative structure: 'The Man who Dreamed of Faeryland', for example, employs its three twelve-line units as containers for distinct phases of the story being told, with repetition of syntax adding to the sense of structural similarity between stanzas: these twelve-line units in fact pull together a sequence of rhymes in which one pattern simply repeats (*abbacddceffe*). This straightforward progression of rhymes is often present in Yeats's narrative verse, and it is to be distinguished from the more artfully interlocked patterns of rhyme employed in the later stanzaic poems. The later Yeats relies especially upon the *ottava rima* stanza which, with its *abababcc* rhyme-scheme, seals up a repeating progression of two rhyme sounds with a last, and importantly a new rhyme in the concluding couplet.[8] Byron's *Don Juan* shows how well this form is suited to the staging and pacing of narrative, but demonstrates also how the *ottava rima* stanza can be used to contain personal reflection and digression without allowing such things to overrun. If one tries to imagine a poem like *The Prelude* written in this stanzaic form, the meaning (and perhaps also the attractiveness) of such containment becomes clear; it was just this capacity of the stanza which Yeats seized upon and made his own in poems of highly structured and performative meditation.

The Yeatsian stanza is a means of both compression and rhetorical launching, and in this respect it moves further away from what might be thought of as narrative utility. A comparison with Byron's *ottava rima* shows this usefully; first, Byron on European-Gothic:

> Huge halls, long galleries, spacious chambers, join'd
> By no quite lawful marriage of the Arts,
> Might shock a Connoisseur; but when combined,
> Form'd a whole which, irregular in parts,
> Yet left a grand impression on the mind,
> At least of those whose eyes were in their hearts.

We gaze upon a Giant for his stature,
Nor judge at first if all be true to Nature.[9]

Next, Yeats on Anglo-Irish Classical:

O what if gardens where the peacock strays
With delicate feet upon old terraces,
Or else all Juno from an urn displays
Before the indifferent garden deities;
O what if levelled lawns and gravelled ways
Where slippered Contemplation finds his ease
And Childhood a delight for every sense,
But take our greatness with our violence? (*VP* 418)

Byron's procedure is one of narrative description, and the stanza serves him perfectly well, its *ababab* progression of rhymes accommodating a clear syntactic ordering of the evidence, and the final couplet allowing a generalised reflection which, in completing the whole sentence, also completes the significance of what the sentence and the stanza have presented for the reader's attention. The rhymes enact a similar economy, for 'arts' and 'parts' are indeed 'join'd' and 'combined' in the rhyming 'hearts' of the beholders, and the final direct linking of 'stature' and 'nature' comes as a resolution provided for by the preceding conjunctions of rhyming words, even though the syntactic meaning of that couplet maintains its reservations. For Yeats, the same stanza form serves a different purpose: the whole sentence with which he fills the stanza is a single rhetorical question, 'O what if . . . ?', and all the description is contained within the syntactic structure this generates, with the important verb occurring in the last line: 'What if [. . .] take our greatness?' Yeats thus shifts the tone of his stanza from the expository and reflective to the exclamatory and disruptive, partly by changing the balance between the alternating *ab* rhymes of the first six lines and the conclusive weight of the final couplet which must introduce a new rhyme, on 'sense'. The syntax of Yeats's sentence runs into the final couplet, so that the stanza's penultimate line, 'And childhood a delight for every sense', as well as being governed by 'What if ...', requires the reader to carry forward the verb 'find' from 'slippered Contemplation finds his ease'. Syntactically, this seventh line is fully a part of the rest of the stanza, but its now final rhyme-sound looks for an answering rhyme, and Yeats ensures that this is one fully at odds, rather than at its ease, with what has come before: 'But take our greatness with our violence?' The arrival of the verb to resolve the sentence brings with it an unsettling idea and introduces, with the surprise of rhyme, its own element of disruption, the 'violence' that underwrites what has seemed ordered and peaceful. Here, the *ottava rima* stanza is made to function rhetorically and dramatically, its syntax and rhyme-patterns in subtle and energetic counterpoint.

The rhyme-schemes of all Yeats's stanzas, and not just those of his *ottava rima*, are made to work as elements of the composition which embody, rather than simply contain the rhetorical energies of the authorial will. An alternative eight-line pattern, which Yeats uses in 'In Memory of Major Robert Gregory', 'A Prayer for my Daughter', the second section of 'The Tower', and 'Byzantium', has the rhyme-scheme *aabbcddc*: here, the change in the rhyming sequence, which comes with the fifth and sixth lines, often accommodates an important turn in syntax or thought. The ten-line stanza of 'All Souls' Night', the second and third sections of 'Nineteen Hundred and Nineteen', and the second section of 'Meditations in Time of Civil War', which rhymes *abcabcdeed*, again establishes a division within itself, between the first six and the last four lines, which syntax can either echo or override. Another aspect of Yeats's stanzaic practice of significance here is his tendency to balance longer against shorter lines, a further resource which works alongside syntax and rhyme in the formal configuration of his stanzas. Yet this kind of configuration is seldom a matter of unforced arrangement and accommodation, and is more often a system of pressures and counter-pressures as syntax, rhyme, and line-length set up competing patterns and energies within the stanza.

In the last stanza of section three of 'Nineteen Hundred and Nineteen', Yeats considers desolation and powerlessness, but the stanza he uses enables him to do something with the futility he sets out to contemplate:

> The swan has leaped into the desolate heaven:
> That image can bring wildness, bring a rage
> To end all things, to end
> What my laborious life imagined, even

The half-imagined, the half-written page;
O but we dreamed to mend
Whatever mischief seemed
To afflict mankind, but now
That winds of winter blow
Learn that we were crack-pated when we dreamed. (*VP* 431)

The complex counterpointing here is to powerful rhetorical effect, and it relies upon the basic shapes that make up this ten-line stanza structure, if only to transcend and reform them. The clear syntactic break occurs between lines five and six, while the change in rhyme-pattern from *abcabc* to *deed* comes a line later; what is more, the *d* rhyme, 'seemed', is sounded early in line six, 'O but we dreamed to mend', and the last line of the stanza returns to that same pre-emptive word for its rhyme in 'when we dreamed'. Earlier in the stanza also, Yeats works to reduce the initial symbolic spectacle through internal rhyme: 'That image can bring wildness, bring a rage' sounds out the 'rage' in 'image', and its shifting of emphasis from the visible symbol to the personal will is intensified by the chain of internal echoes that join 'end', 'end', 'imagined', and 'half-imagined' in the next three lines. The weakness of 'even', stranded at the end of the fourth line, is an important one, for its faint rhyme and its unemphatic rhythmic position in the line help to throw emphasis on to 'The half-imagined'. The effect of Yeats's stanza is to transcend the already apparently transcendent image of desolation with which it began: when 'The swan has leaped into the desolate heaven' is fed into this ten-line matrix, it is transformed into a drama of rage, finality, and imagination in which the ordering authorial voice is the victor, triumphant in its disillusion.

Yeats's stanzaic patterns are dramas of order, and it is vital that they make their formal procedures visible if the poems' rhetorical projects are to succeed. If the Yeatsian stanza makes a point of form, so to speak, then Yeats's authorial voice also has to be seen to win out over the patterns of inevitability which such forms might embody: the poet's determination confronts, as it were, the determined patterns of his stanzas. Thus, Yeats will not shift away from, say, *ottava rima* to a different eight-line configuration within a poem, or vary the sequence of rhymes from one stanza to another; the sense of closure, of formal completeness, which critics often notice (and sometimes deplore) in his poetry, is always a battle won rather than an accommodation easily engineered. For Yeats, stanzaic form is a matter of performance, and his stanzas acknowledge the design they carry.

III

When modern Irish criticism chafes under the designs which Yeats's poetry seems too palpably to have upon it, it tends to see form as an issue that can be dealt with straightforwardly. A crude simplification of the common argument might be that Yeats forces himself upon the reader by using, with great rhetorical skill, those strict forms which have their corollaries in the social and political orders for which the poet was, by the end of his career, a keen partisan. Ronald Bush's useful answer to this kind of argument, that 'despite Yeats's conservative themes, it was from the beginning clear to at least some readers that his art was rooted not in totalitarian poetics but in structures enacting the competition of value',[10] might well be applied to the specifically Irish turns which the quarrel with Yeats has taken. Yet the attraction of this argument from corollary is very strong, for it enables critics to locate certain values in contemporary literature by reference to Yeats as a negative example. Thus, Seamus Deane's *Celtic Revivals* (1985) employs its profound scepticism with regard to Yeats's claims on Irish critical and literary practice in readings of contemporary poets like Heaney, Mahon, and Thomas Kinsella, all of whom are shown to have escaped from the dangerous legacy in one way or another; David Lloyd's *Anomalous States* (1993), which attacks Yeats in one chapter (quoted above), attacks Heaney in another for his supposed investment in the kinds of 'identity' so discredited by the older poet. There is commonly a sense amongst critics that Yeats's poetry is somehow implicated in contemporary Irish poetry, whether for good or ill, and that present artistic phenomena, no less than present political troubles, need to be measured critically against ideas and tendencies which Yeats is seen especially to represent.

Northern Irish poetry since the 1960s has been interpreted as unusually technically-controlled, a critical observation which can easily slide into the backhanded compliment, or worse, particularly when form is understood as a kind of political limitation. If Northern Ireland produces a formalist poetry, then the political shortcomings of the place itself can be associated with the lowered revolutionary horizons of the verse. Hence the insufficient awareness of, or rather suspicion of, the notions of form and order which that poetry reveals. In his 'General Introduction' to *The Field Day Anthology Of Irish Writing*, Seamus Deane looks with irony towards Northern Irish respect for poetic order; in delineating what he calls 'The aesthetic ideology', with its high valuation of 'reconciliation' in art and 'a harmonious and triumphant wholeness', he gives short shrift to ideas of 'order':

> The idea that that which is chaotic, disorganized and 'rude' can be converted to order and civilization was shared by English colonial writers and English literary critics, at least until very recent times. It is also shared by those who see a connection between northern [*sic*] Irish violence and the northern Irish literary 'revival'. The literature—autonomous, ordered—stands over against the political system in its savage disorder. The connection here is as interesting as the contrast. Ultimately, any key political term is exchangeable with any key literary term.[11]

Deane's caricature here would seem to relate to his conception of Northern Irish critics (such as Edna Longley perhaps, who has discussed the precise placing of a main verb in a Derek Mahon poem as something which 'enacts art's therapeutic transformation').[12] Order in literature, in Deane's account (or parody), becomes merely a bolt-hole from the 'disorder' of the 'political system'. But Deane's parting shot—'any key literary term is exchangeable with any key literary term'—describes his own practice better than that of any supposed antagonist, and ignores the implications of the 'autonomous, ordered' idea of literature which he sets out to mock. It is Deane, and not the critics who pay attention to poetic form, who links 'the northern Irish literary "revival"' with ideas of autonomy and order, as though with those of self-government or strong policing.

Nevertheless, Deane's arguments are as influential as they are representative with regard to Northern Irish writing, and their foundations in the nationalist (or post-colonial) critiques of Yeats are unmistakable. Against such a background, the position of a poet of such contemporary eminence as Seamus Heaney is bound to be an interesting, and in some ways a delicate one. The 'best Irish poet since Yeats' tag can become a journalistic convenience which causes some critical embarrassment in this context, and Heaney's less discriminating critical enthusiasts do little to help matters: as one American fan has written, 'Mantles obfuscate as well as illuminate, and Yeats's mantle on Heaney is both burden and honor'.[13] Heaney, for his part, has honoured the burden of Yeats with considerable aplomb; while his 1978 essay 'Yeats as an Example?'[14] combined acute appreciation of Yeats's formal essence with entertaining meditation on Heaney's own poetic development and needs, more recent writing by Heaney has set itself in relation to the prevalent use of Yeats as a symbol for extra-literary anxieties and resentments. It is significant that Heaney's attentions now have turned to the issue of Yeats and form, something addressed explicitly in poem xxii of the 'Squarings' sequence in *Seeing Things* (1991):

> Where does the spirit live? Inside or outside
> Things remembered, made things, things unmade?
> What came first, the seabird's cry or the soul
>
> Imagined in the dawn wind when it cried?
> Where does it roost at last? On dungy sticks
> In a jackdaw's nest up in the old stone tower
>
> Or a marble bust commanding the parterre?
> How habitable is perfected form?
> And how inhabited the windy light?
>
> What's the use of a held note or held line
> That cannot be assailed for reassurance?
> (Set questions for the ghost of W. B.)[15]

This is a poem in touch with recent Irish critical debates on the subject of Yeats, but it is also a piece of writing which carefully ironises such debates as a series of 'set questions' which the dead poet, addressed by them as if he were a schoolboy with something to prove, will of course never answer. The questions are, then, like Yeats's own questions in poems, not intended for response (compare 'What's water but the generated soul?' in 'Coole Park and Ballylee, 1931'); rather, they set up a series of uncertainties, or possibilities, of relevance to Heaney himself. The central question, 'How habitable is perfected form?', touches on the most delicate point, the issue on which Yeats's harshest critics settle, but about which Heaney, as a poet of real substance, cannot entertain such unhesitating prejudices.

In a series of lectures in honour of Richard Ellmann, published as *The Place of Writing* in 1989, Heaney turns to the issue of Yeats's forms, and in particular the *ottava rima* stanza, where 'the place of writing is essentially the stanza form itself, that strong-arched room of eight iambic pentameters rhyming *abababcc* which serves as a redoubt for the resurgent spirit.'[16] Heaney's metaphoric line of thought here runs on the 'habitable' qualities of Yeatsian form (playing of course with the Italian root of 'stanza' as 'room'), and the use of 'redoubt' is felicitous, bringing together an evocation of Thoor Ballylee and the implications of the 'redoubtable' inhering in the poetic attitudes Yeats chose to house there. It may be a further dimension of Heaney's phrasing here to play the 'redoubt' of Yeats's form against the doubts which it faces down. Heaney continues by praising the felt physicality of the stanza form in Yeats's poems:

> In these poems, the unshakably affirmative music of the *ottava rima* stanza is the formal correlative of the poet's indomitable spirit. The complete coincidence between period and stanza which he had begun to strive for compounds utterance with architecture, recalls Milton's figure of the poet as one who builds the lofty rhyme and also recalls Yeats's own stated desire to make the tower a permanent symbol of his poetic work, 'plainly visible to the passer-by' (*ibid.*).

The 'indomitable' Yeats (who of course demanded of future Irish poets that they should keep the race itself 'indomitable') is formally protected in Heaney's reading, having 'created a fortified space within the rooms of many powerfully vaulted stanzas' (*ibid.* p. 35). To follow Heaney's metaphor, it seems that inside such fortifications Yeats can be 'assailed', whether 'assailed by the mocking echo of his own doubting mind'(*ibid.*, p. 33) or perhaps by assailants with critical or political doubts of their own about the Yeatsian enterprise. 'What's the use of a held note or held line | That cannot be assailed for reassurance?': to assail can be 'to make a violent hostile attack upon' (*OED* v. 2), but this does not sit comfortably with 'reassurance'; the word can mean also to 'speak or write directly against'(*OED* v. 4) or 'to attack with reasoning or argument' (*OED* v. 5), and it may be that the line Yeats holds in his stanzaic fortifications can, for Heaney, withstand such questioning reassuringly. And yet, of course, this very idea is itself placed within the context of a never-to-be-answered question, one addressed to a spirit rendered indomitable in its stanzaic redoubt.

The delicate balances described and put into operation in Heaney's metaphorical dealings with Yeats are in contrast to the formulations of the critical assailants: Deane, for example, writes of how 'in the end the actuality overbore the symbolism, and left [Yeats's] poetry hysterical when he let his feeling run free of the demands of form, and diagrammatic when he imposed wilfully formal restraints upon his feeling.'[17] This is very confident criticism, not just with regard to its command of 'actuality', but also about the distinction between 'demands of form' and 'formal restraints', the first good, the latter wilful. Introducing the selection from Yeats in *The Field Day Anthology of Irish Literature*, Heaney was presented with a task requiring considerable diplomatic gifts, not least in the matter of Yeats's redoubtable forms, regarded elsewhere as sinister and wilful. Nevertheless, Heaney makes a point in his Introduction of celebrating the Yeatsian command of form: 'poems like "Among School Children" and "A Dialogue of Self and Soul" go beyond the lyric's usual function of giving perfected form to a privileged state of mind and achieve an effulgent, oracular impersonality'; 'Yeats's essential gift is his ability to raise a temple in the ear, to make a vaulted space in language through the firmness, in-placeness and undislodgeableness of stanzaic form.'[18] Far from functioning as a code-word for a set of ideological positions (including formalism), Yeats is here insisted upon as a producer of palpable—and valuable - poetic forms which possess in themselves a degree of 'oracular' authority. Like Auden, Heaney maintains a distance from the Yeatsian posturings in politics and culture which did not, perhaps, quite find their monumental forms, and in which the poet is 'silly like us'; but he does insist on the legitimate authority of the perfected forms of the poems themselves:

> It is an impersonal command that is obeyed when a poet seeks to make the poem a thing, thrown free of inchoate inwardness. It is an impersonal law that enforces itself when the ear recognizes a rhythm as inevitable (*ibid.*, p. 790).

This does not accord at all well with the widespread suspicion of form elsewhere in evidence in Irish literary theory, but it does constitute, all the same, an extremely important theoretical contribution to the debate among critics on the significance of form in poetry, whether the poetry being assailed is that of Yeats himself or the work of his too-visibly orderly successors in Northern Ireland.

Heaney links the issue of form with the values of impersonal authority and artistic inevitability, and in so doing he lays bare his own
identification with the Northern Irish 'revival' and the kinds of
poetic practice which the poets of Heaney's place and generation
can be seen to prize.

The earlier writings of Derek Mahon and Michael Longley, like
those of Heaney himself, emerge from what might be called a
broadly formalist school of poetic value. Influences which poets of
this generation had in common, besides Yeats, could contribute to
an interest in stanzaic form: Philip Larkin, Louis MacNeice, and
Robert Graves seem all to have had significant roles in the early
poetry of the Northern Irish poets. Both Mahon and Longley make
use of stanzaic form in their early writings in ways that clearly owe
something to Yeatsian precedent, even if the poets remain far from
Yeats in their rhetoric and subject-matter. It would be possible to
argue that the formalism of both Mahon and Longley in their earlier
work is a consequence of a sense of the 'impersonal command'
which Heaney was to formulate much later in his pondering of the
Yeatsian example; but it is necessary also to notice that Longley in
fact moved *away* from the Yeatsian big stanza in his later writing,
and that Mahon complemented his larger stanzaic structures with
other, miniaturised forms, in which Yeatsian 'impersonality' is put
under very severe strain. Where Heaney has moved closer to the
idea of poetic form as the poet's 'redoubt', both Mahon and Longley
seem to have started from this point, and moved on from it to other
destinations.

The stanzaic art of the early Mahon is one of extraordinary
assurance and accomplishment, and the poetry of his first volume,
Night-Crossing (1968) is distinguished by its ability to match stanzaic
form with syntactic period, and to counterpoint these concerns with
rhyme, a technical assurance which is altogether in keeping with the
book's overall tone of nonchalant disillusion. Mahon's forms in this
work do seem to announce their own defensive, or protective function in a mode of performance, of self-drawn rule and limitation,
which has its own precedent in Yeats's tendency to make stanzaic
form acknowledge the design it embodies. In a poem like 'Day Trip
to Donegal', for example, a very simple pattern of rhyming couplets
is gathered into six-line stanzas (*aabbcc*), and the poem's procedure is
thus structured in a way compatible with narrative progression
(each stanza presenting a new, encapsulated stage in the gradual re-
telling of the day's events), but also, with its containment of syntax

within the six-line unit, offering the stages of a narrative as the stages
of a lyric argument or meditation. Within each stanza, an initial
statement of narrative information ('We reached the sea. . . ', 'We
left at eight. . . ') gives way to reflection by the third couplet, as here
in the poem's second stanza:

> Down at the pier the boats gave up their catch,
> Torn mouths and spewed-up lungs. They fetch
> Ten times as much in the city as here,
> And still the fish come in year after year—
> Herring and whiting, flopping about the deck
> In attitudes of agony and heartbreak.[19]

The wonderful, offbeat rhyme of the last line is all the better for the
stanzaic discipline which will enforce a snapping-back to narrative
sequence afterwards, as a new stanza gets underway ('We left at
eight, drove back the way we came. . . '). In this respect, at least,
Mahon's excision of the original (1968) third stanza improves the
poem, cutting away as it does six lines of reflection on the fate of the
landed fish. Each stanza of 'Day Trip to Donegal' shapes itself to a
diminuendo, and the staging of the stanza is as a series of narrative
events that diminish to the point of paralysis; by the final stanza
(where the poet has passed from a narrative of the events to a recol-
lection of sleep), the poem's structure drifts open, into a 'mindless'
reception of the elements:

> By dawn I was alone far out at sea
> Without skill or reassurance (nobody
> To show me how, no promise of rescue)
> Cursing my mindless failure to take due
> Forethought for this, contriving vain
> Overtures to the mindless wind and rain.[20]

Mahon's couplets are distinctly unclosed by now, and his syntax
hurries across the rhymes and line-endings to produce a final resolution which is almost the antithesis of a Yeatsian certainty and
determination: where Yeats's elaborately interlocked rhyme-
schemes propel his stanzas towards the declarative, Mahon's hushed
couplets fade down towards the repeating 'mindless' with an
exquisite artistry.

Mahon's stanzaic assurance, then, is visible early in his career: poems like 'In Carrowdore Churchyard', 'Preface to a Love Poem', and 'An Unborn Child' display an acute sense of the stanza as not merely a container for a series of lines but as itself a vital aspect of the poetry's meaning. In absorbing—ultimately from Yeats—the performative energies of stanzaic organisation in poems, Mahon succeeds in accommodating a rhetorical elevation which, without its resource of stanzaic pattern, might run astray. Edna Longley, in an essay on Mahon's use of poetic form which displays powerfully the extent of the poet's reliance on and mastery of the stanza, writes of how his 'stanzaic skill serves a poetry of statement pushed to prophetic extremity: not full-throated Yeatsian declamation, but the rhetoric Yeats might have produced had he entered more fully into either the *fin de siècle* or the modern city.'[21] The point is an important one, for Mahon's poetry shows how the stanza, understood as a performative element in poems, can shape the rhetorical diminuendo as readily as the Yeatsian crescendo. The central point in Mahon's writing in which this understanding of poetic form is put to proof is 'A Disused Shed in Co. Wexford', a poem which might well be seen as his finest single achievement, and one which is unmistakably in contact with Yeats, on the level of form as well as the more obvious level of its subject-matter.[22] The poem confronts one of the later Yeats's most characteristic places of attention, the Big House, but it does so from the angle of the marginal, the neglected and the decayed. The mushrooms waiting out decades of history in their shed 'Deep in the grounds of a burnt-out hotel, | Among the bathtubs and the washbasins' constitute a radically reduced version of Yeats's 'delicate feet upon old terraces'. However, Mahon's procedure in the poem, though it accommodates and, in a way, transfigures this reduction, is to adopt the ten-line stanza of Yeats's grandest constructions. On the other hand, it is also possible to observe that Mahon's stanza deforms that of Yeats by mutating his rhymes, then scrambling their regular orders. The rhymes of 'A Disused Shed' are often frail ('hotel'/ 'keyhole', 'washbasins'/ 'rhododendrons'/ 'silence', 'star'/'desire', all in the second stanza alone), and the patterns of their deployment through the stanzas are not regular ones. The vaulting of the chamber, to adopt Heaney's metaphor, has been replaced by something apparently ramshackle, though in its own way resilient.

Yeats's stanzas are crucially dependent on regularity of rhyme-scheme; partly, this is because their rhetorical direction is itself reliant on the clinching effect of the seemingly conclusive, or (as it were) the inevitable rhyme. For Mahon, on the other hand, the rhymes will not necessarily arrive on time: the absence of pattern in Mahon's ten-line stanza is wholly in keeping with the attention which the poem pays to things which have failed to find a place in other patterns, whether these are the forgotten inhabitants of the shed itself, or the 'Lost people of Treblinka and Pompeii', who also have their place in the poem. The fourth stanza offers a good example of Mahon's ability to discover an energy in rhyme and its stanzaic distribution which can almost reverse the Yeatsian rhetorical drive:

> There have been deaths, the pale flesh flaking
> Into the earth that nourished it;
> And nightmares, born of these and the grim
> Dominion of stale air and rank moisture.
> Those nearest the door grow strong—
> 'Elbow room! Elbow room!'
> The rest, dim in a twilight of crumbling
> Utensils and broken pitchers, groaning
> For their deliverance, have been so long
> Expectant that there is left only the posture.

The fullest rhymes here have to make contact over a long distance—'strong' / 'long', 'moisture' / 'posture'—while other rhymes are carefully etiolated: 'flaking' / 'crumbling' / 'groaning', 'Nourished it' / 'moisture'. There is a fineness of technical self-awareness in Mahon's structuring of the stanza, where the final word, 'posture', itself takes up a proud and resilient position, having been 'so long | Expectant' of its much-delayed rhyme with 'moisture'. Allowing for the designed frailty of Mahon's rhymes, this stanza might be described in terms of its rhyme-scheme as *abcbdcaadb*; comparing this with Yeats's ten-line pattern (*abcabcdeed*) reveals how completely Mahon scrambles Yeats's more regular design, but it also shows that Mahon works to set up connections between the beginning and the end of the stanza, rather than to complete his initial sequence of rhymes with a final—and potentially conclusive—new pattern. Mahon reserves this conclusive-ness for the end of his poem, where the mushrooms find their voice in a full rhyme:

'Let the god not abandon us
Who have come so far in darkness and in pain.
We too had our lives to live.
You with your light meter and relaxed itinerary,
Let not our naive labours have been in vain!'

The intrusive 'light meter' is also, perhaps, the light metre whose
tenuous rhymes the mushrooms' 'pain'/'in vain' speaks up against:
here, as in Yeats's stanza, the seventh and the tenth lines rhyme,
sealing an elaborate rhetorical construction. But the conclusive
energy, in Mahon's poem, is at least partly, and painfully, ironic: it
carries a plea that speaks from a condition of near-ultimate weakness
and vulnerability. The poem's form both protects and embodies a
'good faith' which announces and enacts its own precariousness and
frailty.
    'A Disused Shed in Co. Wexford' might well make Seamus
Deane's description of Northern Irish literature—'autonomous,
ordered'—seem heavily ironic, for it opens up an aspect of form in
poetry where the order of stanzaic form relates obliquely to all but
the most extreme autonomy. Again, the Yeatsian forms create the
possibility of Mahon's technical discovery, while they remain quite
distinct from it. Deane has written of how 'the formal control of
[Mahon's] poems is one expression of a kind of moral stoicism, a
mark of endurance under pressure',[23] but this seems better to describe Yeats's formal procedures: in Mahon's case, 'formal control' is
apart from the stoicism it serves to contain, always a potentially
ironic frame for the kinds of endurance to which the poems bear
witness. Thus, the musicality of Mahon's poetry can be an unsettling property, just as its syntactic flexibility and command may
sometimes contrast starkly with the bleakness of perspective
actually on offer. To say that these things redeem such bleakness, or
even abolish it, is to miss the irony implicit in Mahon's performative order. Seamus Heaney is so well attuned to the liberation
offered by Yeats's different formal command that he misses, like
Deane, the full irony of Mahon's practice; in reading the conclusion
of 'A Disused Shed', for example, Heaney takes for granted Mahon's
freedom from the situation the poem embodies:[24]

Here he makes the door of a shed open so that an apocalypse of sun-
light blazes onto an overlooked, unpleasant yet pathetic colony of

mushrooms. What they cry out, I am bold to interpret, is the querulous chorus that Mahon hears from the pre-natal throats of his Belfast ancestors, pleading from the prison of their sectarian days with the free man who is their poet-descendant.

The reading here is not 'bold', merely weak and inadequate, not least because it is hardly free itself from 'sectarian' reflexes; it also reads Mahon's poem as if it were the staging of a Yeatsian 'apocalypse'. The echo of Auden on Yeats ('In the prison of his days | Teach the free man how to praise')[25] perhaps indicates where Heaney's critical attention really lies. However, the failure of the reading here, which like Deane's interpretation conflates Mahon's forms with Yeats's, also suggests that the issue of form in Northern Irish poetry, along with the problem of Yeatsian precedent which is always carried in its wake, remains perilously close to a variety of extra-literary corollaries and analogues, such as the casual, matter-of-fact sectarianism which Heaney's remarks let slip.

Simply to protest against the critical stirring-up of such analogues and corollaries in Northern Irish poetry would be disingenuous in some respects, for they do exert degrees of pressure upon writing since the 1960s which mean that they cannot be ruled out of discussion of the achievements of poets like Heaney, Mahon, and Longley. However, the kinds of autonomy, or of order, which poetic form carries into this poetry are various, and embody different aspects of the Yeatsian performative modes which are (sometimes ironically) their precedents. In the case of Michael Longley, an early exploration of stanzaic form gave place, through the 1970s and after, to an approach which sought simpler kinds of poetic architecture. *No Continuing City* (1968), Longley's first full volume, presented a poet of astonishing technical self-confidence, its rhymed and meticulously measured stanzas owing debts to George Herbert as much as to Yeats. In several poems, Longley's typographical layout, with its symmetries of variously indented lines in rhymed stanzas, serves to emphasise the tight order of the writing itself, and an element of self-consciousness inheres in such feats of balance. In one stanza of 'The Hebrides', for example, Longley seems to measure the distance between his aesthetic practice and the world in which it has to be exercised:

> Dykes of apparatus educate my bones
> To track the buoys

Up sea lanes love emblazons
To streets where shall conclude
My journey back from flux to poise, from poise
To attitude.[26]

Where Mahon's 'Day Trip to Donegal' brings flux in to the stanza
and unsettles the balance of order which it accommodates, Longley
here makes a display of form in an accommodation of the flux
which the sea represents, ending in the 'poise' and 'attitude' of
urbane, conclusive poetic shape and rhetorical control. This 'journey back' is mapped out in terms which suggest very clearly what
might be understood as a Yeatsian faith in the resources of poetic
form: from the 'flux' of the given thing, the disordered world which
the imagination perceives, to the 'poise' of a learned discipline and
verbal self-control, finally to the 'attitude' which will combine all
the elements of the poet's enterprise in one performative act of self-
definition. This long and intricate poem is much concerned with the
proper point of observation for the poetic eye, and with the correct
degree of 'poise' for the poetic voice to adopt; like others of
Longley's earlier poems, its rationale is in part a programmatic
impulse, a gaining of bearings for the poetic excursions still to come.
In the light of this, the extent to which 'The Hebrides' needs to
examine its own procedures, its own degree of 'poise', is important,
revealing as it does the irony, or anxiety, which is already implicit
for Longley in such displays of order. By the end of the poem, all
balance is precarious as formality and formalism both come into
view:

Granting the trawlers far below their stance,
Their anchorage,
I fight all the way for balance -
In the mountain's shadow
Losing foothold, covet the privilege
Of vertigo. (*ibid.*, p. 43)

Here the achieved formal balance of the stanza holds within it the
ambition of the poetic voice to lose its balance—and these two
things are themselves, so to speak, put into a kind of 'balance' in the
poem's formal containment and resolution. Almost every phrase in
the stanza might bear an ironic charge: is the poet really 'Losing
foothold', for instance, and does he indeed 'fight all the way for
balance' if 'vertigo' remains a coveted 'privilege'? Here, at a time

before the full force of the word 'order' could have become apparent for Northern Irish poets in its extra-poetic senses, Longley is already fighting shy of the Yeatsian formal 'stance', even in the process of proving himself capable of it.

There are many aspects to Longley's development after his first volume which, while they are often suggested or foreshadowed there, take his characteristic modes of writing away from the 'poise' and 'attitude' contemplated in work like 'The Hebrides' towards forms less obviously structured and self-conscious. One aspect of this development is the change in Longley's stanzas from rhymed to unrhymed arrangements of lines. In a 1985 interview, the poet looks back on these changes in terms which show how far the issue of form, and its vocabulary, have become charged with tensions elsewhere perceptible in the matter of the poetry itself:

> In terms of what's happening now I would be regarded as very conservative and traditionalist. I resent being called that. I do believe that poetry releases the tendencies of the language, and two of those tendencies are a drift towards patterns and rhyme. Rhyme is one of the attributes of language. I rhyme very little now, I don't know why that is. I don't think there are arguments for or against rhyme. It's a basic fact that it's one of the things that words do, and when I'm writing I like to embrace as many of the things that words do as possible . . . My interest in form is a bit like the devotion of those monks in their cells illuminating manuscripts in the Dark Ages.[27]

The idea that 'poetry releases the tendencies of language' is a characteristically benign insight, but 'a drift towards pattern' suggests that poetry also controls those tendencies; Longley here presents his development away from overt forms of control as a move towards greater acceptance of what are essentially impersonal forces and tendencies. Yet there is present here a sense of 'poise' in the acceptance of this impersonal activity, and Longley's alignment of 'interest' with 'devotion' suggests how far the issue of poetic form might be seen as resonant in a poetry which does, inescapably, have its dealings with 'Dark Ages', of one kind of another, nearer home. In allowing that rhyme can be present or absent in poetic expression, Longley still insists upon the 'patterns' which give rise to the poet's formal devotion; the observation that the poems on the page are still 'the same old oblongs and squares' does mean that 'It's almost as if the formal sense is now built-in' (*ibid.*, p. 20). The acceptance of 'the formal sense' entails, for Longley, a rejection of the more overtly violent forcings of language into form which the Yeatsian precedent embodies; it does, however, continue to provide for other kinds of patternings which are not without their own performative dimensions.

The control of syntax in the lines of poems, its shaping, turns, delays, and conclusions across the lines and within the regulated gatherings of lines into stanzas, may be all the more marked in Longley's later work for its being so often unrhymed. The absence of rhyme removes from many of Longley's poems the powerfully dramatic aspects of Yeats's stanzaic forms, as well as the capacity for calculated let-downs and surprises of Mahon's unstable, scrambled rhyme-schemes. Instead, Longley conveys a sense of the self-generating sentence, of 'the things that words do', in his precisely-timed unravellings of syntactic structure, producing very often a coincidence between syntactic period and stanza. In 'Carrigskeewaun', for example, five separately titled stanzas each deploy a sentence over six lines, and the tight uniformity of the poem's design is rendered almost unobtrusive by the absence of rhyme. In the fourth stanza, *'The Wall'*, for instance:

> I join all the men who have squatted here
> This lichened side of the dry-stone wall
> And notice how smoke from our turf-fire
> Recalls in the cool air above the lake
> Steam from a kettle, a tablecloth and
> A table she might have already set.[28]

This is exquisitely paced, and subject to a strict understanding of syntax, line, and stanza: the sentence which the six-line unit contains allows subordinate elements to assume prominence by their position within the stanza, so that the ordered statement from outside ('I notice how smoke recalls steam') is counterpointed by a domestic interior ('She might have already set a table'). The control here creates a balance between the outdoor site of the initial declaration ('I join all the men') and the indoor world mapped by the sentence's subordinate clause; the pivotal point comes in the middle of the stanza, when after the third line 'notice how' finds its verb in 'Recalls': the symmetry between wall and turf-fire, steam and table, is vital to the equilibrium of the whole. Without rhymes, syntax and shape become performative elements, even if what they perform is a balancing-act rather than a rhetorical declaration.

However personal their accents and emphases, Longley's poems take their forms in the knowledge that form in poetry is something more than personal. Heaney's formula ('It is an impersonal law that enforces itself when the ear recognizes a rhythm as inevitable') might well be applied also to Longley's unfolding syntactic periods and their timed conclusions. In *Gorse Fires* (1991) the insistently individual voice is couched in increasingly elaborate syntactic structures, and in the adaptations of Homer in that volume (where the personal and the narrative voices coincide), complex lyric constructions are housed within single sentences: 'The Butchers', for example, carries a sentence over twenty-eight long lines. Seldom, if ever, are Longley's procedures in this respect visibly forced; however, the artistic success of his poetry consists in a sense of rightness, of achieved measure and balance, at which each poem seems to arrive, and this is a point where the affinities between 'inevitability' and order' in perfected form are of some importance. Longley's formal containments are by now very far removed from Yeats's dramatic performances, but their calm insistence upon order, even though it is an order presentable in some ways as one inherent in the properties of words themselves and their structures in speech, is nonetheless a gesture with aspects of 'impersonal' meaning and authority.

Longley's forms are 'habitable' then, and more often the poetic equivalents of the stone-built cottage than the architecturally-imposing Big House. Of all the poets of his generation, it is Longley who comes closest, in his handling of formal design, to an absence of self-consciousness; though even this must be, of course, itself an achievement of artistic purpose, and as such might perhaps be said to remain complicit with the view of literature as 'autonomous, ordered' which still fuels critical suspicion of Yeats and others. Like other poets from Northern Ireland, Longley has done something with the formal influence of Yeats which differs greatly from simple mimicry and which precludes, at the same time, wholesale acceptance of Yeats on the terms he offered to posterity. In learning to 'Sing whatever is well made', Longley and Mahon learned that the 'well made' can allow for modes in which Yeats's performances are scrambled and re-pitched. In his poem 'Architecture', another piece made up of separately-titled stanzas, Longley presents four habitations which miniaturize Yeatsian grand dwellings and bring them into close contact with the nature Yeats occasionally scorned: thus, there are different small houses 'on the Seashore', 'on the Bleach Green', and 'Made out of Turf'. The six-line stanzas do rhyme (unusually for Longley in the late 1970s):

The House Shaped Like an Egg

Do you pay for this house with egg money
Since its whitewashed walls are clean as shell
And the parlour, scullery, bedrooms oval
To leave no corner for dust or devil
Or the double yolk of heaven and hell
Or days when it rains and turns out sunny?[29]

Longley's rhyme-scheme here (*abccba*) seals his stanza into a tight circle, and is a long way from the rhyme progressions, always complicit with the moving-forward of argument, of Yeatsian stanzas. Here the last line, with its own movement from darkness to welcome light, provides in its rhyming connection to the point of departure in the first line a liberating contrast to the fifth line ('Or the double yolk of heaven and hell') with its packed Neoplatonic riddle once used by Yeats to cap a stanza of 'Among School Children' ('Or else, to alter Plato's parable, | Into the yolk and white of the one shell' [*VP* 443]). Longley's house presents in itself an image of order and self-containment which neglects altogether Yeatsian architecture but which, like Longley's poetry itself in miniature, encloses and preserves a clean space, formal and impersonal.

The impersonalities of Paul Muldoon's poetry mingle, like those of Longley, with autobiographical elements; yet Muldoon, from an younger generation of poets, is also a more challenging critical case as regards his understanding of, and uses for poetic form. For Muldoon, the line between form as perceived stylistic pattern and form as impersonal intellectual grid is often deliberately unclear: in collections like *Quoof* (1983) and *Meeting the British* (1987) the formal concerns of stanza and rhyme are never far from view, but their function, or the relation between them and the business in hand of their respective poems is often problematic. Even in long narratives like 'The More A Man Has The More A Man Wants', Muldoon uses the fourteen-line stanza which, often standing alone as a sonnet, is his characteristic form. These sonnet stanzas can have lines of any length and can rhyme, according to highly individual and often apparently improvised criteria, in any order. The New Critical shib-

boleth of the indissolubility of form and content, which most subsequent critical theory makes a point of viewing with suspicion, is
perhaps true in too general a sense to be of much critical use: the
intimacy between form and meaning is not easily ascertainable,
though successful poetry does arguably enable the critic to guess at
the existence of some such relation. In Muldoon's case, form is
paraded in front of the reader, blatantly emphasised as something
created or imposed, while at the same time a show of offhand non-
chalance surrounds the various feats of unlikely rhyme and sometimes apparently arbitrary stanzaic organization. Are Muldoon's
sonnets more properly parodies of sonnets, or even, so to speak,
'deconstructed' sonnets? On the larger scale, in his book-length
Madoc (1990), Muldoon has produced a narrative which makes a display out of its 'meaning' by giving square-bracketed titles to each of
its many short sections, in the form of philosophers' names. As with
the shapes of his poems themselves, this makes authorial working
and shaping so visible as to become problematic, and form can start
to appear as, rather than an enabling means, an hermetic and continually self-defining end.

Difficulties such as these may seem to stand at a considerable distance from the issue of Yeats's influence; yet Muldoon represents a
point in Northern Irish poetry at which the reception of Yeats has
been pursued all the way to an elusive (and allusive) irony. In this,
Muldoon follows poets like Longley and Mahon, taking their ways
with poetic form a stage further, to a situation in which the full
implications of poetic form as poetic performance can be re-
addressed. Here, Yeats is inescapably present, and Muldoon allows
him to enter the long, self-circling '7, Middagh Street' in *Meeting the
British* as a shifting, flexible, and richly adaptable point of reference
of the different speakers whose monologues make up the poem. It is
one of '7, Middagh Street''s numerous ironies that the poem is set
inside a house that is for all the speakers a temporary home, a
makeshift address far from the architectural embodiments of 'deep-
rooted things'. Instead of being 'Rooted in one dear perpetual place',
then, the seven voices of Muldoon's poem find themselves thrown
together to share moments of transition, and their surroundings are
almost incidental to this situation: 'In itself, this old, three-storey
brownstone | Is unremarkable' ('Carson').[30] In the monologue given
to 'Wystan', Muldoon's Auden reflects on how 'The roots by which
we were once bound | are severed here', and finds himself con-
templating the recently-deceased W. B. Yeats in terms which re-

situate the poet in a 'ruined tower' rather than the 'malachited Bal-lylee' of the Irish poet's ideal/real dwelling. As often in '7, Middagh Street', engagement with Yeats happens through allusion and quota-tion:

> As for his crass, rhetorical
>
> posturing, 'Did that play of mine
> send out certain men (*certain* men?)
>
> the English shot. . . ?'
> the answer is 'Certainly not'.
>
> If Yeats had saved his pencil-lead
> would certain men have stayed in bed? (*ibid.*, p. 39)

Yeats's question in 'The Man and the Echo' is rendered 'crass, rhetorical' here partly by formal intervention, as 'Wystan' fractures the original iambic tetrameter couplets of Yeats, deploying his own truncation and full rhyme to interrupt their all too 'certain' momentum. The last question here parodically adopts a regular tetrameter couplet of its own to expose the outlandishness of Yeats's 'posturing'. Other snippets from Yeats are subjected to similar dis-tortion through quotation (or near-quotation) throughout the poem: 'Gypsy' [Rose Lee] for example, remembers advice as 'Never, he says, give all thy heart; | there's more enterprise in walking not quite | naked' (*ibid.*, p. 44). The effect is in part parodic and satiri-cal, but it is achieved by locating the Yeatsian raw material in a for-mal element to which it is not equal: Muldoon's relentless formalism can devour Yeats's original forms, often to comic effect.

'7, Middagh Street' in 1940 presents Muldoon also with a sugges-tive parallel to other poetic addresses and dates—most of all, per-haps, to 'Coole Park and Ballylee, 1931', for Muldoon's cast are aware of their own roles as 'the last romantics' of their period, and are all casting backward glances over finished phases of their lives and careers. The 'old, three-storey brownstone' is the site for a debate in which Yeats provides one topic, as well as a near-constant subtext, and the terms of this debate are drawn from the issues raised in (the real) Auden's 'In Memory of W.B. Yeats', especially the quarrel between the idea of art as autonomous and that of art as agent, which seems to be present in the famous line 'For poetry makes nothing happen'. 'Wystan' elaborates on one reading of this apparent statement throughout his monologue, but later 'Louis' [MacNeice] is made to throw the idea into reverse: 'poetry *can* make things happen— | not only can, but *must*' (*ibid.*, p. 59). It is worth noting that, just as Muldoon's Auden develops his rejection of history from his rejection of the 'crass, rhetorical' Yeats, Muldoon's MacNeice produces his endorsement of art's capacity for action after quoting Yeats's 'In dreams begin responsibilities'. The two stances (each, in its way, 'rhetorical') seem to be set poles apart, just as they are situated at opposite ends of the poem itself; but Muldoon's formal design means that the poem is potentially circular rather than linear: the last line of 'Louis' runs back into the first of 'Wystan', in the same way that each of the seven monologues picks up its predecessor and runs into its successor, by starting, and completing, a quotation. As Edna Longley has observed, 'This suggests that the poet's dilemmas endlessly circumnavigate, rotate on their own axis, perne in their gyres';[31] this spiralling is in part perhaps parodic of Yeats, but it might be said just as well to be authentically Yeatsian in its ability to make form enact a complexity to disarm the demands for a kind of fixity and coherence which art cannot satisfactorily supply.

Muldoon's 'gyres', like Mahon's and Longley's stanzas, and like Heaney's critical constructions of vaulted stanzaic rooms, offer a use of Yeats's forms which is something other than either ideological grudge or formalist imitation. The various ways of absorbing Yeats as a formal precedent in Northern Irish poetry show how unworkable and unsatisfactory is the critical attempt to see form as narrowly symptomatic in the writing of poetry, whether of political attraction to 'order' or cultural delusions of 'autonomy'. Much of the misunderstanding of Northern Irish poetry sees in a supposed formalism only a set of abstractable assumptions and prejudices, and these can be perceived in Yeats as well, given the same quality of misunderstanding. But the central fact which such approaches ignore is that of the flexibility and the changing nature of poetic form: in Yeats's hands, as much as those of his successors, form and performance are constantly moving, shifting modes that set the authorial will a fresh challenge each time a new poem has to be written. Poetic form is in that sense 'living' rather than 'dead', dynamic rather than static, for its kinds of order do not stand still, and they are never finally 'perfected' while they can still be inhabited. In the context of the critical quarrel with Yeats, and in contrast to the empty, unserviceable rooms of theoretical distrust and resentment, poets from Northern Ireland have demonstrated just how 'habitable' his forms remain.

NOTES

1. W. H. Auden, 'In Memory of W.B.Yeats', in Edward Mendelson (ed.), *The English Auden: Poems, Essays and Dramatic Writings 1927-1929* (London: Faber and Faber, 1977), pp. 241-3.
2. Seamus Deane, *Heroic Styles: The Tradition of an Idea* (Derry: Field Day Publications, 1984), repr. in *Ireland's Field Day* (London: Hutchinson, 1985), pp.49-50.
3. Denis Donoghue, *We Irish: The Selected Essays of Denis Donoghue, I* (Brighton: Harvester Press, 1986), p. 66.
4. John Wilson Foster, *The Irish Review* 2 (1987), p. 111.
5. Declan Kiberd, 'The War against the Past', in Audrey S. Eyler and Robert F. Garratt (eds), *The Uses of the Past: Essays on Irish Culture* (Newark: University of Delaware Press, 1988), p. 38.
6. Clair Wills, *Improprieties: Politics and Sexuality in Northern Irish Poetry* (Oxford: Clarendon Press, 1993), p. 26.
7. David Lloyd, *Anomalous States: Irish Writing and the Post-Colonial Moment* (Dublin: Lilliput Press, 1993), p. 80.
8. See Helen Vendler, 'Yeats and *Ottava Rima*', *YA 11*, 26-44.
9. Lord Byron, *Don Juan* Canto XIII (1823), in Jerome J. McGann (ed.), *The Complete Poetical Works* (Oxford: Clarendon Press, 1986), V, p. 544.
10. Ronald Bush, 'The Modernist under Siege' (*YAACTS 6, 5*).
11. Seamus Deane, 'General Introduction' to Seamus Deane (ed.) *The Field Day Anthology Of Irish Writing* (3 vols., Derry: Field Day Publications, 1991), 1, p. xxvi.
12. Edna Longley, 'The Singing Line: Form in Derek Mahon's Poetry', *Poetry In The Wars* (Newcastle upon Tyne: Bloodaxe Books, 1986), p. 179.
13. Henry Hart, *Seamus Heaney: Poet of Contrary Progressions* (Syracuse: Syracuse University Press, 1992), p. 1.
14. Seamus Heaney, *Preoccupations: Selected Prose 1968-1978* (London: Faber and Faber, 1980), pp. 98-114.
15. Seamus Heaney, *Seeing Things* (London: Faber and Faber, 1991), p. 78.
16. Seamus Heaney, *The Place of Writing* (Atlanta: Scholars Press, 1989), p. 29.
17. Seamus Deane, *Celtic Revivals: Essays in Modern Irish Literature 1880-1980* (London: Faber and Faber, 1985), p. 38.
18. Seamus Heaney, 'William Butler Yeats (1865-1939)', *The Field Day Anthology of Irish Writing* II, p. 788.

242   YEATS, FORM AND NORTHERN IRISH POETRY

19. Derek Mahon, 'Day Trip to Donegal', *Night-Crossing* (London: Oxford University Press, 1968), p. 22.
20. *Ibid.*, p.23. Mahon's later revisions of this stanza are found in *Poems 1962-1978* (Oxford: Oxford University Press, 1979), p. 17, and *Selected Poems* (Harmondsworth: Penguin Books, 1993), p. 21.
21. Edna Longley, 'The Singing Line: Form in Derek Mahon's Poetry', p. 175.
22. Derek Mahon, 'A Disused Shed in Co. Wexford', *Selected Poems*, pp. 62-3.
23. Seamus Deane, *Celtic Revivals*, p. 165.
24. Seamus Heaney, *The Place of Writing*, p. 49.
25. W. H. Auden, 'In Memory of W. B. Yeats', *The English Auden*, p. 243.
26. Michael Longley, *Poems 1963-1983* (Edinburgh: Salamander Press, 1985), p. 42.
27. Michael Longley, 'The Longley Tapes' [Interview with Robert Johnstone], *The Honest Ulsterman*, 78 (1985), p. 19.
28. Michael Longley, *Poems 1963-1983*, p. 97.
29. *Ibid.*, p. 153.
30. Paul Muldoon, *Meeting the British* (London: Faber and Faber, 1987), p. 52.
31. Edna Longley, 'The Aesthetic and the Territorial', in Elmer Andrews (ed.), *Contemporary Irish Poetry: A Collection of Critical Essays* (Basingstoke: Macmillan, 1992), pp. 65-6.

SHORTER NOTES

Professor Augustine Martin

A. Norman Jeffares

THOMAS AUGUSTINE (GUS) MARTIN, who died of septicaemia followed by a heart attack on 16 October 1995, was born in Leitrim in 1935, his father a postmaster in Ballinamor. He was educated at Mount St Joseph's, the Cistercian college at Roscrea, Co. Tipperary, and at University College, Dublin, where he added to his BA an MA and PhD. He taught at his old school before returning to the Anglo-Irish Department at UCD in 1965. He married Claire Kennedy; they had four children, Grainne, Breffni, Niamh and Aengus. Gus was devoted to them all.

A co-founder of the Association of Teachers of English, Gus Martin played a significant part in the 1950s in reforming the school syllabus in English literature, getting modern Irish short stories, poems and novels included in it. Later he became a branch chairman of the Association of Secondary Teachers in Ireland.

When he joined the staff of UCD, he brought to the Department proven teaching ability, superb communicative skills, enthusiasm and overflowing energy. All these qualities informed his subsequent appointment in 1979 as Professor of Anglo-Irish Literature and Drama. He was determined to do well by the many postgraduate students who came from many parts of the world to work in the Department, and to do well, too, by the University, insisting on rigorous standards of examining. An excellent lecturer, he conveyed the enjoyment of literature, especially modern Irish literature, not only eloquently but stimulatingly. He knew how to kindle interest and how to encourage students to develop their own scholarly and critical powers. He liked people and was curious about them in the way that he liked literature and was curious about it. He read widely and kept his teaching fresh and lively: it was irradiated by a sense of fun, an ability to let others share in his discoveries.

His interest in the teaching of literature in school as well as university continued; he kept up his contacts and friendships in the world of secondary education; and some of his publications were intended to aid schoolchildren to appreciate literature, among them *Soundings* and *Exploring English*. His anthology of short stories published in 1967 was, for example, planned for the Intermediate examination syllabus. He saw the point of good critical introductions which could supplement the work of teachers.

His writing for a more mature audience reflected his liking for modern Irish writing. He edited James Stephens's *The Charwoman's Daughter* in 1972 and followed this with an admirable critical study of Stephens in 1977. His short life of W. B. Yeats, published in Gill's Irish Lives in 1983, was revised and expanded for the 1990 edition published by Colin Smythe Ltd. This is an admirable introduction to Yeats, lucid, sympathetic and, though brief, inclusive. It was followed by an edition of Yeats's poems in 1989. This interest in Yeats led to many fine lectures, particularly at the Yeats International Summer School in Sligo (of which Gus was Director from 1978 to 1981).

I have many memories of Gus going back over the thirty years of our friendship: some of the sharpest of them are linked to his visits to the Summer School, of his frequently diving naked into the swimming pool at dawn, of his singing—he had a very pleasant voice—at the Imperial Hotel, well into the small hours. He exuded a fine appetency for the good things of life, his intensely blue eyes lighting up with delight at the sight of a friend or at some piece of wit or absurdity. A generous man, he was given to hospitality: he was a giver and creator not a taker.

Gus's approach to literature and politics was not narrow: it was enriched by overseas experience. He taught at Hofstra University in 1974 and was a Research Fellow at Miami University, Ohio, in 1980. He lectured in Belgium, Canada, Denmark, France, India, Japan, the Lebanon and Singapore, as well as in various institutions in the United Kingdom and the United States. His lecturing skills spilled over into television and radio programmes. Out of the latter came *The Genius of Irish Prose* (1983), the Thomas Davis Lectures that he organised in 1984 for Radio Telefis Eireann. *Winter's Tales from Ireland* was a similarly inspired collection. In all he devised and presented fifty programmes for Irish educational television.

Despite the occasional apparent chaos of papers on his desk and the endless kindly answering of telephone calls, Gus was an efficient administrator, almost despite himself. He got things done. In 1987 he set up the annual James Joyce Summer School in Joyce's old University College in St Stephen's Green, Dublin. Out of the lectures at its first session he edited *James Joyce: The Artist and the Labyrinth* (1990). He presided over this school with bonhomie and unobtrusive proficiency. He had of course innate political as well as administrative skills. He was elected twice to the Irish Senate, in 1973 and 1977. He was Vice-Chairman of the Irish Cultural Relations Committee of the Department of Foreign Affairs (1979-82) and—a post that gave him great pleasure—Chairman of the Board of Directors of the Abbey Theatre (to which he had been elected in 1983) from 1985.

Gus was instrumental in raising the funding to purchase Patrick Kavanagh's archives and install them in UCD, travelling to the United States to collect the material and bring it safely back to Dublin. That was typical of his ability to see something through. He was a professional. If you asked him to write an article he would deliver it on time and at the agreed length. He was writing a life of Kavanagh, and I discussed some of what he had written with him. He was frustrated because it was going more slowly than he had expected; there was a great deal of material to order and I suggested that he should get study leave in order to clear the decks for its completion. He did get the leave, but not having the necessary ruthlessness to refuse the non-stop demands of others on his time and attention, he did not get as much written as he had hoped. But, in a recent phone conversation he told me he had managed to make progress and was more buoyant about bringing it to a conclusion fairly soon.

Buoyancy was an essential part of his nature. He managed to make a joke about losing a finger in the fathers' team in a tug of war at a school sports' day. He was knocked off his bicycle some years ago by a careless car driver and despite several operations endured a great deal of pain. He never complained of this nor of recent troubles with his health—he had developed a blood disorder. 'Ah, you just forget it' he said to me the last time I was with him in Belfield. 'Let's go and have a jar'. What he could not forget was poetry. He could quote poems seemingly endlessly. His memory was superb. So indeed was his gift for friendship.

A. L. Burt's 1898 Edition of *Irish Fairy and Folk Tales* 'Edited by W. B. YEATS'

Colin Smythe

IN 1988, I was preparing to issue a reprint of our edition of W. B. Yeats's two collections of Irish fairy tales, *Fairy and Folk Tales of the Irish Peasantry* (1888) and *Irish Fairy Tales* (1892), that we had first published in 1973 under the title *Fairy and Folk Tales of Ireland*.[1] At about this time, as a result of my bibliographical work on W. B. Yeats, when I first held a copy of the book in my hands, I discovered that the text of A. L. Burt's edition of *Fairy and Folk Tales of the Irish Peasantry*, published in New York in about 1898 under the title of *Irish Fairy and Folk Tales*, contained a number of stories that had not appeared in earlier editions of the book. I did not know then whether or not these had been included with Yeats's concurrence or at his behest, so I decided to add the five stories to our next printing, which appeared that year. To my embarrassment, I subsequently noticed that there was another story—the first in Burt's edition—which I had missed, I suppose, purely because of its position as the first story in the book. I therefore added it to our 1992 printing.

This omission was all the more puzzling to me for the following reason: Burt's edition was first mentioned in the second edition of Allan Wade's *Bibliography of the Writings of W. B. Yeats*[2] (which I am presently revising for Oxford University Press),[3] where it is listed as no. 212A. The

248

entry states that 'Except for the addition of *The Fate of the Children of Lir* at the beginning, and the deletion of the dedication, the contents are the same as No. 212': I had added the stories missed by Wade, but missed the only one referred to in the entry. *Wade* (1958) also stated that 212A was published in 1902, but there was an earlier edition published not later than 1898, judging from the title page which gives an address that he left in that year. Here is a brief description:

IRISH FAIRY | AND FOLK TALES | EDITED AND SELECTED | BY W. B. YEATS | [line illustration] | *PROFUSELY ILLUSTRATED* | A. L. BURT, PUBLISHER, | 52-58 DUANE STREET, NEW YORK.
19 x 12.7 cm.; pp. xvi, 416, followed by 2 pp. of advertisements.
Copies exist both in red-brown cloth and in green cloth, with pictorial design in pink, black and yellow on front cover and on spine; white end-papers; all edges trimmed. The contents are in the main the same as the 1888 edition, but the dedication page and notes have been deleted, and the six unsigned stories added. Yeats's contributions, however, apart from the removal of the notes, remain unchanged. There are full-page line illustrations facing the title-page and pp. 60, 88, 120, 196, 210, 318, as well as numerous smaller ones. The 1902 reprint, described in the 1958 and 1968 editions of the *Bibliography* as being the first printing, has the bottom two lines of the title page changed to 'A. L. BURT COMPANY, | PUBLISHERS, NEW YORK.'
  The insertions are as follows:
'The Fate of the Children of Lir' (pp. 1-9): the first story in the collection, before Yeats's note on the Trooping Fairies.
'The Black Horse' (pp. 57-64): printed between Letitia Maclintock's 'A Donegal Fairy' and Yeats's note on Changelings.
'Morraha' (pp. 80-93): printed between Yeats's 'The Stolen Child' and his note on the Merrow.
'The Greek Princess and the Young Gardener' (pp. 113-124): printed between T. Crofton Croker's 'Flory Cantillon's Funeral' and Yeats's note on the Solitary Fairies.
'Smallhead and the King's Sons' (pp. 194-209): printed between 'The Fate of Frank M'Kenna' and Yeats's note on Witches and Fairy Doctors.
'The Leaching of Kayn's Leg' (pp. 301-321): printed between 'King O'Toole and his Goose' and Lady Wilde's 'The Demon Cat'.

As the result of being given a paperback called *Celtic Fairy Tales*, a modern reprint[4] of two collections called *Celtic Fairy Tales* and *More Celtic Fairy Tales*, selected and edited by Joseph Jacobs, both illustrated

by John D. Batten and first published by David Nutt in 1892 and 1894, I
found the source of the six stories, and can therefore conclude that Burt's
edition was published without Scott's knowledge or permission. All but
one (that on the title page)[5] of the illustrations in it, and the six stories
they illustrate, had been taken from *More Celtic Fairy Tales*.

In October 1893, Walter Scott issued an illustrated edition with twelve
pictures by James Torrance and called it *Irish Fairy and Folk Tales*,
thereby avoiding confusion between it and the unillustrated 1888 edition.
The new edition was published in America in 1895 by Charles Scribner's
Sons, who imported English sheets and bound them in the USA. At this
time, if a book had not been produced in the USA it was not protected in
the United States and could be published by anyone,[6] unless it was officially first published in the United States, with two copies being
delivered to the Library of Congress (hence the later importance of John
Quinn to Yeats, Lady Gregory and J. M. Synge, for example, when he
published limited editions of their works to obtain US copyright protection for some of them before they were published in Britain).

The fact that the source of none of the stories and their attendant
illustrations is acknowledged in the Burt edition, and that Burt's name
appears nowhere in Yeats's correspondence, would confirm the supposition that this was a work put together by Burt who, seeing the success of
the Scribner import, decided to issue a similar edition himself. Of course,
Yeats had been paid a flat fee for the work, and so had no financial interest in what was happening on the other side of the Atlantic, and Scott
would have seen no reason to mention it to Yeats even had he known
about it. Scribners, too, knowing the terms of the US copyright acts,
would not have thought the matter worth mentioning.

To improve the saleability of his book as an independent publication,
however, Burt inserted the stories and their illustrations at almost random positions in the text, with little thought for the subject-matter of the
sections in which they were placed, although it must be said that he
never put a story in the middle of any group of stories: they were always
just before a section or subsection.

While Yeats's text of *Fairy and Folk Tales of the Irish Peasantry* could
easily be reset, it was not possible for Burt to use James Torrance's paintings had he wanted to, because they could not be adequately reproduced
without the originals: they were halftone reproductions of paintings,
while Batten's were line-drawings that could easily be copied

Burt therefore took Yeats's collection as being the most likely to sell
to the American Irish market, used the title of the Scott/Scribner
illustrated edition, added six stories and sixteen illustrations from Jacobs'

book, and as a final flourish put a picture of two old voyeurs and a languishing lady on the title page. He must have thought it an unbeatable combination, and the strategically-placed stories and their illustrations certainly give the book the impression of being 'profusely illustrated'.[7] I have now restored the volume in our fifth edition (1995) to its original form, with an explanatory note.

The sources for the tales given below are quoted from Jacobs' notes at the end of the volume, and are as follows.

'The Fate of the Children of Lir': 'Abridged from the text and translation published by the Society for the Preservation of the Irish Language in 1883. This merely follows the text and version given by Professor O'Curry in *Atlantis*, iv.'

'The Black Horse': 'From J. F. Campbell's manuscript collection now deposited at the Advocate's Library in Edinburgh (MS.53, vol.xi). Collected in Gaelic, February 14, 1862, by Hector MacLean, from Roderick MacNeill, in the island of Menglay: MacNeill learnt the story about 1840 from a Barra man.'

In the Trooping Fairies section: about an enchanted horse who finally regains his human shape.

'Morraha': 'The second story in Mr W. Larminie's *West Irish Folk-tales*, pp.10-30. The framework was collected from P.McGrale of Achill Island, Co. Mayo. The story itself was from Terence Davis of Rendyle, Co. Galway. There is evidently confusion in the introductory portion between Niall's mother and wife.'

In the Changelings section: it is a tale within a tale, principally about card-games, the loser's penalty, and the story of the recovery of a king's children stolen by an ogre.

'The Greek Princess and the Young Gardener': Kenny, *Fireside Stories of Ireland*, Dublin: M'Glashan & Gill, 1870, pp. 47-56.

In the Merrow (woman of the sea) section.

'Smallhead and the King's Sons': Mr. Curtin's 'Hero Tales of Ireland', contributed to the *New York Sun*.

In the section on Ghosts.

'The Leaching of Kayn's Leg': MacInnes, *Folk-Tales from Argyleshire*, vii., combined with Campbell of Tiree's version.

In the Saints and Priests section: although there are references to churches and masses, not one saint or priest is mentioned in the story.

NOTES

1.   First published, with a foreword by Kathleen Raine, in 1973. In the 1977 printing we added a list of Yeats's sources that had been compiled by Mary Helen Thuente. The edition was temporarily licensed to Pan whose edition was published in 1979 and reprinted in 1981 and 1984. Since Yeats's works came out of copyright (temporarily), the two works have been published in a single volume by the Slaney Press (a division of Reed International) under the highly original title *The Book of Fairy and Folk Tales of Ireland.*

2.   The second edition was published by Rupert Hart-Davis in 1958. Allan Wade had died on 12 July 1955, so the rest of the work was principally carried out by Hart-Davis himself. The entry remained unchanged in the third edition (1968), edited by Russell K. Alspach.

3.   Oxford took over the Soho Bibliography Series, of which Wade's bibliography had been the first volume, after Rupert Hart-Davis retired and his eponymous company was sold to Granada (later bought by Collins, now HarperCollins).

4.   Published in 1994 by Senate, an imprint of Studio Editions Ltd., London, who somehow claim copyright on it. It is difficult to see on what they base their claim. According to the blurb of this edition, the stories had been 'rewritten to appeal to the widest possible audience', but I find no evidence of any rewriting: as far as can be seen it is a straight facsimile reprint.

5.   The illustration appears to be signed H. J. Farr.

6.   Under the 1891 US International Copyright Act, 'copyright protection was granted to authors of such foreign countries as gave copyright protection to citizens of the United States on substantially the same terms as similar rights were granted to its own citizens'. However, until ratification of the Geneva Convention in 1961, works by Americans first published in the USA were in general not protected in the UK, although some secured it through being published in Canada within fourteen days of US publication (P. F. Carter-Ruck and E. P. Skone James, *Copyright, Modern Law and Practice* [London: Faber & Faber, 1965]). British authors were automatically protected in Britain wherever in the world they were first published, so to protect their dramatic works in the USA it was essential in the 1890s for works to be first published there if they were to gain protection under US law. To protect the US printing industry, after ratification of the Convention there was still a restriction that one could not import more than 2,000 copies of a book produced abroad. If one did, then copyright protection was lost. J. R. R. Tolkien's *The Lord of the Rings* suffered this fate, so that for a while, until agreement was reached, there were two paperback editions on sale, one of which had on the back cover a statement over a facsimile of Tolkien's signature stating that this was the only licensed edition and those who believed in authors receiving royalties for their work should buy this, not any other edition.

7.   A facsimile of Burt's edition was published by Dorset Press, New York, in 1986.

W. B. Yeats, Austin Spare and *Eight Poems* (*Wade* 114)

Colin Smythe

THE POEMS—'The Dawn', 'On Woman', 'The Fisherman', 'The Hawk', 'Memory', 'The Thorn Tree', 'The Phoenix', and 'There is a Queen in China'—were first published in the February 1916 issue of *Poetry* (Chicago), and later in the first issue of *Form*, officially published in April 1916. The first issue of *Form* had been planned for February publication, but it was delayed and as the poems had to be published in Britain at the same time as *Poetry* to secure US copyright, they were published prior to the first number's issue, and in a manner that gave Yeats not a little cause for heartburn. That its production was subject to a number of complications can be adduced by the following bibliographical description:

EIGHT | POEMS | BY | W B YEATS | Transcribed by | Edward Pay | Published by | "FORM" | At The Morland Press Ltd. | 190 Ebury Street London S.W. [*The whole title page printed in red*]
[*a*]. Japan Vellum copies (with no watermark) 28.5 x 19.8 cm.; [*b*]. Dutch handmade paper copies (made by F. J. Head & Co., with their initials and unicorn watermark), 30.5 x 21.0 cm., numbered 1-8; [*c*]. Italian handmade paper copies (watermark with 'A. D. 1470' and figure reading a

large sheet of paper, maker not given), 28.8 x 21.6 cm., numbered 9-130; [*a*], 20 pp.; [*b*] and [*c*], 24 pp., all pages unnumbered. [*a*] comprises the title page in red, verso blank, pp. [1-2]; text, the titles of the poems and the initial letters to each stanza printed red, the rest black, pp. [3-19]; the words "LONDON | January | 1916 | E. P." in red, p. [20]. [*b*] and [*c*] have an additional outer sheet wrapped round to create a 24 page book, so that the pagination now comprises a silhouette of a nude figure by Austin Spare in red, verso blank, pp. [1-2], the inner pages as before, pp. [3-22], followed by a blank page, verso printed red with profile of a head facing right and in [*b*] the words 'THIS EDITION | is printed on | HandMade Paper | manufactured by | F. J. HEAD & CO. | 21 Gt. Russell St. | LONDON W. C.', while in [*c*] the words 'Manufactured by' are missing, pp. [21-22]. At the bottom of the title page there is normally a slip attached which appears, according to Wade, in two forms—typed and printed. The former states

> This edition is an exact facsimile of certain pages in the quarterly periodical, FORM. The responsibility for the caligraphy [*sic*] and design rests entirely with the proprietors of FORM.

The latter

> This Edition is a facsimile of certain pages in the quarterly periodical "FORM." The responsibility for the caligraphy [*sic*] and design rests entirely with the Proprietors of "FORM."

In spite of Wade's statement (in every edition of the *Bibliography*), I have not yet seen a copy with the typed label,[1] but should they exist, it is most probable that they were sold before those having the printed slip and would be exceptionally rare. It has been suggested that the typed version is as a result of insufficient copies of the printed version being produced, and that the shortfall was made up by typing a quantity, but for the reasons given below, I think this unlikely.

Eight Poems was issued in cream card covers, lettered in black on front cover POEMS | BY | W· B· YEATS | [design of ten dots arranged to form an inverted triangle], and sewn with black woollen thread. The inside covers of most copies of all three versions are printed in black as follows:

Of this Edition only 200 copies are available
for sale of which this is No. [handwritten]

Dutch Hand-made   (8 copies) 4/-
Italian Hand-made   (122 copies) 3/-
Jap-Vellum   (70 copies) 2/6
                    Sole Agents:-
              The Poetry Book Shop
                35 Devonshire Street
                 Theobalds Road
                  London, W.C

All three Dutch hand-made paper copies known to me are signed by
Yeats and dated by him April 17 1916. The Columbia University copy
has the 4/- price crossed out, and 'signed by author 21/-' written in.
Some copies printed on other papers also have this or a similar correction.

On the inside back cover is printed:

ERRATA.

"Memory," line six should read
"mountain hare."
"Thorn Tree," second page, two
lines from the bottom should end
"Old men's blame."

Some copies of each issue have no printing on the inside covers, and these
are stapled rather than sewn. Some have the Errata notice but have no
printing on the inside front cover.

The British Museum Library copy is evidently an advance, for it was
received on 15 February 1916, produced and lodged to synchronize with
the magazine publication of the poems in America. It is printed on Japan
vellum, and lacks both the outer four page sheet and the printing on the
inside surface of the cover.

Some time in January or early February 1916, Yeats wrote an undated
letter to Austin Osman Spare, co-editor[2] of *Form*, from Stone Cottage in
Sussex, which he was sharing with Ezra Pound for the winter. He was
grateful to have *Eight Poems*, 'so admirably transcribed' by Pay, but with
Watt's help, asserted his rights to 'another copy or two'.

It was very gallant of you to put so fine a title page to a little pamphlet published for copyright necessities. I have found two errors which are I almost conclude irremediable. I only draw your attention to them, because, one of the titles in red not being added makes me see an unlikely chance that the pages are not unalterable yet.

MEMORY line six should red [sic] "mountain *hare*" (it is printed wrongly "here" [)] THORN TREE second page, two lines from the bottom should end "*old men's blame*", "old" has been omitted.

The faults may have been in my type-script. So please dont think me fussy in the matter. Only the first error is very injurious, and I dare say a clever reader will notice what is wrong. I only feel tagic [sic] about errors in my books.[3]

The copy he had been sent was printed on Japan vellum and therefore lacked Spare's nude figure, and it would appear that the first he knew of the illustration was when he was sent and saw it on a Dutch hand-made paper copy on which the missing title and initial letter to 'There is a Queen in China' had been inserted, but that did not, as yet, have the errata printed on the inside back cover, or the limitation notice on the inside front cover. The British Library Japan vellum copyright receipt copy is similarly corrected, so it is probable that Yeats was sent the illustrated copy at this time or soon after, when Spare had not yet been restricted to 200 copies.

While Yeats was prepared to write a tactful letter to Spare, doubtless to ensure that the corrections he wanted were carried out, his private view of the production was very different, and his accumulating annoyance began to have more general outlet when, in his 26 March letter to Lady Gregory, he wrote:

A man has issued, by mistake he says, by design I suspect, a pirated edition of some of my recent poems. He had proposed to make technical publication as his magazine *Form* was delayed and the poems were coming out in America. I got in a rage and limited him to 50 copies. He wrote this would ruin him and that he had not enough to eat. I did [not] believe [him] and told Watt who was acting for me to be firm. Then Ricketts[4] said he would pay any loss the man was under. I gave way at once, not wishing to have Ricketts pay, and now Ricketts says he misunderstood the situation. I feel I have rather injured Cuala, which should have all my first editions, and myself because the pirated edition is pretentious and has a vulgar drawing (which Ricketts had not seen) (*L* 609).

In one of John Quinn's copies, printed on Dutch handmade paper,[5] Yeats wrote:

> I think this picture vulgar. I had no responsibility for the pamphlet, which was issued by 'Form' to whom I gave eight poems free. These[6] delays made 'technical publication' necessary to secure my copyright and pamphlets like this are what they call 'technical publication.' If you want to reproduce a poem you should print it not write it, and if you do write it you should not break your lines. W. B. Yeats. April 2, 1916.

While Yeats received his first corrected copy in the second half of February, or at the latest in the first week of March, Harold Monro of the Poetry Bookshop received the edition about six weeks later, for he wrote to Spare on Wednesday 12 April:

> Thank you for your two letters Aprill [*sic*] 3rd and April 6th. I received the 200 copies of Yeats' Poems on Monday [presumably 10 April]. I am fixing up the whole matter with Squire.[7] There are two troublesome points. One of them is that I am sure that an edition of this kind should not be bound with wire, but with thread. Squire absolutely agrees with this, and I am proposing to have the whole dition [*sic*] threaded. The second is that Yeats tells me he stipulated for a notice to be put in to the effect that he was not responsible for the format and style of the book. He has asked me to promise to insert a notice. I have therefore arranged the wording with Squire and am having a slip printed.
>
> With regard to *Form* I am very sorry that you have to adopt the policy of only allowing those who pay the full subscription to have copies. I have now sent you cash for one subscription and asked you to enter another one for us. I should now like to apply for one more, making two for the Poetry Bookshop for which I enclose cash.

This letter, and Yeats's dated signature on the Dutch paper copies, tends to confirm Allan Wade's belief that the publication date of *Eight Poems* was in April, presumably around the 17th. As to the periodical itself, Howard S. Mott Inc., in its catalogue no. 210, listed a copy of *Form* with a John Lane review slip, requesting that no notices appear before 28 June, and while there is no absolute proof that Lane's review slip came from Lane with the issue—this is the only mention I know of Lane's connection with it—an entry in Charles Ricketts' diary for Saturday 24 June 1916[8] reads 'First copy of Form', so this would indicate that it was published in the last week of June. Too, as Ricketts got the Yeats poems for Spare to publish, it is likely he would receive a complimentary copy promptly, as soon as it arrived from the printers.

Yeats inscribed two copies of *Eight Poems* belonging to Lady Gregory, both now in the Berg Collection of the New York Public Library. In one, a Dutch handmade paper copy with the inside front cover blank and slightly wider than usual, he wrote:

> I am not responsible for this pretentious publication. It is a blunder or a piracy by the Magazine "Form" which had then to make technical publication for reasons of copyright.[9]

In the other, on Italian handmade paper and without a slip on the title page, he wrote:

> These 8 poems were in pamphlets to secure an English copyright. The edition which was not the format publication I intended but this elaborate pamphlet caused a quarrel between me and Form. I thought it an injury to Cuala. WBY

In the Buhler sale there was a copy on Italian handmade paper, inscribed by Yeats on the front cover:

> I gave these poems to the designer at the request of Charles Ricketts, R. A. W. B. Yeats June 1935. I don't like the work. The red woman is a brute.

In an out-of-series copy on Dutch paper signed by Yeats (now in Penn State University) he wrote in more forgiving mood, however:

> This work was brought out without my leave, & through a misunderstanding. It is not a form of publication or decoration that I would have chosen.

And in a Japan vellum copy in his own library, he wrote:

> This pamphlet was brought out by a magazine called 'Form' to save my copyright as the poems were being published in America & the magazine was delayed.

In another copy given by Mrs Yeats to the Library of Trinity College, Dublin on the occasion of an exhibition of the poet's books in 1956, he had written:

> I am not responsible for this foolish picture or anything else in this book but the writing. A foolish or intrepid young man got them to publish a pamphlet of poems to secure the copyright for me as his magazine was postponed and my poems were coming out in America. I then found he had got this book printed instead of binding up a few sheets and so making 'technical publication'. I got in a rage and took steps to stop him and he wrote that I would ruin him and a friend interceded. So now the book is out worse luck. W B Yeats.

From Monro's letter it would be reasonable to assume that he would have made absolutely sure that after all the 200 numbered copies he received had had the wire staples removed, they were then sewn and had the printed label stuck to the title page. I would guess that wool was used as a means to mask the staple marks, but in most cases the thread has suffered much from the passage of time. All sewn copies I have seen show the staple punch holes. However, the high number of unnumbered, disclaimerless, stapled copies indicates that many more copies were produced, of which the Poetry Bookshop—and Yeats—knew nothing. These copies must be regarded as out-of-series, produced as they were without Yeats's permission.

As the 1911 (and subsequent) British copyright acts stated that the British Museum (alone of the six copyright receipt libraries) has to receive a copy of every work on the best paper, finished and coloured as the best copies and in the best binding,[10] it is probable that the seventy (or more) Japan vellum copies were the earliest printed, and may have been the only copies originally planned and extant in mid February, with the Italian and Dutch handmade paper copies being produced as an afterthought as part of the money-making exercise.

From the evidence it would appear that that Yeats's view of Austin Spare is correct, and that while he only handed over 200 copies to the Poetry Bookshop, he had become ambitious, and actually produced many more copies of each which, however, he was unable to hand over to the Poetry Bookshop because of the poet's limitation, even had he thought of doing so.

Although it is doubtful that Yeats would have been interested in bibliographical pedantry, he would certainly have been outraged had he known the full extent of Spare's sales of 'out-of-series' copies, as he felt guilty that these poems had not had their first non-periodical publication in a book issued by the Cuala Press. Regardless of how much he knew, or suspected, it is very obvious that the matter irritated Yeats for the rest of his life whenever he saw copies of the offending publication.

To consider publication dates: the copies were first issued to protect copyright, the poems having to be published first in the UK as everything hinged on the date they were received by the British Museum Library. Yeats must have received a copy before that sent there, as it contains the requested corrections, but no one else appears to have done so until the stock arrived at the Poetry Bookshop in April. Regardless of the dates that Yeats received copies—he received other 'advance' copies, probably in March as a result of his request—it would seem that the official publication date must be considered to be in April, possibly the 17th, the date Yeats signed the Dutch paper copies.

As to the 'pamphlet' itself, only the sewn and numbered copies are truly 'in series' and all others, including the copyright copies and those sent initially to Yeats, are advance and/or out of series. From those known numbered copies, it would also appear that all had a printed slip inserted, except a block probably given to Yeats by the Poetry Bookshop before the labels arrived from the printers, who gave them out to family and friends, including no. 114 (belonging to Lily Yeats), no. 118 (to P. S. O'Hegarty), no. 121 (to Oliver St. John Gogarty), and no. 122 (now in the British Library).

With regard to the question of the date of those with typed labels, I consider it unlikely that the printers produced too few labels—every printer worth his salt normally printing a number of 'overs', but as copies would appear to have been sent to Yeats before Monro got the printed slips, he may well have sent out a few with the basic text typed in to comply with the poet's requirements, possibly for review (although none are known). It is possible that the copies mentioned above were sent to a Dublin bookseller, from whom they were bought, but as they would certainly have had a 'responsibility' slip inserted, I consider the latter scenario unlikely.

The numbered copies checked and used as the basis for the conclusions given in this article are nos. 2, 3, 34, 199 (Harry Ransom Humanities Research Center), 6 (Columbia University), 21 (University of Colorado, Boulder), 26 (P. & B. Rowan, Belfast), 31 (Bernard Quaritch), 43 (Clark Memorial Library), 50 (University of Florida, Gainesville), 59 (Mills Memorial Library, MacMaster University), 64 (Wellesley College), 67 (Library of Congress), 70 (National Library of Ireland), 71, 121 and 178 (Colby College), 78 (Beinecke), 79 (SUNYAB), 87 (Princeton), 114 (Anne Yeats), 118 and 189 (Kenneth Spencer Research Library, Univ. of

Kansas), 122 (British Library), 139 (Wesleyan), 145 (University of California, San Diego), 151 (University of Massachesetts, Amherst), 152 (Huntingdon), 155 (McCabe Library Swarthmore), 165 (Oberlin), 170 (Cornell), 185 (Harvard), 186 (Olin Library, Mills College) and 192 (Michigan State University, East Lansing). All are sewn and all but three (114, 121, 122) have labels, all of which are printed.

I have descriptions of the following out-of-series copies: seven on Dutch (unicorn watermarked) paper; nine on Italian (AD 1470 watermarked paper), and six on Japan vellum. All but one of these have been stapled only, the single exception may have been one of a very few extras sewn in case any copies got damaged and needed replacing. Limitation notices appear in four of the seven unnumbered Dutch copies and four of the nine unnumbered Italian copies, while none of the unnumbered Japanese vellum copies have the notice. None of the out-of-series copies have labels. It can be assumed that Spare quietly sold off all these as and when he could.

The fact that some of the unnumbered copies have been printed on the inside front cover can be accounted for by the normal system of printers always printing a few more copies—'overs'—than required.

To end: the second issue of *Form* (April 1917)[11] contained the following apology on the inside front cover:

> It is a matter of great regret to the editors of *Form* that a confusion of responsibilities led to a misunderstanding of the exact conditions of Mr. Yeats' copyright in his poems published in the first number, and to the consequent infringement of American copyright in them held by the magazine POETRY, published monthly in Chicago. POETRY, which printed these poems in February, 1916, owned the American serial rights, and *Form*, being an international quarterly, could not legally sell its first issue in America except through arrangement with the editor of POETRY. This necessary consent was not obtained. The editors and publishers of *Form* feel that the forbearance of the editors of POETRY in not exercising their rights under the law of copyright evinced good feeling and kindness of the highest order, of which we are thoroughly recognisant.

Perhaps the last words should be left to Ricketts, whose diary entry about his copy of *Form* partly quoted above, continues, laconically, 'The literary contributions are better than the artistic'.

NOTES

1.   One completer of my questionnaire indicated that his library's copy had a typed
      label, but as he included a photocopy, I saw that it was, in fact, printed. I am
      most grateful to the following owners for permission to quote the inscriptions
      in their copies of *Eight Poems*: The Henry W. and Albert A. Berg Collection of
      the New York Public Library (Astor, Lenox and Tilden Foundations); Anne
      Yeats; The Board of Trinity College, Dublin; The Library of Pennsylvania State
      University; and Professor George Mills Harper. I am most grateful to the fol-
      lowing for completing my questionnaire: an anonymous member of staff
      (Poetry/Rare Books Collection, SUNYAB Library), Peter Berg and Mildred
      Jackson (Michigan State University Library, East Lansing), John Bidwell (Clark
      Library, UCLA), Anthony Bliss (Bancroft Library, University of California,
      Berkeley), J. P. Chalmers (HRHRC), Cathy Cherbosque (Huntingdon Library),
      Linda Claassen (Mandeville Dept of Special Collections, University of
      California, San Diego), Lynne Farrington (Cornell University Library), Edward
      Fuller (Special Collections Librarian, McCabe Library, Swarthmore College),
      Lisa Gedigian (F. W. Olin Library, Mills College), Rick Gekowski, Vincent
      Giroud (Beinecke Rare Book and Manuscript Library, Yale University), War-
      wick Gould (Royal Holloway, University of London), Charles E. Greene (Prin-
      ceton University Libraries), Terry Halladay (Wm. Reese & Co., New Haven,
      CT), Professor George Mills Harper, Carmen R. Hurff (University of Florida
      Libraries, Gainesville), John D. Kendall (Head, Special Collections, University
      of Massachusetts, Amherst), Patience-Anne W. Lenk (Colby College Library),
      Charles Mann (Chief, Rare Books & Special Collections, Pennsylvania State
      University Libraries, University Park), Linda M. Matthews (Head, Special Col-
      lections, Robert W. Woodruff Library, Emory University, Atlanta, GA), Wil-
      liam L. Mitchells for Alexandra Mason (Kenneth Spencer Research Library,
      University of Kansas), Alice Morgan (Special Collections, University of
      Colorado Libraries, Boulder, CO), Megan Mulder (Wake Forest University
      Library, Winston-Salem, NC), Timothy D. Murray (University of Delaware
      Library, Newark), Milton McG. Gatch, Robert K. O'Neill (Burns Librarian,
      Boston College, Chestnut Hill, MA), Ruth R. Rogers (Special Collections
      Librarian, Wellesley College), Donald W. Rude (Texas Tech University, Lub-
      bock, TX), Dina B. Schoonmaker (Head, Special Collections, Oberlin College
      Library), Rob Shields (Library of Congress), Roger Eliot Stoddard (Curator of
      Rare Books, Harvard College Library), Elizabeth A. Swaim (Wesleyan
      University Library), and Cynthia Wall (Newberry Library, Chicago).

2.   *Form*'s other editor was Francis Marsden.

3.   I am indebted to John Kelly for the copy of this letter and that from Harold
      Monro.

4.   Charles Ricketts (1866-1931), artist and connoisseur, friend of Charles Shannon,
      had just declined the position of Director of the National Gallery, London.

5.   Lot 11592 in the sale of John Quinn's library in 1923-24. There were over
      12,000 lots, which realised $226,351.85—a poor price as $111,000 of this came

from his Joseph Conrad collection, contained in 230 lots.

6.   Probably 'Their delays'. The transcriptions in the Quinn catalogue of Yeats's inscriptions are not always accurate. For example, Yeats rarely used full stops in his signature, yet they appear in every one given.

7.   J[ohn] C[ollings] Squire (1884-1958, Kt. 1933) was Literary Editor of the *New Statesman* at the time. In 1919 he established the *London Mercury*, in which much of Yeats's later work was to appear.

8.   Ricketts & Shannon Papers, *B. L. Add MS.* 58107.

9.   This wording is echoed in his inscription on another copy, now in the possession of Professor G. M. Harper: 'I have had nothing to do with the publication of this pretentious pamphlet'.

10.   Section 15 of the 1911 Copyright Act was not repealed by the 1956 Act or the Copyright, Designs and Patents Act 1988 [Ch.48], and remains in force.

11.   In spite of describing itself as 'A Quarterly of the Arts', this was only the second issue, appearing a year after the first. Following my completion of the main draft of this essay, I read 'Some New Light on W. B. Yeats' *Eight Poems*', by Donald W. Rude and L. Layne Neeper, in *Analytical & Enumerative Bibliography*, n. s. 3:1 (1989), 11-15. This covers some of the same ground as, and quotes some of the material in, my essay, but is presented with different aims in mind: beyond noting its existence, I have therefore not seen the need to make any reference to its contents.

REVIEWS

'An Heroic Dream'?

John Kelly and Ronald Schuchard, editors, *The Collected Letters of W. B. Yeats, Vol III 1901-1904* (Oxford: Clarendon Press, 1994) liv + 781 pp.

Michael J. Sidnell

As the second volume of the *Collected Letters* to be published, Volume Three (1901-1904) of this magnificently-conceived project discloses with greater clarity than Volume One (1865-1895) some of the implications of the editorial choices. And it will be of great interest to see how far these choices are confirmed in Volume Two (1896-1900) when its appearance closes the chronological gap, for the consequences for Yeats studies, biography and the editing of letters may be considerable.

   This volume of the poet's letters, given the kind of documents they mostly are and the ways in which they are presented here, decentres biography; or, rather, it adds momentum to a collective project that has been under way for some time and that challenges some assumptions of the life-writing genres of which Yeats has been the subject, not least his own autobiographical constructions. Letters written later in Yeats's career are accomplished performances of his imaginative self-begettings and are thus more seductive emanations from imagined centres; but, in these letters, written in his thirty-fifth to thirty-ninth years, he was only tentatively beginning that labour of re-making the self which became a necessity when the world broke faith with him and he stopped loving it. In *CL3*, Yeats is still mostly preoccupied with keeping himself before his publics, by whatever means, and with the images of him that they reflect.

267

Two such are the morally and culturally suspect neo-pagan projected by some bigoted and vociferous Irish antagonists and—its antithesis—the wonderfully encouraging image of the spell-binding Irish orator and poet, created (on the basis of his own careful rehearsals and John Quinn's brilliant public relations) by his American auditors and adulators.

Such images were formative of Yeats's more finished selves but even the later volumes in this edition will contribute to the decentring effect if they sustain the scope and scale of the annotation here undertaken. For a second, no less powerful, decentring force is the extensive annotation, generously supplied, meticulously researched, tentacular, which brings to bear the realities of the other persons, the events and accidents—'that wrong of wrongs, | Those undreamt accidents' (*VP* 321)—by which the channels of Yeats's life are being cut. For *CL3* is by no means simply, or even mainly, a collection of Yeats's letters.

The volume contains two main texts, both multiple. One consists mostly of Yeats's writings in various letter-related genres: personal letters, brief notes, invitations, drafts of letters, letters to the press, epistolary dedications to books, business documents, memoranda, and (the items not written by Yeats) summaries of the deduced contents of non-extant letters. The other main, multiple text, mostly by John Kelly and Ronald Schuchard, but studded with quotations from a great variety of sources, is the one mostly printed in small type at the foot of the page. Throughout the volume, the editors' commentaries and researches are pursued with a thoroughness that goes well beyond the requirements of their immediate occasions to constitute a writing not dependent on Yeats's thoughts, words and deeds for its interest. Frequently, the annotations quote or otherwise indicate the addressee's initiative or response, thus opening another subjectivity to the reader's view, which may, indeed, readily be extended yet further, since many of the letters written to Yeats in this period (by Quinn, Gregory, Maud Gonne, AE, Bridges, Frank Fay and others) have been published elsewhere.

The editorial text might be re-arranged in other ways than under numbered notes subjoined to each Yeatsian document, as it doubtless will be in some electronic or other form, and as, indeed, it already is by means of the very detailed index.[1] When all the volumes of letters are done, their massed editorial texts should be a major source of information not just about Yeats but, *inter alia*, about hundreds of other figures of his time and place, about manners and convictions, about publishing and theatre and about literature. But this textual aggregation will contain a degree of repetition, accepted by the editors as the condition of making each volume self-sufficiently, as well as amply, annotated. It would appear that the cumulative effect of repetition may be hard to manage and that, ultimately, the publication of the notes in some combined and separate (electronic?) form that eliminates repetition will be more convenient and enable great economies.

Since the editorial text is so extensive—longer than Yeats's—and will doubtless be read closely by most of those who are likely to read Yeats's letters in this form, it was rather absurd to bow to a typographical decorum whereby it is printed so much smaller than the Yeatsian one.[2] But the typographical ratios will hardly determine the ratios of interest between subjects as they emerge from the juxtaposition of letters and annotations for, in many cases, the annotations are much more interesting than the perfunctory Yeatsian note that they annotate. What organizes the two multiple texts formally is, of course, the chronological order of the letters.[3] But historical time passes slowly in the economy of this volume and the scale of the topical axis is proportionate to that of the chronological one: from January 1901 to December 1904 in seven hundred or so pages. In this respect the volume resembles another book concerned with 1904—Joyce's *Ulysses*—which, not insignificantly, is put to use in the annotation of this one.

The phenomenon of editorial decentring has crept up on us partly unawares, as something that the age has demanded in recognition of multiplicity, and in response to its unappeasable appetite for information and to the advent of the means—economic, technical and the sheer accumulation of inter-related data—of supplying more diverse matter ever more amply. The editors of *CL3* make no claims to be doing anything different from previous editors of letters but the effects of the scale and the ratio of its two texts make it different from most earlier collections of letters and its purposes and principles are, of course, quite distinct from those that motivated Wade's 1954 collection and led him to make 'the notes as brief as possible' (*L* 18).

One eponymous subject of a collected letters, who also happens to be a subject of exceptional eminence in this volume's perspective, has already been named. He is the addressee of the following example of a common epistolary usage of the time:

> Nassau Hotel
> South Frederick St
> Dublin

Dear Mr. Joyce: Lady Gregory begs me to ask you to come & dine with her at the Nassau Hotel tomorrow (Monday) at 6.45. to meet my father.

> Yrs sny
> W B Yeats (*CL3* 242)

Along with related items of correspondence, this note attests to Yeats's kindness to Joyce and—prompted by Lady Gregory—his promotion of the younger writer's interests. The Yeats-Gregory invitation generates two editorial notes and is linked to the section on Joyce in the Appendix. The first editorial note alludes to the opening performance of the Irish Literary Theatre, to *The Day of the Rabblement* and to Ellmann's account of the first meeting of Yeats and Joyce. The second note admits to doubt as to whether the dinner actually took place and, in support of the suggestion that it might have, goes on to retail an anecdote from Gogarty's *It Isn't That Time of Year At All* about Gogarty and Joyce encountering J. B. Yeats in the street and trying to borrow two shillings from him.

Joyce makes regular appearances throughout the volume in both texts and, thanks to the precision and fullness of the index, he is easy to track. One revealing incident, recorded in a letter, has the obliging Yeats vainly trying to cash a money order for Joyce at some expense of time, shoe-leather and frustration. This provides an opening for the editors to quote Stephen Dedalus' difficulties—of a rather different order—with the cashing of his mother's money order. On other occasions, *Ulysses* (in Gabler's 1984 edition) is used to gloss its prototypes when they turn up as characters in Yeats's letters—John F. Taylor the orator, Oliver St.John Gogarty, Thomas W. Lyster and Richard Best (both of the National Library of Ireland), William Henry Brayden, editor of the *Freeman's Journal*, Mrs. Joyce, and Sceptre the 5-year-old that failed to win the Gold Cup in 1904. Such links between Yeats's letters and Joyce's fiction marvellously confirm the insights of 'The Wandering Rocks'.

A particularly amusing anecdote from the life, about Joyce making mock of the editor of the *Academy*, is re-told here. By contrast, the style, economy and convictions governing Ellmann's edition of Joyce's letters, and his ideas about biography, were such that he included the anecdote only in his biography. Throughout the editorial text of *CL3*, anecdote after anecdote gaily lightens the way, bringing its characters to life as the letters themselves only occasionally do.

Joyce is one of the ten persons (about half as many as in *CL1*) included in the 'Biographical and Historical Appendix'. Characteristically, we get a brief life of the subject followed by some paragraphs on his relationship with Yeats throughout their lives. In the entry on Joyce, mutual admiration, deliberate differentiation and artistic complementarity are the main themes. A few of the literary links are mentioned but not such major ones as the mass of allusions (including those to the first meeting of Yeats and Joyce) in *Finnegans Wake* to "my allaboy brother, Negoist Cabler, of this city, whom 'tis better ne'er to name, my said brother, the skipgod, expulled for looking at churches from behind, who is sender of the Hullo Eve Cenograph in prose and worse every Allso's night (*FW* 488). There may be occasion to mention the importance in Joyce's life and *Ulysses* of 'Who goes with Fergus' and the links between Yeats's stories and Joyce's in *CL2*; and in a later volume the importance to Yeats of the Joycean model (as Yeats understood it) of fictional autobiography, which would strongly affect his self-representations in several genres, including letters. There is no compelling reason for an edition of letters to undertake such a review, but the Appendix entries and annotation make such extensive forays in this direction that the actual selection of materials and and the perspectives of the editors' observations become noteworthy.

Among the other people included in the Appendix are Padraic Colum, Edward Gordon Craig, the Fay brothers, Arthur Griffith, John Synge—all but one of them, not surprisingly, collaborators in the theatre, as were two of Yeats's three great patrons: John Quinn, Annie Horniman and Lady Gregory. Quinn gets a cogent resumé of his career as (apart from being a high-flying lawyer) an extraordinarily discriminating patron of modern writers and painters. The editors' summing up is a little flaccid: 'Nevertheless, without Quinn the history of modern literature would not only have been different, it would have been poorer' (p. 731). The reservation about Quinn that they have overcome has to do with his pretensions in offering to correct Curle on Conrad, the prose of Sherwood Anderson and T. S. Eliot's punctuation. Presumably, Quinn's corrections of Yeats's proofs are taken to be more positive contributions to literature. Like Gregory and Horniman, Quinn expressed himself through his very active secretarial assistance, as well as through financial patronage and, of course, through such cultural 'productions' as Yeats on tour and the Armory Show. He wanted to be involved in the making itself and, as these letters (and his to Yeats) amply demonstrate, he was, indeed, a large contributor to the construction of 'Yeats'.

Annie Horniman self-consciously hoped to become not merely a philanthropist but an artist and she appears to have supposed—not altogether ridiculously—that one did this by collaborating with artists. But she found herself in another, less congenial role—that of a 'middle-aged, middle-class, suburban, dissenting English spinster' (p. 712), according to the editors. Their description probably implies, though rather obliquely, her great integrity and dislike of humbug. But humbug, alas, is what she gets in Yeats's one letter to her in this volume. (Was it that Yeats *saw* so much of Horniman that he rarely wrote to her?) But because so many of the letters to other people are about theatre business, Miss Horniman is often referred to—she has to be! And, of course, she has provided the editors with the momentous event with which this-volume concludes, thus ensuring her prominent place in it despite the paucity of letters to her.[4]

The entry on Lady Gregory is the most complex one in the Appendix, attempting to address the psychological bases of her relationship with Yeats in terms of 'mother-son', 'hostess-protégé', 'patron-artist' and a reciprocal triad of relationships in which Yeats was the provider (p. 706). Though the editors convincingly portray Gregory and Yeats as authentically complementary personalities and writers, their hypotheses of the 'had they not met' variety indicate a firmer attachment to the idea of essential selfhood than the evidence, including that of the letters between these (and other) correspondents warrants. In letters in this volume we see how ambivalent both are about how their collaborations are to be negotiated and presented to the public, as with Yeats's musings about whether or not *The Travelling Man* would be needed to fill out a volume of *his* plays. Michael Field is a comprehensible literary couple but as joint authors (of letters included here amongst other writings) Yeats-Gregory remains mysterious.

The editors' running annotations allow room for many persons other than those included in the Appendix to appear as more or less independent figures in the Yeatsian chronicle, and they provide frequent vistas of a world that did not arrange itself round the poet. Among the figures sketched in biographical notes, a fairly representative sampling might include: Gordon Bottomley, who is not quite adequately or accurately presented in terms of the flow between his work and Yeats's, which was not entirely one-way; Thomas MacDonagh, who is succinctly sketched as a literary figure in his own right, as well as a character in Yeats's work; and Henry D. Davray, who, in connection with a nondescript letter by Yeats, is illuminated as a significant intermediary between writers in English and readers in French, and as a translator of Yeats amongst others.

The editors do not insist on their evaluations of the persons, doings and writings they mention but neither are they shy about their opinions. They enjoy the human comedy and are willing to make summary judgements of deeds and works: that a dramatic experiment by Matthew Arnold 'produces wooden formality rather than passionate intensity' (p. 7); that Florence Farr exhibited 'mercenary behaviour' in charging for lessons (p. 253); that Augusta Gregory had a 'patronizing air' (p. 733). With a period flavour, perhaps, they discriminate between a 'poetess' (Ethna Carbery) and a 'poet' (Katharine Tynan), an 'authoress' (Sibell Lilian, Countess of Cromartie) and an 'author' (Olivia Shakespear).

The editors' gendered terms may be associated with Yeats's own concern, in this phase of his life, with the development of a masculine style and his suspicion that there was something 'effeminate' in 'the modern passion for the lyric' (p. 309). When Whitley Stokes, the Celticist, declared Yeats's 'verses . . . as emasculated as Burne Jones' knights' (p. 127) he was, at least, speaking Yeats's critical language. And that the theosophist Eleanor Blanche Elliot may have displayed an inordinate 'passion for the lyric' is suggested by H. W. Nevinson's report that she rehearsed Yeats's lyrics so assiduously 'that her husband cried out in his sleep '"Impetuous heart, be still, be still"' (p. 264). These are some of the many instances in which quotation is engagingly used for the purposes of characterisation. Others are: Virginia Woolf's remark that her aunt, Lady Anne Ritchie (Thackeray's daughter), would be 'the unacknowledged source of much that remains in men's minds about the Victorian age' (p. 355); or the quotation from the memoirs of William Stanton Pyper, the journalist and author of an unpublished book on the Boer War, who recalled in 1924 that in the late 1880s 'we could not help feeling that [Yeats] had already begun to act the part' (p. 22); or, Masefield's report that Mrs. Old (whose decisiveness in the matter of a gas stove significantly raised her employer's standard of living) declared, late in life, that she would 'never forget the blessed days with Mr. Yeats at Woburn Buildings' (p. 55). Such items convey the editors' own pleasure in their work and will surely heighten that of their readers. And the plenitude of its citations, not least those of the many newspapers and periodicals that have been so diligently scanned, make this book a richly valuable source, quite apart from Yeats's letters.

As to the letters here reproduced, a few of the originals survive only in print, others are typewritten by Lady Gregory or a stenographer, most are handwritten by Yeats and a few by Annie Horniman, usually in ink. They are written on various sizes, colours and qualities of stationery, from Coole Park letterhead to leaves torn from an exercise book. They are frequently undated and, though not always very legible, use many detectibly idiosyncratic misspellings and insufficient punctuation. In some cases, their envelopes have survived.

The editors always indicate the form of the document, whether typed or written by Yeats or someone else, and report on the envelope and its postmark whenever possible. They assign dates, as precise as the evidence allows, and note the present location of the document and a previous printing, where appropriate. The type of stationery is occasionally mentioned by Yeats himself but not by the editors. But their principle of retaining Yeats's spelling and punctuation, wherever practical, has the effect they aim at of representing 'the immediacy and personality of his correspondence' (p. xxiii). And it often suggests his pronunciation, as in his particularly expressive spelling of 'fateague' and his very common substitution of 'ea' for 'ee' in such words as 'sleep' (but not in 'endeed'). The handwriting remains, of course, out of editorial reach, though important cancellations are represented. (The editors would have done well, though, to have allocated one of the twenty-two illustrations to the reproduction of a letter—the draft letter to Maud Gonne, in which the appearance of the document is so critical, would have been an obvious candidate).

Between the writing of most of the letters included in *CL1* and those in *CL3*, Yeats apparently developed the habit of following the salutation with a comma or a colon, instead of no punctuation at all. (Perhaps *CL2* will mark the transition.) But this can scarcely be called *the* habit since, having decided for *some* punctuation, he vacillates between the comma and colon without rhyme or reason. His draft letter to Maud Gonne is an instance of his use of 'Friend' in the salutation. Others include a few letters written to Lady Gregory, mostly during the winter of 1902-1903, when Gregory becomes briefly 'Dear Friend' and 'My Dear Friend'. What is the meaning of this transition? More puzzling, what is the meaning of Yeats's reversion, not without inconsistencies, to (mostly) 'My Dear Lady Gregory'? His valedictions vary within a certain range ('Yrs snly', 'Yours very sincely', 'Yr ever', 'Yours alway', 'Your aly', 'Yours affectley', 'Yours') but they are followed by the most invariable feature of his letters: whether he is writing to a stranger, a sister or a friend the signature is consistently 'W B Yeats'.

And what of Yeats's parts in the brief but busy chronicle of this volume? The selection in the Appendix implies that the keyword is *theatre*, for not only are most of the persons in it associated with the theatre but so also are all four of the non-personal entries: 'Abbey Theatre', 'Irish Dramatic Movement', 'London Theatre Societies' and 'Psaltery'. But the last of these headings, which covers one of the less known—though critical—aspects of Yeats's career, has more to do with *performance* than theatre. And *performance* would embrace more of the activity recorded in this volume, including the tremendous energy that Yeats put into getting himself published to the best effect, his lecturing, his inclination to speech-making before the curtain, and his newly-adopted Nietzschean bearing in the world.

'Speaking to the psaltery' put Yeats in a performative role in which the expense of the self was a dramatic, as well as a lyrical manifestation. It was associated with the recital of narrative poems, the two modes constituting an attempt to develop a personal, 'poetical' centre, a conception of unity of being much simpler than that of selves held in tension, which would displace it. The period covered by this volume is Yeats's phase of the troubadour at its most intense, practical and, maybe, pathetic. After 1904, as the verse-speaking program faltered, his project of a series of long narrative poems written for performance was finally abandoned in favour of more conventionally theatrical productions, which come to dominate in this volume and in which he tried to imbue dramatic performance with some of the values of epic and lyrical recital.

As to pathos, the image, in *On Baile's Strand* (1903), of the chicken feathers, which are the Fool's share of the stolen chicken and with which Cuchulain wipes his son's blood off his sword, was an emblem of the ambivalences of ambition, success and failure in this period of Yeats's life. And like much else, the emblematic feathers appear to be traceable, in this volume, to dialogic origins. Yeats tells Lady Gregory how he was studying Pamela Colman Smith's designs for *Where There Is Nothing* and found that a design for Act I was 'a little humdrum', largely owing to his own conception of the scene.

> Suddenly while I was looking at it it occurred to me that it could all be made fantastic by there being a number of bushes shaped Dutch fashion into cocks and hens, ducks, peacocks &c. Pamela began sketching them at once. It can be supposed that these fowl have been the occupation of Paul Routledge's ironical leisure for years past . . . . (p. 267).

Yeats goes on to tell Lady Gregory how he proposes to introduce some comedy into the play. Strongly disapproving, she picked up the fowl motif:

> What frightens me is your joy of creation, you are like a Puppy after a chicken, when you see a new idea cross the path, tho' it may but end in a mouth full of feathers after all—(p. 268).

Yeats's letter was published long ago by Wade but, of course, without reference to Gregory's reply, from which we may surmise the dialogic links between the results of Paul's 'ironical leisure', those achieved by the Fool and Cuchulain in *On Baile's Strand* and Gregory's (and Yeats's) fear for Yeats.

Most of Yeats's theatrical ambition and activity was focused on Dublin but he was by no means inattentive to developments in England that were congenial to him. A 'literary' theatre was no less his objective than an Irish one, and Irishness and literariness did not always consort closely enough together for his liking. Whether to attempt Irish themes in an English literary theatre or—to use Yeats's own main approbative term—to attempt 'poetical' drama in an Irish theatre gravitating towards realism and bedeviled by religious censoriousness were options he kept open, especially at this time.

In England, literary theatre, under various banners, brought Yeats into association with the likes of Sturge Moore, Laurence Binyon, Gordon Bottomley, Florence Farr, Charles Ricketts, Gilbert Murray, Edith Craig, Gordon Craig, Allan Wade (whose career is worth a fuller note), and Bernard Shaw—to all of whom he wrote letters printed here. Shaw he thought of, for a few months, as a great potential asset of the Abbey-to-be but the shifting perspectives of *John Bull's Other Island* were by no means compatible with the Yeatsian project, as Yeats had to make clear—but not too clear—in his letter to Shaw, one of the most carefully wrought in the volume. (The editors seem to have overlooked the previous partial printing of it, by the way.) With a stroke of comic genius, apparently unconscious, Yeats concocted a major obstacle to the production of *John Bull's Other Island* out of its requirement of two English actors.

The rising stock of the Hudson's Bay Company enabled a permanent theatre in Dublin by putting Annie Horniman in a financial position in which she felt able to endow a theatre for Yeats. Yeats's artistic endeavours in preparing the ground for the new theatre, which would affect so many artistic and more ordinary lives, took impurely entrepreneurial, managerial, political and educational forms. Hating James Cousins' *Sold*, Yeats set about suppressing not just the play but its author: 'Every encouragement we give him as a writer will only bring trouble on us in the future.'(p. 387) There is little doubt that the trouble Yeats envisaged was corruption of taste; bad, popular plays driving out 'poetical' ones. But the trouble that most beset him, especially in the theatre, but also as a writer and nationalist generally, was religious antagonism.

The Countess Cathleen dispute still rankled and even *The Land of Heart's Desire* was thought dangerous. And the animus of Irish reviewers became such that, at Lady Gregory's suggestion, Yeats made it a rule not to have his books sent to them. This was on the occasion of attacks spurred by one of the pro-pagan sentiments that he was prone let slip from time to time. The offending remark was in his Preface (for which she had paid him the goodly sum of £10) to her *Cuchulain of Muirthemne*. The Irish papers 'evidently had an idea they shd be a sort of truffle dog where you are concerned, to scent out heresy however concealed',

Gregory wrote (342). It was not surprising, however, that such views should emerge and offend, since he and Lady Gregory had, as she reported, 'found startling beliefs & came to the conclusion that Ireland is Pagan, not Xtian' (p. 321). That conclusion animated Yeats's work as an Irish writer and, as he was often told and deeply felt, alienated him from a part of his nationalist public in Ireland.

One of his strongest and most fortifying impressions of America, as he repeated to several correspondents, with great wonder, was the religious tolerance he found there:

> Tomorrow I speak at St Pauls another Catholic College—in Ireland neither Catholic nor protestant college would let me among its students I suspect—here I find a really wonderful large tolerant spirit. One Catholic Proffessor was told that I was a pagan & said `There is a great deal that is very good about paganism' & now he has arranged for four lectures I believe,—& yet I think people are very pious here. Yet Catholics go without protest to the state schools in New England where the protestant Bible is read every day & there are a hundred Non-conformists & Jews in Notre Dame where all the teachers are priests. There are some intolerants but they seem to be fading out (CL3 526-27).

He wrote this almost a year after Maud Gonne had decided to marry Major John MacBride and, simultaneously, to be received into the Roman Catholic Church. In this manner she betrayed Yeats and what he conceived to be their cause in two inseparable ways, as he emphasised in the anguished draft letter to her reprinted in this volume (pp. 315-317). One betrayal was 'to marry one of the people' and thus abandon her membership in a 'superior class', a status that had enabled her to serve the people and influence them. The other betrayal was give up a 'heroic discipline' in surrendering her soul to priests. Yeats's sense of loss was by no means solely sexual and he compensated for it, apparently, by bonding closer with Lady Gregory. He had lost the closest ally and companion he thought he had, one who authenticated for him their nationalist cause: she had gone over to a dangerous and implacable enemy. CL3 lists Maud Gonne as the recipient of twenty-five letters from Yeats but the harsh fact is that the volume includes none at all that she received. What we have is the one distraught draft and twenty-four traces of letters, mostly found in the letters from her that Yeats kept. That the missing letters are so represented is entirely to the editors' credit and the readers' advantage. It is also a strong indication of the way in which this edition reaches beyond Yeats's letters to the lives that he shared.

NOTES

1. In the index to *CL1* 'italic page-references indicate passages where the subject is particularly discussed' (p. 525) but *CL3* does not continue this practice.
2. An alternative both typographical and editorial, which will be close at hand for many readers of *CL*, is *LTWBY*, which annotates by means of a single note prefixed to each letter and in the same type.
3. And, of course, the note numbers, which rather annoyingly—though quite conventionally—preserve the integrity of each document at the expense of the duplication of numerals on a single page. Even the proof-readers occasionally slip up with this numbering system, as at p.95, where there are two notes "1", two notes "3" but only one note "2", while at pages 207-8 the typesetter was apparently defeated by the system.
4. There is a trace of another letter to her from Yeats in the volume and he is also a signatory to a formal letter of thanks from the Irish National Theatre Company to her.

W. B. Yeats, The Hour-Glass: *Manuscript Materials* edited by Catherine Phillips (Ithaca and London: Cornell University Press, 1994) xxxviii + 362 pp.

Richard Allen Cave

Another fine volume has been added to the Plays Series in the Cornell Yeats—Catherine Phillips's edition of the manuscript materials relating to *The Hour-Glass*. To date the series has focused on the late plays where we have been in a position to study through the manuscripts how Yeats as a mature dramatist developed, refined and endowed with a purposeful theatricality what was already a complex inspiration. *Purgatory* and *The Death of Cuchulain* took possession of Yeats's mind from the moment of conception *as plays*. With *The Hour-Glass* we find the apprentice playwright painstakingly working to shape an idea into a dramatic form. For a start the project was not so much self-generated as suggested by a friend whom the manuscripts identify as John Eglinton. This is the first volume in the series that allows us to watch not simply a play take shape but Yeats discovering not only the intricate constituents that go to the making of a successful dramaturgy but also how to deploy that dramaturgy for what were in time to be highly innovative and deeply personal ends. The manuscripts offered here cover a period of over twenty years, during which the original prose version as acted by the Irish National Theatre Company in March 1903 was steadily transformed into the mixed prose-and-verse version that did not take its final form until 1922. The popularity of the play in the Abbey repertoire after December 1904 enabled Yeats to study it regularly in performance and try out subtle changes of emphasis to alter the impact of visual and verbal details and moments of staged action that vexed him. Catherine Phillips lists some forty-four known manuscripts relating to the play (often little more than scraps); twenty-four cover the evolution of the prose version and a further twenty relate to the second mixed version. Space did not allow for facsimile reproduction and transcription of them all; but judiciously she selects to demonstrate how each version reached its recognisable shape then offers the earliest printed format of each version (the *North American Review* printing of the prose version in 1903; and the printing in Gordon Craig's *The Mask* of 1913 of the mixed version),

279

against which she sets variant readings in an *apparatus criticus* drawing on the intervening group of manuscripts in both instances where the changes, though significant, are not substantial. Further material is included relating to the translation of sections of the dialogue into Latin in the scenes between the Wise Man and his pupils; while the three appendices print 'The Priest's Tale' from the first volume of Lady Wilde's *Ancient Legends, Mystic Charms, and Superstitions of Ireland*, which was Yeats's principal source; his draft of a song for the pupils to sing during entrances and exits; and his initial attempts at a preface for each of the versions on publication. The editing is exemplary and we are given a remarkably full picture of Yeats as playwright at work in consequence: the sheer tenacity of the man, the refusal to rest easy with compromise, the creative response to criticism (from others such as AE and Craig; and from his own rigorous, appraising eye and ear) are now available to us in minutest detail, so that we can readily appreciate just how and why the apprentice became in the fullness of time a mature dramatist and a great innovator within the European tradition of theatre. The evidence of a dedicated ambition which this volume reveals on a careful reading is breathtaking.

The enduring popularity of the play from the first performances was, to judge by the material shown here, both gratifying and problematic. It was not long since the public fracas over *The Countess Cathleen* and here was Yeats attempting another allegorical drama about the nature of faith, wisdom and doubt. Clearly he had to proceed with care to avoid a hue and cry yet again from the likes of Hugh O'Donnell, particularly as he wished to draw from the narrative a less tritely moralistic theme than that proposed by Lady Wilde's version. The characterisation of the Wise Man's atheism was crucial and Yeats seemed reluctant at first to invest him with a measure of dignity or sympathy which would make his ultimate predicament truly tragic. The climax comes at the moment of the Wise Man's death when he on impulse decides to trust blindly in God's compassion, which proves his saving grace; but the earliest acting versions considerably marred the impact of that moment by twice anticipating its significance, when the Wise Man knelt first before the Angel immediately on its appearance and then again before the Fool on realising that Teigue alone has remained uncontaminated by his teaching. As Yeats came to realise, this pattern of movement risked suggesting that the Wise Man's doubt was not really the product of deep-reaching thought and a passionately-held conviction. (Yeats deliberately avoided any suspicion of the kind which Lady Wilde's account promoted, that the Wise Man's free-thinking led inexorably to loose-living; rather he wished to examine the distinction between unquestioning faith like the Fool's and an instinctive faith that wins out over genuine intellectual doubt.) To lessen the dramatic stature of his central character in this way was ultimately to subvert the significance of his final decision, which requires him to abandon a lifetime's rigorously sustained principle.

What is of interest is how slowly Yeats gained the courage to effect the necessary changes. He even took the precaution in first staging the piece to ensure that the leading actor in the company, Frank Fay, played the oppositional role of the Fool, which would have invested Teigue with the heroic charisma that Fay was popularly seen to bring to the parts he acted. Though Yeats quickly saw that he had stacked the cards too heavily against his protagonist, he proceeded cautiously in rectifying the balance. By the time of the *North Atlantic Review* printing, he had removed the incident of the Wise Man's kneeling to the Angel; but in *The Mask* the revised, mixed text still has the Wise Man, conscious that the sands in the hour-glass are running out, *seizing* the Fool in desperation as he utters the words 'I kneel to you . . . you are the man I have sought. You alone can save me' (ll.557-8). Though the stage-direction specifies the *seizing*, there is no further direction requiring the actor actually to kneel. Holograph corrections subsequently removed even the stated verbal intention to kneel, but not before the play had run through two Cuala printings in 1914; the text of this passage as established in *Collected Plays* was seen first in the London 1916 printing of *Responsibilities: Poems and a Play*; and it was not until 1922 in *Plays in Prose and Verse* that Yeats actually drew full attention to the fact in his short preface to the mixed version. He was not to be troubled by likely audience reaction to *The Herne's Egg* or *Purgatory*. The suggestion is that the affair over *The Countess Cathleen* was a more vexing issue that rankled over a longer period of time than Yeats chose to admit.

With both versions of the play, the opening and the ending posed the most problems and underwent the most substantial revision. Little survives of the earliest sketches for the play beyond a rough attempt at the encounter with the Angel; but two extant typescripts show how seemingly from the first Yeats decided to start the play with his two protagonists: the Wise Man is busy perusing his vast tome in quest of a passage which begins: 'There was a time when men thought that the truth could be found through dreams and visions'; he meditates a counter-argument as the Fool enters in quest of pennies. This opening immediately establishes a series of oppositions (between dreams and reason, between the Wise Man who lives in the mind and the Fool who lives in the body) which the play will develop but the exposition does little more. The text that was prepared for the 1903 printing of the prose version would appear from a number of pieces of evidence to ante-date the first performance but already the opening has changed: what the Wise Man is now searching for in the tome is the text he wishes to base that day's lesson on for his pupils; it is the Babylonian beggar's account of 'two living countries, the one visible and the one invisible'. This realises the oppositions mentioned above, but does much more besides: there is the context of the lesson and all that that now implies about the extent of the Wise Man's influence as teacher (which is the occasion for the Angel's visitation) and the text quoted from the tome, instead of merely stating the fact of religious vision, actualises that vision as a part of the beggar-author's experience. The begging Fool who now enters is sensed as representative of an on-going tradition of belief and insight; and wisdom is presented as not exclusively the property of the learned. This in turn intimates an arrogance and intellectual snobbery in the Wise Man, which the play will relentlessly challenge. The exposition now has psychological depth and the oppositions a consequent vitality, though the effect is to make the Wise Man appear coldly cerebral and superior when he engages the Fool in conversation and takes a somewhat patronising stance.

Once Yeats embarked on revising the play wholesale to eliminate any possible intimation that the Wise Man had to 'humble himself to the Fool [before he could] receive salvation as a reward', the more he saw the need to humanise the character. This however posed a further problem in that too characterful a Wise Man might destroy the formal allegorical style Yeats had pursued both in the writing and in the staging of the play. Early drafts of the mixed version show Yeats already exploring a different kind of opening sequence for the pupils, who are seen trying to decide on the subject for the day's lesson; one is curious as to the Master's whereabouts and is informed that he is within the house talking with his children. This immediately establishes a different, domestic image of the Wise Man as father and husband yet it was quickly cancelled, perhaps because it introduced a sentimental note at odds with the general tenor of the play. (Similarly an attempt to make Bridget a more complex and agreeable figure in one revision by offering more insight into her marriage and by allowing a more relaxed and genial tone into her dialogue with her husband was not developed into the acting version, again presumably because of the risk of such a scene reaching for sentimental pathos in the playing.) Instead Yeats concentrated on exploring the pupils' response to their Master, their awe (rather than fear as in the prose version) of his prodigious intellect and their affection for him as their instructor; this beautifully establishes the extent of the Wise Man's influence without it initially inviting any critical response. Instead of the stark visual opposition of Wise Man and Fool of the prose version, Yeats now worked to perfect a more intricately symbolic tableau: the Fool chances to enter while the pupils are struggling with the vast book and they hit on the idea of deploying him as lectern, spreading the volume over his back while he holds his arms out to support it 'like a golden eagle in a church'. The Fool now supports the great book of wisdom in which the young men will find the strange writing by the Babylonian beggar and he is associated (wittily by the fourth pupil without anyone on-stage realising its particular significance) with the eagle, emblem of the most visionary of the four writers of the gospels. Now it is the young pupils who unthinkingly patronise the Fool, treat him as a toy or chattel by objectifying him as the lectern, which frees the Wise Man of the elitism that circumstance invested him with in the prose version.

By the time we reach the text Craig printed in *The Mask* Yeats had also successfully integrated a wholly new theme into this opening sequence: the relation of chance and choice in human affairs. The play starts with the pupils' need to find a topic for the lesson, but the fourth pupil at first displaces that subject with an account of his previous night's dream in which he felt urged to argue with his teacher over the existence of God till he is derided by the first pupil for his presumption. But that theme is restated in a different form with the Fool's arrival, since the young men need his help to lay the book out in a position where one of them can turn the pages while another with closed eyes chooses a passage at random as the basis of the lesson. What chance presents them with in the writings of the Babylonian is a more specific challenge to the Wise Man's atheism than the fourth pupil voiced but it reasserts the subject of the dream. Twice the seemingly irrational enters the world of the play, before the Angel's visit sets that academic world at hazard; crucially it now does so without either the Wise Man or the Fool being yet associated with the oppositional forces of reason and vision. In this way Yeats avoids investing his two central characters with overly representative labels, which would make his later subtilising of their positions more difficult to achieve. This is now the exposition of a master-dramatist: it states much inventively, but it intimates more which the development of the play will steadily bring to the surface. The central theme of the play is sounded but indirectly and in a fashion that teases the imagination into a rapt engagement with the ensuing action.

The first extant typescript of the complete play has the Fool admit to conversing with angels and the Wise Man rejoice in finding one who believes in God, before dying while urging the Fool to pray that the pupils may be given a sign that will 'save their souls alive'; the Fool summons the pupils who gather in time to witness the emergence of the butterfly, which one of them realises is their teacher's soul. This with minor changes is the version that was first printed in America in 1903; but Yeats quickly began adjusting this ending (generally by annotating a copy of Bullen's English edition of 1904, which appears to have been used as prompt copy in the Abbey and which incorporates material that was first published in the 1907 theatre edition). The chief alteration was, of course, to re-introduce the Angel who appears at the doorway where 'she' stretches out her hands and closes them again as the Fool describes her actions, supposing that she will release the butterfly 'in the Garden of Paradise'. Interestingly (and presumably once again to avoid any risk of sentimentality in this close or a wrong note of piety) there exists a holograph but unpublished additional speech given to 'A Young Man' which would end the play on a provocatively paradoxical note: as the Fool envisions the release of the butterfly in Paradise, the man asserts brusquely: 'There is nobody there . . . there is nobody in the door'.

It would be interesting to know whether Yeats consciously studied Marlowe's *Dr. Faustus* at some point before revising the ending for the mixed version though as always what appears at first sight a potential influence on Yeats has been quite transformed by him till his inspiration exists in a kind of dialogue with the original. The most significant change is to keep the pupils off stage for the close (though in one of the drafts Yeats experiments with having the Fool toll the bell that would summon them into the room throughout the Wise Man's dying speeches, which he presumably later decided to cut as provoking too elegaic a quality inviting pathos, which would detract from the courage of the Wise Man in the moment of his death, as Yeats had come to conceive it). This decision helps to focus attention in the revised text on the Wise Man's consciousness as it approaches the moment of death. As rewritten, that process of rendering the self absolute for death is full of dramatic surprises (especially for an audience familiar with the earlier version). Where before the Wise Man had found in the Fool a genuine believer and died in a measure contented; here the Fool proves evasive and *fey*, eluding the Wise Man's efforts to get a positive answer to his questions. Earlier Teigue spoke of angels; reminded now of his former words, he does not directly deny them but intimates that his mind wanders and is not to be trusted. Yeats had trouble getting the tone of this strange disclaimer right.

At first Yeats experimented with a flat denial that carried an undertone of subservience: 'No, no what should poor Teigue know,

Teigue that is out in all weathers, Teigue that sleeps in the fishers' loft, poor Teigue the Fool' (versions of this recur in the manuscripts and in Craig's printed text). It was not until the 1916 text published in *Responsibilities and Other Poems* that Teigue's reply took final shape: 'Oh no. How could poor Teigue see angels? Oh, Teigue tells one tale here, another there, and everybody gives him pennies. If Teigue had not his tales he would starve'. This is fool's talk indeed, admitting Teigue's sharp eye for the main chance, which undermines the Wise Man's hopes and expectation. The passage gives point retrospectively to that curious moment in their first scene alone together where the Wise Man describes Teigue as the butt of everyone's orders and imitates people bidding the Fool be gone or stand or else sit in the corner, all of which the Fool performs to the letter like a puppet. Teigue now admits he does as he is bidden to do in hope of financial reward; it is an honest admission, but not at this moment the reply the Wise Man seeks. Yet *had* he answered as the Wise Man wills, the Wise Man would have been duped and not saved. Teigue's reply seems cruel in destroying the Wise Man's hope, but by so doing he throws the Wise Man back on himself in his abject loneliness. And it is out of that awareness that the Wise Man submits to the divine will whatever may occur and becomes himself the sure believer, prepared to accept that all his speculation may be naught but wind. (Marlowe's Faustus by contrast surveys that void but is too focused on his own terror to be capable of such courage.) In that final speech the Wise Man reaches a tragic dignity too intense for the subsequent image of his soul as butterfly to seem either bathetic or overly pious. By conveying the significance of the last moments through the rhythms of the Fool's chatter, Yeats also keeps sentimentality firmly at bay. How much does the Fool ultimately know or understand? How much is he indeed wandering in his wits? It took much redrafting before the subtle psychological shifts of this version were encompassed with such confidence. As Catherine Phillips argues in her introduction, Yeats was shocked when he saw the first performances of the prose version by how cowardly he had made the Wise Man appear; despite numerous minor revisions to the close, it took a wholesale revision of the play before he drew a portrait that credibly conveyed intellectual courage to his satisfaction.

The shape of the main body of the play remained virtually unchanged from the first version to the second, except for one telling detail where we find Yeats returning to an original inspiration which (during an early revision) he had chosen to cut from the prose text. In the second scene with the pupils after his encounter with the Angel, the Wise Man is desperately seeking for one student unaffected by the force of his teaching and he rages at them ('Out, out or I will beat you with my stick') because one and all 'answer me with argument'. The Young Men roar with laughter and, in the earliest surviving typescript of the play, one of them observes 'How well he plays his part; he is like the monk when he had nothing more to say' (referring to a one-time opponent, whom the Wise Man had publicly bested in argument). The words, 'his part', are scored through and 'at faith' substituted in their place; and so the line remained in the 1903 American edition and in subsequent printings of the prose text.

While 'plays' initiates the idea of conscious acting which 'part' endorsed; the substitution of 'at faith' draws the focus of attention back to the crisis of belief which the Wise Man is experiencing but which the pupils choose to interpret as a trick to test their perceptions. Early in the drafts of the mixed version after the Wise Man tells his pupils of the Angel's visit, one of them comments that their master appears to be 'pressing that old claim' of visionaries and martyrs to have a gift of inner seeing; a second agrees 'How he imitates their trick of speech | And air of mystery'. The Wise Man reiterates that 'something incredible has happened' and, as if taking up the implications of 'imitates' from the earlier speech, the First Pupil next comments: 'What a fine mummer he is | And what a man he is'; the two lines were immediately cancelled but their governing idea was retained and elaborated: 'You d think the way he says it that he felt [it] | Theres not a mummer to compare with him'. With slight modifications the lines have remained in this form right into the volume of *Collected Plays*, except that the initial idea of the Wise Man's brilliant way with imitation was extended and shared between three speakers ('How well be imitates their [visionaries and martyrs] trick of speech'; 'Their air of mystery'; 'Their empty gaze') as if he affected the whole group of pupils with his passion and excited their applause for his mimicry. The moment now has complex resonance: so meticulously has the Wise Man shaped his pupils' modes of perception that they judge his tragic declamations as farcical caricature. The Angel had observed that 'Hell is the place of those who have denied; | They find there what they planted and what dug' and this is now the Wise Man's exact and exacting experience: his sincerity is praised as a virtuoso display of *acting*, duplicity, a calculated trick to trap the unenlightened and culturally insensitive.

The moment is a great challenge for an actor in performance, to make the pupils' assessment of their master's intention plausible, while nonetheless sustaining the profound pathos of the Wise Man's predicament.

Between the two version of *The Hour-Glass* Yeats had completed *Deirdre* in which he had begun to experiment with consciously deploying the idea of *acting* to extend the thematic and symbolic significance of the stage action (Yeats's Deirdre is a consummate actress, adopting roles first out of sheer fear to persuade Naisi to quit Conchubar's lodging while there is still time and later with Conchubar to calm the King's suspicions, to gain access to the murdered Naisi's body, and to achieve her intention of commiting suicide). Acting in *Deirdre* is the key to define the heroine's complex psyche. To use acting metatheatrically as an aid to characterisation in this way dates back to Shakespeare and Jonson. With *The Hour-Glass* Yeats deployed the device for a more original but wholly organic end that brought more clearly into prominence his philosophical argument.

This sequence of revisions to the mixed text highlights an aspect of the whole conception of the play that Yeats had steadily strengthened over the years: a powerful sense of the alienation and consequent experiential anguish that must accompany the loss of a communal faith. Some of the most tellingly dramatic incidents in *The Hour-Glass* occur where the characters' words or actions show how they are wholly engrossed in their own selves and personal ways of seeing. There is the stage image in the prose version (the germ of this conception was present from early in the drafts) of the Fool sitting on a stool by the door throughout the Wise Man's search for a believer amongst his pupils '*reckoning on his fingers what he will buy with his money* [the four pennies he has just tricked the Wise Man into giving him]'; or later the equally powerful image which, unlike the last instance was retained into the mixed version, of the Fool blowing on a dandelion to 'find out what time it is', which seems so callous a gesture to the Wise Man, who is all-too-conscious of how the sands are rapidly running out in the hour-glass. A further example is the uncomprehending Bridget, harassed by her children and her daily chores, who, when offered her husband's intimate confidences about his spiritual terror, blithely supposes he just needs 'somebody to get up an argument with'. The incident about the Wise Man's supposed acting is another of these moments, and perhaps the darkest of all, since the pupils' reaction, which appears so cruel, is actually well-intentioned, an expression in this instance of a deeply felt admiration. Despite its allegiance to the genre of morality play, *The Hour-Glass* in the second version is decidedly modern in its tone, pitched as it is with such unerring skill between the tragic and the comic as these episodes demonstrate. Faith may win out in the end, as in all true moralities, but it is no easy victory, given the conflicting perspectives onto events which Yeats's revisions brought to the play; the only witness, disturbingly, to the final apotheosis in the mixed text is (to use the theatrical term) a zany.

The whole history of revision to the play could (from a theatrical viewpoint) be seen as necessary to bring the text into line with what for the initial audiences would have been the remarkable innovation and modernity of its staging. Yet the potent simplicity of the setting for the original production in 1903 was clearly not a part of Yeats's first conception. The earliest manuscript draft opens with a leaf in Lady Gregory's hand evoking a far more traditional kind of stage picture to represent a medieval scholar's sanctum:

> A large room with a door at the side into an inner room—A desk with a chair in middle—An hour glass on a bracket on the wall—A creepy stool near the door. Some benches—An astonomical globe—A blackboard. A large/ancient map of the world on the wall—Some musical instruments. Floor strewed with rushes.

With only minor variations this was the stage direction incorporated into the 1903 American edition; indeed only the text printed in *The Unicorn from the Stars and Other Plays* in 1908 began to amend the text to bring the direction for the setting into line with actual Abbey Theatre practice. While this is simple enough in its requirements, it is still more akin to standard nineteenth-century pictorial ways with stage design with its superfluity of illustrative detail (globe, blackboard, map, instruments, rushes) than the setting created for Yeats by Sturge Moore from an idea of Robert Gregory's, which included within a stark box set only such features as were given a purposeful function by the dramatic action: desk, chair, hour-glass, bell and two simple entrances. It is difficult to determine at this date who precisely was responsible for the originality of the first setting: Sturge Moore certainly proffered a sketch (see letter 5 in *TSMC*) which survived amongst Yeats's effects as did Gregory's watercolour; but how much the idea for the stark precision of this was influenced by Yeats himself (or more likely by Charles Ricketts, whose subsequent practice as a stage designer it anticipates in remarkable detail) remains open to question. Assigning the invention to its rightful author is, however, less important than appreciating the design itself for what it achieves, since it broke with current theatrical conventions in the boldest ways, dispensing with painted scenery and making an aesthetic virtue of what was an economic necessity. Yet interestingly Yeats continued to allow the printed text of the prose version to encourage readers to imagine a more traditional style of setting.

As Catherine Phillips shows in her introduction, it was the acquisition of a set of Craig's miniature screens which was the spur finally to goad Yeats into revising the play substantially; the screens allowed Yeats effortlessly to experiment with stage design and *The Hour-Glass*, as staged using the mixed text in January 1911 within an arrangement of the full-sized screens by Craig himself, was the Abbey's most successful deployment of this highly innovatory device. It was perhaps the most completely satisfying staging of one of his plays that Yeats was to see until his work with Ninette de Valois on the dance plays in the late Twenties. It was only with the text printed appropriately in Craig's journal, *The Mask*, in 1913 that Yeats finally gave directions for a 'scene' which reflected the challenging starkness that had boldly confronted audiences since 1903:

THE WISE MAN'S house. An Hour-glass on a stand and a big chair with a great book on a desk before it.

Nothing is admitted to the playing space but what the dialogue will invest in time with a precise dramatic function. Here are the roots of that modern functionalism in stage design which was steadily to become the dominant practice within twentieth-century art (as distinct from commercial) theatres. By 1911 Yeats had at last created a text that properly matched the daring modernity of its setting; and by 1913 he found the courage to admit as much in print. In many ways it is with this production and this publication rather than with the *Four Plays For Dancers* that Yeats gained his maturity as practising dramatist.

W. B. Yeats, The Herne's Egg: *Manuscript Materials*, edited by
Alison Armstrong (Ithaca and London: Cornell University Press,
1993) xxxi + 205 pp.

Richard Allen Cave

Deciphering the elderly Yeats's holograph poses formidable problems.
He frequently abbreviated words, especially when attempting to modify
phrases already written out in full, or truncated them to an initial letter
followed by a line or flourish that vaguely intimates the noun, epithet or
participle intended. What appears on the page often has the look of an
aide-memoire, made in the heat of composition, designed to assist the
poet's processes of recall when he should feel sufficiently confident of the
overall shape of a work to wish to transcribe it into typescript ready for
more detailed local revision. With the surviving manuscripts of *The
Herne's Egg* the problems facing an editor intent on an accurate transcription are further augmented by Yeats's ill-health on the one hand (the
writing shows clear evidence of waning physical stamina) offset on the
other by that irresponsibility he remarks on in several letters at this time.
This was the result of his extreme confidence in the play once the
scenario was completed, which seems to have stimulated in him a
wonderful exuberance at his own Rabelaisian daring; and this in its turn
urged him on to periods of creative fervour that more than once sapped
his energies to the point of requiring that he submit to days of total rest.
    Long stretches of the play (such as the dialogue between Congal and
the Fool in the final scene) were set down with such a clarity of purpose
that they hardly needed even modest revision at the point of being trans-
ferred to typescript. Other sequences show Yeats simply repositioning
blocks of largely unmodified text at the transcription stage (as in the
speeches for the three young girls at the close of scene two, where they
watch Attracta enter her mystic trance, seize the hen's egg and go whirl-
ing away in 'long leaps' towards Tara), where Yeats appears to wish to
heighten the dramatic climax of the episode by giving a clearer
psychological progression to the ideas that lie behind the girls' musing
about Attracta's strange behaviour and about the nature of her forthcoming, promised union with a god. In the drafts the focusing of the

290

audience's attention on the fact that it is a hen's egg that Attracta has picked up (which is necessary for a proper understanding of why the plot-line subsequently develops as it does) and the comic squabbling between Agnes and Jane (the character was ultimately named Kate) about whether Herne and Priestess are to couple in 'the blazing heat of the sun' or in 'blue black midnight' are interwoven, whereas in the typescript the speeches have been subtly re-ordered so that the two themes are now carefully distinguished.

The changes also show Yeats getting a firmer control over the complex shifts of tone he is attempting in this episode: in the manuscript version the mundane, the mystical and the farcical are bewilderingly confused. One could argue that this has a dramatic point in a play that sets out deliberately to leave an audience guessing for much of the time whether they are watching a farce or some profound mystery drama or *auto sacramental*. The revisions that led to the typescript show Yeats more purposefully manipulating his audience's emotional responses: we now move from awe at Attracta's possession and weird, inexplicable dancing to the matter-of-fact, as the girls talk of the hen's egg; but that tone begins rapidly to shade into the grotesque, as they ponder whether the egg is about to undergo some kind of transformation; then the grotesque moves into the downright hilarious as two of the girls start arguing fiercely over the circumstantial details involved in mystical sex between a woman and a bird, till Mary halts the wrangling with an ecstatic vision of how Attracta at the moment of consummation will lie in the bride bed 'full of his [the Herne's] might | His thunder bolt in her hand'. These had been the concluding lines of the scene in the draft; but the revisions now give them a startling prominence. Yeats had originally written 'joy', but changed it almost immediately for the more resonant 'might'. Sexual consummation is here envisaged as embracing not only personal transcendence but also visionary potential, insight and power (all qualities that Attracta possesses when she later comes out of her trance in scene five). But beyond these intimations the revision of 'joy' to 'might' in all its rich ambiguity brilliantly creates a context for the final line to be heard| read both literally and as bawdy innuendo. Yeats's greater control over the tone of the episode in the typescript allows him to move the scene inexorably towards this conclusion which deftly holds the earthy and the sublime in an exquisite poise. All the components of the scene were there intact from the first draft; but the final line is now fully *placed* dramatically as the masterstroke that it is, expertly preparing the attentive audience to interpret everything that is to follow on those two levels: liberatingly profane and awesomely sacred.

Generally Yeats was confident of the tone he sought after right from the first. It is noticeable, for example, how quickly he settled on the short, sharp lines of the opening scene with their patterning of ideas and rhythms, immediately suggestive of a world of jocular sparring and male bonding, a time of thoughtless fisticuffs between well-matched, easy-going rivals, into which religion and sex are about to be introduced with devastating consequences. Yeats at this stage of his career can create a dramatic situation that encompasses at one and the same moment the specific, the historical and the archetypal with consummate ease and an admirable succinctness, while critically placing it all in respect of an audience's reactions by adopting a tone of genial satire. As an exercise in exposition, the opening scene is a model of dramatic artistry. The same is true of the edgy atmosphere instantly evoked at the start of the final scene. Here we have a whole new character (the Fool) and set of bizarre stage properties (lid, pot, spit and stones), yet their seeming zaniness we are taught promptly to re-read by Congal as ominous. For the first time in the play his speech is devoid of martial vigour; because his physical self is wholly exhausted, imagination and conscience have taken over his mind and are now controlling his mode of perception; everything he encounters is to him a possible manifestation of the Great Herne's power against which he must hold himself continually on guard. He is alert with fear to a degree that has sapped all his customary energy. The fact that this highly complex mood is realised within seconds of playing-time allows Yeats to move the dramatic action towards Congal's suicide with an implacable speed. Implacability was what excited Yeats most about great tragedy (though he considered the structuring of Sophocles' *Oedipus the King* near-perfect for the ways it provoked a sense of relentless implacability, he had dared in completing his own adaptation of the Greek original massively to cut the final sequences of the play to enhance that very quality) and he achieves it here at the close of *The Herne's Egg* with a consummate skill—consummate, because the manuscripts up to the point of Congal's final soliloquy show that the scene came into being with an absolute precision and needed scarcely any modifying at a subsequent stage of composition.

The most heavily revised and re-written sequences are interestingly the two major confrontations in scenes two and five between Congal and Attracta, where Yeats seems uncertain for some time about the tone he is seeking to capture. This is partly because he appears unsure at first quite how to characterise Attracta, whether in fact to present her as in the drafts Congal initially sees her: as mad, frigid, obsessed and withdrawn. To do this would, of course, seriously undermine Yeats's metaphysical intentions with the play, since the audience would be invited to mock her, perceiving her from a wholly worldly perspective. If Congal's view of Attracta were endorsed in this way, then there would be no scope for her to challenge him and his arrogant self-possession; and that would leave Yeats little room to effect any kind of development with Congal's character. In consequence the metaphysical agenda devised for the play would have no roots in a credible psychological realism. Yeats needed to find a tone for each of these roles that would invest their speeches with a creative ambiguity: it was imperative that the audience should not be disposed to judge either of them too quickly.

It is tempting to speculate whether it was at this point that Yeats made one crucial change in his conception of the play. At first Yeats spoke and wrote of *The Herne's Egg* as his first, full-length three-act work for the theatre (the manuscripts actually divide the action into acts and scenes). The initial drafts of the second scene do suggest such a spacious scheme: there is an attempt to individualise the three old soldiers, Mike, Pat and Mathias, who accompany Congal to the hernery; Mike is more loquacious than he was to become with subsequent revisions; Congal is much given to philosophising and metaphysical speculation, after first commenting on the time of day and his army's hungry state; while Attracta rhapsodizes about the many priestesses and women before her who died in seeking union with the Herne in order to confirm his miraculous immortality. In revising the episode Yeats cut whole sections of his text rigorously, paring the whole scene down till it made its points with trenchant vigour. (There is a quite different process of revision at work here from that described above for the sequence between Attracta and the three girls which ends this scene, where there is little attempt to trim the length of the action only to re-order its development.) Though Congal in the typescript is given all six men from his army, only Mike speaks in this scene (the rest are characterised individually later through the form each of their objections takes to Congal's command about raping Attracta—a passage in scene four (ll.125-136) that, significantly for my purpose here, Yeats was still revising between the typescripts and the 1938 London printing of the play, presumably at proof stage). Mike in one early revision at his first speaking is given the name 'Mantis'; it is not clear whether this was accidental or deliberate (if accidental, then it could have been a creative Freudian slip); certainly he is not so named again. 'Mantis' with its close approximation to 'Manto' carries classical resonances suggestive of 'prophet' or 'seer'. It would be appropriate given the saga context of the play and its source material for a king like Congal to be accompanied in all his dealings by a Druid advisor, the like of Cathbad who counselled Conchubar. What is curious is that 'Mantis' appears as designating the speaker on the first occasion that the character utters a one-word riposte to Congal, calling him to order. Cancelled drafts for dialogue later in the scene show Yeats crossing out Mike's name above more expansive speeches and assigning them to Pat or Mathias before cutting the material altogether. It appears that Yeats chanced upon what he realised he could develop as a superb running joke in respect of Mike's role: the single-word imperatives that usually stop Congal's flow of thought dead in its tracks to make him realise that there are often other ways of interpreting the situation in which he currently finds himself. It is wholly in keeping with the absurdism of the play that a seer's authority and voice of command should be so reduced to cartoon-like propor tions.

The decision to curb Mike's utterance to these comic exclamations served in time another useful function. As Yeats cut Congal's speeches quite drastically to highlight one or two central ideas, so he needed a means of effecting some necessary psychological transitions to account for Congal's shift of focus. Mike's disruptions made this possible without breaking the comic tenor of the sequence; the effect is to suggest that Congal is capable of deep thinking only at Mike's prompting and that off the battlefield he is at a loss without Mike's shrewd guidance; and shrewd his interjections certainly are by the time the play has reached the typescript stage. In its finished form Congal's relationship with Mike now affords a creative parallel to Attracta's with the Great Herne as, later in the scene, she becomes possessed by the god and moves 'like a doll upon a wire': destiny is shaping their several lives, but as yet the intimations of its absolute power are kept firmly within the bounds of comedy.

The cutting of Congal's dialogue leaves his role in this scene with three main motifs: the trespassing on sacred territory in quest of the eggs (which is still in the genially rough manner of his encounter with Aedh in scene one); his attempts to justify his actions to Attracta after being riled by her enigmatic servant Corney, who refuses to be impressed by any show of power on Congal's part; and his sudden perception of her not as Priestess but as woman. Yeats seems to have found immediately the idea of the hilarious reiteration of the word 'principal' to define Congal's embarrassed efforts to explain why he wants the eggs; and the struggle to aggrandise himself in this way is a perfectly judged characterstroke. In the early drafts, however, the comic effect is somewhat dissipated by a protracted description of the eggs as a *worthless* novelty: 'A thing of no accont | Mere rubbish that my men | Have set their fancy on'. Congal further disputes Attracta's right to possession of the eggs on the grounds that 'nobody has a claim on rubbish' ('claim on' was revised to 'right to' before the whole passage was cancelled). While the illogic of all this (why make such a fuss about nothing!) is funny to some degree, it does delay the development of the central focus of the episode, which is the impact of Congal and Attracta's meeting on each other. The repetition of 'principal' exactly captures Congal's insecurity matched with his characteristic desire to brave it out; by cutting all the ensuing speech, except for its central idea that the men feel themselves important enough to merit dining off a 'certain novelty or relish', the momentum of the action can move swiftly on to Attracta's stern refusal and Congal's manifest shock at anyone daring to challenge his authority.

Yeats at first gave Attracta a quite lengthy justification for her response, referring to 'Rules made centuries ago' by the 'first father' of that Herne-god who is to be her husband. But the lines gave him obvious dissatisfaction as they were worked and re-worked (the manuscript text here cycles around this exchange for four pages, new attempts at Attracta's speech often disrupting Yeats's drafting of Congal's outraged reaction to being refused). The problem lies in Attracta's explaining her conduct, since this infers that she has taken full notice of Congal and is matter-of-factly addressing him direct. Almost immediately after this Mike is to deride her as 'Mad!' and clearly that outburst needs some motivation. The revisions to Attracta's speech steadily eliminate any suggestion of a wish to explain her conduct; what we are left with is a wholly depersonalised, hieratic utterance as if it is the voice of some sibylline power which deems itself above question. This voice shows no recognition of Congal or his worldly authority; there is no attempt at any human engagement and no invitation to reply and establish a dialogue; the speech is exclusively an expression of Attracta's status as priestess and guardian of the hernery. Congal's unthinking swagger has met its match in Attracta's cold, detached dedication to her calling. At once Yeats has achieved the means credibly to provoke Mike's jeering dismissal of Attracta and force Congal to take a proper look at his antagonist. Mad she may be, but her beauty and presence move him suddenly to an eloquence that has no need of Mike's inspiration as he endeavours to find an acceptable psychological motivation for what to him is strange, because unfeminine, behaviour.

Congal is the arch male chauvinist, but circumstance has compelled him to notice Attracta as an individual; he has listened to her words and now tries to understand the terms of her vocation as Bride of the Herne. The speech in which Congal imaginatively re-interprets Ovid's account of the various metamorphoses Zeus underwent in pursuit of his rape of Danae and Leda came to the page if not fully formed at least sharply defined and requiring scant revising and reordering of lines, though again Yeats carried on re-writing the speech over several pages of manuscript till the complex ideas achieved clarity of expression without losing the sense that Congal's mind is here struggling with modes of thinking that are quite new to him. (It might be argued that one of the cancelled versions of the lines describing Leda—'What moonlike dreams groped for pale feathr | When Leda lay upon the grass'—presents her predicament more graphically and in a manner that effects a more certain verbal parallel for the lines describing Danae than the rendering in the published text. 'Groped' has an experiential immediacy that is more highly evocative of passionate desperation than the rather bland substitution: 'What rose against the moony feathers' and it totally eclipses in a manner proper to drama the vivid image defined in the phrase, 'dragged down the gold', which relates to Danae.) Congal here denies that the sacred has any place in life; but in so doing he is trying to express a degree of compassion for Attracta as far as his limited experience can encompass some explanation of her distinctive presence and aura. Her very being (aloof, coldly passionate in her commitment to her faith) is beginning to awaken in him a dormant imagination. The soldierly swagger remains, but he leaves the scene a changed, because inwardly troubled, man. Deftly Attracta is established in the revised version as otherworldly; she is completely untouched by the encounter. That chance meeting has set going a process of transformation in Congal: the total ease of physical well-being which characterised his exchange with Aedh in the opening scene has been shattered beyond repair. Revision has clarified the two central characterisations in a manner that is now wholly and incisively dramatic rather than descriptive, expansive and literary, which are the epithets that define the original tenor and method of the scene.

In Scene Five we find Yeats again in the processes of revision seeking to establish and sustain an appropriate tone for Attracta's speech. She has at first a new quiet confidence which supports her conviction that she has been wedded to the Herne; she has acquired a new physical self-possession too, as with Corney she gathers the remains of the eggs to return them to the hernery. Congal, on entering, observes the change in her and patronisingly congratulates Attracta on becoming 'all woman', clearly seeing himself and his men as responsible in raping her for making her this model of femininity. His tone is quite devoid of moral conscience; he even needs to be reminded by Mike that some expression of thanks is due for all their pleasure. (Yeats's ear for styles of male chauvinist banter is unerringly exact.) Attracta is calmly disbelieving, asserting her perception of the truth: 'My husband came to me in the night'. And when this statement is laughingly challenged by Congal, her assurance is immediately transformed into the hieratic tone of her first appearance, a tone assumed now as of absolute right.

This is, however, to write of the scene in its final form. What seems to have given Yeats most difficulty in composing the encounter was the mounting grandeur of Attracta's voice of authority to the point where her vision of the metamorphoses to be undergone after death by Congal's soldiers carries conviction. The bursts of thunder that seal her decrees about the future destinies of the men must, in terms of theatrical performance, be worked up to if they are to afford a genuine climax to the action and not be reductively comic. Revision once again chiefly took the form of extensive cutting. Yeats at first sought to find words to allow Attracta to describe the moment of her mystical union with the Great Herne. Initial thoughts in the form of images such as 'I parted the great curtain of his bed' were quickly excised as presumably too prosaic, literal and worldly, while self-consciously wrought phrases such as 'Pure clove to his purity', since they serve only to make Attracta sound artful, went in favour of a complete simplicity of statement: 'I lay beside him his pure bride'. Yeats seems to have written himself steadily into the awareness that what to Congal and the audience seems an incomprehensible mystery verging on the absurd has to Attracta's perceptions been *direct* experience. As for her there is no mystery, then there is no pressure on her to explain, define or justify; and all words or phrases that intimated a degree of defensiveness on her part had of necessity to be eliminated. A totally unquestioning, utterly transparent and exact mode of expression has in the context an unchallengeable power. All is stark precision; there is no place for the least touch of human feeling. So secure was Yeats with the bald and bold expressiveness of this voice in Attracta, once he had attained it, that the final moments of the scene where Attracta summons Congal to the holy mountain clearly flowed unimpeded from his pen and needed relatively little correction.

What is of note is that Yeats attempted at some stage (by way of a revision subsequently discarded) to condense the last lines of the scene where Congal makes a compact with Attracta to come to Slieve Fuadh at the full of the moon. In the revision, after Attracta has voiced her wish to have 'one man there among Gods' acknowledging her new-found status as bride of the Herne, she bids him 'get a swift hors' and Congal agrees: 'I come'. The final two lines in this version read:

Atratt

acknowledging my marrage

Congal

Because I am in terror of the Thunder

This ends the scene on a note of ambiguity: Congal has agreed to do Attracta's bidding, but she seeks to ascertain his motive for agreeing. Has he finally accepted her perception of things? Does he believe that she underwent a transcendental union? Immediately Congal cuts short such a line of thought by offering a more prosaic, self-centred reason for submitting to her request. In this version the focus is on character and psychological motive. In the final state of these lines, the moment of making the contract is wholly ritualised as Congal thrice asserts, 'I will come'. First he acknowledges that he knows the place appointed and so will come; secondly he asserts that whatever the outcome, even death, he will come; thirdly and most importantly he admits that he is 'terrified' and so will come. The relating of 'terrified' to the recent thunder is now omitted, so that the word is released from a contextualising that potentially renders it comic; in consequence it gains a much more ominous resonance. The effect in performance is that Congal is overwhelmed by the strangeness of the experience he is going through; it is as if he is possessed and so 'under the curse', as Attracta says is his current condition. There is no courage, none of his customary derring-do bravado in his electing to follow Attracta to the mountain. The patterned speech with its repetitions suggests rather that Congal has relinquished all effort to control and define experience, because he no longer possesses the necessary confidence or certainty to do so. His mind is expanding into hitherto untravelled ways of thought. Is he accepting the possibility of fate and destiny? The scene now ends on a very different kind of ambiguity from the revision discussed above: the compact is effected and it is powerfully endorsed by the ritual mode, which leaves Congal's precise motive undefined. This creates a narrative dynamic which carries over into the next scene, where we quickly discover that Congal's motive had little directly to do with his perception of Attracta's identity. What has possessed Congal's mind is the idea of a sequence of three conquests between himself and the Herne for supremacy. That he should in the moment of his death finally appeal for help to Attracta is all the more moving for its contrast with Congal's continuing obsession with the Herne; and that appeal cuts through Attracta's cold detachment to touch in her the wellspring of pity, which excites her to attempt to frustrate the Herne's intentions as to their several futures. As they become more human in their suffering, so the Herne as shaper of all the grotesque action is revealed as shamelessly cruel and malign. It is in that revelation that the full tragic potential of the play is made manifest. The matching of tone with thematic purpose and dramatic strategy, which is shown by this revision to the last lines of Scene Five, is meticulous and demonstrates Yeats's absolute control of the subtler kinds of structuring required of drama.

A similar mastery of structuring is evident in two other notable revisions. Attracta's song, which in the final version of the play provides the climax to Scene Four, makes its first appearance in the drafts as a kind of soliloquy between the departure of Congal and his men in Scene Two and the arrival of the three girls in which Attracta voices more private fears of the mystical marriage that she had so proudly talked of with Congal: 'Shall I that seemd so great in my thought | Shrink to a bird that a bird has caught | Shrink to a beast that a beast holds tight'. In several cancelled drafts of part of Scene Four Attracta on entering in her tranced state sang a brief ditty in the fashion of a nursery-rhyme prophesying Congal's ultimate fate: 'What shall he do with a Hernes egg | what with a table legg | Play the fool for that is the rule | How shall he die? At the hands of a fool'. Single stanzas of the song, which through copious revision are moving steadily towards the final version, are initially situated throughout the episode in which Congal persuades his men to engage in the rape and sets up his 'court' to give 'judgement' about the proper ordering of the event. In this way the dramatic focus shifts repeatedly between the scheme for the rape and the vision of the mystical marriage. It is not clear at what point between drafts and typescript Yeats took the decision to amalgate these bursts of song into one sustained lyric, but there is no denying the greater force of the revision. Throughout discussion of the rape Attracta now stands silent, her great eyes staring in an unseeing trance; she seems wholly victimised, vulnerable and pathetic, mortified into a catatonic state by the threat to her person of this gang of drunken louts. The uneasy comedy of the scene is nicely calculated to keep an audience's response on the right side of revulsion.

Now it is only when Congal removes the egg from Attracta's grasp that she 'wakes' from this state. The 'waking' marks a significant shift of perspective: it is as if we have moved inside Attracta's consciousness and away from the social reality of her predicament to a place where in the depths of her being she is seeking to prepare herself for an experience of the transcendental, to allay her innermost fears, and find the calm of mind in which she might properly accept what she believes to be her destiny. The fact that this moment is realised in dramatic terms as song suggests its otherworldliness, its confrontation with what is not natural. (The choice of a song strengthens the parallel with the Virgin Mary's 'Magnificat', the better to emphasize the differences attending Attracta's fate.) If she cannot *accept* (in the sense of opening herself to) the Herne, then that coupling too will be an invasion, a rape of her person and her psyche. The extended song focuses an audience's attention on Attracta with an intensity that was not possible when the stanzas of the song were distributed throughout the scene. We are at once in two time-scales, two modes of perceiving reality: in both the woman is likely to be cast in the role of victim to male dominance. The scene as finally realised offers now a precise structural parallel with the conclusion of the following scene, as analysed above, where Congal also enters a state akin to trance as he senses his awareness being invaded by a force which lies beyond his powers of definition or his ability to resist. He like Attracta comes to know himself as victim.

The second notable revision came late in the process of creativity, after the initial 1938 printing of the play. In itself it is the slightest of adjustments, yet its impact *theatrically* is momentous and proof (if proof be needed) of Yeats's superb control of tone and of the various constituent arts that contribute to the creating of a performance-text. Attracta at the close of Scene Five bids Congal join her on the holy mountain 'when the moon is full'. Throughout the process of composition, Yeats appears to have envisaged the final scene opening on a nearly darkened stage as Congal meets and fights with the Fool and Attracta journeys to the mountain with Corney; a stage direction requiring a change in the lighting state, '*The moon rises*', was positioned immediately after Congal has attempted suicide at the moment that Attracta joins him on stage; the tragi-comic ending in which Attracta struggles to frustrate the Herne's plan to effect Congal's rebirth as a donkey was imagined at first as being played in an eerily intense light. But Yeats suddenly changed that. He cancelled the direction for the rising of the moon and revised the opening description of the final scene so that not only the moon's radiance suffuses the whole of the stage action ('*the moon has just risen*'), but the moon itself has to be clearly visible on the backdrop and presented in a very particular style: '*the moon of comic tradition, a round smiling face*'. The face of a genial joker now presides over all Congal's earnest self-examination and all the pain of his death and the misery of Attracta's efforts to redeem his soul from the Herne's manipulations. That expression of a profound and cynical indifference to human suffering inevitably affects an audience's response to the final actions of the play. The Herne has had his sport with Congal and Attracta and the moon is the god's representative: withdrawn, superior, amoral. For all the grotesqueness that occurs throughout Scene Six, however absurd the behaviour of Congal and Attracta, the presence of that grinning moon ensures that an audience never ceases to view them with compassion. Just as the revisions concerning Attracta's song in Scene Four and Congal's compact in Scene Five invest each of the characters with an unexpected tragic dignity, so this revised detail relating to the stage design for the last scene serves to endorse and augment their tragic stature. Yeats's hold on the structural development of character in drama is both assured and subtle. The change seems small, hardly perhaps noticeable to the casual reader; but in terms of performance the consequences alter the whole tenor of the ending, as the farcical and the tragic are placed in a wholly new relation to each other. Perspective challenges perspective, making the judgement implicit in our response to the action far from easy to gauge.

Alison Armstrong's editing of the manuscripts for *The Herne's Egg* is a fine work of scholarship both in its attention to detail and in terms of her making chronological sense of some ten items comprising holograph and typescript drafts, annotated proof sheets and a heavily revised copy of the initial published volume to illuminate the processes whereby this complex and disturbing play came into being. Previous volumes in *The Cornell Yeats* set formidably high standards and this edition matches up to its predecessors admirably. There is just one textual crux that Alison Armstrong's otherwise vigilant eye has overlooked, which merits some comment in the annotations. It is a problem that came to my personal notice only when directing the play and which a careful viewing of this edition partly helps to resolve. There are a number of occasions in the play where in the haste of composition Yeats appears not to have bothered to check certain minor details: eg., he seems to have been unsure at different times just how many soldiers Congal has in his army and what their names are; and the matter was not resolved when the play went into print. One soldier, James, is not listed in the *dramatis personae* of the earliest editions, though he is given dialogue in Scenes Four and Five. Malachi is listed and is assigned some entrances and exits and he is given a single speech in Scene Four; he is included in the list of soldiers entering in Scene Five, but does not speak and is not included in the roll-call of those who claim they raped Attracta. The play continually refers in these later scenes to 'seven men' (including Congal himself) as involved in the rape and the god's curse; but if both James and Malachi are counted in with the other soldiers who have substantial portions of dialogue to utter, then the correct number of the army would be eight. Most directors tend to conflate the roles of James and Malachi rather than make a joke of the matter along the lines that either Congal or Mike cannot count the numbers that comprise their army. Most of this material is discussed in the annotations. But there is one other incident where Yeats might be accused of being somewhat slapdash. It occurs just before Congal and his men leave in Scene Two after acquiring the hernes' eggs by force and commandeering Corney and his donkey to transport them. Congal has just been ritually cursed for his sacrilege but is indifferent to his fate, believing his person so becursed that 'There is not a quarter of an inch |To plaster a new curse on'; he leaves advising Attracta: 'Take to your bosom seven men'. The passage was clearly revised between manuscript and typescript so that Congal's long speech is twice disrupted: once by Mike's ejaculation, 'Pickled!' to describe Congal's predicament; and once by an aside from Corney, 'Wriggling rascals!' which is his dismissal of Congal's claim to be impervious to more cursing. The passage was further revised between typescript and the 1938 edition to give us the text as published in the *Collected Plays* so that Corney's speech now reads simply 'Luck!' while Congal's is more heavily emended to read:

> Adds that your luck begins when you
> Recall that though we took those eggs
> We paid with good advice, and then
> Take to your bosom seven men.

The crux is the ascription of the single word of ejaculation, 'Luck!' Such monosyllabic utterances have been established by now as a running joke in respect of Mike's truculent character. Invariably after one of these interruptions Congal takes note of the fact that Mike has influenced the drift of his thinking and generally begins his next sentence with 'He says . . .'. This is precisely how Congal continues speaking after Mike has disturbed his musing on being cursed with the word, 'Pickled!' While the sardonic aside 'Wriggling rascals!' is wholly in keeping with Yeats's characterisation of Corney's refusal to keep 'a civil tongue' in his head even in the presence of armed men, the revision of this speech to 'Luck!' would seem to require that it be ascribed to Mike (particularly since Congal's next speech begins with 'Adds that . . .'). There is no plausible psychological motive for assigning the speech to Corney, particularly when characterisation and the comic artistry of the scene all suggest that preferably it should be given to Mike. The prime focus of Yeats's revision to the passage in preparing the play for the 1938 printing is obviously Congal's speech, which is sizeably changed to give a better shape to the flow of ideas, but the new movement in his thinking required a suitable prompt. It is truer to the patterning of the scene and the relationship which Yeats has carefully built up between Congal and the man who is clearly his chief of staff for the simple word 'Luck!' to be assigned to that man, namely Mike. Yeats in hastily revising the speech omitted changing the speaker. Whatever one's view in the matter, the passage does require comment. This is, however, a minor cavil in respect of what is in every way a superb editorial achievement.

W. B. Yeats, The Wind Among the Reeds: *Manuscript Materials*, ed. Carolyn Holdsworth (Ithaca and London: Cornell University Press, 1993) xxxvi + 220 pp.

Warwick Gould

The central symbolic obsession of *The Wind Among the Reeds* dates from 'Ephemera | An Autumn Idyll' of 1889 '"The innumerable reeds | I know the word they cry, 'Eternity!' | And sing from shore to shore, and every year | They pine away and yellow and wear out, | And ah, they know not, as they pine and cease, | Not they are the eternal—'tis the cry."' (*VP* 81 v.). Yeats had noted down the title early in the notebook used for many drafts of the poems of this collection (Holdsworth, p. 156) and rather incautiously announced it to D. N. Dunlop as early as October 1893.[1] Nora Hopper then used the phrase as title of a poem in *Ballads in Prose* which began 'Mavrone, Mavrone! the wind among the reeds'. The final stanza, including the line 'Play hide and seek with winds among the reeds' was incorporated into the cover design and repeated on the verso of the half-title. Yeats's reaction was surprisingly magnanimous (*CL1* 426-7 & nn.), but later he was to complain rather more vigorously when Katharine Tynan published *The Wind in the Trees: A Book of Country Verse* in 1898. Her reply was a barely believable attempt to blame her publisher, Grant Richards (*LTWBY* 37-38), but she was probably right that the clash redounded more to her disadvantage that to Yeats's.

There was (and is) no copyright in titles and Yeats suffered less from these clashes than from the awkward publicity thus accorded his continued delay in producing this long-promised title, which had been announced so regularly by Elkin Mathews that a *Today* paragraphist despaired in March 1899

Nowadays I do not measure the growth of age by my birthdays. I measure it by the periodical announcement of Mr. Elkin Mathews that he is 'shortly to publish' Mr. W. B. Yeats's poems, 'The Wind in *[sic]* the Reeds'. Time has sobered me considerably since I first read the announcement in a dim, long-buried year. And the volume never comes. Mr. Yeats is a mystic and a symbolist, so, perhaps, is Mr. Mathews, and the announcement may be a weird and cryptic hint that new poetry nowadays is like the wind: periodically passing over our lives, though neither men nor publishers may capture it. Or is Mr. Yeats's poetry not to be issued in the ordinary way on paper, but circulated on the breezes some favouring night when London is sweet below the stars? What really does Mr. Mathews mean?[2]

Yeats's infinite capacity for taking pains is most clearly shown by the slow preparation of every aspect of *The Wind Among the Reeds*, but also in his refusal to compromise with any dealings with Mathews which might have resulted in a meaner-looking book or in a meaner royalty for himself. Much of the story of delay, compounded by doubt, suspicion, rivalry, and sheer circumstance, in the production of *The Wind Among the Reeds* has been told by James G. Nelson in his *Elkin Mathews: Publisher to Yeats, Joyce, Pound*,[3] Correcting and expanding Nelson's account (upon which Holdsworth wholly relies) is too lengthy a task for a review and must await *The Collected Letters* Vol II, involving as it does the complex relations of the poet, the publishers Elkin Mathews and John Lane, and Althea Gyles, the designer of the cover and frontispiece portrait—abandoned before publication—of the poet.

Althea Gyles's wrap-around design for *The Wind Among the Reeds* is her finest and most restrained design, and the implicit narrative of the sequence spills out onto the covers. The symmetrical pattern of reeds on the top board, with its lozenges and triangles, forms the net of the fisherman in 'The Fish' (then called 'Breasal the Fisherman'). From front cover to back the pattern changes from order and the intended entrapment of the beloved, to chaos, tangle and escape. The fire of the front cover is replaced by water on the back, just as one of the central symbolic 'principles of mind', Michael Robartes, is 'fire reflected in water'.[4] The process of reading is thus prefigured in the boards themselves, as 'the pride of the imagination brooding on the greatness of its possessions', and the subject of contemplation is further symbolized by the spinal design of the 'hyssop-heavy' sponge on a reed: a remarkable image of a sexual passion envisaged as Christ's Passion.

The despatch of the frontispiece offers a clue to how Yeats's bibliographical mind set was working. Finishing the book was on his mind, cost on Mathews', and the frontispiece was shelved. To the modern eye, however, the self-image remains personal and is subversive of the totality of the book. Rose symbolism, after all, belongs more with *The Secret Rose* or the named section of *Poems*: after the long gestation of *The Wind Among the Reeds* this frontispiece could have come to seem a little outdated. Yeats-as-mage looks outward, blowing his rose-leaf against invasive forces, but the image accords neither with the text's aspiration to impersonal mastery of immanent moods nor with the deep human suffering at the centre of each lyric.

Above all, as it is not possible to detect in Yeats's letters any regret at the loss of the frontispiece, it is hard to think it the focus of the book's 'moods'. A book essentially of 1896-98, its 'painful stillness' is something from which Yeats had only recently and briefly escaped into that decisiveness which facilitated the book's final arrangements in the late summer of 1898. Though about to plunge back into crisis in December 1898, when he might have married Maud Gonne but for some strange failure of nerve,[5] he was, for the moment, over the misery of the Olivia Shakespear/Maud Gonne impasse of 1897. This had been projected, redeployed into the artful, self-rupturing narrative of the lyric sequence, as John Harwood has shown.[6] Given the acutely autobiographical—even confessional—nature of the lyrics which were added to the manuscript from 1895 onwards, Yeats might have found the occultation of his identity into the symbolism of a cover design more acceptable than a frontispiece portrait. The book's opening appeal ('And Niamh calling *Away, come away:*') summons us to the *topos* of 'The Wanderings of Oisin' yet again, and poem after poem speaks of the fatality of knowledge until in the last poem of the volume Mongan, sober again after 'ale from the Country of the Young' can 'weep because I know all things now' (*VP* 177). *The Wind Among the Reeds* is not a book about fatal books but a fatal book in itself, and it created among its already esoteric readership an inner order of readers who read Yeats's new poems by the lamp of older ones.

Holdsworth oddly chooses to record the reception of the volume as 'hostile', 'somewhat hostile', 'administering a caustic', and as critical of 'literary elitism'. Yet John Davidson praised Yeats's 'living and intellectual regard for what is at most only a faded mythology' and—with some wit—the reviewer for *The Critic* saw the volume as 'prose sequence of Celtic fairy tales' with a 'poetic chain of comment thereon'.[7] William Robertson Nicoll averred that the poems 'must live whatever become of empires. They will live with love and sorrow and death'. 'Aedh wishes for the Cloths of Heaven' was 'worth all the poetry Mr. Kipling has ever written or ever will, and . . . those who do not see this saying to be true will never understand at all in any proper way what poetry is'.[8]

Most surprisingly ignored is the fact that *The Wind Among the Reeds* won the 25 guineas offered by *The Academy* for the best volume of poetry of 1899—the contemporary equivalent of the Booker Prize.[9] The

Cornell Series typically eschews critical comment from its editors and warns the reader not to expect it (p. v), but this one, who shows no particular liking for the volume, does not restrain herself.

> The poems become so elaborate, finally, that nearly half of the 1899 volume consisted of prose notes, which look like Yeats's ingenious but futile attempt to make simple again what may have been simple to begin with (p. xxi).

Yeats took a calculated risk with his notes (45 of 108 pp). These replaced his initial idea of an extended commentary, but preserved the essay-like amplitude he needed for excursions into folklore. One motive was certainly his worry over 'reckless obscurity' (*VP* 800). A revision of *The Celtic Twilight* and his 'big book of folk lore' with Lady Gregory were—somewhat indistinguishably—on his mind at this time and the notes embody Yeats's reading of J. G. Frazer's *The Golden Bough* (1890), Count Goblet D'Aviella's *The Migration of Symbols* (1894), Sir John Rhys's *Celtic Heathendom* (1892) and numerous Irish authorities. Henry-D. Davray, his French translator, was told that these 'really elaborate essays in the manner of *The Celtic Twilight*' were 'made out of quite new material'. Above all, the deployment of longer notes (some of which were rewritten from headnotes to periodical printings of individual poems) under groups of titles of particular poems or such subjects as '"Aedh," "Hanrahan" and "Michael Robartes" in these Poems' gave Yeats the chance to convey to readers—initiaites or willing neopyhtes—the strategies by which he wished the book to be read, within its own textual compass, and within the wider textual horizons of his other books, and of his sources and analogues in earlier writers.

> They have given me a good deal of trouble & will probably make most of the critics spend half of every review in complaining that I have written very long notes about very short poems. I am in hopes however that others will forgive me the poems for the sake of the valuable information in the notes. It is a way of getting the forgiveness of the philistine which may serve as a useful model.[10]

Yeats had wanted to deploy an occult, symbolist theory of folklore as evidence of 'the most violent force in history' (*Au* 400), the 'embodiment of disembodied powers . . . age after age' (*VP* 810), but while his gamble paid off, his forecast was not entirely misplaced. E. Nesbit was puzzled by the 'wide wilderness' of notes while Francis Thompson thought their 'clumsy expedient' created 'wanton difficulty' and compounded the 'arbitary . . . imagery' which 'darkened' the poetry.[11] The reviewer in *Literature* doubted if the charm and dubious etymology of forty pages of notes was justified by 'fewer than forty poems'.[12]

Arthur Symons, a dependable logroller, found the 'delightfully unscientific vagueness' of the notes also possibly ineffectual.[13] Stephen Gwynn found the notes 'excellent foppery'.[14] Fiona Macleod, however, saw the notes as 'the prose equivalent of the verse . . . Yeats turns us round and shows us the other side, where the roots grow and the fibres fill with sap'.[15] A[nnie] M[acdonnell] respected the intertextual intentions whereby the 'old friends' of *The Secret Rose*, Aedh, Michael Robartes and Hanrahan had turned up again. She saw in 'these poems of faërie, the perennial human interest of pain'.[16]

T. S. Eliot would come in time to find the notes a useful model for the construction of *The Waste Land*, but by 29 September 1902, Yeats was wondering about the notes, telling Elkin Mathews 'I may want to revise. Those notes have always annoyed me', yet added 'I wont touch them now' (*CL3* 231-32). *The Poetical Works of William B. Yeats* (1906) was very carefully rearranged for his new American audience, and THE WIND AMONG THE REEDS becomes a section title for the poems of the 1899 collection, clarified or simplified for this new readership. The incorporation of *The Wind Among the Reeds* into a collection revealed that Yeats had 'A Cradle Song' in that volume-unit as well one of identical title in THE ROSE.[17] Breasal, Hanrahan, Michael Robartes, Aedh and Mongan disappeared from the titles and their identities merge as 'He', 'The Lover', and 'The Poet'. This was a decision which Yeats did not reopen.[18]

Hand-in-hand with this went the temporary abandonment of separate notes to the various volume-units, including those to *The Wind Among the Reeds*. Instead, the 'Legendary and Mythological Foundation of the Plays and Poems' (to which the various notes, including those from *The Wind Among the Reeds* fined down in Volume II, 'Dramatical Poems') was a single root for the flowering of both volumes. Yet it was curiously retrospective, and the elaborate essay-notes to *The Wind Among the Reeds* are casually if internationally dismissed as 'fragments of ancient mythology common to all lands'. These, for 'a long time' had had for their author

a very intense, a very personal importance, and they are too much woven into the fabric of my work for me to give a detailed account of them one by one' (*VPl* 1283).

The notes were restored (in a somewhat truncated form), for *The Collected Works in Verse and Prose* (1908), when Yeats had come to see what has tended to be overlooked since then: that *The Wind Among the Reeds* was by nature a secondary creation, a De Quinceyan involute of his early works, an obsessive and recurrent imbrication of redreamt dreams. Delay, far from being merely a matter of a disorganised designer, mean and quarrelsome publishers, transatlantic printing and a fire in the Boston Bookbinding Company, had been central to the writer's whole enterprise.

> When I wrote these poems, I had so meditated over the images that came to me in writing 'Ballads and Lyrics', 'The Rose', and 'The Wanderings of Oisin', and other images from Irish folk-lore, that they had become true symbols. I had sometimes when awake, but more often in sleep, moments of vision, a state very unlike dreaming, when these images took upon themselves what seemed an independent life and became part of a mystic language, which seemed as if it would bring me some strange revelation. Being troubled at what was thought a reckless obscurity, I tried to explain myself in lengthy notes, into which I put all the little learning I had, and more wilful phantasy than I now think admirable, though what is most mystical still seems to me the most true. I quote in what follows the better or the more necessary passages.[19]

This was anything but a retreat from the commitment to mysticism some might have welcomed and showed a deepened self-awareness of a demonstrably lengthened textual personality. Twenty pages of these closely-set notes are found in *Poems: Second Series* (1909), but by the time of *Later Poems* (1922) Yeats had cut them to five pages, carried forward to *Collected Poems* (1933).

Is it really the case that no manuscripts and proof material survives of *any* of this material? If so, why does the editor not tell us? Some prose headnotes are included in the setting copy or corrected proof for periodical printings, and these are duly reproduced. Those to 'The Desire of Man and of Woman' (for *The Dome*, June 1897) and 'O'Sullivan the Red upon his Wanderings' for Henley's *New Review* (August, 1897) are cases in point (pp. 72-3; 158-161). The poems are rewritten as 'Mongan Laments the Change that has come upon Him and his Beloved' and 'Hanrahan Laments because of his Wanderings' in *The Wind Among the Reeds* (1899), while relevant sections of their prose headnotes are incorporated into one of the longer combined endnotes to the published volume (*VP* 153, 171, 806-7).

Prose headnotes to periodical printings are included in the collations even when no manuscripts of those versions survive. Examples include the prose headnotes on 'The Valley of the Black Pig' (to 'Two Poems concerning Peasant Visionaries', *The Savoy*, April 1896—see *VP* 161), 'Aodh pleads with the Elemental Powers' (*The Dome*, December 1898—see *VP* 174) and 'Song of Mongan' (*The Dome*, October 1898—see *VP* 177) but there is no information on manuscripts of the endnotes expanded and rewritten from them for the 1899 volume (*VP* 808-9, 811-2). Such information is crucial because of the strategy adopted by Yeats when he abandoned the prose commentary and grouped his notes in the way he did, a method which he was to adopt with later volumes.

Without much curiosity as to Yeats's creative economy, Holdsworth deals with the simultaneous existence of the lyrics in differing states in prose and verse collections and the changes to the canon in subsequent reprintings (pp. xxvii-xxviii), but fails to ponder the fundamental questions that the editing of these manuscripts might have raised. What is the entity the manuscript materials of which are being edited and presented—is it a group of *poems*, or is it a *book*? If a book, issued in 1899 and kept in print until 1911 by Elkin Mathews, what of its subsequent history? What of its history as a volume-unit of *The Poetical Works of William B. Yeats, Poems 1899-1905*, and subsequent collections for which its prose texts disappear, reappear and mutate?

This 'total book' is—in the symbolical rather than the decorative tradition—the most successful *grimoire* of its period and so the changing cover designs and various states of the abandoned frontispiece have a textual status. They should have been represented as such in this volume, since Yeats was as involved in their programmes as ever an author could be, as indeed he was in Gyles's talismanic designs for his other 'total' books of the nineties, *The Secret Rose* and *Poems* (1899). While George Bornstein's *The Early Poetry: Volume II* made an effort to record the (spine and top board only) cover designs for *Poems* 1895 and 1899, this volume contains neither the cover design nor the abandoned frontispiece. She deals only fleetingly with the matter of the cover design (failing to record that it was redrawn for the 1903 vellum bindings in which certain earlier copies of earlier states were rebound) and even more cursorily with the frontispiece, omitting to record that the original drawing is extant (in the British Museum).

The edition is based upon Holdsworth's 1983 PhD from Tulane University, which acknowledged in its title (though not in its actual compass) the object of her concern: '"The Book of my Numberless Dreams": a Manuscript Study of W. B. Yeats's *The Wind Among the Reeds*'. Then, however, as now, Yeats's prose notes and the various paratextual and bibliographical features of that entity are ignored.[20] At the outset of the published volume, Professor Stephen Parrish, who is in no doubt that these are the manuscripts of a *book*, adds a very important note on the format of this edition.

> The record of the growth of this book [i.e., *The Wind Among the Reeds* (1899)]—that is, of Yeats's 'creative process'—is not complete until it is carried from the earliest recoverable drafts of the poems up through the form the poems took in the first printing of the book (p. xxxv).

Parrish explains that while post-1899 variants can be traced in *VP*, Holdsworth has also included all surviving post-1899 manuscript work to provide 'a complete record of Yeats's work on his book up to its publication in 1899 and a full record of manuscript work on it thereafter' (*ibid*). The poem titles of the first edition are privileged over subsequent reworkings of titles, and the volume-arrangement and contents are those of 1899. For subsequent changes in poem-order and canon one must also consult *VP*.

The editor's own introduction is imprecise and tired. 'Yeats wanted to write poems, however, not outbursts, and he was careful to control his emotions as he transformed the prose subjects into poetry' (p. xxv). 'Any woman with whom Yeats was emotionally involved would, at this point, have been metamorphosed into an archetypal woman' (p. xxx). So much for the Muses' anvil. Her language does not really get to grips with the issues dominating Yeats's book. What, for instance, is meant by 'general apocalypse'? Private shorthand takes over in references to '*Wind* poems', and 'Lady Augusta Gregory' appears before being reintroduced (correctly) as 'Lady Gregory' two paragraphs further on, following a sentence which might serve as a sample of the editor's style: 'Another of Yeats's friends, fortunately, had provided more impetus for the completion of the volume than simply raising queries' (p. xxiii).

One manuscript from *The Flame of the Spirit*, Yeats's transcription of 'Dedication of John Sherman and Dhoya' (also known as 'A Salutation' or 'Aedh tells of the perfect Beauty') is not shown here (pp. xxvii, 132-5; c.f. *YA 11* 131) while 'Your Pathway' also from *The Flame of the Spirit* is misquoted on p. 181, where 'Tread gently most tenderly' should read 'F̶o̶l̶l̶o̶w̶ Tread gently, tread most tenderly,' (c.f., *YA 11* 134). The 'Macmillan reader' who marked up sheets for Yeats's inspection is unidentified by Holdsworth in her text (pp. 152-5) but acknowledged (p. xxvii) to be Thomas Mark (see *VSR* xxii & ff.). These 1931-32 proofs (of *Mythologies and the Irish Dramatic Movement* and *The Poems*) were prepared for the unpublished *Edition de Luxe* (here misidentified as the 'Coole Edition' [pp. xviii]).

Many of the manuscripts are found in the '1893 notebook' formerly in the collection of Michael Yeats. Holdsworth is not quite right in suggesting that Yeats 'fashioned' the book himself (p. xvii). He told Katharine Tynan, he had 'had the book made to fit' Maud Gonne's 'cherry-coloured brocade and tarnished gold' slip-on cover (which she brought from Paris and which made the book look like a 'mediaeval missal'). Tynan also observed that the volume had 'such thick paper as one finds in *éditions de luxe*, and . . . must be rather uncomfortable to write upon'.[21]

A transcription of 'Subject for a lyric', the last of the prose subjects in the 1893 notebook and dateable to well after the publication of *The Wind Among the Reeds*, is confusingly included. In describing an occasion when Maud Gonne 'came here from the railway' and 'lay resting in my big chair' (p. 201), Yeats refers to Lady Gregory's gift of a leather armchair for 18 Woburn Buildings (*Au* 408). Maud Gonne remembered it as a 'new expensive addition to his furniture' when recalling May Gonne's wedding and the writing of 'Adam's Curse' in 1902 (*SQ* 320-1), but the earliest reference I have found to this 'huge leather armchair' is in the anonymous 'A Poet at Home' in T. P. O'Connor's *M.[ainly] A.[bout] P.[eople]*, 20 October, 1900. The 'Subject' suggests Maud Gonne in transit, as when she came from Paris to lecture in Liverpool on 12 December 1900, or when she arrived from Dublin to spend the last night of the century with WBY. She wished him to read *The Shadowy Waters* to her, the last lines of which perhaps account for the collocation of 'eagle', 'heavens' and 'faun' [Yeats's spelling] in Part I of the 'Subject'. The swan, eagle and fawn also suggest the period of the writing of 'The Withering of the Boughs', 'Under the Moon' and 'Baille and Aillinn'. Either way, 'Subject for a lyric' belongs to that period when Yeats's poetic armature had been broken.

Holdsworth's doctorate appeared one year after Phillip L. Marcus's ground-breaking *The Death of Cuchulain: Manuscript Materials including the Author's Final Text* established the editorial principles for the Cornell Yeats Series. It is not only that editorial thinking has become influenced by the History of the Book as a field of study since Marcus's principles were first hammered out, but that he had devised them to suit the editing of the manuscripts of a single play and a late one at that, with a short and concentrated history of revision.

This edition is not without its uses for the reader interested in the surviving avant-texte of certain poems. It is not, however, up to the high standard of the Cornell Series. The General Editors might look again at the editorial principles to be applied to complex volume-units of verse and prose with long histories of authorial rethinking.

NOTES

1. D. N. Dunlop's 'Interview with Mr. W. B. Yeats', *Irish Theosophist* II:2 (15 November 1893), 147-49 [i.e., 14-15], misdated in *I&R* 22 and *UP1* 301).
2. Yeats kept the cutting from *To-day* 22 March 1899, 242 (*NLI MS.*12145).
3. Madison: University of Wisconsin Press, 1989.
4. *VP* 803. Holdsworth finds this note 'a murky psychological statement' (p. xxvii).
5. 'The Cloths of Heaven' was the last poem written for the collection, which was being printed by the time of the crisis of December 1898. See Deirdre Toomey, 'Labyrinths: Yeats and Maud Gonne' in Deirdre Toomey (ed.), *Yeats and Women (YA 9)*, 95-131.
6. In *Olivia Shakespear and W. B. Yeats: After Long Silence* (London: Macmillan, 1989), pp. 59-82.
7. *The Speaker*, April 29 1899; *The Critic* (New York), September 1899.
8. Writing as 'Claudius Clear' in *The British Weekly* 1 June, 1899, 125. The comments were recycled in the Dublin *Daily Express*, 3 June 1899, 3, and Nicoll's column sparked off a newspaper controversy from which Yeats kept a number of cuttings (*NLI*).
9. *The Academy* commented in 'Our Awards for 1899' that Yeats's prose style though 'poetised' was of a 'true prose-rhythm, with none of that terrible bastard movement—like blank verse gone very much to the bad—which makes most writing of this sort anathema'. Reading the *praise* which followed perhaps helped Yeats to change his poetic style. According to *The Academy* Yeats stood alone as poet: 'a poet he is, and—to our thinking—a poet only. In everything else he suggests the poet. As poet he suggests nothing outside poetry—the simple essence; not poetic embodiment of this thing or that, but just poetry. His is not a large or wide gift. It is . . . an exceedingly contracted gift . . . authentically his and no man else's. . . . Mr. Yeats has practically recognised this. He has known that his gift was small; he has known that his gift was narrow; he had known that his gift was *his* gift . . . he has held to it and within it, unswerving and contented . . . In proportion as he becomes, or tries to be, his power passes from him. It is when he is obeying the dictates of an emotion . . . as insubstantial as a gust of the night, that he achieves his most delicate and evanescent charm. With a true instinct of his prevailing quality he calls this latest book *The Wind Among the Reeds*. No less frail and mysterious than such a wind is the appeal of Mr. Yeats's best verse' (20 January 1900, 63).

10. ALS Northwestern University, 21 November [1898], cf. *Wade* p. 48. Davray reviewed the book in *Mercure de France*, July 1899, 267.
11. *Athenaeum* 15 July 1899; *The Academy* 6 May 1899.
12. *Literature* 29 April 1899.
13. *The Saturday Review* 6 May 1899.
14. *The Spectator* 8 July 1899, 54.
15. *Daily Express* (Dublin) April 22 1899.
16. *The Bookman* May 1899.
17. It remained 'A Cradle Song' until after *Later Poems* (1922). The problem came to light in *Selected Poems* (1929). 'The Hoisting of the Sidhe' [*sic*] went unnoticed.
18. It allowed him to capitalize upon the apparent death of Michael Robartes (as recorded in 'Rosa Alchemica' [*VSR* 148-9]), by bringing him to life in *The Wild Swans at Coole*, and reusing him in *A Vision* (1925) and later.
19. *VP* 800. The cut passages are recoverable in *VP*, but a broad summary might be helpful. Yeats cut entirely the notes entitled '"Aedh," "Hanrahan" and "Michael Robartes" in these Poems', '"A Cradle Song". "Michael Robartes asks Forgiveness because of his many Moods"' and '"Michael Robartes Bids His Beloved be at Peace"'. Passages within notes were cut, such as those from 'A solar mythologist' to 'little at a time' (in the note to 'Mongan laments the Change that has come upon him and his Beloved' and 'Hanrahan laments because of his Wanderings') from 'It is possible' to 'different countries' (in the note to 'The Valley of the Black Pig'), from 'Two Birds' to 'forgetfulness' in the note to 'The Secret Rose', which removes the entire history of Cuchulain, recoverable from Lady Gregory's *Cuchulain of Muirthemne*. In the same note, the gesture to Yeats's source for Caoilte mac Rónáin ('I am writing away from most of my books') is made more triumphantly evasive: 'maybe I only read it in Mr. Standish O'Grady, who has a fine imagination, for I find no such story in Lady Gregory's book'. The same note is now further cross-referred to Yeats's own *Deirdre* (*VP* 814).
20. Yeats assembled, transcribed and despatched the press cuttings for the third (1900) edition.
21. *The Sketch*, 29 November 1893, p. 256.

W. B. Yeats, The Wild Swans at Coole: *Manuscript Materials*, edited by Stephen Parrish (Ithaca and London: Cornell University Press, 1994).

Wayne K. Chapman

The 1919 Macmillan edition of *The Wild Swans at Coole* was an artistic triumph wrought from complex personal experience. At the verge of his greatest accomplishments, Yeats combined three bodies of work. One was the lyric poetry of a dejectedly ageing man, as we read in the 23 poems of *The Wild Swans at Coole* (Cuala Press, 1917). Another was the spousal love poetry that began to emerge in *Nine Poems* (privately printed by Clement Shorter, 1918). And the third was a new, discursive type of verse that drew from the the philosophical explorations of *Per Amica Silentia Lunae* (Macmillan, 1918). Among poems he wrote about Maud Gonne in 1915, 'His Phoenix', 'A Deep-Sworn Vow', 'Broken Dreams', and 'Presences' show that he was troubled by the death of his love for her and by realization that Iseult Gonne, to whom he proposed marriage in 1916 and 1917, would have thought him an old man. The ebullience of poems written after his marriage to Georgie Hyde Lees in October 1917 is one with his enthusiasm for her adventure in automatic writing and their industry in marketing manuscripts to publishers and collectors to earn a living in Oxford from 1918 to 1921. The relevance of these facts to the making of *The Wild Swans at Coole* (1919) is not lost on the editor of this fine edition of the manuscripts. The arrangement of facsimiles, transcripts, and textual variants follows an introduction that is enlightening on a selection of poems that represent most important facets of the 1919 collection. Indeed, it is hard to exaggerate the value of this essay as an introduction to the 43 poems and 136 manuscripts documented in the book.

Like the best of Curtis Bradford, whose work on the title poem the first exhibits improve greatly, Parrish's essay responds to the organic process by which poems develop from their origins. In this case, a recurrent origin turns out to be the Maud Gonne Notebook of 1912-1915 (*NLI* 30,358), which, though listed only once in the editor's Census of Manuscripts, contains drafts or fair copies of ten poems, prose subjects for four, and a provisional Contents that anticipates the 1917 collection in a

315

surprising way. Although much remains to be said about 'Easter 1916' in its making and later stationing in the canon, Parrish rightly guesses that prudence demanded substitution of 'The Wild Swans at Coole' for the Rebellion poem, the effect being a radical revision of Yeats's original design for the book his sisters published in 1917, after the displaced poem had been discreetly printed by Clement Shorter for collectors and friends. Parrish is also insightful on Yeats's exercise of tact in the descriptions of Mabel Beardsley and Maud Gonne, respectively, in 'Upon a Dying Lady' and 'Broken Dreams'. Similarly, Yeats's good judgement is shown in a revision of 'His Phoenix' and in a note in which he reported deliberating with Oliver St. John Gogarty on a point of diction: whether 'privacy' or 'chastity' were the better word in a poem that paid tribute to Maud Gonne. The essay acknowledges Yeats's well-known afterthought, stanza VIII in the elegy 'In Memory of Major Robert Gregory', about the young man's courage. (The addition, as manuscripts show, was coerced by Gregory's widow.) Furthermore, since my transcriptions appeared in *YA 8* (1991), I see that another fragment has been recovered to confirm that the dialogic of 'The Phases of the Moon' was not at first that of Robartes and Aherne though related to early scribblings in the *Vision* papers owned by Michael Yeats. Decidedly, all this news merits heralding.

Parrish's introduction addresses two other matters that should be mentioned here because of their bearing on the volume's reconstructions. The first concerns Yeats's surrender of manuscripts to pay his father's debt to John Quinn, who thereby gained possession of forty holographic copies of poems from *The Wild Swans at Coole* before they joined the Berg Collection in the New York Public Library. Many of these manuscripts—'freshly made fair copies . . . [and] drafts salvaged from the work of composition' (xxvii)—the Yeatses posted to Quinn in a 'bundle' in July 1919. Regrettably, Yeats's 'concocted' manuscripts, as Bradford called the fair copies, are sometimes all that remains of the genetic record.

Secondly, the manuscripts of the title poem itself are presented more thoroughly and accurately than Bradford managed in his pioneering study, *Yeats at Work* (1965), which missed Yeats's first sketch (on three consecutive leaves of what is now *NLI* 30,416) and an important preliminary fragment on which Yeats records the metrical pattern he worked out for the poem's unique stanza. Unsorted in Parrish's arrangement, the complete verse drafts that Bradford labels A, B, and C (scrambled B, A, C among the nine leaves of *NLI* 13,587[1]) do not reconcile easily with the arbitrary order of the file. Nevertheless, with the Cornell volume, 'The Wild Swans at Coole' manuscripts become more accessible and achieve greater comprehensiveness than before, including a valuable account of the fair holograph that Shorter received for *The Sphere* and also of a later one of 'Sept 1917' that Quinn came to own after *The Sphere* and the *Little Review* had published the poem in stanza order 1-2-5-3-4 and bearing witness to the date on which Yeats made, in Parrish's words, perhaps 'as brilliant a single revision as [he] ever made' (xxix). (Few of Yeats's readers will know before this that Yeats published *any* work in *The Sphere*.)

Thoroughness and faithful observance of the editorial principles developed by Parrish and, with his oversight, other editors of the Cornell series give this book gravity and style. I find no inconsistent use of graphics within transcriptions as I have in the *Michael Robartes and the Dancer* volume (see p. 322 below). Each poem is represented by no less than one set of facsimiles on facing pages; and particularly interesting typescripts are sometimes reproduced just because they *are* interesting, such as the one entitled 'The Phoenix' (later 'The People'), which Ezra Pound revised for *Poetry* (Chicago) in 1916. Photographs and transcripts are usually arranged chronologically except when the archival sequence is itself disorderly (as in *NLI* 13,587[1]) or when dissevered units such as the early Cuchulain fragments of 'The Phases of the Moon' are situated late as if by chance. (Should not strict chronology be followed whenever possible? Should not loose folios be presented in reconstructed sequence?) Much of the book's scholarship stands modestly half-concealed in the fine print of its *apparatus criticus*, where most of the materials listed in the Census and all known printings up to 1919 (and sometimes beyond) are systematically collated. Perhaps the finest example of Parrish's competence in this line is his treatment of Yeats's frequently revised epigram, 'The Scholars'. Presenting four versions in facsimile and transcript, Parrish transcribes two more in the apparatus: one as revised in a copy of *Later Poems* (1924) and the second as written in Yeats's Rapallo Notebook C, in a diary entry of 1929. Variants are compounded from a revision in a copy of *Later Poems* (1922), from a typescript and galley proof for *Poetry* (Chicago), and from four publications between 1915 and 1919. All necessary dedication, ironically, to twelve lines that pay no respect to anyone who would '[e]dit and annotate' them.

Given the book's many strong points, there are two faults that I note here to improve its use as a resource. The first involves compensating for omissions in the collations of several poems associated with *The Sphere* in 1917 or with *Nine Poems* in 1918. The first of three sets of proof sheets housed in the Berg Collection (call them 'NYP [1a]' to distinguish them from the others) contain unique texts of five poems, only one of which had been printed in *The Sphere* though in an altogether different format and character font. Among the five unrecorded texts—'Men Improve with the Years', 'The Collar-Bone of a Hare', 'Lines Written in Dejection', 'A Deep-Sworn Vow', and 'In Memory [of Alfred Pollexfen]'—none but the last is cited in the apparatus and integrated in the list of variants. More significant omissions occur in 'To a Young Beauty', 'Solomon to Sheba', 'Tom O'Roughley', 'A Song', 'The Living Beauty', 'The Cat and the Moon', 'Under the Round Tower', and 'A Prayer on Going into My House', eight of the lyrics in *Nine Poems* for which Yeats's corrected typescripts, joined by the printer's annotations in pencil, exist in the Kenneth Spencer Research Library at the University of Kansas. It seems probable that these materials were unknown to the editor because, among other materials, they were missed by Conrad Balliet in *CM*. Nevertheless, James Helyar and I did discuss the typescripts in *YA 10* (1993): 225-6, 231, and 236, including the reason Shorter's copy text for 'To a Young Girl' got separated from the lot. Especially interesting are the peculiarities one finds in 'The Cat and the Moon' typescript, where correspondence with the private printing is frustrated by textual anomalies in line 10 (TS reads 'And lifts'; *9P* reads 'Lifting'; and *WSC (19)* reads as in TS) and line 15 (TS revised from 'this courtly' to 'her courtly'; *9P* reads as emended; and *WSC (19)* reads 'that courtly').

The second reservation I have concerns the frequency of supposedly indecipherable words in some manuscripts, ones written at points in the composition where authorial intention is least clear. Parrish's treatment of the last six lines of the Cuchulain fragment of 'The Phases of the Moon' gives query marks for eleven out of nineteen words in one segment. He reads 'those crude ragged men', instead of 'that crude ragged man', because he envisions speakers in much the same circumstance as in the later version (only with other names) without acknowledging the influence of *The Only Jealousy of Emer* and, I believe, Yeats's adaptation of an incident in Lady Gregory's *Cuchulain of Muirthemne*. The indecipherable words on leaf 14ʳ lines 17-19 of the manuscript are plainly keys to the function of the two speakers with respect to each other. My view is that Yeats redeployed from provisional work on the play the substance of the Platonic song of 'Mine Author', simultaneously changing speakers and the setting to counterpoint 'Ego Dominus Tuus'. The tentative beginnings of 'The Wild Swans at Coole', 'A Prayer on Going into My House', and 'On Woman' (in the prose subject in Appendix II) give other opportunities for readers to interpret the facsimiles for themselves.

As a reference work, this book gives valuable assistance to scholars on matters by no means conclusive in Yeats studies. In the spirit of complicit reading manifest in the series' commitment to 'the greatest possible fidelity in transcription . . . to illuminate Yeats's creative process' ([v]), I offer, for example, a solution to an issue of interest to students of that process who marvel at options he sometimes recorded for possible later use. At the end of stanza 3 in the 25 May 1914 draft of 'On Woman', Yeats wrote: 'If I repeat first lines[,] begin repetition | with 'The[re] is no friend but woman['']'. (This emends Parrish's 'If I [?repeat] four lines begin [? ?] | with The is no friend but woman'.) Rather than a possible reference 'to the opening lines of another text, now lost' (135), Yeats's note records his thought that a fourth stanza might be made by repeating the first one with substitution in the first line. Thus, 'May god be praised for woman | That gives up all her mind . . . [etc.]' (*NLI* 30,358, 55^v, lines 1-8) might have become 'There is no friend but woman | That gives up all her mind[!] | A man may find in no man | A friendship of her kind | That covers all he has brought | As with her flesh & bone | Nor quarells with a thought | Because it is not her own' (lines 44-51 if Yeats had bothered to write out the alternative ending). It seems for the best that Yeats did not pursue this circular, choral strategy although it does appeal to an ear sensitive to the kinetic properties of lyric poetry. Let it be noted that this new reading of his manuscript only slightly refines the solid transcript provided by the editor and that it is based on just one example from a rich yield of photographic reproductions.

The number and significance of texts in the volume generally pay dividends for the effort one invests in them. Yet, in fact, one owes a very great debt to Parrish's skill and painstaking labour assembling all but a few of the extant materials from which developed *The Wild Swans at Coole* lyrics of 1919, including the prose subjects of four of them from the Maud Gonne Notebook and the manuscripts of three related poems that Yeats left unpublished ('Am I a fool or a wise man', 'What could there be but those & these', and 'Reprisals'). In the end, this useful book will go down as a tribute to the poet, whose gift is everywhere in evidence in the methods and decisions we see him exercising as a writer between 1912 and 1920.

W. B. Yeats, Michael Robartes and the Dancer: *Manuscript Materials*, edited by Thomas Parkinson, with Anne Brannen (Ithaca and London: Cornell University Press, 1994).

Wayne K. Chapman

As the fourth volume in the Cornell Yeats Series to be issued on the poems and, with Carolyn Holdsworth's edition of *The Wind Among the Reeds* manuscripts, only the second to focus entirely on a single collection of verse, this book continues the valuable exhibition of Yeats at work that its antecedents have introduced (and I think too of Parkinson's own example in earlier studies). It might seem tactless to say that the book is perfunctory where *W. B. Yeats, Self-Critic* and *The Later Poetry* gave excitement (in 1971) with every remarkable insight on 'vestiges of creation' culled from Yeats's manuscripts. Yet, unlike the copious tomes of George Bornstein's *The Early Poetry* (vols. I and II), the Parkinson and Brannen addition to the series gives the impression of scholarship arrested before completion, and Thomas Parkinson's untimely death is the main cause of problems which the reviewer hesitates to point out. Still, in the short time of my acquaintance with him, he did feel that a law of diminishing returns operated in Yeats's manuscripts. Thus, I think this wise, inspiring, and generous teacher drew little enthusiasm from revisiting the stimulus that first roused him as a student of modern poetry.

Small enough as a body, the fifteen poems of *Michael Robartes and the Dancer* stand in their customary order but arranged according to the layout and reconstructed sequence of the manuscript materials themselves—of which forty-six documents are recorded in the volume's census, many of these finding a place in the secondary apparatus. The primary feature of the book, as with others in the series, is the photographic reproduction of seminal or particularly interesting materials (sometimes including specimens from typescripts or proofs) joined with the editors' transcriptions, notes, and collations against selected base texts. All but one of the poems, 'A Meditation in Time of War,' are found in holograph in the National Library of Ireland's file MS. 13,588(1)-(16), often beyond the initial drafting stage and so fairly legible. Unfortunately, the editors make no use of, or reference to, subfiles (1) and (16), containing corrected preliminaries and notes for the 1921 Cuala Press edition of the poems (especially interesting on 'An Image from a Past Life' and 'The Second Coming', two of the most complete sets of manuscripts in the volume)—an omission less serious, to be sure, than a similar one in *The Wind Among the Reeds* volume. In the exceptional poem, 'A Meditation in Time of War', Parkinson and Brannen reproduce facsimiles of the two existing holographs, from the Maud Gonne notebook of Christmas 1912 and the Yale typescript of 'Demon and Beast', on which it was delivered to *The Dial* for publication in 1920. (Regarding the latter poem, the editors misread as 'Nov 23 1915' the date 'Nov 23 1918', the usual one that is given by Mrs. Yeats in her copy of *The Collected Poems* [*YL* 2323], in the typed list of dates based on her authority [MS. 30,166], and in Ellmann's chronology [in *The Identity of Yeats*].) In the best tradition of the Cornell series, the editors have opened to Yeats's readers materials only partially described in a few scholarly works of a generation ago—in this case, mainly Jon Stallworthy's *Between the Lines* (1963). Early studies of Yeats rarely consulted collections outside his private one. Now we have, aggregated from ten collections, another means by which to observe how textual genes in Yeats's poetry evolve into a body of work.

Among the book's strengths, the high resolution of its camera-work and the readability of its textual transcripts and collations are probably as good as any in the series. First of all, the transcripts support facsimiles more than they presume to be strictly diplomatic renderings of content; therefore, transcripts tend to capitalise and spell as Yeats 'intended' rather than as he actually wrote (see point 1 of 'Transcription Principles and Procedures' [xxvii], which extends considerably the licence to interpret pre-texts). Secondly, not fond of using the foot of the page for brief notes (as Marcus and others have done with greater frequency), the editors produce a kind of simplicity that is almost always elucidated by corresponding photographs. Although critics of the procedure will note that the editors' transcriptions *depend* on the assumption that the photographs will *always* be there (an unwarranted assumption, as the *The Hour-Glass* volume and *The Early Poetry* II have recently shown), it is not inherently bad that an editor with Parkinson's experience should help the reader read. For one thing, Parkinson's assuredness imparts a vast improvement to Stallworthy's hasty interpretation of 'The Second Coming' manuscripts—an interpretation that has exercised great influence on scholarship (on Donald Torchiana and Patrick Keane, for instance)— but fails to recover most of the prose sketch and much of an early verse folio (see Parkinson and Brannen 150-3).

Of course, while the degree to which an editor chooses to annotate might reflect individual preferences, there are times when, to subvert a proverb, less is *not* more. If there was ever justification for a note, it was to defend the puzzling redating of 'Demon and Beast' (based on a character formed like a capital 'S' more than an '8' or '5'); the decision merits comment because of the evidence against it. A greater mistake—only compensated for by material drawn on elsewhere from the private collection of Michael Yeats—is the subordination of a complex revision of 'Solomon and the Witch' worked out on facing pages (326-7) in a copy of *Later Poems* (1922; *YL* 2382) owned by Anne Yeats. Understandably, the editors felt it necessary to report the sequence of revisions *below the line* (in the apparatus) as they interpreted it. After all, because the premise of the volume restricts its contents to 'recoverable drafts through the form the poems took in the 1921 volume' (*Michael Robartes and the Dancer*), they were not obligated to report the revisions at all. Still, since the material is more interesting, difficult, and layered with revision than anything of its kind in the book—than, for example, the corrected proof copy of 'The Leaders of the Crowd' (see p. 110)—some means of presenting the original, perhaps in a photographic appendix, might have preserved the sovereignty of the manuscript over that of the editors on this point. Again silently, they seem either to have overruled or ignored some of Edward O'Shea's plausible readings in *YL* on several supposedly indecipherable wordings.

Likewise, there is an inconsistency in the way graphics are used in the transcripts at various points in the book. The problem is usually avoided altogether by allowing photographs to speak for themselves on interpolations Yeats made with lines and arrows. While transcriptions are kept as clean as possible, a note, either at the foot of the same page or (at left) beneath the facing exhibit, will comment on most occurrences. On page 63, the transcript omits Yeats's marginalia and defers to the adjoining copy of the first leaf of 'Under Saturn' nearly all sense of his rewriting; nevertheless, on page 169, in recording the first draft of stanzas I-III of 'A Prayer for My Daughter', Parkinson and Brannen fully replicate Yeats's marginal strokes in their transcript (the only time they do so in the complicated sequence)—and to excellent effect. Evidently deemed extraneous to verses penned on the first page of 'An Image from a Past Life', the doodle of a tree and seven variously positioned numbers (ranging from '2' to '5') are not mentioned at all in the editors' account although the numbers might represent the lengths of lines Yeats anticipated for the seven-line nonce form he developed while drafting the poem. For the reader, such experiences teach that one must depend on the pictures and one's own eyes.

In sum, this book is valuable from a documentary standpoint, is interesting technically, but is defective due to circumstances that have prevented its editors from grasping issues some of the manuscripts pose. The introduction exhibits a tendency to disengage from a subject before developing it to a conclusion and demonstrates an only partial acquaintance with recent scholarship on the poems. The influence of 'The New Faces' on 'A Prayer for My Daughter' (see my own article, *YA* 6 [1988] 108-33), is unnoticed both in the introduction and in the presentation of stanzas that Yeats recast in the octave of the later poem and used in the original ending. Parkinson speaks of the poet's 'ruthless sacrifice of personally meaningful imagery' (xxiii) regarding an improvement effected by cutting three stanzas about Coole Park from this poem, but the editor says nothing about Yeats's equally personal reasons for self-censorship. The point matters in the final movement of the introduction (xxiii-xxiv), as it does in the way Stallworthy's error is perpetuated in the arrangement of holographs (167-89). Donald Davie and Conor Cruise O'Brien, voices of the 1960s, prevail in the discussion of Yeats's ordering of the poems while Edna Longley's reading of *Michael Robartes and the Dancer* as a political work has been missed (see *Studies on W. B. Yeats*, ed. Jacqueline Genet, 1990). And so, too, one feels, an opportunity has been missed to connect Yeats's draft lists of titles (see xix-xxi) with a detailed account of the publication history of the poems in newspapers, magazines, and private printings. In Yeats's relationship with the publisher Clement Shorter and poet Dora Sigerson Shorter there are reasons practical as well as political for the supposedly 'shrewd and cunning way' Yeats allied himself with the revolutionaries by publishing his Rebellion poems in 1921, as letters accompanying some of the manuscripts will testify. In a way, *Michael Robartes and the Dancer: Manuscript Materials* begs completion by the devout audience to which it speaks, having brought to the board another tantalizing section of the puzzle.

Elizabeth Butler Cullingford, *Gender and History in Yeats's Love Poetry* (Cambridge: Cambridge University Press, 1993), 334 pp.

Edna Longley

This fine critical study remakes Yeats and his poetry for the new *fin-de-siècle*. Its focus on gender takes in much more than the 'love poetry'—a sub-genre which, in any case, should be understood as a metonymy rather than a self-contained category. Elizabeth Butler Cullingford is most provocative where she anatomises Yeats's imaginative androgyny, where she charts the interpenetration of sexuality and the occult in different phases of his work, and where she reveals him, in his Crazy Jane drag, as the mad woman in the Irish attic. My one reservation concerns her insistence on citing all the possible theoretical angles. Here, conscientious scholarship meets the vogue for the multivocal—at times, to the detriment of clarity. The book's unresolved subtext might be 'Theory and History in Cullingford's Criticism', and this has some negative as well as positive consequences. For instance, I find her deployment of feminist theory generally more productive than her occasional forays into the 'post-colonial'.

Cullingford vindicates Yeats's record as a 'female identified' artist who 'loved, liked, collaborated with, and respected women—most of the time' (p. 9). Her first chapter, on 'anxiety of masculinity', begins by stressing his dependence on powerful women, and quotes Maud Gonne's remarkable letter of 1911: 'Our children were your poems of which I was the Father sowing the unrest & storm which made them possible . . . You and Lady Gregory have a child also *the theatre company* & Lady Gregory is the Father who holds you to your duty of motherhood in true marriage style' (*G-YL* 302). Cullingford then reads Yeats's early poetry in the light of gender-ambiguity and a reaction against Victorian patriarchy which incorporates all his familiar objects of detestation: 'Desire, in "The Man who Dreamed of Fairyland", destroys what society has defined as masculinity' (p. 17). So the courtly-love icon does not merely put woman on the pedestal to which Gonne preferred a platform: 'Yeats, disciple of William Morris, would have seen the poetic recovery of the goddess as a project compatible with advanced socialist and feminist thought' (p. 42). Yeats, indeed, went beyond Morris in criticising 'the heroines of all the

neo-Romantic London poets' as 'essentially men's heroines, with no separate life of their own' (*L* 46), and he interpreted Samuel Ferguson's
mythic females as made of sterner stuff—Irish *dominatrices*, perhaps.
However, Cullingford's language does not sufficiently allow for Yeats's
sense of difference and dissidence from Morris's socio-political project. It
is not surprising, as her later chapter 'Venus or Mrs Pankhurst' observes,
that 'No Second Troy' should draw on 'anti-suffrage propaganda' and
'take back with one hand what it gives with the other: the exceptional
woman is acknowledged, but her freedom to constitute herself as a subject through political action is denied, and her frustrated power is defined
as destructive' (p.82). Cullingford underlines the ambivalence of Deca-
dent male androgyny when she says: 'Womanly men were more acceptable than mannish women'; but Elaine Showalter's *Sexual Anarchy: Gender and Culture at the Fin-de-Siècle* takes the politics of this theme further.

Yet Cullingford is surely right to highlight Adorno's claim 'that the
historical relation of individual to society in the lyric poem "will be the
more perfect, the more the poem eschews the relation of self to society as
an explicit theme and the more it allows this relation to crystallise
involuntarily from within the poem"' (p. 73), and also Hélène Cixous's
regard for 'men who are capable of becoming woman', 'poets who let
something different from tradition get through' (p. 6). (The latter is,
more broadly, poetry's *sine qua non*.) In Yeats's *Liebestod* of the 1890s 'an
inherited generic trope reanimated by the rise of feminism intersects with
Yeats's private pathology, and is intensified by the unavailability of
Gonne' (p. 46). This apocalypse, within which the New Woman figures
as creator, destroyer and deeper challenge, had its most complex artistic
results (and hence cultural implications) in the 1920s. In her nicely-named
chapter 'Crazy Jane and the Irish episcopate', Cullingford combines close
reading, social history and Bakhtinian theory to demonstate that Jane 'is
rooted in the repressive social and religious circumstances symbolised by
her antagonist the Bishop' (p. 227). In 'Crazy Jane on God'

> Yeats marshals all the power that anomaly, ambiguity, and hybridisation
> can provide. An old woman's sexual desire is out of place in the cycles of
> generation. Unmarried and past childbearing, Jane lacks a Catholic justifi-
> cation for her sexuality . . . Post-menopausal desire is rare in the love
> lyric: Crazy Jane's lust violates generic expectations (pp. 234-5).

This reading, backed up by Cullingford's earlier discussion of the controversy surrounding 'Leda and the Swan', suggests that Yeats's recoil
from the barren Senate and 'Holy Church' (*L* 746) towards 'the great

creators' (*VP* 831) found, among the resources of his poetry, the prototypical female 'satirist' who has done much to undermine Catholic justifications since 1970. May Irish feminism take note. It might also note Cullingford's fascinating account of Yeats's relations with Dorothy Wellesley and her lesbian circle which 'theorised lesbianism in terms of androgyny: the woman in man and the more socially transgressive man in woman'. Thus, in the 1930s, the ideas of Virginia Woolf helped to renew 'Yeats's identification of poetry with femininity' (p. 269).

Yet was this identification really 'suppressed', rather than protected, by the 'masculine poetics' of his middle years (and which inform his dialectic to the end)? Here Irish politics and gender politics may conflict rather than converge. After 1916 Yeats associates Gonne and Markiewicz with a destructive, triumphant, masculinised rhetoric; his poetry, with a principle that is female, powerless, constructive: 'I count those feathered balls of soot | The moor-hen guides upon the stream, | To silence the envy in my thought . . .' (*VP* 424). If 'Easter 1916' criticises Constance Markiewicz, without 'question[ing] the right of male patriots to engage in argument' (p. 124), it is because women patriots might have been expected to conceive a different brand of politics. Like other commentators, Cullingford allows male-identified republican women to monopolise the image of the Irish political female. Further, her contrast between Markiewicz as 'a pleasing object of aesthetic contemplation' and as a victim of 'argumentativeness and social concern' is hardly Yeats's, although it suggests how women were bound up with the self-image of his poetry and with its image of Ireland. He struggled, not always successfully, to deconstruct the opposition between poetry and rhetoric into a truly androgynous aesthetic and an alternative social vision. Thus the concluding image of 'On a Political Prisoner' is, most fundamentally, nostalgic for the first principles of the literary and national movement: 'With all youth's lonely wildness stirred' (*VP* 397).

Cullingford, however, may be anxious to placate some recently shrill voices:

> A feminist critique of the figure [Mother Ireland] should not be interpreted as complicity with the revisionist impulse, nor as a blanket rejection of Irish nationalism. Nationalism, as Said and [David] Lloyd insist, had its progressive decolonising historical moment: the repressive, anti-feminist Free State created by bourgeois nationalists was not the inevitable consequence of the Republican ideals of 1916 (p. 55).

Nor was the Spanish Inquisition the inevitable consequence of Christian ideals. Here subtle frameworks that derive from Cixous or Bakhtin, and for which Cullingford finds persuasive contexts in Irish culture and Yeats's writings, are replaced by a rhetoric which denies context except to one 'moment', reduces historiography to 'impulse', and imputes fellow-travelling ('complicity') to the views of other academics. 'Bourgeois nationalists' (Lloyd's term in *Anomalous States: Irish Writing and the Post-Colonial Moment*, 1993) occludes the role of republicanism in splitting suffragism, and of Catholicism in preventing a utopian outcome in the 1920s. Thus Cullingford offers divergent versions of the relation between feminism (in theory and practice) and twentieth-century Irish society—elsewhere she refers to 'the totalising monoglot discourse of Irish Catholicism' (p. 244)—without developing the debate from her own perspectives, as she is well-equipped to do. At certain points, a sudden convulsion seizes the text and its precisions collapse into jargon:

> As a white, male, middle-class, Protestant citizen of the British Empire, with an acknowledged debt to canonical English writers, [Yeats] belonged to the dominant literary tradition. As a colonised Irishman, however, he was acutely conscious of repression and exclusion' (p. 6).

Yeats enjoyed having the best of both worlds and asserting the literary dominance of a secessionist Dublin. The Irish tried harder than the English to repress and exclude him. Cullingford's automatic writing of the term 'colonial' needs to be qualified with reference to sources outside the field of discourse (e.g., Liam Kennedy's article, 'Modern Ireland: Post-Colonial Society or Post-Colonial Pretensions?' (*Irish Review*, 13 [Winter 1992/1993], 107-21). A resort to comparative economic history might also temper the romanticism of 'Woven into the hem of the Irish Rose is the narrative of the oppressed' (p. 72).

Fortunately, such convulsions are rare, and may have been unassimilated afterthoughts in a rich book that raises questions about the deepest sources of Yeats's art. Cullingford is alert to the difficulty of eradicating 'essentialism', where gender or androgyny is concerned, and her answer is to 'reinsert [the issues] into history and into material practice' (p. 37). This enables her to examine Yeats and gender with an eye that that analyses rather than accuses, and to elicit where he genuinely 'lets something different from tradition get through'. But although she confirms, yet again, the indissolubility of sex and art (not only for Yeats), perhaps we could find less fraught metaphors for the mysterious transaction between responsiveness and architectonic that occurs whenever Woolf ceases to be 'Virginia' or Yeats a 'bundle of accident and incoherence' (*E&I* 509).

Edna Longley, *The Living Stream: Literature and Revisionism in Ireland* (Newcastle Upon Tyne: Bloodaxe, 1994). £9.95 paperback. 302pp.

Bernard O'Donoghue

In the first issue of *The Irish Review* in 1986 (edited by Edna Longley and others), Roy Foster, who is the commonest nomination for the leadership if not the invention of Irish historical revisionism, asked with characteristic elegance: *quis revidebit ipsos revisores?* Assuming that revisionism, with twenty years of authority behind it, was paradoxically now the norm in Irish historiography, Foster, concerned that it will itself harden into an unchallenged monolith, invites new revision. *The Living Stream* is part of Edna Longley's contribution to the debate, but it starts from a different point. Longley argues that Irish literary criticism has not yet undergone its primary revision and that the unregenerate nationalist and—to a lesser extent—unionist monoliths are still the norm there.

If literary criticism has some catching up to do, Longley has been working on it. The greatest virtue of her earlier critical collection *Poetry in the Wars* (1986) was its refusal to detach literature from its sociopolitical context, despite her passionate commitment to the autonomy of the artistic. Both of these principles were borne out in her 1988 study of Louis MacNeice, from whom they had partly been derived in the first place. But the main title of *The Living Stream* recognizes an earlier inspiration for Longley's aesthetic politics, in lines from Yeats's 'Easter 1916' containing an image of fluidity that she has touched on often before:

> Hearts with one purpose alone
> Through summer and winter seem
> Enchanted to a stone
> To trouble the living stream. (*VP* 393)

Longley sees the most imperative obligation for the revisionist critical enterprise to be the breaking of the spell of that inflexible singleness of purpose, continuing Yeats's battle against the curse of 'opinion' as

328

described in 'Prayer for my Daughter' and 'On a Political Prisoner'. Side-stepping with a cursory acknowledgement the problems that all three poems present to a declared feminist, Longley finds Yeats's lines here to be a perfect expression of the critical principles that she has been developing since her admirable annotated editions of Edward Thomas: the virtues of MacNeice's 'flux' as against dogma, and of his humanism in the face of the ideological campaigns of the literary modernists and the political radicals of the first third of this century.

Her heroes are well known, and they are all prominent again: Mac-Neice himself and Muldoon for their complex political non-alignment (like that of Thomas and of Keith Douglas who are less prominent in this Irish context); John Hewitt for his socialist struggles against sectarian and dogmatic pieties; Durcan and Kennelly for their facing down of various forms of violence. There are other aspects to Longley's aesthetic; for example, flux is not only opposed to the negativity of dogma: it is also to be held in balance with a formal principle of pattern. In the last essay, 'The Room Where MacNeice Wrote "Snow"', Longley identifies a school of MacNeice, answering to the pluralism of that poem and proposing for membership three very different Northern Irish poets: Mahon, with his 'rage for order', Muldoon with his linguistic ellipticism, and Carson with his sociological riddling.

The Living Stream has two components. It is a welcome reissuing of a number of earlier essays by Longley, some of which have already attained classic status: for example the powerful polemic 'From Cathleen to Anorexia', a penetrating analysis of the various uses of femininity within the long traditions of male-dominated Irish writing. The book's other element is a vigorously combative 60-page introduction, 'Revising "Irish Literature"', which is the clearest declaration so far of Longley's critical credo; only the last of this Introduction's six sections performs the normal prefatory function of introducing the essays. The first essay, 'The Rising, The Somme and Irish Memory' (1991) uses the year 1916 to illustrate a subtle contrast between Catholic and Protestant Irish commemorative practices. Longley argues that Catholic representation is iconographic while Protestant is textual; hence Catholic living-rooms have pictures of Pádraig Pearse's profile while their Protestant counterparts feature the text of 'The Ulster Covenant'. This theme is returned to in other essays, arguing that Catholic/nationalist figuration aspires towards future refulfilment of past models (Longley believes that religious terminology must not be ducked: she even praises Tom Paulin of Field Day, one of her great *bêtes noires*, for this), while Protestant piety is more purely focused on the past. These general insights are often expressed with great economy: 'the Protestant equivalent of martyrology is a biblical narrative of persecution (paranoia rather than masochism)'.

It would be hard to name anyone writing in Northern Irish literature—or any other area of English writing, for that matter—who is Longley's equal in this kind of aphoristic insight (ironically enough, Tom Paulin's *Minotaur* is perhaps the closest: indeed his incrimination of the monolithic state there has much in common with Longley's championing of creative flux against monumentalism). *The Living Stream* is full of unforgettable—and often savage—one-liners: 'It sometimes seems as if Protestants have to die for Ireland before being allowed to live here'; 'The great advantage of living in Northern Ireland is that you can be in three places at once'.

Of course, if Northern Irish revisionist criticism is to be, in Seamus Heaney's phrase, adequate to its predicament, it is not going to be all epigrams. No less clear than Longley's heroes are her villains: the post-colonial critics, non-Irish commentators (especially those from the greater Ireland beyond the sea), and the proponents of a unitary pan-Gaelic view of Irish literature. The integrity of the Irish quarrels in the book sometimes suggests a more depressed Yeats formula: 'more substance in our enmities | Than in our love'. The long introduction is Longley's most sustained battle so far with Field Day, drawing on her *London Review of Books* review of the *Field Day Anthology of Irish Writing* in 1991 to accuse it of nationalist bias. Predictably, her own corrective can lean too far the other way in defining canons and contexts: for example, she proposes three literary environments which shaped Northern Irish poetry of the 1960s: 'the English/British dimension'; Hewitt's 'Ulster regionalism'; and 'Trinity College Dublin' which foregrounded 'Anglo-Irish literary traditions'. Without going so far as to suggest Irish language classes, some Gaelic component might have been allowed. Again, the excellent (and wittily titled) 'When Did You Last See Your Father? Perceptions of the Past in Northern Irish Writing 1965-1985' might have noted that father-fixation in Irish writing goes back to Joyce and Yeats at the start of the century. And the heat of battle can lead Longley to an uncharacteristically reductive crudeness of diction: 'dumping on MacNeice for having ventured across the Irish Sea' for example (Longley is not always so protective of the literary Wild Geese; it tends to depend on who they are and where they go).

These aberrations are the more noticeable because Longley is a marvellously acute and appreciative critic, as is well known from her exemplary comparative readings of Thomas and Frost. These strengths are evident in abundance here, especially on Muldoon's *Madoc*. She has the alert reader's eye for an outstanding line caught on the wing, such as Heaney's 'Ghosting the trenches with a bloom of hawthorn'. For a controversialist with an inclination for satire, her literary temper is very often positive. At the end of her Introduction Longley places the would-be revisionist's dilemma with great clarity: 'Whereas Irish historiography has long been led by scholars bound up with Ireland's changing condition, homegrown literary criticism, though now increasing in influence, has been overwhelmed by the international fixation on Joyce and Yeats'. As critic, she has always been generous before the poets, arguing, for instance, that there is more to be learned about Northern Ireland by reading Muldoon than the history books. In fact, though there are plenty of Irish poets around these days (no doubt part of what Longley calls 'the European Poetry Mountain'), good Irish critics are much thinner on the ground and to be cherished. It may be that the confrontationalism of Irish criticism is in direct proportion to the crucialness of the venture: what Longley calls 'an inter-disciplinary burden not only borne by historians'. Her most formidable opponents are combative too: Deane, Paulin, Eagleton. They can be seen to be in some ways engaged in the same corrective enterprise; none of them, for example, would deny the term revisionist in *some* sense; all would reject the term 'essentialism'. At the very end of her Introduction Longley relates the difficulties of Irish Studies to uneasy origins, divided between Enlightenment empiricism and 'the discursive tradition of "talking about Ireland" which grew up with nineteenth-century Nationalism'. Both have their place; and she concludes 'At the moment Irish literary studies (including this book) are uneasily caught between the two'. With its gracious parenthesis this is an appropriately acute conclusion to a brilliant and invigorating book, one which is of crucial importance for readers of Irish poetry and of the politics of Irish culture.

Dan H. Laurence and Nicholas Grene (eds.), *Shaw, Lady Gregory and the Abbey* (Gerrards Cross: Colin Smythe, 1993) xliii + 211 pp.

James Pethica

This skilfully compiled volume of correspondence, journal entries, memoranda, press materials and other documents bearing on the public and private relationship between Bernard Shaw and Lady Gregory is aptly titled. Though the friendship between the two writers was anchored in deep mutual regard and genuine affection, it nearly always required the fuel of literary controversy for it to reach true intensity, and moments of crisis at the Abbey Theatre consequently loom almost omnipresent over the writers' transactions, like the third term of a triangular relationship. Shaw and Lady Gregory were first drawn together as allies during the *Blanco Posnet* affair of 1909, and their exchanges thereafter were largely centred on and cemented by episodes of artistic debate or difficulty: the campaign to recapitalize the Abbey after the withdrawal of Miss Horniman's subsidy in 1910; the protests against *The Playboy of the Western World* during the Abbey's American tour of 1911-12; opposition to *O'Flaherty, V. C.* in 1915; and the rejection of O'Casey's *The Silver Tassie* in 1928. Lady Gregory also enlisted Shaw's support during the furore over the Dublin Municipal Gallery of Art in 1912-13, and, with rather less success, in her long-running campaign for the return of the Lane pictures.

Outside of such controversies, however, the friends met and corresponded relatively infrequently. With Shaw—who had emigrated for good in 1876—adamant that 'the first business' of Irish intellectuals was 'to get out of Ireland', and Lady Gregory a late-blooming Nationalist who defined her work as 'preparing for Home Rule', it was inevitable that there should be much that divided them politically, strategically and personally. The material presented in this volume offers much evidence to suggest both how and why the friendship flourished nonetheless.

Most striking is the practicality and independence each valued and came to admire in the other. Shaw had, in his own words, 'orphaned himself' in response to a childhood troubled by his father's drunkenness, his mother's neglect, the bankruptcies, suicide and madness of near relatives, and, most of all, the unorthodox role played by George Vandeleur

Lee in his family life. Left with lasting difficulty in forming close emotional attachments, and in enduringly conflicted reaction to the proprie-
ties of Ascendancy culture, Shaw resolutely remade himself as a
workaholic man of business, promoting himself—as writer, critic,
socialist thinker and polymath—with a self-reliant zeal that would always
savour of narcissistic compensation. For Lady Gregory, childhood was
also troubled, and in later life she would rarely refer, and then only critically, to her evangelically strict, misogynist mother, or her authoritarian
father. While she never rejected her Ascendancy roots, she, too, proceeded to remake herself substantially. First, through marriage, she trans-
ferred her loyalties to a more accomplished and cultured family, buying
into its history and values so thoroughly that she would come to write of
Coole and its traditions as if they were part of her own, rather than an
acquired, family history. Then, following the death of her elderly husband when she was only thirty-nine, she built a new career through her
energetic patronage of Yeats, her activism in the theatre movement, and
her work as a folklorist and dramatist.

Being each accustomed to roles as an outsider—Lady Gregory as a
well-connected Unionist turned 'rebel', and as a woman in overwhelmingly male literary circles; Shaw as a displaced Irishman playing
enfant terrible to the British masses—the writers had much in common to
unite them. For Shaw, it was Lady Gregory's determined character
which seems to have held the greatest appeal, and he repeatedly voices in
these letters a collegial admiration for her personal strength. It was not
merely that she was, like him, a tenacious battler, vowing during the
1912 *Playboy* troubles, for instance, that she 'would sooner go to my
death than give in', but that she also possessed in his view a powerful
talent for subverting 'established institutions, by simply walking in [her]
heavy amiable way through every prejudice'. For all his criticisms of the
Ascendancy, Shaw retained a weakness for 'the grand manner', and was
hence also admiring of her willingness to disregard class position and personal pride when she took on the myriad and often demeaning tasks
necessary to the Abbey Theatre's success. In 1910 he memorably dubbed
her 'the charwoman of the Abbey', a phrase that she immediately
embraced as a high compliment.

For her part, Lady Gregory likewise admired Shaw's pugnacious
qualities, and she quickly came to appreciate his populist instincts, often
turning to him as her advocate of last resort when other avenues of per-
suasion had failed. As she would write in a 1918 Journal entry, 'When
you're in doubt lead trumps say cardplayers, and when I'm in doubt I
lead G. B. S.' His mercurial and flamboyantly unconventional per-

sonality also undoubtedly added to his appeal. As her first biographer, Elizabeth Coxhead, shrewdly noted, Lady Gregory always had 'a certain weakness for a rake'. From the *savoir faire* of her husband Sir William Gregory and later of John Quinn, to the self-dramatizing romanticism of Wilfrid Scawen Blunt and the artistic pose of the young Yeats, the men with whom she formed her closest relationships invariably had a streak of showmanship or commanding personal presence. Shaw seems to have quickly sensed this tendency in her and played up to it, for this volume shows him to have been a deft and frequent flatterer with a expert sense of how to appeal to her vanity: 'She always tells me what to do, and I just do as I'm told'; 'I always find out what she wants, and then advise it'; 'Lady Gregory has me on a string and I can't do anything without her leave'.

Yet for all that the writers had in common, their friendship seems ultimately to have succeeded precisely because neither was, nor intended to be, in any real sense dependent on the other. For Lady Gregory, at the height of her literary success when they first became allies, and long-established in her close partnership with Yeats, Shaw readily became a 'trump card', an advocate she could turn to in moments of need, but both writers recognised that her prime loyalties—to Yeats, to the Abbey, and to Ireland—would inevitably limit the intimacy between them. With his habit of ironic self-distancing, and conscious that his disdain for orthodox Nationalism would always be a source of contention between them, Shaw indeed seems to have preferred that the relationship should be modest in scope. He was well aware of the manipulative side to Lady Gregory's personality, and was clearly unwilling to be drawn by the bonds of friendship into serving her agenda too closely. In 1917, for instance, he would acidly—and astutely—observe that the Abbey had repeatedly produced his work only 'as a stopgap in a desperate emergency', and in 1921 he would turn down her request for a Abbey benefit lecture with the impatient comment 'if the child needs so much nursing it had better die.' However much he admired her strength of purpose, he was never slow to voice exasperation when he became its intended victim, complaining in his letters at her 'frightfully obstinate' opinions, and denouncing her as 'the most obstinate and unscrupulous devil on earth'. During an anxious period in her negotiations over the sale of Coole land in 1920, he even went so far as to twit her over the methods she habitually used to get her own way, mercilessly ventrilo-quizing an imagined speech in which she reproaches her tenants as 'a pack of greedy grabbers that would turn a poor widow out of house and home and rob her little grandson etc etc etc etc etc; so shoot me or dhrownd me in the lake an' be dam to yez; for I'll stand by me homestead as Parnell tould me, God be with him in glory.'

Passages like this epitomise the dynamic at the heart of the friendship. Shaw, self-confident and discriminating in his sense of her character, repeatedly blends sincere admiration with direct or implied criticism, and almost always manages to remain either ironic or flattering in doing so. His ventriloquization, for instance, displays a knowing recognition of her guile in portraying herself as 'grande dame and lone widda', but at the same time signals appreciation and approval of her methods. His characteristic tone throughout is essentially conspiratorial. The 'obstinate' or artful Lady Gregory, he seems to say, is a persona that he can see through, yet he thoroughly respects and values her nonetheless, particularly as his partner in a fight. There is little point in posturing with each other, his letters imply, for we each understand the other's limits too well. Even in passages which seem merely playful, a perceptive, part-critical, part-flattering Shavian voice repeatedly emerges. His well-known poem for Catherine and Anne Gregory, for instance, quietly figures Lady Gregory as a benevolent tyrant who threatens her grandchildren with 'merciless whippings' and throws her maid 'over the bannisters'. In economical fashion the poem praises her strength and energy while humorously acknowledging the potentially dictatorial dimension to her 'beneficent rule'.

This Shavian voice was one which Lady Gregory clearly relished; not least, perhaps, since its penetrating directness was in sharp contrast to the always mannered indirection which typified her dealings with Yeats. Shaw not only played mischievous devil's advocate for her—who else would have dared suggest in 1925 that she 'sell Coole' and move to Scotland?—but was also willing to criticise her on matters of extreme personal sensitivity when circumstances merited. A 1919 letter of rare unleavened seriousness is a case in point. Urging her to send her grandson Richard somewhere other than 'that obsolete and thrice accursed boy farm' Harrow School 'which is an evil tradition in the family', Shaw insists that it would be a 'crime' and 'unthinkable' to send him 'to such a place'. The letter expresses his frank and doubtless highly discomforting opinion that the Gregory tradition she cherished had in fact been broken as soon as her son Robert had married 'a Welshwoman' and 'bec[o]me a painter', and that this break was irremediable however much she might think otherwise: 'You cannot patch it up again'. Although Robert had been killed in action on the Italian front little more than a year earlier, Shaw was not prepared to spare her feelings in making his point, observing bluntly that 'Robert was just on the verge of being overbred: one more generation as fine drawn as that would have produced something that might have been pretty and would certainly have been effete.'

His advice was promptly ignored, and Richard Gregory was sent to Harrow, but it was the kind of directness Lady Gregory rarely received from other friends. For Yeats, in particular, never able to fully come to terms with the bonds of debt and emotional dependency which linked them so closely as friends and collaborators, such candour was never possible. Where Shaw was resolute in both his criticisms, as here, and in his praise—calling her simply 'the greatest living Irishwoman'—Yeats was almost always obtuse or uncertain, dampening the edge of his criticisms to save her feelings, and too often excessive in his praise in ways which savoured of insincerity.

For her part, Lady Gregory seems to have had an intuitive and effective sense of how to respond to Shaw's volatility and directness. The material presented in this volume suggests that she never sought to engage directly with his polemical side, or pressed for greater intimacy in their friendship than circumstances allowed. Her warm relationship with Charlotte Shaw, whom she often met separately in London and elsewhere, attests to her level of ease, being in marked contrast to her obvious disdain in earlier years for Lucy Hyde, Cottie Yeats, Violet Russell and other 'non-creative' wives of literary men of whose talents she was possessive. She was quick to acknowledge her appreciation of Shaw, signing herself 'Yours affectionately' within weeks of their first exchange of letters, and showed herself to be an astute judge of the character underlying his fierily irascible public persona, dedicating her play *The Golden Apple* to him as 'the gentlest of my friends.' 'Peace' and 'ease' recur as the dominant terms in her journal entries describing Shaw's three visits to Coole and her own to Ayot St. Lawrence. Meeting only occasionally, and working in largely separate spheres of influence, they were able to relax when together, reading one another's work without competitive strain, and enjoying mutual interests with a refreshing lack of posturing.

Dan Laurence and Nicholas Grene have edited this volume expertly, presenting a wealth of material, much of it previously unpublished, with judiciously comprehensive annotation, and an accompanying critical narrative that contextualizes the material nicely. If there is one topic passed over too quickly in their Introduction, however, it is the matter of Yeats's impact on the Shaw-Gregory friendship. Shaw and Yeats, they note, had 'little sympathy' and 'not much appreciation of each other's writings' but were 'never antagonists'. This unduly downplays the latent hostility towards Shaw that remained marked in Yeats's writings throughout his career. Yeats, the junior and largely ignored dramatist when *The Land of Heart's Desire* shared the bill with Shaw's *Arms and the Man* at the Avenue Theatre in 1894, seems never to have overcome a degree of envy at Shaw's popular success, his imperious personality, and his precursive sexual success with Florence Farr. In *The Trembling of the Veil* in 1921, Yeats would describe Shaw as 'the most formidable man in modern letters'—glowing words that reek of rivalry—only to demolish him in the same paragraph with his memorable depiction of Shaw as the cold force of mechanistic logic, 'a sewing-machine, that clicked and shone'.

Laurence and Grene also quote a 1940 letter in which Shaw remembers learning for the first time during his first long stay at Coole in 1910 'what a penetrating critic and good talker [Yeats] was; for he played none of his Bunthorne games, and saw no green elephants, at Coole', and imply that this meeting smoothed the course of the future relationship between the men. Yeats, however, was notably absent during Shaw's subsequent visits to Coole in 1915 and 1918, and was never invited to Ayot St. Lawrence despite Lady Gregory's many visits there alone. Shaw's reminiscence, indeed, seems intended mainly as an elliptical compliment to Lady Gregory's influence, since it implies that it was only 'at Coole' that Yeats ever fully relaxed his pose with Shaw.

In general, as this volume shows, Yeats seems to have been left deliberately out of discussion in Lady Gregory's dealings with Shaw: she mentions him sparingly in her letters, and Shaw evidently had little inclination to do otherwise. Some level of jealous competition over her attention was certainly involved between the men, but Yeats's pre-eminence in Lady Gregory's life was sufficiently clear for all parties to have recognised the value of silent accommodation. (Ironically, her annotations to the only surviving photo showing Yeats and Shaw together with her at Coole shows her attention centred on her grandson Richard rather than on either of her two celebrated and strong-willed guests.) Yeats's only significant mention of the subject to Lady Gregory is in fact one of the most intriguing passages in this volume. After meeting Shaw during an early phase of opposition to *O'Flaherty V. C.*, he reported Shaw's comment that 'if Lady Gregory was in London, she would fight'. Shaw, he noted, didn't want a fight over the play 'but thought you would do it out of love of mischief. I told him that was a misunderstanding of your character.'

Lady Gregory appears to have offered no comment on these contrasting interpretations of her character, since Yeats's confiding and somewhat possessive appeal to their greater intimacy, and Shaw's admiring and conspiratorial recognition of her rebellious side would have both been satisfying to her. As Shaw and Yeats in their different ways doubtless both came to appreciate, it was ultimately best that her friendships with these two remarkable but incompatible men should have been largely conducted in separate tracks.

Mary K. Greer, *Women of the Golden Dawn: Rebels and Priestesses* (Rochester, Vermont: Park Street Press, 1995) pp. 490.

Alex Owen

Mary Greer has written an extraordinary book. It charts the inner—or, visionary and spiritual—lives of four women who were involved in their younger years with the late-Victorian magical Order, the Hermetic Order of the Golden Dawn. Greer takes as her subjects the actress and writer Florence Farr, Annie Horniman, who provided the financial backing for Dublin's Abbey Theatre and went on to become a successful owner-manager in England, Moina Bergson Mathers, the artistic sister of Henri Bergson and High Priestess to the Golden Dawn's 'Chief', and Maud Gonne, the Irish patriot and long-time unrequited love of William Butler Yeats. These women, of whom only two (Farr and Horniman) were obviously important members of the organisational hierarchy of the Golden Dawn, are placed at the centre of a revisionist narrative which argues both for their position 'as the true heart and soul of this magical Order', and for the enduring difference that an early exposure to and training in ritual magic made in their own lives (p. 1).

As Greer correctly notes, we are now familiar with the basic history of the Hermetic Order of the Golden Dawn, a secret and strictly hierarchical society founded in 1888 and dedicated to the 'rejected' knowledge of Western hermeticism. Ellic Howe produced his accurate and enormously helpful standard account in 1972, many of the Order's secret and most cherished documents have now been published, and scholars continue to mine the relationship between the imaginative creativity and magical endeavours of the Order's *adepti* and luminaries. Chief among the latter was W. B. Yeats, and it was in part the recognition that the Golden Dawn and its system of magic were integral to the evolution of his literary imagination that first prompted scholars to pay close attention to the Order itself. As Greer also suggests, however, accounts of the Golden Dawn have tended to emphasise the importance of male initiates and their contributions, and it is this aspect of the Order's history that Greer implicitly addresses.

While we already know that Florence Farr and Annie Horniman held high office in the Golden Dawn, and a good deal about their participa-

tion in the wrangling and power struggles that went on within the
Order, Greer fleshes out their intuitive and instrumental role in an evolving and deeply serious magical undertaking. The Golden Dawn offered
initiates a systematic training in Astrology, Alchemy, Cabala, and divina-
tion, and encouraged an elite inner or Second Order to experiment with
the techniques of psychological magic. What Greer succeeds in giving us
is an illuminating and detailed account of the part played by Farr and
Horniman in the development of the Order's complex rituals and practices, and the extent to which the organisation and teachings of the
Golden Dawn were shaped by their extensive knowledge and experience
of things magical. Indeed, as Greer reminds us, by 1897 only Samuel Mac-
Gregor Mathers and his wife, Moina Bergson Mathers, out-ranked
Florence Farr in the Order, and she had jurisdiction over the London,
Bradford, Weston-super-Mare, and Edinburgh Temples (or local organisations). George Bernard Shaw, Florence Farr's advocate and lover in the
1890s, was infuriated by what he saw as her diverting metaphysical interests and refusal to take her acting career seriously, but Greer understands
magic and is able to show how and why it formed the central core of
Farr's life. Indeed, it is Greer's grasp of the arcane realities of the Golden
Dawn's teachings and cosmology that makes her handling of both Farr
and Horniman so illuminating. Greer is able to explain the significance
and appeal of the Golden Dawn for these women in ways which elude
the otherwise useful biographies written by Josephine Johnson and Sheila
Goodie.

    One of the most successful aspects of the primary research for the
book is Greer's reinstatement of the gifted Moina Bergson Mathers, often
an enigmatic and shadowy presence in other accounts, as a vitally important figure in the Order's history and that of subsequent magical developments. Moina (born Mina) Bergson Mathers emerges here as a woman of
great spiritual power and vitality, one who worked closely with her husband to create what has become the foundation for much current magical
Work. Moina's difficult but productive years with MacGregor Mathers
in Paris (when they began to 'restore' the Egyptian mysteries) are
recovered, as is her life in London following his death in 1918. Along
with Farr and Horniman, she assumes here a central place in the history
of modern magic. Finally, although Greer cannot make the same case for
Maud Gonne, she argues convincingly for the often unwelcome and half-
denied richness of Gonne's spiritual life and the importance of the magical experiences that she shared with Yeats. Although Maud Gonne's formal involvement with the Golden Dawn following her initiation in 1891
was brief, she worked with Yeats and the Matherses on the rituals for

Yeats's Celtic Mysteries in the 1890s, and pursued her occult work into the twentieth century. As Greer demonstrates, Gonne's tortuous relationship with Yeats was largely conducted on the spiritual plane and relied in large part on the kinds of imaging techniques taught in the Golden Dawn.

The great strength of this book for those interested in the Golden Dawn itself is that it provides a nuanced sense of exactly what it was that adepts *did* in the Golden Dawn, and a feel for the quality of the noumenal experience that lay at the heart of the Order's arcane learning. Greer's clear and informed decoding of magical practices and procedures, and her recreation of the kind of inner experience that constituted the real allure of participation in a secret magical society, are invaluable even for those of us who have read the published documents and accounts. Equally, however, this is not a book about the Golden Dawn *per se*, but rather one which argues for the enduring legacy of its magical training for four very different but inherently fascinating Victorian women. Most particularly, and perhaps also the most valuable for those who have already read widely about Farr, Gonne, and Horniman, Greer is interested in the relationship between the inner and outer—the ways in which the secret (but not necessarily private) spiritual and visionary experiences of these female magicians interacted with their public lives and work. It is Greer's combination of skills—scholarly and esoteric—which make this account so unusually insightful and compelling.

It is, though, precisely this combination of the academic and occult which will deter some readers. Mary Greer is a *believer*. She brings to her account an insider's understanding of ritual magic, and she incorporates her considerable practical knowledge of tarot and astrology into her analysis of the four women and the structure of her narrative. I find this a facilitating means of entry to an otherwise often dispiritingly opaque occult Victorian world; others might be less impressed. There will also be some resistance to Greer's penchant for an American cultural feminist approach to her subjects. I find, for example, Greer's framing discussion of these unique but in some ways quintessentially Victorian women in terms of archetypal 'feminine types' (p.8) or 'embodied archetypes of empowerment' (p. 388) alienating and unnecessarily reductionist, as well as strangely at odds with her lucid evocation of the tensions and ambiguities that marked these women's lives. But I also accept that Greer has her own agenda in writing the book and that this has to do with a particular feminist vision of recouping and honouring what she calls women's 'tales of experience' and 'songs of wisdom' (p. 9). That language might read a little awkwardly for those of us schooled in a different brand of feminism, or, indeed, not schooled in feminism at all, but it does nothing to obscure the importance of Greer's achievement. If *Women of the Golden Dawn* is a labour of love and an unusual read it is also a valuable, meticulously scholarly, and well-written analysis of the impact of magic on four important Victorian lives.

Phillip L. Marcus, *Yeats and Artistic Power* (Basingstoke and London: Macmillan Academic and Professional, 1992), 263 + xiii pages.

Paul Kirschner and Alexander Stillmark, eds., *Between Time and Eternity: Nine Essays on W.B.Yeats and his Contemporaries Hofmannsthal and Blok* (Amsterdam and Atlanta: Editions Rodolpi, 1992), 170 + xi pages.

Richard Greaves

Phillip Marcus finds a new focus for a study which fully justifies the declaration made on the jacket that this is 'the post-deconstructionist era'. The readings of poems, tracing of sources and influences, and references which suggest a great deal of further reading make this book of interest to Yeats specialists *and* more general readers.

Building on his *Yeats and the Beginning of the Irish Renaissance* Marcus examines 'the relationship between art and life and the importance of the concept of art's shaping power to [Yeats's] aesthetic of national literature'. Yeats's conception of himself as a bardic poet is particularly important to Marcus's theme. Standish James O'Grady believed that it was the Greek bards who sang a great civilization into existence. Though Marcus is cautious about just when Yeats read O'Grady, the claims for his influence are convincing. Marcus shows how *The King's Threshold* links Shelley's idea of the poet as legislator with the power of the poet in the Irish bardic tradition in making Yeats's claim for the rights of poets. His references to this play form one integrating thread for his book.

Marcus re-enters the controversy about the order of *Last Poems*, claiming that the presence of the plays at the end of *Last Poems and Two Plays* makes so great a difference to the way the volume reads that the order of the poems here cannot be relied on as a guide to how Yeats would have wanted them ordered in his *Collected Poems*, and that Richard J. Finneran and A. Norman Jeffares are wrong to be guided by the table of contents he drew up for the volume of plays and poems. (We are referred to Marcus's 'Yeats's "Last Poems": A Reconsideration' [*YA* 5 3-14] for his reasoning.)

343

There are many helpful readings of individual poems. Marcus reconstructs the background of 'The Dolls', for instance, with references to Yeats's 1909 journal, to see the poem's political level as 'a sort of palimpsest'. His suggestion of how we might read the poem offers an example of how references to a half-submerged level can add to meaning: 'what began as a poem grounded in parochial Irish concerns moved increasingly during the process of composition towards an exploration of ontological questions involving Neoplatonism and "incarnation"'.

Yeats's revisions are another way in which poems are subject to change in time, and sometimes as an effect of the impact of the world on the poet. Marcus suggests that the revision of 'holy quietude' to 'measured quietude' in 'To Ireland in the Coming Times' might have been provoked by 'increased Catholic political power', but that the word 'measured' also looks forward to 'The Statues' and 'Under Ben Bulben'. This further suggests the constant shaping of his work by Yeats which makes a nonsense of any attempt to read his poems without a sense of the author. Marcus demonstrates throughout his sense of the author by his references to Yeats's letters, essays and articles and by so often situating the poems in relation to the events and circumstances of Yeats's life. By seeing the movement from early hope and confidence in artistic power, through discouragement, to the gaining of a new confidence which builds on the poet's recognition of what it is possible to achieve, he can see the work as a whole without reducing its complexity. Yeats confronted his doubts about the efficacy of artistic power in his poems, but in 'The Municipal Gallery Re-visited' he demonstrated his 'renewed faith in the power of art', and in 'Under Ben Bulben' his 'resurgent' confidence.

Marcus also recognizes Yeats's sense that there is a popular audience and an exclusive audience. There was already a literature for the people; *The Secret Rose* was an attempt to reach the few. He hoped to reach the many through the few, but sometimes hankered after a direct route, as in the involvement with the theatre which was to force him back to the more indirect approach when the Abbey audience showed a taste for the realism so at odds with his own aesthetic of artistic power.

'To a Wealthy Man' and 'To a Shade' show Yeats's belief in the influence of art on future generations. In 'The Fisherman', Yeats imagines his ideal audience. Marcus finds in 'The Curse of Cromwell' 'an address from the modern poet to his readers, to that audience without whom artistic power is impossible because it is in their experience of the text that life intersects with art and can be changed by it'. Yeats's poetry embodies its aesthetic, accepting (for the most part) that its most significant effects are deferred rather than immediate (and the more significant for being deferred), and setting out to engage with—to have an effect on—the world *by* creating its own audience and *through* the audience so created. What both demands and enables the creation of the work becomes part of the work created.

Marcus's conclusion refers heavily to Seamus Heaney. Heaney's implication that the realm of 'the ludic' and 'the self-inculpatory' is a 'sanitized realm' suggests that much recent literary theory encourages literature to cop out, even insists that it should. Marcus sees it as no surprise that 'a theory that seemed to sever the connection between text and world' should have failed to maintain popularity for long. In moving into a post-deconstructive era, 'critical theory and practice of all types, from "old-fashioned" to avant-garde, could re-establish or reaffirm as appropriate their "relationship to the actual" by devoting themselves to the study of artistic power and the problems that inevitably accompany it.' Here is the book's manifesto; one which it justifies and lives up to. Accepting that literature does affect life means taking a risk for authors, theorists and teachers; but to deny the possibility of artistic power because it might be used for evil—or by attempting to deny that literature *can* engage with the world—is for author, critic, theorist and teacher all to deny their portion of 'the responsibility of informing' the 'general conscience of mankind'.

Between Time and Eternity collects papers from a symposium held in the Institute of Germanic Studies in London: six are on Yeats, two compare Yeats and Hofmannsthal, and one compares Yeats and Blok. Time is the general theme. The comparative essays make no case for direct influence (Avril Pyman's essay on Blok specifically rules it out). Alexander Stillmark points to similarities between Yeats and Hofmannsthal as lyrical dramatists, and he and Hubert Lengauer acknowledge that the comparison was suggested by T. S. Eliot. Lengauer rather brings up short the game of comparisons, sensing the threat of disappearance into 'a sort of common ground or well-trodden path of harmonious comparative literature'. The caution is wise: interesting as some of the similarities and associations between the three are, it is difficult to see any openings for further work here.

Paul Kirschner describes well the duality of Yeats's feelings about time, how in 'Byzantium' Yeats shows himself caught 'between the desire to escape space/time and an inescapable solidarity with all that exists in it.' He and Barbara Hardy both show how a clearly intelligible reading of a poem need not be unsubtle. Hardy uses a comment from the Preface of the Yeats-Ellis *Blake* about the companionability of myth as her starting point. But this is a companionability which can be 'terrifying', as Hardy's reading of 'Her Vision in the Wood', in which we 'sense and follow the generation of a myth', demonstrates.

George-Denis Zimmermann realizes, with Kirschner, that 'art cannot ignore time', though those who see a pattern in events might think (wishfully or not) that they have a kind of power. Zimmermann, too, refers to Yeats's occasional apparent indecision between an elite and a mass audience. 'As usual, he was trying to cope with a dilemma by first choosing one pole, then trying to recover the other'. It is this ability to recognize the co-existence of opposites that allows the cataclysm to be celebrated as the possible new beginning, 'a reconciliation of nihilism and hope'.

Jacqueline Genet picks up the theme of polarity in indicating that art bridges the gap between the visible and invisible worlds. She is aware of Yeats's attraction to both. 'His central subject remains the nature of the disincarnated world and its relation to the incarnated world'. Genet is particularly good on the blending of esoteric and mythological sources as part of Yeats's creative process. Like Hardy—and Marcus—she recognizes the power of the past in the present and the part in this of the self-conscious use of myth, 'which anchors the work that creates it in tradition', and locates the creation of poetry at 'the trysting-place of the human and the superhuman, of the living and the dead'.

Andrew Roberts draws on Genette in examining Yeats's use of the iterative in 'Reveries'. In using it to suggest the recurrence of event or of narration, Yeats gives to his memories the same form of truth as folk-belief and myth, which are also told repeatedly. This is, then, a part of Yeats's creation of the tradition of himself. The argument would need to be more tightly made to be thoroughly convincing.

Hugh Epstein deliberately sets out with what is (certainly in the case of Yeats) a suspectly intrinsic approach. His reference to Heaney's 'Yeats as an Example' suggests that Heaney would have preferred Yeats's *Collected Poems* to end with 'Under Ben Bulben'. This is either a misreading or careless phrasing: Heaney wants 'Cuchulain Comforted' at the end. His quotation from 'Wheels and Butterflies', which he takes from Ellmann's *The Identity of Yeats* is so inadequately introduced as to be confusing. As a whole, the book does have some well-expressed ideas and judicious readings, but there is nothing excitingly new.

Stan Smith, *The Origins of Modernism: Eliot, Pound, Yeats and the Rhetorics of Renewal* (Hemel Hempstead: Harvester Wheatsheaf, 1994), pp.x + 270.

Richard Greaves

Stan Smith draws on the theories of Bakhtin and Kristeva as he exposes the contradictions at the heart of Literary Modernism. He shows particularly well the involvement of the poetry he examines with contemporary history even as it tries to escape into a search for origins.

> For Modernism stands in dual relation to its time. On the one hand it expresses the age's will to power, to recuperating like Eliot's Tradition 'all the past', in an act of cultural conservation which identifies with the triumphal processions of the victors. On the other hand, its fractured discourses and interrupted narratives figure the reality of an historical order of exploitation founded in the inequalities of class, race, nation and gender, in exclusion, privilege and, ultimately, massacre.

Smith recognizes the centrality of Pound to Modernist poetry, and brilliantly analyses the process of projection which leads Pound to condemn others in *The Cantos* for the divorce of order in the state from beauty in art, when the responsibility lies within himself, who failed to connect the tradition he admired with its history of exploitation. Smith also soundly relates *The Waste Land* to its historical moment: 'If cities and selves merge into and slide through each other in this poem, this only reproduces the shifting, malleable, interpenetrating frontiers of a Europe in post-war flux.' Eliot's sense of the need for homogeneous culture is the more understandable in this light.

Turning currently popular theory to marvellous account, Smith explains how Modernist texts register the disruption caused by the challenge of the periphery to the declining metropolitan 'in terms of a shifting interplay of *polyphony* and *intertextuality*—the one a democratic, open-ended responsiveness to the many voices of the present, the other a closed, autocratic celebration of the unitary text of tradition.' In the case of Yeats's *The Tower*, the combination of intertextuality and polyphony leads to an incorporation into the poetry of a sense of failure, as allusiveness in itself denies the possibility of spontaneous self-sufficiency. Smith illuminates the radical ambiguity of language in distinguishing between Yeats's idea of the 'self-delighting *self*-sufficiency of Homer' and the sufficiency of the image of the swan with which he is 'satisfied'. There is a kind of sufficiency which *merely* suffices, which is *not* sufficient. For Yeats, '[w]hat the poet may achieve . . . is a *sufficient* unity'. Smith recognizes the conflict between the desire for 'unity of utterance' and the need not to dismiss conflict; but 'sufficient' here suggests compromise, and so a stilling of conflict. I prefer to keep all as a paradox which cannot be resolved without the loss of that conflict which is indispensable: unity is only possible as the object of a drive.

Chapter 9 was first published as 'Porphyry's Cup: Yeats, Forgetfulness and the Narrative Order' (*YA5* 15-45) and Smith has added to his original piece Wayne Chapman's discovery of the source of '"mine author sung it me"' (*VP* 373) in Milton's *The Doctrine and Discipline of Divorce* (see *YA8* 65-66). The third of the book's chapters specifically on Yeats chides earlier accounts of his relationship with Maud Gonne for being too concerned with 'the role he overtly assigns her'. This might well be fair, yet Smith does not altogether avoid romanticising her in another way as New Woman and revolutionary socialist and nationalist. More attention to the realities of their personal relationship now available in *The Gonne-Yeats Letters 1893-1938: Always Your Friend* (1992) would have been in order here. Smith's reading of the last two lines of 'Reconciliation' seems to disregard Yeats and Maud Gonne's physical affair in 1908. His reading of 'King and No King' also falls short in its lack of regard for biographical detail. The thing lost in this poem is close, surely, to the thing half regretted in 'Words': Smith overcomplicates.

Smith certainly runs the full gamut of current critical discourse, from 'always-already' through 'interpellation' to 'signifier and signified', but I wonder if the non-originariness of origins is becoming a little cliched now—or maybe the point *is* the radical belatedness of us all. He notes the retrospective nature of the term 'Modernism', and that Bernard Iddings Bell's *Postmodernism and Other Essays* was published in 1926, so that 'the term 'postmodernism' in a book title predates by a year what is generally thought to be the first comparable usage of 'Modernist', in the title of Graves's and Riding's *Survey of Modernist Poetry*.' The point is an amusing one. I would draw attention to R. A. Scott-James's *Modernism and Romance* (1908), though its use of the term *is* rather different from its use by Riding and Graves.

P. Th. M. G. Liebregts, *Centaurs in the Twilight. W. B. Yeats's Use of the Classical Tradition* (Amsterdam, Atlanta, GA: Editions Rodopi, 1993).

A. Norman Jeffares

This long book is not an easy one to review. Through its author's desire to be exhaustive it leaves the reader exhausted, wishing that someone had edited it rigorously, for it is excessively self-indulgent in its tendency to summarise, to spell everything out and to make nods and becks in the direction of other scholars and critics without, however, always going the earliest scholarly or critical discoveries about Yeats's writings. The Introduction tells us how limited previous discussions of Yeats and the classics have been, no nods and becks here: the author is going to proceed in a chronological rather than a thematic way. This method certainly has its points. As its author asserts, the book is an extension of and a complement to a thematic account of Yeats's classicism by Brian Arkins, *Builders of my Soul: Greek and Roman Themes in Yeats* (1990), the most complete study heretofore (and one written at reasonable length).

What do we get then? A 'General' Introduction of five pages tells us, somewhat inelegantly, what the author will do. The first chapter, 'A Classical Education', discusses the role of the classics in Victorian education and then examines the evidence relating to the knowledge of Greek and Latin that Yeats gained at his schools in England and Ireland. Rightly described by E. R. Dodds, a Belfast man who became Professor of Greek at Oxford, as one of those 'who are incapable of assimilating any language ancient or modern other than that into which they are born', Yeats was always insecure about his classical knowledge and largely used translations (the same was true of his knowledge of French—he made vain attempts to learn it in the late 1880s and again in middle age). He developed an antipathy towards Latin civilization while admiring Greek, and thought, in later life, that in Ireland Irish and Greek should be taught together.

The second chapter 'The Nineteenth Century Matrix', deals with the pull of Arcadianism and Aestheticism upon the early Yeats. Here, citing Wilde's comment in 'The Decay of Lying' that 'the highest art rejects the burden of the human spirit', the author lapses into the currently fashionable use of the subjunctive when he tells us that this sentence of Wilde 'would not have appealed to Yeats with his passion for life'· Critics often use 'would' where they try to convey the certainty of the indicative without proof. This is parallel to the Wardour Street style of biography: 'as X climbed the hill he would have paused to look back for the last time over the scenes of his childhood'. In such a case the biographer doesn't know if X did pause to look back: only if he did know would he have written 'he paused'.

The discussion in this chapter ranges over Theosophical teaching, Platonism, Neo-Platonism and the effect of Pater's *Plato and Platonism* (1893) and his *Marius the Epicurean* (1885). The author argues convincingly that Yeats's knowledge of classical philosophy and Greek myth cannot be detached from his studies in the occult. There is an allusion to 'the Westcott Hermetic Library which Yeats certainly knew and used'. He also used, of course, the actual library of the Theosophical Society in Dublin: the late H. F. Norman knew about the nature of his reading there. A not very relevant and very obvious discussion of symbolism is followed by an attempt to link elements in 'The Wanderings of Oisin' with the *Odyssey* in a somewhat roundabout way via Thomas Taylor's translation of Porphyry. Perhaps a simpler explanation might suffice: that Yeats had read the *Odyssey* in translation and indeed, as his school friend Charles Johnston recollected, had stumbled through some of it in the Greek with the aid of a crib in High School. There are obvious comments on the influence of translations of the Irish cycles and some of the books written upon Celtic subjects in the latter quarter of the nineteenth century. Yeats's use of 'Homeric' as a term of praise is examined; he wanted Irish writers to study Homer alongside Celtic mythology. The author emphasises the effect of the Rhymers' classicism and that of the French symbolists upon Yeats, who moved firmly from epic to lyric, hoping that he could create through intensity, compression and repetition of symbols an epic-like effect.

The third chapter deals with Yeats's early poetry and prose fiction. His use of Helen as a symbol is discussed at length: much of this is description of the poetry. *The Celtic Twilight* is handled next; there the author fails to draw the unstated links between Homer, Raftery and Yeats himself, though he does emphasise Yeats's realisation of the role of oral tradition in both Greek and Irish civilisation. The section on Hanrahan and hedge schoolmasters pads out the chapter somewhat, though that on *The Secret Rose* has some useful aperçus.

Chapter four discusses Yeats and the theatre, dragging together disparate material: it smacks of the card index approach. The fifth chapter,'Mediumships, Spirits and the Imagination', moves from Yeats's essay on Swedenborg to *Per Amica Silentia Lunæ* suggesting some new sources for Yeats's views of the after life, but also dragging in some material unneccessarily. Yeats's approach was complex, multi-layered, and cannot therefore be easily reduced to obvious order without risk of excessive simplification. This chapter calls for ruthless pruning.

With 'The Daimon in Yeats', the sixth chapter, we are into the world of *A Vision*. The author shows the poet using (mainly) the Platonic tradition to reinforce his own concept of the Daimon. This is Henry More/Blavatsky country: Plutarch, Apuleius, Neoplatonists, Cambridge Platonists, Hermes Trismegistus and, of course, the old women of Soho. Heigh ho, we are off on the magic roundabout, the automatic script.

We return to the plays and poetry from 1914-1922 in the seventh chapter. A lot of story telling here: but More, who paraphrased Giralamo Cardano (rather than any Irish shapechanging) is used to gloss Fand's change of shape. This chapter does not relate so much to the classics as offer the author's notes upon the plays, though Plutarch is offered as a source for parts of *The Player Queen*. There is a good deal of spelling it out (and repetition of the work of others) when the poetry of 1914-1921 is treated, though some new linkages are made.

In the eighth chapter the author considers the contribution of the classics to *A Vision*, taking seventy-nine pages over it. Approximately nine of these pages offer us some new source material: there is a good deal of repetition of the work of other scholars (not always acknowledged). Again, an Editor's pencil would have greatly benefited the book.

The ninth chapter begins with descriptions and very obvious comments on the poems in *The Tower* and then goes on to *The Winding Stair*. Various points arise. Is there any *proof* of a connection between Plotinus, *Ennead* v.2.1. and Yeats's well/fountain imagery in 'A Dialogue of Self and Soul'? Sometimes, perhaps, he should be given credit for creating his own images? Again, there are identifications of sources made earlier by others but not acknowledged here. In view of Yeats's difficulties with languages other than his own it may be worth commenting that Yeats's translation of *Oedipus at Colonus* described as being made 'with the aid of Jebb and a French translation by Paul Masqueray' actually depended greatly upon Mrs Yeats's translating Masqueray's version into English for her husband. This chapter also smacks very much of thesis techniques, though it lacks adequate chapter-and-versing of other scholars' work.

'Last Will and Testament', the tenth chapter, adds yet more summarising, making the point that *The King of the Great Clock Tower* and *A Full Moon in March* are 'not only new works in Yeats's oeuvre but also interpretations of earlier works'. The section on *The Herne's Egg* and Super-natural Songs attempts to blend classical and Indian sources, alluding to the 'horniness' of Danae and Leda to gloss the 'lonely lust' of *The Herne's Egg*. This is typical of the approach which involves spelling out 'The Three Bushes'. Again in the discussion of 'Parnell's Funeral and other Poems' and *New Poems* we are presented with ideas already treated by others. The 'Old Rocky Face' of 'The Gyres' is, incidentally, related not only to Delphi, but to the 'cliff that's christened Alt' in 'The Man and the Echo'.The author points out a connection between the 'What matter' of 'The Gyres' and a comment of Plotinus, *Ennead* 111. 2.15, 'What does it matter when (men) are devoured only to return in some new form?' The comments on 'What Then?' rather force the issue: again, Yeats should be given credit for his own creativity! There is a long discussion of 'The Statues', which could have been cut severely.

The conclusion makes the usual ritual gestures in the direction of fash-ionable (and often incomprehensible) critics before going on to a heavily didactic use of Claes and his 'typology of specific intertextual phenomena·' After the synchronic intertextual survey we are given a diachronic approach, the author wishing, he says, to provide 'a general framework to the several more specialised scholarly studies published the last thirty years·' This book is often merely a gleaning exercise, and it could have done with much more winnowing.

Dwight H. Purdy, *Biblical Echo and Allusion in the Poetry of W. B. Yeats. Poetics and the Art of God.* (Lewisburg: Bucknell University Press, 1944) .pp. 169

A. Norman Jeffares

The Introduction tells us that the author will examine Yeats's knowledge of the tradition of converting the Art of God to the Art of Man; then treat the poetics of Biblical allusion in Yeats's lyrics; after this place Yeats's poetic practices in the context of Romantic and Victorian scriptural rhetoric. A brief Afterword considers the significance of Yeats's use of Biblical texts: he learnt from Biblical poetry without submitting to it.

The nub of the book is, therefore, in Chapters two to five, where the author links passages and imagery in specific poems with Biblical sources and with other poems by Yeats. He draws attention to many associations and linkages in a stimulating way, and he has supplied an admirable and most useful pair of Appendices which list all Yeats's allusions that he has found and the echoes he has selected, the first according to poems (arranged chronologically) and the second, similarly arranged, to Biblical echoes.

The author thinks that Yeats in his poetry of the nineties not only wanted to displace the Bible by Celtic myth, but also to 'legitimize' Celtic myth through it while be also used the Bible's poetic language either in direct echoes or allusions, sometimes ironic.(Some of the Biblical allusions pointed outhave, of course, been mentioned by earlier commentators whose work is not always acknowledged: this, however, is the first specialised work on the part played by the Bible in Yeats's work). At times, as the author puts it (not very clearly, for his language sometimes clogs up, in the currently fashionable jargonised academic style) 'this triplemindedness amounts to the intertextual theme of the one poem in these volumes to .use what Conte calls reflective allusion, a similitude in which the two voices of the poet and the used text coincide.' After the turn of the century Yeats tended to be more ironic and in the case of Biblical echoes and allusions reversed the Biblical usage. The author regards 'The Hour before Dawn', 'The Cold Heaven' and 'The Phases of the Moon' as explorations of antithetical revelations: in the period from 1902 to 1919 Yeats was making his allusions ironic, he thinks, by diminishing the force of his Biblical sources through humour, contrast or parody, or else by employing reversal—the allusion placed within a context which is contradictory) or else by expanding the llusion, giving it a position in his own system of thought in such ideas as those of cyclical history, of the anti-self, of rebirth, and others which derived from occult lore.

In the fourth chapter seven poems are to be examined (actually there are eight since 'Vacillation' is discussed at the beginning and end of the chapter)—'The Second Coming', 'Sailing to Byzantum', 'Meditations in Time of Civil War', 'Nineteen Hundred and Nineteen', 'A Prayer forMy Son','A Dialogue of Self and Soul' and 'Blood and the Moon'. The author rightly dismisses the superficiality of Ellmann's and Bloom's treatments of 'The Second Coming', arguing persuasively that the poem's echoes from and allusions to the Bible are strong, making it dependent upon them for its effectiveness, the blend of seventeenth century sacred language with that of the twentieth giving the poem its peculiar force (particularly to readers brought up in the Christian tradition). The author-regards Yeats as doing more to absorb than imitate Biblical ideas, language and rhythms; he is transforming the Biblical material 'into his own sacred book'. In dealing with 'Meditations in Time of Civil War' the author makes the obvious point that irony underpins the intentions of the poet, but he stresses some linkages between Biblical text and poetic effectively. He thinks that Yeats did not want 'to replace scripture with his own 'Bible' but to retain it while creating his own sacred texts. The combination of Biblical passages and poems continues, accommodating the idea of vacillation which is ultimately part and parcel of the poet's intellectual and emotional make-up. After writing 'Vacillation' Yeats seems to the author to have blended Biblical texts with sensuality, and to have used them to criticize his own poetry.In chapter five, however, a desire to emphasise the prevalence of references to Biblical texts sometimes runs too strongly, as in the surprising (in view of the book's emphasis on Blake and Shelley influencing Yeats's Biblical echoes) comment on the lines, from 'Crazy Jane talks with the Bishop', 'Love has pitched his mansion in | The place of excrement'. Here the Blakean source—'For I will make their place of love and joy excrementitious'—is neglected, in favour of an idea put forward by M. L. Rosenthal and Sally Gall, that the place of excrement is the stable of Luke 2.7. The 'mansion', of course,is derived convincingly from John 14.23. The treatment of 'The Choice'is not very satisfactory because the author is determined to see the poems in terms of irony. This prompts a query about the treatment of 'A Prayer for Old Age.' *Is* it derived from 1 Corinthians, 19-25, with its contrast of wisdom and foolishness; does it relate to Corinthians 4.10, 'We are fools for Christ's sake'? The Shakespearean fool comes to mind here, particularly the fool in *King Lear*. Similarly in the discussion of 'The Gyres' and 'The Man andthe Echo' Shelley's Ahasuerus is not considered as a source for the seer: how do we know that 'Old Rocky Face' is a God? When the author says that his appendices list 'all' of Yeats's Biblical allusions and selected echoes perhaps we should have translated this into 'all' those which he has discovered himself: there may be more to be noticed; some of his listings may not be accepted by others—though I reiterate my praise of their usefulness.

The sixth chapter deals with the very different ways that D. H. Lawrence and T. S. Eliot used the Bible in their writings. Yeats is regarded as more closely related to Romantic rather than Victorian forebears. The Afterword suggests that Yeats marks the end of a tradition because of the decline of the Bible as a sacred text in our time. Dr. Purdy has done a service to many modern readers who will get more from the texts of Yeats's poems by realising their relationships to Biblical texts. The reverberations of the Bible's rhythms and images, its words in their rhetorical arrangements, enrich our awareness of the complexity of Yeats's poetic sensibility and skill, the various imaginative levels at which he worked, words obeying his call and echoing the man's aesthetic efforts to surmount the problems posed by contemplation of time and the hereafter.

The Entire Pancake

Edward Larrissy, *Yeats the Poet: The Measures of Difference* (Hemel Hempstead: Harvester, 1994) 226pp + xii. pb

Deirdre Toomey

Edward Larrissy is interested in Freemasonry, Protestantism, Orientalism, Occultism, Celticism, Gaelicism, Fenianism and much, much more. In a mere 226 page book addressed to an undergraduate readership, we have what Flann O'Brien called 'the Entire Pancake'. At times when reading this monograph, I found myself in the position of one undergoing instruction in Atomic Theory from Sergeant Pluck. The 14 page introduction, which might have clarified Larrissy's enterprise, leaves the reader in a state of confusion. The 'difference' of the title is claimed as both Derridean *différance*/deferral, and plain old English difference. It is as if Larrissy had conceived his striking title without thinking of this problem and decided *post hoc* to justify an ambiguity. The only stable conclusion one can grasp from the introduction is that the author is hoping to have it both ways—to be a close reader and/or a deconstructive critic, but also a contextualising cultural critic. This is a convenient decision which allows Larrissy to wander any way he pleases.

The monograph proper begins badly with a discussion of Freemasonry. Larrissy admits that there is 'no evidence that Yeats was ever a Freemason in the sense of belonging to a lodge that called itself Freemasonic': apart from the weird qualification, this is correct. Yeats was an Irish Nationalist and a member of the IRB from c. 1886: he could not have joined an organisation identified with English Imperialism. Larrissy cannot abandon this non-issue and surrounds Yeats with a flurry of Masonic or pseudo-Masonic associations. Thus, Yeats's uncle was a

Mason, as many Irish protestant males were, Masons came from miles around to Pollexfen's funeral and Yeats was moved by the spectacle, and (*most sinister of all*) Yeats went to a Masonic concert in Sligo in 1898 and hissed at a comic song. Finally, according to Larrissy, the Golden Dawn is a 'Masonic order'.

Although the Order of Golden Dawn had degrees modelled on Masonic degrees, it was a Christian Cabbalist Order with a Rosicrucian Inner Order, which practised ritual magic. It was not a Masonic Order. Masons do not practise magic. Larrissy cites Maud Gonne's (1938) assertion that she left the GD because of its Masonic symbolism; but when she left in 1894, her reasons were that she disliked its 'semitic symbolism'—a very different issue, related to her own frank anti-semitism. Yeats was at a Masonic concert in 1898 because he was living off his uncle, who invited him along. For that matter I have attended a lecture at the Quatuor Coronati Lodge (no. 2076), but as far as I am aware I am not a Mason—nor indeed much interested in Masonry. It is hard to discern the *value* of all this fuzzy, associative thinking. Larrissy tries to suggest at one point that Yeats's assumed interest in Masonry was related to a wish to 'imbue Irish Nationalism with a sense of craft and mystery'. But the IRB had had 'craft and mystery' in abundance since 1858; Yeats had taken the Fenian oath and was too well acquainted with the IRB world of codes, passwords, plotting and secrecy (though no aprons).

The first chapter continues with a discussion of the value of Gaelic scholarship and the Celtic Church to Irish Protestants. This massive and fascinating subject is dealt with in two pages and the chapter scrambles rapidly to a conclusion in which the Irish Druids can be seen as being 'Magicians practising Eastern religion and magic in the West, like the speculative Masons of the Golden Dawn'. Well, up to a point, Lord Copper.

Chapter three contains an unusual but welcome element in a short book on Yeats, a discussion of *Mosada*, a text that is typically ignored. Larrissy begins by announcing that under the work's 'orientalism' is a 'displaced handling of Irish themes', then provides a flat plot summary confusingly interrupted by a reference to Leo Africanus, Ramon Lull and Yeats's later North African interests. This is part of a counterproductive attempt to make *Mosada* into an Irish poem. It is read as being full of Protestant anxiety and in doing so Yeats is relocated from the West of Ireland to the North: to see Yeats as 'half way between Protestant and Catholic Ireland' in Sligo is unconvincing. Larrissy points to the fact that Sligo town was largely Protestant; but the proportion of Protestants to Catholics in Co. Sligo (1891 census), is close to that in Co. Cork. A 1%

advantage to the Protestants in Co. Sligo over those in Co. Cork doesn't seem striking enough to mobilise exceptional paranoia about the Catholic Church. This reading of *Mosada* is based on some rather coarse associations, i.e., that the Inquisition can be transparently equated with Irish Catholicism in the consciousness of the young Yeats. Yet the lover transformed into a monk is a stock motif of the Gothic and *Mosada* seems to derive from decadent-romantic pseudo-Jacobean chamber drama, particularly that of Beddoes. *Death's Jest Book* (partly set on the 'African Coast') gives a good deal of this 'oriental' nexus:

> 'Whither should a student in the black arts, a journeyman magician, a Rosicrucian? Where is our country? . . . to the shores of Egypt . . . in that Sphynx land found Raymond Lully those splinters of the philosopher's stone . . . there dwell hoary magicians. . . .'[1]

The account of *The Countess Cathleen* shows a laudable wish to set the play in the context of a real famine, yet the famine which is referred to (1898 not 1897) and with which Maud Gonne was involved, was long after the composition of the play. Larrissy could have rescued this point by seeing the importance of the 1898 famine to the first performance of the play in 1899, but instead rapidly swerves in search of the 'fatal woman', drifting into an oblique argument, one very appropriate to Niamh, but wholly inappropriate to Cathleen, an emphatically non-supernatural being. The confusion here is again the result of a tendency to proceed by an associative mode; *The Countess Cathleen* is written for Maud Gonne, Maud Gonne was seen by starving peasants as 'The Woman of the Sidhe', the 'Woman of the Sidhe' in Irish mythology could be fatal, therefore Maud Gonne and Cathleen and Ireland (also typically symbolised as a woman) are somehow fatal, vampirish. There is no real argument here, merely a string of associations—a method stimulating in a seminar, but decidedly less so in a monograph. Again, in the discussion of *The Wanderings of Oisin*, a desire to make critical response to the poem more exciting leads to Larrissy's dragging in Freud on the *unheimlich* (and Lacan, for no discernible reason). Freud specifically excludes the wholly supernatural narrative from his discussion. The tales which Freud deploys, such as 'The Sandman', involve the irruption of the uncanny into a very mundane, domestic and *heimlich* world.

Chapter four opens with a brief but interesting and confident discussion of Blake, Yeats and Cabbala, then progresses, via a disorienting excursus into Yeats's dislike of the new bourgeoisie of early C 20th Ireland, to a less happy account of the Golden Dawn. Yeats's section title

'Crossways' is deemed to refer to the Paths of the Tree of Life. This seems unlikely; the word means 'byways' in Hiberno-English. Certain poems in this section to do have clear references to the Tree of Life, 'The Two Trees ' being an obvious example, but not every 'path' or 'pathway' in the early poems can carry a Golden Dawn interpretation. On such hopeful readings, Larrissy hangs a discussion of the Path of the Serpent and of the Arrow [*Samekh*]. I cannot agree with his interpretation that the divine lightning will descend on the Adept if he or she follows the Path of the Serpent, rather than the path Samekh: this stems from an over close reading of a very short extract from *Is the Order of R.R. & A.C. to Remain a Magical Order?* (1901). Larrissy has presumably not read the full text and therefore assumes that 'sacred leaves' is Yeats's coded reference to the Path of the Serpent. He is unaware that earlier in the pamphlet Yeats has stated:

> It is not merely an ascent, that has for symbols the climbing of the Serpent through the Tree of life and of the Adepti through the Degrees that we know of, but a descent that is symbolised by the Lightning Flash among the sacred leaves [and] that should be symbolised . . . by the Obligation spoken on the day of Corpus Christi.

Thus Yeats excudes the possibility of interpreting 'sacred leaves' as a reference to the Path of the Serpent. *Is the Order of R.R. & A.C. to Remain a Magical Order?* is a document concerned with the weakening of the magical power and organic unity of the Order by the creation of groups working by themselves. The pamphlet is less a personal interpretation of the Tree of Life than a summary of an ideological quarrel. Larrissy's monograph—intermittently—seeks to *contextualise*, and such a context should have been noted. (George Harper reprinted the text in *Yeats's Golden Dawn* [1974]).

A brief but genuinely interesting account of Yeats's relationship with Blakean ideas of the demonic and the 'husk' drifts into a discussion of the mixed genres and themes of the early collections and to mad figures in early poems. Larrissy's assumption that King Goll is the 'type of the crucified poet' would have been very strongly supported if he had informed his readers that in its first printing the poem was illustrated by a reproduction of an impressive water-colour by J. B. Yeats of Yeats as King Goll playing his harp, (which suggests a measure of identification).

Chapter five is a discussion of 'The Rose' in early Yeats. The result is a mare's nest full of red herrings, in which we move with disturbing rapidity from *roisin dubh* and the Jacobites to the Rose Croix Order of

Sâr Peladan. Larrissy has a real concern for Yeats's cultural context, but is continually hampered by sketchy knowledge. Thus Yeats's understanding of Rosicrucianism came not, as Larrissy suggests, from A. E. Waite (although he had obviously read *The Real History of the Rosicrucians*), but directly from the Golden Dawn, which had a Rosicrucian Inner Order. Larrissy also surrenders to his worst habit, that of offering a line of argument in which he expresses no belief: thus we have a page of discussion of the Virgin Mary and Rosa Mystica, despite the *caveat* that Yeats did 'not really' draw on this association.

The first section of the monograph concludes with a Chapter on 'Fin-de Siècle Fenianism and *The Wind Among the Reeds*' a rich and potentially rewarding subject. A desire to see in these poems an expression of Yeats's political radicalism is something with which I am wholly in sympathy. Larrissy's approach is to identify the 'Aedh' of *The Wind Among the Reeds* with a companion and rival of Fionn Mac Cuil, Goll mac Morna, originally named Aedh. Thus, by association with the Fianna, the poems become 'Fenian'. This is to assume, firstly, that the only Aedh in Irish history or mythology whom Yeats could have been referring to was Goll mac Morna, previously known as Aedh. Even if we grant that 'Aedh' in *The Wind Among the Reeds* is, in Richard Finneran's phrase, a 'specific allusion' this seems rash. Irish mythology is awash with Aedhs. And were we (unecessarily I think) to seek a specific source for the 'Aedh' of the poems, a more obvious choice would be Aedh Slane, High King of Ireland. Rebirth, as in the Mongan poems, is a powerful theme of the volume and Aedh Slane was born first as a lamb, then as a silver trout, finally as a human. On the slender peg of such source hunting a 'Fenian' interpretation of the volume is hung. If one is seeking overt 'political poems' in the volume, one finds them directly in 'Aedh thinks of those who have Spoken Evil of his Beloved', which relates directly to contemporary radical politics. The slanderers whom Yeats condemns are two of the most marginal men in Irish politics, Mc'Carthy Teeling and Frank Hugh O'Donnell, both of whom had been attacking Maud Gonne as a spy and worse. To identify the Fenian-INA element in the mythological poems would require considerable acumen. But one would have to begin by informing the student reader that in the period 1897-8 Yeats was President of the '98 Centennial Association of Great Britain and France and heavily involved in Nationalist politics; further that he was still a member of the INA, a dynamiting splinter group of the IRB. One would then have to isolate the element of of *political* Armageddon in poems such as 'The Valley of the Black Pig' and link it with ideas of a final war of independence in Ireland and prose pieces such as 'War'.

The second section of this monograph opens with a close reading of Yeats's poetic output from 1900 to 1910 and is a welcome relief. Even when I disagree with Larrissy's readings, I can see that he demonstrates real pedagogical skills, which one would like to have seen more widely deployed in a book directed at undergraduates. Yet by p. 107 lucidity and helpfulness is abandoned for an opaque analysis of Yeats's lunar symbolism, following on from a reading of 'Adam's Curse'. At no point does Larrissy inform the student reader that Yeats was a serious and highly competent astrologer and that this might have some bearing on the matter. (The waning moon of the poem is an astrological indication of spiritual exhaustion.) The chapter ends with a brisk ride on a hobby horse, 'orientalism' as expressed by Yeats's *lapsus* of 'Ramon Lully' for 'Nicholas Flamel' in *The Green Helmet*. If we are to take the slip seriously, we could interpret it as expressive of Yeats's unconsious sense of how mismatched he and Maud Gonne are, by pairing Flamel's wife with a Catalan mystic. Yet in lines 385-386 of 'Rosa Alchemica', Lully immediately precedes Flamel and Pernella; thus if the astigmatic Yeats had glanced at this text, when producing copy for *The Nation* an eye-jump might have produced this odd couple.

'Framing Ireland' rapidly runs through *Reponsibilities*, in the style of a teacher making a comment here and there as the volume is discussed in a seminar, with a scatter-shot effect. Some readings indicate a substantial distance from Ireland. Thus 'September 1913' is read as an attack on small Catholic shopkeepers, yet Yeats makes clear in his first printing of the poem in the *Irish Times* that it is presented as a response to the refusal of Dublin magnates, such as William Martin Murphy, to support the Lane Gallery. However the political anger and despair in the poem surely derives from the actions of the same 'Masters of Dublin', led by Murphy, Dublin's premier capitalist, who were preparing to beat striking workers and their families into submission in the Dublin Lock-out: the strike had begun 26 August 1913. In Russell's words, these employers decided to 'deliberately, in cold anger . . . starve out one-third of the population of this city'. Russell and Yeats did indeed dislike the narrow, bigotted, cultural programme associated with the new Catholic bourgeoisie—and one only has to look at *The Leader* or *The Catholic Bulletin* to see why— but Larrissy's is an unacceptable reading of the poem and one distant from Irish history.

Then, via a brief discussion of associationism in Yeats's ideology, we move with bewildering speed to Eagleton on Yeats and Maud Gonne and Freud on the Death pulsion. It is as if anything which crosses the author's mind gets into the book. The useful and sensitive reading of 'In

Memory of Major Robert Gergory' which follows seems to be written by a different person. In a study aimed at undergraduates, the discussion of 'Easter 1916' must be crucial. Larrissy, the seminar rooms of the '90s before his eye, predictably sees insult in the account of Constance Markiewicz. He scolds Yeats for not thinking Pearse a great poet and for patronising MacDonagh. He equivocates on MacBride, but does not tell the students why 'drunken vain-glorious lout' should not be read as mere vulgar abuse. Yeats had been aware for 11 years of MacBride's sexual assaults on his step-daughter Iseult Gonne, with whom Yeats was now in love: he wrote the poem in July 1916 at Maud Gonne's house in Normandy. An interesting reading of the second section of the poem seeks to link it to Blakean notions of the terrible, although I could have done without the comparisons with *Dracula*. And Elizabeth Cullingford's and G. F. Dalton's discussions of 'terrible beauty' are prior to Carmel Jordan's. Larrissy's account of the final section of the poem underestimates the force of *domestication*—'as a mother names her child'—at the end of a poem which accepts blood sacrifice.

In 'Reflections on Yeatsian Occultism', Larrissy, after a brief excusus into Orientalism and Catholicism, turns to the genesis of *A Vision*. He quotes George Yeats's remark to Suheil Bushrui, that the sand diagrams in the fictions surrounding *A Vision*, were derived from Golden Dawn practices. This leads Larrissy to conclude that 'if so, there is an obvious Rosicrucian source for them . . . Robert Fludd . . . there is no other occult writer who pays so much and such learned attention to geomancy'. This argument is bewildering to me. If George Yeats directed Bushrui to the GD (of which she had been a member since 1914) she was trying to be as open and helpful as possible. Why did Larrissy not investigate Regardie's *Golden Dawn Rituals*, which have been in print since 1937 and in paperback since 1986? George Yeats was not telling Bushrui the source of the geometry of *A Vision*, but giving him the source for its fictional presentation in sand diagrams. Moreover, any chase after Fludd is irrelevant, unless Fludd can be shown to have strongly influenced George Yeats when she was developing the symbolism of the automatic script, or Yeats when he was systematising what she had developed. Yet another blind alley is explored, that of the origin of 'Giraldus'; Larrissy wishes to force an association with Giraldus Cambrensis, so that a 'Celtic' element can be introduced. From this point on any pretence of coherent argument is abandoned and within a page we find ourselves—via Duns Scotus Erigena—dealing with W. J. Mc Cormack on Ferguson's *Hibernian Nights Entertainments*, which is deemed to be of relevance to a discussion of *A Vision* because of the *Arabian Nights* allusion. The very brief account of the symbolism and progress of the automatic script would have been assisted by a reading of George Harper *et al*, *Yeats's Vision Papers* (3 vols Macmillan, 1992). Larrissy finds misogyny in *A Vision* by a series of arguments or rather associations. He concludes that 'Yeats's artistic metaphor for *A Vision* is steeped in misogyny'. What does this mean? Well 'gyres and cubes' remind Larrissy of Cubism and Vorticism, which remind him that for Pound and Lewis, Vorticism had a phallic dimension. And Yeats *must* have known this.

In his concluding chapters, Larrissy wastes paper worrying about the renaming of Yeats's tower. He is shocked that Yeats called his house *Thoor* rather than the correct *Tur*. (Yet Larrissy does not concern himself at all with Ballylee versus *Baile ui Laoi*). Is he greatly distressed when he travels round Ireland to find that almost every place-name is, in English, corruptly or phonetically spelled? That we have, say, Ballynoe, or Ballina, rather than the correct *Baile Nua*? Or that many Irish surnames (such as my own) are universally mispronounced? It is hard to see what undergraduates will make of this sterile wrangle with Yeats and Hiberno-English. Larrissy's indignation on behalf of a fictive 'nationalist Irish speaker' could be put into perspective by a reading of the naming of a house in *The Dalkey Archives*. A discussion of the 'Big House' is marred by a bizarre equation of Martyn's vast Norman and neo-Gothic Castle with Yeats's tumble-down tower, bought for £35. I once again remind myself that this is a book directed at undergraduates; there is no *discussion at all* of the poem 'The Tower'. Indeed one thing that is absent from this monograph is any consistent communication of the sense that Yeats is a great poet. Larrissy's 'discussion' of 'Sailing to Byzantium' is paradigmatic of his method. He begins with the assumption that the poem begins simply with a rejection of Ireland (as in the early MS drafts), rather than of Ireland as representative of mortal life—'*That* is no country . . .'. Then, paying little attention to the poem's argument, form or texture, he rides his hobby horse off to P. W. Joyce's *A Social History of Ancient Ireland*, Gibbon and *Don Juan*. The discussion concludes with some source-hunting. He insists that the idyllic Ireland of the first stanza of the poem is based upon Ferguson's 'The Fair Hills of Ireland', ignoring more obvious materials such as the account of *Tír na nOg* in Midhir's appeal to Etain, used in *The Wind Among the Reeds* (VP 805). In contrast Larrissy's suggestion of Blake's bent and aged man (Blair's *The Grave*, *Jerusalem*) as a source for the 'paltry thing' of this poem is genuinely stimulating.

The concluding chapter partly concerns itself with arguments about sexuality and might have been assisted by a reading of Elizabeth Cullingford's *Gender and History in Yeats's Love Poetry* (1993). Larrissy's last six pages, which struggle to pull together all the threads of this heterogeneous monograph, are largely unintelligible despite some very aspirational prose.

NOTES

1.   The Muses Library Beddoes was later edited by a friend of Yeats's youth–Ramsay Colles. Colles (a subscriber to *The Wanderings of Usheen*) was to go into print in his journal the *Irish Figaro* in 1900 as saying that *Mosada* was a great work, but that from then on Yeats's writing had deteriorated consistently.

'It is no time to discourse, the town is besieched!'[1]

Declan Kiberd, *Inventing Ireland* (London: Cape, 1995). 720pp.

W. J. Mc Cormack

The latter half of 1995 was dominated by two major events in the Irish political calendar. After years of preparation, the Dublin government brought the issue of a right to divorce before the electorate in a referendum, a proposal carried by the slenderest of majorities. A week later, President Bill Clinton of the United States visited Belfast, Derry and Dublin to add his weight in the cause of peace, and to boost his chances of re-election in 1996. Between these two events a full-page advertisement appeared in national newspapers, addressed to the prime ministers in London and Dublin, urging them to take all steps etc. to advance the peace process. Among the many signatories, drawn from the ranks of public life and what passes for an intelligentsia, was that of Dr Declan Kiberd.

The previous Sunday, he had written a post-referendum column in *The Tribune* pointing to the closeness of the result and to 'an intellectual silence' which had contributed to the near-run-ness of the thing. On the topic of intellectual silence, he certainly knew what he was talking about. This most articulate commentator on Irish culture had remained discreetly mute throughout the referendum campaign. With one bound he was free, not only to pontificate on his own silence as a remote phenomenon but also to urge sovereign governments towards their duty. What had freed him was a Catholic Church defeated at the polls, however narrowly. He was only free conditionally, of course, free to speak to the great powers rather than those elements—Sinn Féin and the

Unionist parties—who were more obviously blocking progress towards a permanent peace. The monumentality of the advertisement and the dignity of the addressees exactly reflected the scale of the power ranged against reform of southern Ireland's constitution—the scale of the Catholic Church. There's no point in hectoring the illegals if you have just escaped from the supra-legal, nothing to be gained by pleading with those you have earlier characterised as 'boot-faced'. Better express and repress on a grand scale.

On several occasions as I read Declan Kiberd's mighty and witty book, I wondered when I would wake up and find myself back in the college debating society. His jokes are delivered at just the right pace to keep each constituency in the audience enthralled, embarrassed or enthralled by the embarrassment of others. Adverbs roll off the tongue—alternately, generally, happily, judiciously, paradoxically, repeatedly—usually to the effect of keeping the sense of what is said available in multiple form so that audience 'take-up' is maximised. Or, to change the perspective, one's first experience of *Inventing Ireland* is that of the tolerant, bewildered stranger button-holed in a lounge or bar and entertained beyond endurance and the last bus. It is great stuff, all too great.

Yet mighty the book undoubtedly is. Its thirty-five chapters—not to mention ten interchapters—amount to more than seven hundred pages, including notes and an index. The earliest author treated at some length is Geoffrey Keating, the latest Brian Friel, figures who also signify the book's inclusive attitude to languages; Gaelic and English are repeatedly considered together and to good effect. The author of *Synge and the Irish Language* (rev. ed. 1993) once again puts readers in his debt on the topic. A chapter on 'Lady Gregory and the Empire Boys' is revealing, sympathetic, inconclusive and oddly disengaged with the chapters on Yeats. Generally speaking, women are considered to the extent which a repressive history allows, and Kiberd compensates for the absence of a more numerous company of women writers by attending with intellectual and emotional insight to theories of androgyny and feminism. The whole enterprise is, with the proper reservations and qualifications, a tribute to the gaiety of nations.

On the topic of nations, an odd discrepancy emerges between the book's dust-jacket and its title-page. According to the latter, *Inventing Ireland* is just so named, having no subtitle. But according to the former, the subtitle reads 'The Literature of the Modern Nation'. The extended title would appear to signal a restricted field of operation, a partitioned area, with the nation largely but not exclusively identified with the southern Irish state established in 1921. Thus Seamus Heaney, Derek

Mahon, and John Montague are admissible, but Medbh McGuckian isn't, and Michael Longley features once in a sentence about the influence of W. H. Auden. When Louis MacNeice gets a passing mention in despatches, he is a critic of Yeats. A sentence or two are reserved for W. R. Rodgers and John Hewitt, but it is an unintentional irony that the lines of Hewitt's quoted should include these:

> This is my home and country. Later on
> perhaps I'll find this nation is my own.

Discrepancy brings its own illumination. As one reads, *Inventing Ireland* becomes more clearly visible as yet another statement of the proposition that modern Irish literature is the elder twin of modern Irish nationalism or—to be more exact—of the movement which commenced with the election of Charles Stewart Parnell to the leadership of the Irish Party in Westminster. Kiberd has no interest in the novelists of the nineteenth century, of whom he says—simply—that they 'simply repeated the prevailing English methods, in a tradition which stretched from Edgeworth to Griffin, from Carleton to Moore' (p. 342). One wonders why Walter Scott paid such lavish tribute to the author of *The Absentee* as the inspiration which sent him back to the abandoned manuscript of *Waverley* (1814), and notes also how he borrowed more specifically from Sydney Owenson for *The Surgeon's Daughter* (1827). These are not prehistoric and unrecovered arcana. After all, Marilyn Butler has had the audacity to suggest that Thackeray's 'novel without a hero' owed a similar debt to Edgeworth. Nor is the problem limited to the early years of the nineteenth century. George Moore, for Kiberd, is the purveyor of some useful *aperçus*; none of the novels is discussed, not even the ones set in Ireland. Le Fanu, Lever, and Lover might as well not have existed, a fate which James Clarence Mangan successfully wished upon himself, it seems, for Kiberd has at last confirmed it. To dismiss 'sentimental Kick-hamesque novels written to an English literary formula' is to refuse to the nineteenth century that buck-leppin' dialectic of English/Irish mutual invention which Kiberd will repeatedly promote in the literature of more recent years, the literature of a national/post-colonial phase. Nothing else matters, for it has failed to be invented.

Then there is the wretched problem of the eighteenth century. It is an axiom of Kiberd's that no greater galaxy of genius was ever born in (or to) Ireland than the generation of Joyce, Synge, Yeats and Wilde. This is a proposition made the more plausible by a refusal to look any earlier. For surely, the generation (just as loosely defined) of Burke, Edgeworth, Malone, and Sheridan deserves consideration. An even earlier generation

(Berkeley, Goldsmith, and Swift) does get a look in, but its great names feature within Kiberd's treatment of Yeats rather than in their own right. Indeed, the eighteenth and nineteenth centuries as invented by Kiberd have already been invented by the poet; the latter-day inventor might more accurately be termed a Re-Cycler, a term Yeatsian enough to serve.

There are, therefore, several aspects of Kiberd's eighteenth century which give rise to concern. Not the least of these is the mechanical adoption of Yeats's forceful suppression of Victorian Irish literature, at least in the greater man's public utterances. But questions of scholarly procedure are also implicated, together with the political nuances cast by imprecision in this area. For example, it is declared that 'Goldsmith, Swift, Sheridan and Berkeley were all recruited by Yeats in *The Winding Stair* for his pantheon of ascendancy intellects' (p. 449). Whether one concentrates on the volume of that name published in 1929 and containing just six poems, or on *The Winding Stair and Other Poems* (1933), nowhere is R. B. Sheridan to be found. This is hardly surprising, given Yeats's rage against whiggery and the persistence of Sheridan's whiggery even after the French Revolution; what is surprising here is the absence of Burke from Kiberd's list. The matter is further complicated by his characterisation of these heroes as 'hardworking men' and 'impeccable representatives of the Irish Protestant middle class'. Swift's poem on brother protestants cannot have sprung to a mind additionally neglectful of Burke's and Sheridan's Catholic origins (Gaelic also in Sheridan's case). And Goldsmith as hard-working? The sentence quoted is a travesty of scholarship and critical judgement.

One could cite other instances. The discussion of Yeats's attitude to John Locke and George Berkeley reaches the conclusion that 'Blake's well-publicized attacks on the empirical Locke set the republican poet in well-chosen Celtic company, along with Scotland's David Hume' (p. 322). Here the problem lies with adjectives rather than adverbs. That anything of Blake's doing was well-publicised will come as news to literary historians, and the implication that Berkeley was a Celt is—like tar-water—hard to swallow. For, if Kiberd does not intend so to classify the bishop, then there is no 'company' and no 'revolt by the Celtic fringe', just the solitary figure of Hume whose differences with Locke did nothing to discredit empiricism. Finally, if Blake was (indeed) a republican, he was also a stout supporter of revolution, a devastating parodist of Burke, and no friend of Hume's. It seems that we witness not only an inventing of Ireland but of philosophy also. Notions and nations go turnabout in a work where historical exactitude counts for little.

Perhaps these questions lie unfairly beyond the inventor's specialist field. In so far as it is at all important to his argument, he believes of

Edgeworth's *Castle Rackrent* that 'she wrote the book in the aftermath of the Act of Union' (p. 71). Given that the novel was published (albeit anonymously) in January 1800, and that the Union was passed in July and August of that year, successively in Westminster and College Green, the belief seems ill-founded. Indeed the manuscript was prepared for the publisher in October 1798, and composition has been assigned by Butler and others to a date somewhere between 1792 and 1796, with later additions. But perhaps this question lies unfairly outside the inventor's period, the opening of which is signalled by a vigorous and amusing chapter on Oscar Wilde.

Wilde was, so to speak, the buck-lepper of London drawing rooms, and in treating the plays Kiberd elaborates an intricate argument in which sexual and national identities are seen as creations rather than inheritances. Unfortunately, the case is marred by occasional overstatement, misleading terminology and inconsistency. We are told that Wilde's 'essays on Ireland question the assumption that, just because the English are one thing, the Irish must be its opposite' (p. 35). What are these essays? No titles are cited, but through laborious work on the endnotes one can establish that just three pieces by Wilde are implicated. These are (in order of their spectral appearance in *Inventing Ireland*) 'The Critic as Artist' (first pub. September 1890), a review of J. A. Froude's *Two Chiefs of Dunboy* (April 1889), and a passage from 'Some Literary Notes' (February 1889). The last is in effect a review of *Fairy and Folk Tales* (ed. W. B. Yeats, 1888), a book which tells of many wonders including (in Wilde's phrase) 'that Irish giant who swam across the Channel with his head in his teeth.' A mighty book.

Not content with the analogy of sexual and national identity, the argument yearns for concrete embodiment or personification. Thus we are advised that 'Wilde saw his own career as running parallel to that of Parnell, another urbane Irishman who surprised the English by his self-control and cold exterior' (p. 37). Parnell, in this phase of *Inventing Ireland*, serves both as the fated precursor of Wilde the victim and as the long-range founder of Irish independence. But where is the evidence that Wilde had seen his career as paralleling that of the lost leader? Certainly, it is not to be found in Kiberd's book. In the sentence immediately preceding that just quoted, we read that 'when Parnell was at the height of his power in 1889, Wilde wrote in celebration of *his* Celtic intellect which 'at home . . . had but learnt the pathetic weakness of nationality, but in a strange land realized what indominable forces nationality possesses' ' (ibid, original emphasis). When we have traced this to Wilde's review of Froude, we find that the piece nowhere refers to Parnell, or at least nowhere names him. Nor does the sentence most recently quoted have as its subject Parnell's Celtic intellect as implied by Kiberd: Wilde is writing about the general phenomenon of Irish emigration to America and the resulting Irish-American factor in politics. Comparing the ancient Jews in captivity with the exile of the latter-day Irish, Wilde concludes his first paragraph, 'their first practical leader is an Irish American.'[2]

Assuming for the moment that this is not a veiled allusion to O'Donovan Rossa or John Devoy, we can agree that there is a strong possibility Parnell is the unnamed subject. But, however strong, possibility remains nothing more than that. There is of course nothing Celtic about Parnell whatsoever, neither in the strict sense of that term as denoting linguistic practice nor in the looser or fringe sense much indulged in this work. Nor was Parnell Irish-American in any sense other than that he was the son of an American mother and an Irish (non-Celtic) father. Wilde's point might be understood to underline a contrast between the leader and the led, a contrast effected paradoxically by swapping the descriptive tags, a tentative rhetorical device at best. Kiberd's confident assumption that 'Celtic intellect' can be specified as Parnell's Celtic intellect is based on two suppositions, each of which requires the other to be fact rather than supposition. Where is the evidence that 'Wilde saw his own career as running parallel to that of Parnell'? A shred or two would satisfy. For the truly remarkable feature of Wilde's political writings is the *absence* of Parnell's name, a suppression which does not prohibit reference to Michael Davitt or William O'Brien. The most striking feature of Wilde's reference to an Irish-American leader is its indeterminacy.

Kiberd, by contrast, is a very determined writer. When he praises 'the near absolute command of human experience evident in the success of their presentations' (p. 69) one wonders if he has turned to the Greek tragedians for a comparison—in the manner of Fiona Macintosh—with the Irish dramatists. But no; not Sophocles and Aeschylus, but Somerville and Ross are thus praised, with all the suspect effusion of post-referendum intellectuals squaring up to John Major. Later, in a chapter linking Samuel Beckett to Austin Clarke, Brian Coffey, Denis Devlin, and Thomas MacGreevy, we are assured that 'all of the foregoing writers were incorporated, only with immense difficulty and after decades of delay, into the Irish literary tradition' (p. 466). The difficulties were twofold—the provincial outlook (or rather, inlook) of Irish intellectuals, and the larger 'inability of so many liberal intellectuals to respond with warmth to religious writing' (ibid). If we allow that no such inability prevented T. S. Eliot from becoming the hegemonic guru of English Departments from Downing College to Earlsfort Terrace, then the real achievement celebrated in this paragraph turns out to be the *rapid* appropriation of some very recent figures to the reading lists. This academic cosiness retrospectively enlightens an obscure word in the tribute to Somerville and Ross. Despite the hostility of Daniel Corkery and his followers, the ladies of Castletownshend were all the time making 'presentations'—the first syllable is long—*pree*sentations which can safely be deemed acceptable now that Corkery's anathemas are translated into a different code and the RM stories can be sold in Irish-America without apology. In the name of post-colonial 'différance', *Inventing Ireland* welcomes them to the tradition.

At the heart of any such endeavour, one would expect to find W. B. Yeats. As is only proper, Kiberd alludes to Yeats virtually on every page, while also devoting five chapters more specifically to the work. These are dispersed through *Inventing Ireland* in a manner which does not always avoid confusion. While the detail of these five (and other occasional) discussions of Yeats deserve respectful attention, the reader may suspect that s/he has been locked into a system of Celtic boxes. 'Inventing Irelands' is a chapter in a section called *Inventing Irelands* in a book called *Inventing Ireland*. Meanwhile the chapter called 'The Winding Stair' deals largely with *The Winding Stair* to the point where Yeats's authorship and Kiberd's are in danger of convergence. This yo-yo writing is not very inventive, nor is it enhanced by an exuberant taking-up of the hideous coinages, Protholics and Cathestants.

Despite all this, the discussion of Yeats's early poems is fine, especially attentive to the narcissistic tendency evidenced in the poetry up to and including *In the Seven Woods* (1904). Kiberd is never afraid to speak his mind—'many of Yeats's most memorable lines are striking without being lucid' (p. 312)—and the chapter in which this appears ('Revolt into Style') is in itself a solid essay- or lecture-survey of the poet's achievements and limitations. (Chapter of a developing, lucid argument it is not!) If a certain confusion in the end-notes—an accident which can befall the best of authors—is evidence that a longer essay was cut down for inclusion at this point of *Inventing Ireland*, then this is to be regretted. When Kiberd gives himself time to dwell on the poetry he invariably has valuable things to say and do. The linking of 'The Stolen Child' to 'Easter 1916' is delicately achieved, and one only wishes that the book's address of Yeats were less dispersed and less subject to the hearty interruptions of the Re-Cycler.

Treatment of *A Vision* is not so happy. The polished arts of staying 'onside' (p. 360) with every interest group in one's audience are all too evident. How many disingenuous details can be spotted in such a sentence as this—'*A Vision*, however tentative a title, deliberately refers the Irish reader back to the *aisling* or vision-poem, practised by the fallen bards like ó Rathaille to whom Yeats was increasingly attracted' (p. 318)? Even the notion of ó Rathaille (c. 1675-1729) as a fallen bard blurs any historically or stylistically acute understanding of bardic poetry. The habit of discovering parallels between literary and political entities, likewise the indiscriminate use of terms and snatches of quotation, reaches an apotheosis in the declaration that '*A Vision* is a Celtic constitution not solely for Ireland but for all the world, after the rough beast has come again' (p. 319). Despite these idiosyncrasies, there are also specific and unacknowledged debts to earlier critics in the chapter on *A Vision*—to Denis Donoghue, for example. As a matter of practice, Kiberd is not a generous reader of criticism and literary history. The joke is always being told for the first time, and the re-cycled insight is not only first-class but first-hand.

One symptomatic exception to this rule can be found tucked away in a footnote to the interchapter devoted to sexual politics. Having declared that *A Vision* is not an *encyclopaedia fascistica* (p. 320), Kiberd gradually abandons the topic of Yeats's politics. Characteristically, the process involves a modicum of self-reference: 'The universal history of politics and art is rendered in *A Vision* in terms of the original Anglo-Irish antithesis . . .' (p. 321), but the antithesis in question is not quite so original or venerable; indeed it has been just invented by Kiberd himself on p. 318. There the matter rests, until some undeclared unease prompts him to endorse (p. 679 n5) Elizabeth Cullingford's *Yeats, Ireland and Fascism* (1981) as 'decisive' on the ill-mannered business of considering Yeats as pro-fascist. Cullingford had ignored the most damning evidence—e.g. his acceptance of the Goethe Plakette in 1934 and an *Irish Independent* interview of 13 August 1938—but Kiberd goes further and passes over everything in *On the Boiler* (1939) also. In addition, of course, he studiously avoids any reference to the critical debate on this complex historical, philosophical, political and aesthetic question.

Why so? Well, it would be difficult to launch an anti-imperialist criticism, leading to a post-colonialist critique, if Yeats were to be admitted an admirer or supporter of Mussolini and Hitler whose pre-war antics in Abyssinia, Czechoslovakia and Transylvania could hardly be classified among the de-colonising triumphs of the century. Hence the emphasis on Yeats as a national poet (p. 115), together with the early and persistent troping of post-coloniality in *Inventing Ireland*. It is therefore with an anticipation of ultimate illumination that one reaches Chapter 31, 'Post-Colonial Ireland—"A Quaking Sod"'. The opening moves in this debate are familiar, involving Frantz Fanon's *Wretched of the Earth* and citations of Achebe, Naipaul, Ngugi and other Third World writers.

While resemblances between Algeria and Ireland are stressed, differences are ignored as usual, notably historical differences. African, Indian and West Indian authorities feature principally in a loud murmur of 'name upon name', substituting for argument.

A revealing instance of this centres on Kiberd's reading of Aijaz Ahmad, a person virtually missing from the inventory. The phrase 'a nationalism of mourning' is cited twice (pp. 291, 531), first without acknowledgement to any named author but with a end-note attached, then with acknowledgement but without any end-note. Once located, Kiberd's page reference for this pithy phrase directs us no more precisely than to pp. 95-122 of Ahmad's excoriating *In Theory; Classes, Nations, Literatures* (1992). In fact, the phrase occurs (Ahmad p. 119) as a gloss upon a particularly ironic movement or phase of Indian 'nationalism' (the sorrowful quote marks are Ahmad's) involving what is characterised as 'the gigantic fratricide conducted by Hindu, Muslim and Sikh'. Leaving aside the specific distortion created here by quotation of the first phrase without the second, one notes Kiberd's further inability to engage with a book which subjects to a rigorous critique the kind of sloppy thinking about Third World Literature, Nationalism, and Post-coloniality he indulges in. To need a phrase, while needing to suppress the argument it occurs in, is to be in dire straits. So nothing remotely like a theory of post-coloniality as it bears upon Ireland follows; instead we are treated to a few jokes about Harold Macmillan and the Katanga crisis and a distorted account of the Irish educational system.

In the last connection, it is worth noting the claim that 'religion, rather than English literature, was held to be the central subject of study' (p. 554). Surely the Gaelic language served that purpose, for at no time was religion (or any of its sub-divisions) an examinable subject. Kiberd makes generalised claims about the inadequacy of English literature syllabuses in independent Ireland, and employs Quiller-Couch as the epitome of all that was derivative and dull.[3] Once again the scales of expression and repression are indelicately balanced. If it is more or less a fair complaint that no attempt was made 'to imagine how the study of republican poets like Blake or Shelley . . . might constitute a challenge to the Eliotic notion of a royalist, Anglo-Catholic canon' (p. 561), should this not be complemented by acknowledgement that Milton (as sturdy a republican as you could wish for) did hold his place in the Irish curriculum, and that Anglo-Catholicism scarcely featured in the school syllabus. Kiberd is forever setting up straw men, and then tilting at windmills instead. Every don is his own Sancho Panza.

At this point in the assessment of a lengthy and substantial book, the tone should change to one heralding a re-balancing of judgements, a note of congratulation tinged with hesitancy, even a final plaudit. But the issues raised, and the reputation of the raiser, call for something better than comradely trimming. If 'A Vision [was] a Celtic constitution' what are we to make of the 1937 document whose amendment preoccupied many minds in 1995 to the point of near silence? And if *Inventing Ireland* has a comparative agenda involving Nigeria and the West Indies, why has it nothing to say about cultural relations between the Irish Free State and Wales, no comment to make about post-colonial societies in Europe? Norway, Finland, Hungary, Czechoslovakia—even Italy, if one can reach back as far as the Risorgimento—offer viewing-platforms from which the Irish experience might be seen afresh. This is not to require of any cultural commentator—least of all of Kiberd who uniquely combines learning and eloquence in two languages—that s/he scan the globe for neglected opportunities; but it is striking how the post-colonialist discourse boils down to an Anglophone moan—a point upon which Ahmad is eloquent. It might be said of De Valera's constitution that its unstated pretext was differentiation from Great Britain, but such a binary drive in the political field does not necessarily require a similar mechanism in the cultural seminar.

Despite these larger parallels between the constitutional exercises of 1995 and the political unconscious of *Inventing Ireland*, perhaps the most disturbing feature of the book is to be found in its intellectual aerobics—its preference for the regular, but systematically discontinuous, exercise of intelligence upon topics of massive implication. As sound bites dominate what used to be known as political discussion, so Kiberd's humour is turned on and off, lest the reader tire of any sustained argument by a rhetorician who will heckle himself just to double the entertainment value. This, however, is to ignore the sombre implications of such behaviour. *Inventing Ireland* gives dignity to the notion of 'attention span' by assuming a maximum endurable length of about eight pages. One is forever being stimulated, to the point of tedium. There are too many original borrowings—e.g. 'The Empire Writes Back' . . . 'Texts of Laughter and Forgetting'—among the many chapter-titles. Nor does this reduce upon examination into a negligible or personal trait; it signals a disturbing reliance on short-term memory in the audience, as if the influence of Edward Said had to be balanced by that of Gay Byrne. In the wider cultural and social sphere, the phenomenon encountered in Kiberd's re-cycling has grave symptomatic implications. There is a danger that such reliance will energise itself so as to effect a veritable imposition of intermittent amnesia in public discourse, with brevity regarded as top score in matters of attention and memory. In this scenario, Post-coloniality will be the Valium of the People.

The structure of *Inventing Ireland* not only conceals its substantial treatment of Yeats, it also conceals its substantial neglect of Northern Ireland as an entity not only political but cultural also. It is significant that we are introduced to Seamus Heaney as 'one of the most talented poets to emerge from [sic] Northern Ireland' rather than *in* that undeniable place. Surely it is an abuse of analogical reasoning to declare that 'the farm of his childhood thus becomes a colony in which unwanted kittens are purged' (p. 591). Heaney's poem-title, 'The Early Purges', had a resonance in its time which had specific political implications of a Cold War variety. Having said this, one also notes with admiration how Kiberd can pinpoint a near-pornographic aspect of Heaney's early natural descriptions.

The trouble is that, despite being pushed and slapped on the back, Heaney does not fit Kiberd's agenda, and while the poetry is extensively quoted, the results scatter in all directions—warm if platitudinous introductions here, isolated (though telling) points there. At some point, Brian Friel evidently looked like more promising canon-fodder, and thus had a whole (if brief, pp. 614-623) chapter assigned to him. Even in this, however, it proves necessary to concentrate exclusively on one play (*Translations*, what else?), and to exclude all trace of the complaints made by J. H. Andrews about the way in which his scholarly work on the Ordnance Survey was travestied in the play. In Kiberd's only reference to the controversy which followed *Translations*, the source turns out to be Friel himself (pp. 616 and 697 n.7), a singular example of *Sinn Féin amháin*. The dust-jacket puff from Friel does not diminish the narcissistic perfume of the book.

Nevertheless, weighing up *Inventing Ireland*, one's immediate feeling is a pain in the arm. But this is too frivolous a response to so varied, so uneven a book—a veritable curate's omelette. Nothing which Declan Kiberd publishes lacks symptomatic value; the present work, which brings together the results of many years of teaching and lecturing, does reflect the period in which it was composed, as also the moment at which it was published. After nearly half a century of industrious application by hundreds of bibliographers, biographers, critics, literary historians, textual editors and other specialists, this *magnum opus* doubles as yet one more introduction to the topic of Anglo-Irish literature and as a discontinuous (at times disingenuous) special theory.

The fault line between these ambitions reproduces the discrepancy between title-page and dust-jacket—is literature still to be seen primarily as a national issue, both in the sense of mattering to the nation and in the sense of issuing from (or in) the nation? If so, then the fustian barb, 'what ish my nation?' requires a moment's consideration, one which a less repressive attitude towards Aijaz Ahmad would have facilitated. Is it not possible that MacMorris's question should be read historically as a bewildered response to a concept not as yet then viable in the cultural, social, political, and economic conditions of his formative experience? Kiberd does not wait for an answer. But to assume the eternal viability of the concept makes no more sense than the shallow interpretation of Mac-Morris as either a sleeveen or a bit of canon-fodder.

NOTES

1. *Henry V*, 3 ,ii, 48.
2. Richard Ellmann (ed.), *The Artist as Critic; Critical Writings of Oscar Wilde* (London, W. H. Allen, 1970, p. 136). The passage is cited here precisely because Kiberd omits it.
3. See Kiberd, pp. 554-555. My own impromptu analysis of four text-books used in Irish schools for public examination purposes in the 1950s and early 1960s does not bear out Kiberd's imputations of a slavish anti-Irish bias: these are (a) *Simple Lyrics and Story Poems* , Book 1 (Dublin: Browne and Nolan, n.d.); (b) H. L. Doak (ed.) *Intermediate Certificate Poetry* (Dublin: Educational Company of Ireland, n.d.); (c) James J Carey (ed.) *New Intermediate Prose* (Dublin: Gill, 1960); (d) *An Anthology of Prose for Leaving Certificate and Matriculation* (Dublin: Browne and Nolan, n.d.). The first (a) contains 47 items of which 13 are by Irish authors; (b) has 99 items in all, of which 24 are by Irish authors; (c) has 40 items, of which 10 are by Irish authors; (d) has 34 items, of which 6 are by Irish authors. It seems clear that policy generally sought a 20-25% Irish representation in anthologies of English Literature. Among the Irish are such political writers as Wolfe Tone, John Mitchel and Stephen Gwynn, not to mention William Carleton. Among twentieth-century novels, Joseph O'Neill and Francis Stuart are represented. Had Kiberd been at that moment addressing his feminist, rather than his post-colonialist, constituency, and had empirical fact weighed with him to some degree, an impromptu analysis of actual school texts might have served a purpose. Finally—no sign of Quiller-Couch in any of these anthologies.

Publications Received

Barker, Nicolas (ed.), *A Potencie of Life: Books in Society The Clark Lectures 1986-87* (London: The British Library, 1993).

Beckson, Karl, *London in the 1890s: A Cultural History* (London: W. W. Norton, 1992).

Clark, David R., with Rosalind Clark, *W. B. Yeats and the Theatre of Desolate Reality*. Expanded edition, including *Vivien and Time, The Irish National Theatre*, and *The Poet and the Actress* by W. B. Yeats (the last two of which are reprinted from *YA 8*). (Washington, D.C.: The Catholic University of America Press, 1993; first pub.,1965 without additions).

Clarke, Austin, *Reviews and Essays* edited by Gregory A. Schirmer (Gerrards Cross: Colin Smythe, 1995).

Daneluzzi, Sergio, 'Shelley, Yeats, L'Ebreo Errante e L'Eterno Ritorno', offprint from *L'Ebreo Errante: Metamorfosi de un mito*, Quaderni di Acme 21, Facoltà di Lettere e Filosophia dell'Università degli Studi di Milano, 1993, pp. 183-218.

de Petris, Carla (ed.), *Yeats oggi: Studi e richerche* (Rome: Dipartimento di letterature comparate della Terza università degli studi di Roma, 1993). Studies by Enrica Cagnacci, Nemi D'Agostino, Seamus Deane, Carla de Petris, Fiorenzo Fantaccini, Joan Fitzgerald, Anthony Johnson, Andrea Mariani, Ariodante Marianni, Barbara Arnett Melchiori, Giorgio Melchiori, Jan Hendrik Meter, Jacqueline Risset, Franca Ruggieri, Elémire Zolla.

Foster, R. F., *The Story of Ireland*: An Inaugural Lecture delivered before the University of Oxford, 1 December 1994 (Oxford: Clarendon Press, 1995).

Genet, Jacqueline, *Le Théâtre de William Butler Yeats* (Paris: Presses Universitaires du Septentrion, 1995).

Gonne, Maud, *A Servant of the Queen* eds. A. Norman Jeffares and Anna MacBride White (Gerrards Cross: Colin Smythe Ltd., 1994).

Gould, Warwick, "W. B. Yeats and the Resurrection of the Author", *The Library* 16: 2 (June 1994), 101-34.

Innes, C. L., *Woman and Nation in Irish Literature and Society 1880-1935* (London: Harvester Wheatsheaf, 1994).

Hanley, Mary, and Liam Miller, *Thoor Ballylee: Home of William Butler Yeats* with a foreword by T. R. Henn (Gerrards Cross: Colin Smythe Ltd. 1995). Third edition, with additional illustrations (first published by The Dolmen Press, Dublin, June 1965).

Journal of the Eighteen Nineties Society Nos 21 (1994) and 22 (1995).

Keneally, Michael (ed.), *Poetry in Contemporary Irish Literature* (Gerrards Cross: Colin Smythe, 1995).

Lewis, Gifford, *The Yeats Sisters and the Cuala* (Dublin: Irish Academic Press, 1994).

Lewis, Wyndham, *Time and Western Man*, edited by Paul Edwards (Santa Rosa: Black Sparrow Books, 1993.

mac Liammóir, Micheál, *The Importance of Being Oscar* with an introduction by Hilton Edwards (Gerrards Cross: Colin Smythe, 1995).

W. J. Mc Cormack, *Dissolute Characters: Irish Literary History through Balzac, Sheridan Le Fanu, Yeats and Bowen* (Manchester: Manchester University Press, 1993).

Meyers, Stephen W., *Yeats's Book of the Nineties: Poetry, Politics, and Rhetoric* (New York etc.: Peter Lang, 1993).

Midgley, Nick, 'Yeats and the Elements' *Poetica* 43 (Japan), 1995, pp. 67-100.

Murphy, William M., *Family Secrets: William Butler Yeats and His Relatives* (Dublin: Gill & Macmillan, 1995)

Murray, Paul, *A Fantastic Journey: The Life and Literature of Lafcadio Hearn* (Sandgate, Folkestone, Kent: Japan Library, 1993). With a foreword by Roy Foster.

Pierce, David, *Yeats's Worlds: Ireland, England and the Poetic Imagination* (New Haven and London: Yale University Press, 1995). With contemporary photographs by Dan Harper.

Pyle, Hilary, *The Different Worlds of Jack B. Yeats: His Cartoons and Illustrations* (Dublin: Irish Academic Press, 1994).

C. George Sandulescu (ed.), *Rediscovering Oscar Wilde* (Gerrards Cross: Colin Smythe, 1994) pp. xvi + 464. Proceedings of the May 1993 The Princess Grace Irish Library Series 8. Proceedings of the May 1993 conference of the same name at the Princess Grace Irish Library, Monaco.

Schuchard, Marsha Keith, 'Yeats and the "Unknown Superiors": Swedenborg, Falk, and Cagliostro' from Marie Mulvey Roberts and Hugh Ormsby-Lennon (eds.), *Secret Texts: The Literature of Secret Societies* (New York: AMS Press Ltd., 1995), pp. 114-168.

Smith, Stan, *The Origins of Modernism: Eliot, Pound, Yeats and the Rhetorics of Renewal* (London: Harvester, 1994)

Smythe, Colin, *A Guide to Coole Park Co. Galway: Home of Lady Gregory*, with a foreword by Anne Gregory (Gerrards Cross: Colin Smythe Ltd., 1973, 1995). Third edition, revised.

Synge, J. M., *Riders to the Sea, The Shadow of the Glen, The Tinker's Wedding, The Well of the Saints, The Playboy of the Western World, Deirdre of the Sorrows* ed. with an introduction by Ann Saddlemyer (Oxford: Oxford University Press, 1995).

Valverde, Cristina Pérez, El simbolismo celta en *The Wanderings of Oisin* PhD, Universidad de Granada, 1994 (Barcelona: ETD Micropublicaciones, S.L., 1995).

Watson, G. J., Irish Identity and the Literary Revival: Synge, Yeats, Joyce and O'Casey (Washington: Catholic University of America Press, 1994). First published in 1979.

Wilde, Oscar, *The Importance of Being Ernest: a Reconstructive Critical Edition of the Text of the First Production, St. James's Theatre, London, 1895, Annotated and Illustrated from Contemporary Sources and Edited with Introductory Essays on the Play and its Text* by Joseph Donoghue, with Ruth Berggren (Gerrards Cross, Colin Smythe, 1995).

W. B. Yeats, *The Early Poetry Volume II: "The Wanderings of Oisin" and Other Early Poems to 1895: Manuscript Materials*, ed. George Bornstein (Ithaca and London: Cornell University Press, 1994)

................, *The Winding Stair (1929) Manuscript Materials* ed. David R. Clark, (Ithaca and London: Cornell University Press, 1995).

W. B. Yeats, *Short Fiction*, edited with an introduction and notes by G.J. Watson ((London, New York: Penguin Books, 1995).

................, *Writings on Irish Folklore, Legend and Myth*, ed. with an introduction and notes by Robert Welch (London, New York: Penguin Books, 1993).

................, *Derniers poèmes (1936-1939) Édition bilingue, Présenté, annoté, et traduit de l'anglais* by Jean-Yves Masson (Paris: Editions Verdier, 1994).

................, *Collins Gem Yeats Anthology* with a preface, 'W. B. Yeats' by A. Norman Jeffares (Glasgow: HarperCollins, 1995).

Yeats-Eliot Review, XII I (Summer 1993); XII 2 (Fall 1993), contains Shalini Sikka `Yeats and the Upanishads: An Introductory Note' pp. 56-60; XII: 3 & 4 (Winter 1994), Special Double Issue containing papers presented at the National Poetry Foundation Yeats Conference, August 1990.

Note: The following titles all belong to 'Decadents, Symbolists, Anti-Decadents: Poetry of the 1890s', a series of facsimiles and reprints chosen and edited by R. K. R. Thornton and Ian Small (Oxford and New York: Woodstock Books, 1994). Each volume has a short preface and bibliography by the editors.

John Gray, *Silverpoints* (1893) and *Spiritual Poems* (1896).
Lionel Johnson *Poems* (London: Elkin Mathews; Boston: Copeland & Day, 1895).
Arthur Symons, *Silhouettes* (1896) and *London Nights* (1897).
The Book of the Rhymers' Club (1892, 1894) [sic].
W. B. Yeats, *Poems* (London: T. Fisher Unwin, 1895).
................, *The Wind Among the Reeds* (London: Elkin Mathews, 1899); second ed. with errata).